TONY BLAIR

TONY BLAIR

JOHN RENTOUL

LITTLE, BROWN AND COMPANY

A *Little, Brown* Book

First published in Great Britain in 1995
by Little, Brown and Company

A CIP catalogue record for this book
is available from the British Library.

ISBN 0 316 91444 4

Typeset by M Rules
Printed and bound in Great Britain by
Clays Ltd, St Ives plc.

Little, Brown and Company (UK)
Brettenham House
Lancaster Place
London WC2E 7EN

CONTENTS

Preface

One of the first questions of biography is the nature of the author's relationship with the subject. This is all the more significant with an anticipatory political biography, that is, a study of someone who has yet to hold high office. I first planned to write this book soon after the 1992 General Election, because I was impressed by Tony Blair and, like others, thought he would one day lead the Labour Party. I made several films for the BBC about him and the Labour Party, including one about his visit with Gordon Brown to the United States in January 1993. But I do not know him well, except now as a biographer.

I have discussed the book with him, and his staff have been helpful, but I have not interviewed him for quotation, nor have I been given access to his papers or to members of his family.

I interviewed nearly everyone else I wanted to. Quotations which are not followed by footnotes giving the source are from my interviews.

I should like to thank Sean O'Grady, who helped with research, commented on drafts and suggested some historical perspectives; Michael Crick, who allowed me to transcribe his interviews for BBC TV's *Newsnight*; Mick Rawsthorne; Sallyanne Godson; Georgie Grindlay; Adrian Long; Stuart Robertson; Andrew Gordon at Little, Brown and, for his sound judgments, James Stephenson. And thanks to Alex.

INTRODUCTION

A NEW DAY:
21 JULY 1994

The result was announced just after noon. The words 'Tony Blair. Leader of the Labour Party' were projected onto the screen. John Prescott was the new Deputy Leader. Margaret Beckett held back her disappointment. The rest of the hall, including the one Conservative, Tony Blair's father Leo, cheered.

The gift of a little hindsight, and particularly the knowledge of Blair's success in rewriting Clause IV of the Labour Party's constitution, means there is a risk of exaggerating the importance of 21 July 1994 as a turning-point in the party's history. But, even without any inkling of what Blair intended to do, it was evident then that the election was a complete break with the past, that this piece of theatre signalled a revolution in the Labour Party.

First, there was the manner of Blair's accession. This leadership election was the first to be conducted in a way that could definitely be described as democratic. Neil Kinnock and John Smith had been elected not *at* a conference but *by* the conference, the 'parliament of the labour movement', attended by delegates who cast their votes and then waited for them to be counted. This time the voters had already voted 'out there', and the computer-readable forms had been counted. This conference was a ceremony only, a television spectacle to put history, in the form of The Moment, and speeches from the new leadership, on videotape.

Secondly, the cast. Aged forty-one, Blair was the fifteenth, youngest and least naturalised Leader of the Labour Party.[1] He had been in parliament for only eleven years. If he becomes prime minister by 1997, he will be the youngest since Pitt the Younger in 1783.

Thirdly, the scripts, too, were new. It was the first time a Labour politician could plausibly turn the historical tables on the Conservative charge against the party's closed and unaccountable power relations. When John Prescott in his speech contrasted 'the biggest democratic exercise carried out by any party in British political history' with the '185 Tory MPs who elected John Major' – adding, with a theatrical sneer, 'in their smoke-filled rooms' – it carried a ring of truth.

But it was another part of Prescott's speech which highlighted the real change. 'This man, our new leader, has got what it takes. He commands moral authority and political respect. He has the energy and vitality to win people over to Labour.' His voice dropped into melodrama, 'And he scares the life out of the Tories.' After laughter and applause he added: 'And me.' The audience were delighted. 'Sorry, that's not in the script,' he said, looking up at the journalists' section of the hall.

This, of course, was the real surprise. More than in any previous leadership election, the party put winning above all other considerations and chose the candidate most feared by the Conservatives. 'If Blair turns out to be as good as he looks, we have a problem,' said an internal Conservative Central Office memorandum. Margaret Thatcher described him as the most 'formidable' Labour leader for over thirty years.

Blair's acceptance speech started quietly. His voice cracked slightly, but then strengthened as he promised not to rest until the 'destinies of our people and our party are joined together again, in victory at the next General Election'.

He remembered the tragedy which had lifted him so early to leadership. John Smith 'gave our country something important and he gave our party something precious. He showed the British people that public service is still an ideal that can breathe hope into a politics grown weary and cynical.' His legacy was 'a pride reborn . . . We are proud to be Labour.'

But Blair was about to redefine what it was to 'be Labour', adopting a label, 'New Labour', which had been proposed and rejected under Smith. Socialism, or 'social-ism', was 'the power of all used for the good of each'. He promised clarity, but delivered only platitudes: 'I will tell you how it works. Not through some dry academic theory or student gospel of Marxism. It works when every person who wants to, can get up in the morning with a job to look forward to, and prospects upon which to raise a family.' The slide from *how* it works – a difficult question of the means by which socialism can be achieved – to *when* it works – a matter only of describing desirable ends – was achieved with distinctive fluency.

'How socialism works' has always been a predominantly economic question – public ownership, planning, regulation – and Blair's views on the economy implicitly rejected 'the common ownership of the means of production, distribution and exchange' then inscribed in Clause IV. His aim was 'not to abolish the market, but *on the contrary* to make it dynamic and work in the public interest, so that it provides opportunities for all'. With that 'on the contrary' he declared it was not the role of 'New Labour' to constrain market forces, only to re-direct them. One only has to imagine any of Blair's predecessors using that form of words to appreciate that – although Blair had not set out a single policy that was different from his predecessor's – he really was different.

If it was not clear what programme Blair promised, it was certain that he was not promising much, as he made a significant defence of Fabian gradualism:

I say this to the people of this country, and most of all to our young people: join us in this crusade for change. Join us. Of course, the world can't be put to rights overnight. Of course, we must avoid foolish illusions and false promises. But there is, amongst all the hard choices and uneasy compromises that politics forces upon us, a spirit of progress throughout the ages, with which we keep faith.

He ended with an atypical lyrical tribute to those who have changed the world 'through courage and compassion and intelligence, but most of all through hope – the small, broken moments of hope that forever are worth an eternity of dull despair'. This was much admired at the time, although on closer analysis its meaning remains winsomely elusive.

Blair left with his wife Cherie in a blue Rover lent by the GMB union. Margaret Beckett left in the official Leader of the Opposition's car, allowed to her as a courtesy. John Prescott was the third to leave, in a taxi, and the only one to put any small change in the railway signal workers' strike collection bucket.

An hour later, on the steps of Church House, in the precinct of Westminster Abbey, a small crowd waited, holding single red roses and a bouquet. But this was not an English society wedding, it was a party to celebrate the election of a new socialist leader. By ones and twos and little groups, Labour MPs and party dignitaries arrived, fresh and elated, as if they had just done something dangerous.

When Tony and Cherie arrived, the room upstairs was full of MPs and admirers. The host was one of the central figures, not just in the leadership campaign, but in the whole of Blair's career: Alexander Irvine, Lord Irvine of Lairg, the head of the chambers in which Blair trained as a barrister.

Blair gave a short speech of thanks. Speaking without notes, alternately self-deprecating and serious, he set out his priorities at the start of his leadership to a private gathering of close supporters.

He started by thanking his staff, particularly Anji Hunter, his assistant for the previous six years, whom he first met when they were both at school in Scotland. 'I met Anji when I was about seventeen, at a party where we both stayed overnight,' he said, adding mischievously: 'It was my first defeat.'

He thanked his parliamentary colleagues, his family, and Cherie and her family. He had two debts of gratitude to more obscure friends. 'A special word of thanks – from the very depths of my heart – to some people who are down here today from Trimdon, including John Burton and Phil Wilson and many others. It all started with them.' He paused and added: 'It's all their fault actually.'

The next acknowledgement was the only part of his speech which was reported the next day: 'A particular thank-you to a friend of mine called Bobby, who some of you will know. He played a great part and did so well.' Most people in the room were bemused, but thought little of it until the next day's newspapers identified 'Bobby' as Peter Mandelson, the MP for Hartlepool and former director of communications for the Labour Party.

It was a curious private joke, as he acknowledged Mandelson's secret contribution in front of many MPs who were hostile towards him. Blair must have known that these MPs would find out who Bobby was, and that the story would appear in the newspapers. Thus he bestowed his special favour, dividing his closest supporters into the 'some of you' who knew, and the others who did not. In the savouring of victory, there was a trace of arrogance which suggested a detached attitude to his party. There was a similar sense in his public speech after his Clause IV victory nine months later. 'I was not born into this party, I chose it,' he said, trying to underline his commitment to it but at the same time giving the opposite impression.

He must also have realised that the origin of the codename 'Bobby' would be found out. Mandelson was given it by Blair's staff: they liked the image of Blair as John F. Kennedy, and Mandelson was so close to him that he was cast as the former US President's younger brother. Irony never translates well, and it was bound to be seen as an example of the presumptuous self-image of Blair's private court.

Finally, as his speech started to change tone, he thanked all his supporters 'for giving us the chance to build this country again. I meant what I said this morning – just as well, really, since I said it to millions of people.' Then he adopted his intense, urgent style, switching his attention from the election just won to the next General Election:

> I meant what I said about wanting to win power, not to enjoy it, but to change the country, to change its place in the world, to make it a country people are proud of again, to make this country of ours a country where *everyone* gets the chance to succeed and get on. We will win the next election, not by giving up our principles – that's not the business we're in – we're going to get power *through* principle, not at the expense of it. We will win, I am confident of that, but we will have to work for it. We will work for it, without any let-up, from this moment on. I've seen a lot of things over this past fifteen years that I've hated and loathed, and we've never been able to change them. I know that there exists within this group, and within our party, the discipline to make it happen.

To the charge that he was really a Conservative he offered his loathing of the government's – unspecified – actions. To the charge that he was an opportunist, he offered his restatement of principles – equal upward mobility, the chance for everyone to 'get on'. This 'principle' that Blair declaimed so passionately was, of course, nothing more than what used to be referred to as equality of opportunity. Of course, neither Neil Kinnock nor John Smith talked about equality of *outcome* much. But Blair's emphasis on equality of opportunity bypassed the fundamental question of society's obligations to those who cannot succeed and get on, because they are ill, old or simply incapable. Equality of opportunity is as much Conservative as Labour – the meritocratic aspiration which inspired Margaret Thatcher's success.

Blair does have a strong belief in the need for 'social justice' for the less capable. But, both for reasons of electoral positioning and because he has a different world-view, they are not central to his politics. Neil Kinnock understood social aspiration – he wanted everyone who could to go to university – but his authentic voice was also on the side of those who need looking after: 'I warn you not to grow old,' he famously said in 1983. John Smith's sympathy also lay with the widows who came to his MP's surgeries and to whose problems he often referred. Kinnock and Smith both grew out of a tradition in which the view of what it meant to 'be Labour' was not 'getting on', but 'being looked after', by your union, your party and your country.

Despite all this, nothing about Blair was as new as it looked. He was the youngest leader the Labour Party had ever had, but he was only four months younger than Neil Kinnock, when Kinnock was elected to save the party eleven years before. He talked in phrases more familiar to the Right of politics, in a moral language that was utterly unfamiliar to most of the Labour Party that elected him; yet he was reviving the defunct tradition of ethical socialism, an intellectual movement which reached its height just before the Labour Party was born. He was described as a moderniser so extreme that his supporters had feared that he was becoming isolated in the party before John Smith's death; and yet he had just been elected without saying that he intended to change any of the party's policies.

If Blair becomes prime minister, he could herald a turning-point in British politics equivalent to 1945 or 1979, or a dashing of hopes as in 1966. Or he could set a new standard. Blair clearly wants to avoid raising expectations. So his victory could be different in another way, heading an administration which exceeds its own modest targets and breaks a traditional Labour government cycle.

Is he a conviction politician, or is he playing the part of a conviction politician? How did the public-school rebel, the smooth barrister, rise from obscurity to the leadership of a socialist party in just eleven years? And what would he do in power? Those are three of the central questions of this book. Some of the most important characters in the story were identified in Blair's private victory speech – Anji Hunter, Cherie Booth, John Burton and Peter Mandelson.

It has been said that there is nothing that cannot be made to look inevitable when written by a competent historian. I have tried to be competent, but I am unable to present the rise of Blair as predestined. Once in parliament, his rise was smooth and apparently inexorable, a rise bracketed by unexpected events: his selection as a parliamentary candidate when the 1983 election campaign was already under way, and John Smith's death in 1994. Any assessment of Blair so soon after his election to the Labour leadership is bound to lack perspective, but he has impressive qualities which can be discerned now. If he were to be run over by a bus, the outline of the tributes would be clear. He is sincere in his ethical socialism. He has shown bravery in challenging some of his party's assumptions. He is a fine advocate and debater. He shows promise, without making promises. If he does succeed in converting his aspirations into policies in power he could complete the historic rehabilitation of Labour as a party of government.

Note

1. Tony Blair is technically only the fifth Leader of the Labour Party, as that title was adopted in 1978, when it replaced 'Leader of the Parliamentary Labour Party', which dated from 1922. Before then, the leader was called Chairman of the Parliamentary Party, starting with Keir Hardie in 1906, the man usually regarded as the first leader of the party.

PART ONE

FROM ATTLEE TO WILSON

1. CHEERFUL REBEL
School Days in Durham and Scotland, 1953–71

'We had a perfectly good, average, middle-class standard of living.'

Tony Blair's political ambition began at the age of ten, when his father Leo's ended. In 1963 Leo Blair was a university lecturer and Conservative activist looking for a parliamentary seat, when he suffered a stroke. At the age of forty, he found himself unable to speak. It was, says his son, 'one of the formative events of my life'.[1]

According to Canon John Grove, then headmaster of the Chorister School, Durham, 'Mrs Blair arrived at the school one day at about 8.30am – we normally started at nine – saying, "Leo's had a terrible stroke. Would you just look after Tony for the day?" and left him with me. I did my best to console him. He was terribly upset by it.'

The stroke was caused by overwork. Leo was a lecturer in law at Durham University and a practising barrister as well as chairman of the Durham Conservative Association. He had gone to university late, because of the war, and felt he had a lot of catching up to do.

Tony Blair was old enough to understand that his father had unfinished business:

You can only guess now the appalling frustration for him.

He was a highly articulate and tremendously able man, a barrister, lecturer in law and a fledgling politician. And there was a time when he could say only one word. That was: 'Good'. Otherwise he'd have to motion for a cup of tea.[2]

It was three years before his father learnt to speak again. That 'appalling frustration' instilled in Tony Blair the drive to succeed on his father's behalf. 'After his illness my father transferred his ambitions onto his kids. It imposed a certain discipline. I felt I couldn't let him down.'[3]

The Blairs' middle child may have felt the weight of responsibility most. His brother William, three years older, left home to go to Fettes College boarding school in Edinburgh, while his younger sister Sarah developed a form of rheumatoid arthritis just as Leo was getting better. 'My early years seemed to have been spent in and out of hospital in Durham. My father's illness impressed on me from an early age that life was going to be a struggle, that there were a lot of losers.'[4]

The myth of a leader's origins has always been important, particularly in the Labour Party, from Ramsay MacDonald's croft to Harold Wilson's unemployed industrial chemist father.

Leo Blair's life was a self-made one. He had been brought up by foster parents, Glasgow shipyard rigger James Blair and his wife. These were the grandparents Tony Blair knew. He was aware that his father had been fostered, but had no idea who his natural grandparents were – until the *Daily Mail* researched his family tree when he emerged as the likely leader of the Labour Party after John Smith's death.

The story of Tony Blair's real grandparents is a colourful one, although perhaps of limited relevance to all but genetic determinists. They turned out to be actors: Charles Parsons, whose stage name was Jimmy Lynton, and Celia Ridgeway. They played in comedy, music hall and straight drama around the time of the First World War.

Celia led a complicated life. She left home to go on stage

against her parents' wishes. 'She enjoyed the company of men and was married by the time she was seventeen,' says Pauline Harding, the elder of two daughters from her first marriage (and therefore a hitherto-unknown aunt of Tony Blair's). 'Mother was always away and she didn't answer our letters. Our father was wicked to her. He used to knock her about, though I suppose he was fed up with her carrying on. Eventually they were divorced.'

Celia then married again, but most of the time was away from her daughters. Her son Leo was born in 1923, in Filey, Yorkshire, while Celia was on tour in a show with Jimmy Lynton. Her second husband knew that Leo was not his, and divorced her. At a time when the shame of illegitimacy was real, the baby was fostered out to the Blairs.

Jimmy and Celia then got married three years after Leo was born. According to Harding, they tried to get him back in 1936, when he was twelve, but 'he didn't want to leave the Blairs. Mrs Blair was the only mother he knew, and he obviously loved his foster parents. Mrs Blair also didn't want to let him go. So Leo stayed in Glasgow.'[5]

Mrs Blair would not discuss Leo's natural parents, and insisted that he had been born in Glasgow. Leo himself seems to have been unforthcoming about his real story, even with his own children. His adoptive roots were in 'Red Clydeside', and he was secretary of the Scottish Young Communist League between 1938 and 1941. On the eve of the Second World War, Communism attracted many young idealists – Denis Healey was a Communist at Oxford at the same time.

After war broke out, Leo left school, at the age of seventeen, and worked as a clerk for Glasgow Corporation before joining the Army in 1942. He was demobilised, as a major, in 1947, and then went to Edinburgh University to study law. He came back to Glasgow to marry Hazel Elizabeth Rosaleen Corscaden in 1948. She came from a strongly Protestant farming family in Donegal, where she was born in 1923. When her father died, she moved to Glasgow, where her stepfather was a butcher.

When he married, Leo gave his name as 'Blair, formerly Parsons', and he took Charles and Lynton, a combination of his natural father's original and stage names, as his middle names. His first son, William, had his foster father's name, James, and Lynton as middle names, and his own middle names he gave to his second son, although he never told him where they came from.

Anthony Charles Lynton Blair was born on 6 May 1953, in the Queen Mary Maternity Home, Edinburgh. By then, his parents and brother had moved to a small bungalow, 5 Paisley Terrace. His birth certificate records that his father was then an Assistant Examiner for the Inland Revenue – a junior tax inspector. More importantly, he was working for a doctorate in law and hoping to begin an academic career. The family later moved back to Glasgow, and then lived in Adelaide, Australia, for three years, where Leo lectured in law. 'We moved around a lot when I was young, before we finally settled in Durham,' says Tony Blair. 'I never felt myself very anchored in a particular setting or class.'[6] As the family moved to Durham City in the summer of 1958, when he was just five, and stayed there for seventeen years, the feeling of not belonging may have owed more to the uncertainties of upward mobility than geography. In Durham their setting was dominated by the Cathedral and their class was rising middle, but their home was rented and Leo's high status was recent. Leo was not only a university lecturer but also read for the English Bar and began to practise as a barrister.

Tony Blair saw little of his father: 'Dad had a flourishing legal business and was always lecturing around the country. He was also an astute self-publicist, appearing regularly on regional television. I'm sure I saw less of him than my children see of me now.'[7]

The Blairs had nowhere to live when they arrived and Canon John Grove, Headmaster of the Chorister School, offered them an empty flat above the old school. Grove describes conditions in the top flat in No 5, The College, in precincts of the cathedral, as 'very primitive'. They stayed there a few months before moving into a rented house nearby.

A law lecturer then earned a good and secure salary, and both boys went to private schools. William, aged eight, started at the Chorister School; Tony went to Western Hill pre-prep, and followed his brother to the Chorister School in 1961, where they were day boys rather than members of the cathedral choir to which the school owed its origins. The Blairs were well-off, although Grove says 'our fees have always been low compared with many prep schools – a deliberate policy in the past by the Dean and chapter, so that it shouldn't be beyond the range of the clergy. And so if a clergyman can send one son, a lawyer can probably send two.' Tony Blair says: 'We had a perfectly good, average, middle-class standard of living.'[8] This is rather euphemistic code for: 'I may have enjoyed the privilege of private education, afforded to a tiny minority, but we did not live in a country house and go hunting and shooting at the weekend.'

Blair Two, as Tony Blair was known, was considered academically bright enough to skip the lowest form, and came third in the exams at the end of his first year. Brian Crosby, now Deputy Headmaster, took Tony Blair for maths, and remembers him partly because the word 'rhinoceros' once appeared on his test answer sheet. Blair explained cheekily that he knew the longest side of a right-angled triangle was called something like 'hippopotamus', but that that was not right.

Blair Two was a conventional boy. There was little indication of the rebelliousness of his teenage school years. Grove remembers him for his impish smile, and says he was 'a really good sort of small boy to have in prep school – the sort of boy that was the backbone of a school like this'. He was good at Scripture, coming top of his form on a number of occasions and, according to Grove, he was a serious believer. On the day of his father's stroke, Grove says, 'I think he was comforted by what I could offer him, and we said prayers together. Tony is a very strongly religious person – always has been and I think always will be – and that, I think, helped him.'

Tony Blair was good at athletics, and later at cricket and rugby, playing for the school teams in both. He won the school's Scott Cup as 'the best rugger player in 1965–6'.

In 1963 the family moved to 28 Hill Meadows in High Shincliffe, a four-bedroomed house on a new estate in a suburb a mile or two outside Durham. Leo's stroke soon afterwards limited the family's means. 'We were still well-off,' says Blair, 'but not nearly as well-off as we might have been.'[9] Leo remained at the university, which supported him as he made his recovery, and insisted that his wife should not work. 'He had very fixed ideas about that sort of thing, and even though she wanted to get a job to tide the family over this difficult period, he wouldn't hear of it,' says Blair.[10]

His father's zealous Conservatism was one of the dominant political influences of Tony Blair's youth. From the Communist-saturated culture of working-class Clydeside, Leo Blair worked hard to raise himself and his family to comfortable respectability. He became chairman of the Durham Conservative Association, with what his son describes as the proto-Thatcherite politics of Norman Tebbit. 'I was ready to try for any Conservative seat that became vacant,' Leo says.[11] It was no surprise, then, that when he was twelve, Tony Blair should be the school's Conservative candidate for a mock election to be held on 26 March, five days before the 1966 General Election. 'During that week speeches were held in the yard by Christopher Scott (Liberal); Tony Blair (Conservative) and Stephen Dowrick (Labour), the candidates,' records the school magazine, *The Chorister*, July 1966. Canon John Grove remembers:

For about a fortnight beforehand the boys went around canvassing and then there came the election day. And possibly the Fates wanted to say to him, 'Conservative so far, but no further', because on the day he was ill. Somebody else had to stand in and got elected.[12]

According to the school magazine, Richard Stewart took
over as Conservative candidate for the final speeches on the
night before the mock election. 'The following morning, the
polling station (The Hobbies' Hut) was opened and the ballot papers were printed. On Monday, 28th of March, the
Results came through.' Stewart won handsomely with 62
votes to 26 for the Labour candidate and 24 for the Liberal.
Exaggerating the national trend which gave Harold Wilson a
96-seat majority at Westminster, there had been a dramatic
swing from the Liberals to Labour since the previous mock
election in 1964.

Twenty-eight years later, during the leadership campaign of
1994, the event was inevitably recalled by contemporary witnesses. Blair himself said he could not remember it, nor could
he recall whether he had stood as the Conservative under the
influence of his father, or because 'we'd all got parts to play
and that was the one ascribed'.[13] He gave the impression that
he was embarrassed by a party label he had worn long before
most people's political ideas are fixed. After all, Clement
Attlee was a Conservative and Harold Wilson a Liberal, not at
school but at university.[14]

He did not develop settled political views of his own until
he was at least seventeen or eighteen. Although his father's
values were Conservative, and Durham Cathedral city has a
different feel from the surrounding area, he could not have
avoided absorbing something of County Durham socialism.
He claims he was influenced by the strong local traditions,
recalling the miners' galas of the 1960s: 'There was great
pride in the industry and an overwhelming sense of local
community. That feeling has stayed with me ever since: you
don't just create your own space and inhabit it, you share it
with others.'[15]

The mining community of the Durham coalfield had been
bonded by hardship. Seventy-four people were killed in the
Trimdon Grange pit explosion in 1882, and the folk songs of
the area still recall it. 'Firedamp' or explosive gas was one of
the greatest hazards of mining, particularly around the Tyne,

an area well known for its 'fiery pits'. The county council was the first local authority ever to be controlled by the Labour Party, in 1919. Peter Lee was its first leader. *'It was the first time working men had been called to govern in Britain,'* Lee's biographer, fellow Durham miner Jack Lawson MP, wrote triumphantly.[16] The foreword to the 1949 edition of Lee's biography was written by Prime Minister Clement Attlee, who was still the Leader of the Opposition when Blair was born:

> He typified the courage, integrity and humanity of the mining community which he served so well . . . In these days of fulfilment it is well that the younger generation should realise what manner of men won the advantages which they now enjoy and what were the forces they had to overcome.

By the time Blair came to live in Durham, most of the pits in the county had closed. But the tradition of a particular kind of socialism was deeply embedded. The authors of *English Ethical Socialism* identify Lee and his community as central to the tradition, which came through William Cobbett (1762–1835):

> His ideal of the self-improving, sober, industrious, responsible and altruistic working man was passed down so as to eventually form the Thomas Burts, the Peter Lees, the Jack Lawsons and the ethical-socialist convictions of thousands of unknown people like them in the mining villages of Co. Durham, the textile towns of the Pennines and all over Britain in the respectable working-class communities of the first half of the twentieth century.[17]

Lee was born in Duff Heap Row, Trimdon, six miles from the Blairs' home in High Shincliffe. Trimdon was later to become the centre of Blair's universe, his base in the constituency of Sedgefield.

However, Blair's upbringing was essentially middle-class.

His background is often misunderstood, on the one hand because of his 'classless' accent, and on the other because of the connotations of his 'public school education'. The common assumption that the British middle classes only live in Southern England is a further confusion. As the writer and poet James Fenton, who overlapped with Blair at Durham Chorister School, observes, the truth is that his accent and his background are *Northern* middle-class. He says Blair's accent has not changed since he was eight.[18]

Fettes College

One of the boys who was there at the same time as Tony Blair describes Fettes College in the late 1960s as an emotionally bleak place: 'It was a school without a core to it. It had no rationale apart from rugby.' It is one of the best-known public schools in Scotland. Founded in 1870 by Sir William Fettes, its elaborate fairy-castle Gothic tower is a landmark on the outskirts of Edinburgh. Until now its most famous old boy has been Conservative Chancellor of the Exchequer and Foreign Secretary Selwyn Lloyd. It was essentially an 'English' private school in Scotland, where Blair studied A Levels instead of Scottish Highers, and where more boys were confirmed in the Church of England than the Church of Scotland.

Tony Blair won a scholarship to the school, and went as a boarder in 1966, again following in his brother William's footsteps. He started in his brother's Kimmerghame House, but he hated the harsh discipline and the archaic practice of fagging. Junior boys were allocated as 'fags' – effectively servants – to seniors. Blair was fag to a prefect called Michael Gascoigne, now an Edinburgh solicitor, who recalls Blair as cheerful and efficient:

Blair would clean my shoes, blanco my army belt and

polish the brass on it. If I couldn't see my face in it, he would have it thrown back at him. He would also, if it was a games afternoon, lay out my rugger kit on the bed for me, or my whites if it was cricket . . . There was always a requirement for toast, but we insisted that it had to be one inch thick, no thinner, no thicker, with lashings of butter and marmalade. And Blair would steam into the adjoining kitchen where he made particularly good toast.[19]

Although Gascoigne detected no 'truculence or unwilling-ness', Blair found it such a painful experience that he eventually ran away from school. 'I wasn't very happy at the beginning,' he says. 'I think it's not unnatural if you take kids away from home at that age.'[20] He claims that his running away simply meant that he was a day or so late returning to school, a gloss over what was obviously an acutely miserable episode. His father was summoned, not for the last time, to see the headmaster, Dr Ian McIntosh. McIntosh explained that Tony Blair would have to accept the rules, but at the end of his first year Blair was transferred to the new Arniston House, which was just being built, a square, squat collection of white concrete blocks. The house master, Eric Anderson, now Headmaster of Eton, was a liberal who ran his house on 'modern public school lines', which were more congenial to Blair.

Initially, Blair was as conventional and conformist as he had been at Durham Chorister School. He won a place in the school Junior Colts rugby team in his second term, and was captain of the Junior Colts cricket team in the summer term of 1967. His team won seven matches, lost one and drew one. As he grew older, however, rugby and cricket – especially as 'captain of cricket' – were too Establishment for him, and he took up the more unconventional sport of basketball, in which he had the advantage of being tall.

In his second year, aged fourteen, Blair was chosen to play the role of Mark Antony in the house play, *Julius Caesar*. This was a token of his house master's favour, and an early experience of being promoted at a younger age than would be expected. The reviewer for the school magazine, the *Fettesian*, saw potential: 'As the instrument of Caesar's revenge, Blair emerged as a somewhat youthful Antony, but nevertheless a very promising actor who should prove indispensable for school productions in the next few years.'

Eric Anderson taught Blair English literature. He is an expert on Walter Scott, still one of Blair's favourite novelists. But as Blair grew more anti-Establishment, Anderson clashed repeatedly with him over the enforcement of school rules:

> He certainly wasn't a model pupil. It was, of course, the Sixties, and you remember everybody was rebelling a bit and testing the rules to the limit. And Tony was something of an expert at testing the rules to the limit. I think the school rules on smoking and drinking and breaking bounds in particular probably had quite a difficult ride while he was there. He was the sort of boy that you were always struggling with to have his hair cut properly.[21]

Nevertheless, Anderson seems to have channelled some of Blair's energies into his own passion, which was drama. In the public life of the school, it is as an actor that Blair is mainly remembered. Whether or not it had anything to do with the show-business heritage of his secret grandparents, Blair knew early that he could hold an audience. At the age of sixteen, under Eric Anderson's influence, he formed a group with five other boys called The Pseuds, to act in and produce 'contemporary dramatic works'. Their first 'presentation' was 'an evening of contemporary drama' open to any member of the Upper School, featuring Harold Pinter's *The Dumb Waiter* and *Trouble at the Works*, N.F. Simpson's *Gladly Otherwise* and Crompton's *Out of the Frying Pan*.

In the autumn of 1969 Blair played the Cockney 'Drinkwater' in the school play, George Bernard Shaw's *Captain Brassbound's Conversion*. The *Fettesian* review was mixed:

His accent was, on the first night, a little garbled, and often presented the same difficulties of comprehension experienced with the original article. This, however, was soon remedied and the slower, if slightly less convincing accent of the ensuing nights came over very well. His clearer diction, combined with his superb command of the gestures and mannerisms of the insolent, unscrupulous Cockney, provided us with an accomplished and amusing study.

Blair's greatest dramatic triumph was as Captain Stanhope in R.C. Sherriff's *Journey's End*, the Arniston house play at the beginning of 1971. Everyone who saw it seems to remember his performance in this claustrophobic First World War drama, set in the trenches. When the play was first produced in 1928, Laurence Olivier played the part of Stanhope, the company commander who can only fight an absurd war if he dulls his moral senses with whisky. It was a part to be seized with some relish by a seventeen-year-old rebel – the nihilism of the tortured 'war is hell' hero could appeal to the post-1968 generation with heads full of Pink Floyd lyrics. This time the *Fettesian* review was unstinting:

> Arniston were fortunate in having so experienced an actor as Blair for this central figure. From his first entrance . . . Blair brought out the febrile intensity of Stanhope, wiring himself into his ever more circumscribed troglodyte world, speculating moodily on the worm that went down when it thought it was coming up.

A house tutor, Robert Philp, thought Blair's performance was 'brilliant'.

Blair was also a member of a debating society called Paramaecium, which met by invitation at the home of another house tutor, David Kennedy. His name does not appear in the records of the larger school Debating Society, but the subjects it discussed give a flavour of those years. In

1967, Vietnam (the vote was 19–4 against 'deploring US intervention') and devaluation; in 1969, 'This House would make strikes illegal' and 'This House deplores British intervention in Nigeria' (votes not recorded).

However, the dry pages of the school magazine paint a misleading picture, especially of Blair's later years, when he was a charismatic rebel, a leading figure in the counterculture that defines the pupils' real experience of a school. One master has since described him as the school's 'leader of the opposition'. In the sixth form he was flamboyant and aloof. He had a big, lippy mouth like Mick Jagger, and younger boys were in awe of him. He was always just stepping over the limit of the rules, and using his charm to get away with it. 'Hair was a big issue', says Hugh Kellett, two years below him in Arniston House. 'It had to be above the collar and behind the ears. He would put butter and crap on his hair, to grease it down inside the back of the collar. Many of the boys did.' Ties were a big issue as well, and Blair's was always loose. Another schoolfriend, Nick Rydon, says he questioned everything, 'from fagging to the number of buttons that were supposed to be done up on your blazer'.[22] But most teachers, like David Kennedy, a tutor in Arniston House from 1968, found him stimulating:

Some boys are rebellious because they are stupid. Tony was rebellious because he wanted to question all the values we held to. In a boarding school there are obviously lots of rules as to how the day runs and what one does at various times. You had to have simplified sets of rules. And Tony would always question them.

Robert Philp sees Blair's later career as rooted in this schoolboy attitude:

He was always interested in pointing out the defects of the institution of which he was a part, and that kind of analytical stance is probably fundamentally some kind of political stance, even when it isn't attached to any party political feeling.

Blair was never a prefect. His brother had been, listed in the *Fettesian* under the bald heading 'THOSE IN AUTHORITY'. Kennedy says: 'Most boys of his academic standing and personality would have been prefects, but he was against the system.' However, he was an intellectual rebel rather than a simple trouble-maker. He worked hard and read a lot. Philp says Blair was 'not the very cleverest, but he had a good mind'. He studied English, French and History at A Level, and won a place to read law at St John's College, Oxford.

David Kennedy believes that Blair's persona as a rebel was a front, related to his skill at acting, and offers a pointed assessment:

> He was so affable that you couldn't call him reserved, but you never saw his real self. He didn't like to expose himself in case someone spotted a weakness. He could become a prime minister like Wilson, clever but shallow. He was always charming, never sulky or nasty but, to be cruel, he only likes to be in groups where he is the leading light. He has always been conscious of how he appears to other people, the facade is always there. He is very intelligent and calculating. Don't forget that he was a superb actor.[23]

He was a rebel, but a mature and emotionally self-controlled one. He was careful in his disrespect. Most of the time, according to Hugh Kellett, he was only 'on the cusp of trouble'. But Blair's house master, Eric Anderson, left in 1970 to be headmaster of Abingdon school, and his successor, Bob Roberts, found Blair – in his final year – infuriating: 'He was the most difficult boy I ever had to deal with.'[24] Blair had been beaten by prefects, but Roberts was the only master who beat him at Fettes, giving him 'six of the best' at the age of seventeen, for persistently flouting school rules. 'Bob was a very old-fashioned, strict teacher who did not get on with him at all,' according to David Kennedy.

'Masters were very worried about sex, drugs and rock 'n' roll, and Blair looked like all three,' says Kellett. 'He was a big guy, six feet tall at sixteen.' The rock 'n' roll at Fettes was mostly heavy metal – especially Led Zeppelin – which was played in the boys' studies. In October 1970 Atomic Rooster and Anno Domini played a pop concert at the school. As for drugs, there were 'hardly any' in Fettes, according to contemporaries. From Eric Anderson's testimony it would seem that alcohol and cigarettes were the narcotics of choice. And as for sex, 'boys were allowed to "go up town" three times a week, and Blair probably didn't bother getting the slip signed', according to Kellett. The opposite sex was one of the main attractions of 'up town'. Blair's father was once summoned to talk to the headmaster and house master. Leo Blair says: 'He was always nipping over the wall to chat up the girls at the fish and chip shop.'[25]

On his last summer holiday, Blair, aged seventeen, met a girl even more rebellious than he, called Anji Hunter. The daughter of a Scottish rubber plantation manager, and born in Malaysia, she was about fifteen, and was at St Leonard's, a girls' private school in St Andrews, forty miles away. She and Blair never went out with each other, but have been friends ever since. She was expelled from St Leonard's for insubordination in 1971, around the time when Blair left Fettes. Like Blair, she persistently questioned the rules – she just took it further. She went to take her A Levels at St Clare's sixth form college in Oxford, so she was there during his first year at the university. Fourteen years later, she came to work for him as an MP. She is now head of his private office, and one of his closest and most trusted advisers.

Meanwhile, Fettes's own defences against girls had just been breached. An arch note in the *Fettesian* in 1969 welcomed 'three young ladies' as visitors to the Science Sixth. 'This should not be seen – at least not yet – as the thin end of the wedge of co-education, which, while being a cause of regret to some, will no doubt be a relief to others.' The regretters did not have long to wait. In the autumn of 1970, at the beginning of Blair's last year, two girls joined Fettes as full members of the school. One of them was Amanda Mackenzie-Stuart, daughter of an Old Fettesian judge, a crossbench peer. She was in Blair's class, the History Sixth. Now Amanda Hay, an independent film producer, she says: 'I was his girlfriend. He was so bright, so engaging – and very funny. He could get away with teasing the masters and, looking back, I suppose it was because he was cleverer than most of them.' All the boys and masters who have given their opinion express surprise at Blair's future course, but Mackenzie-Stuart may have known him better. She says he was 'not really into politics at the time – it was more Led Zeppelin and Cream – but I was never surprised that he joined Labour. That was always there.'[26]

She is an important witness, because this is the earliest sighting of left-wing leanings. Others speak of his compassion, and his anti-Establishmentarianism, but this is the first inkling that they might take political expression. Blair himself says he has been left-wing (he prefers to say left-of-centre) since he was twenty, two years later.

Blair's relationship with Amanda Mackenzie-Stuart continued for a while after he left school in 1971, and they are still friends. He took a year off before going to Oxford. He spent the time in Durham, London, which he had previously visited only once, and France. He says he 'dabbled in the music business, helping to organise gigs', worked for some months on a building site, and was a 'waiter in Paris for ten days', which was not a success.[27] He also worked, more successfully, for a French insurance company and returned to Britain fluent in French.

Was Blair the typical product of a famous public school? In some ways he was – he emerged with a set of good qualifications and with the confidence that is traditionally attributed to the type. There is little evidence that he was political, but much that he was a bit of a show-off. The dramatic tendencies, later to find more colourful expression through a rock group, and the urge to lead his peers through rebellious example, rather than by being appointed a prefect, suggest that he wanted to 'be something', and seen to be so, rather than crusading for any cause. Blair did not see himself as confident, however. 'The problem with the public school system is that you end up being a highly competent sitter of exams, but you haven't necessarily got much confidence,' he said in 1991. 'The idea of safety first was with me all the way through university.'[28]

At least it can be said that, unlike some other politicians and public figures who went to boarding schools and whose experiences were almost unalloyed misery – Winston Churchill, Neville Chamberlain, Prince Charles – he carved out the space to enjoy himself.

Blair's time at school was more comparable to Clement Attlee's, who said of his time at Haileybury College that it was 'on the whole enjoyable, though there were considerable periods of black misery'. Attlee also rebelled, although Blair's cheerful rebellion was rather different from his. During the Boer War, the relief of Ladysmith in 1900 followed a series of British defeats. 'The news provoked a collective act of patriotic indiscipline in the school in which Attlee eagerly participated,' writes his biographer. He was caned for his part in a celebratory schoolboy march to the local town.[29] Blair's trips 'up town' were for rather more prosaic celebrations.

There are also parallels between Blair's schooldays and those of another Labour leader, Hugh Gaitskell. He went to Winchester, with Douglas Jay and Richard Crossman, in the 1920s. Gaitskell was described by his biographer as a 'quiet rebel', and he was strongly critical of the school's intense pressure against things which 'weren't done':

Junior boys were required to learn, and were examined on, an elaborate private Winchester vocabulary (it even had its own dictionary); and they had to obey strict rules of conduct and costume, enforced by a very irrational system of punishments.[30]

On the other hand, Gaitskell retained some of the ethos of the school, which 'served him well in politics . . . his high-minded sense of duty, his notable courtesy and self-control, his rational style'.[31] Blair's sense of duty came from sources other than Fettes, but his confidence, style and self-discipline are recognisably the product of the British public school system.

Notes

Unsourced quotations are from the author's interviews. Publication details of books referred to are listed in the Bibliography.

1. *Evening Standard*, 16 November 1993.
2. *Ibid.*
3. Martin Jacques, *Sunday Times Magazine*, 17 July 1994.
4. *Ibid.*
5. *Daily Mail*, 27 May 1994.
6. *Observer*, 2 October 1994.
7. Jon Sopel, *Tony Blair: The Moderniser*, p7.
8. *Channel Four News*, 11 July 1994.
9. Martin Jacques, *Sunday Times Magazine*, 17 July 1994.
10. Jon Sopel, *Tony Blair: The Moderniser*, p10.
11. *Times* Diary, 17 May 1994.
12. BBC TV, *Newsnight*, 10 June 1994.
13. *Observer*, 2 October 1994.
14. On going to Oxford University in 1901, Clement Attlee said, 'I was at this time a Conservative', *As It Happened*, p15; Ben Pimlott, *Harold Wilson*, pp47–50.
15. *Scotland on Sunday*, 24 July 1994.
16. Jack Lawson, *Peter Lee*, p121 (emphasis in original).
17. Norman Dennis and A.H. Halsey, *English Ethical Socialism*, p57.
18. James Fenton, *Independent*, 16 January 1995.
19. Jon Sopel, *Tony Blair: The Moderniser*, p14.
20. *Observer*, 2 October 1994.
21. BBC TV, *Newsnight*, 21 November 1988.
22. Martin Jacques, *Sunday Times Magazine*, 17 July 1994.

23. *Sunday Telegraph*, 24 July 1994.
24. *Mail on Sunday*, 22 May 1994.
25. Martin Jacques, *Sunday Times Magazine*, 17 July 1994.
26. Keith Dovkants, *Evening Standard*, 18 July 1994.
27. Martin Jacques, *Sunday Times Magazine*, 17 July 1994.
28. *Harpers & Queen*, January 1991.
29. Trevor Burridge, *Clement Attlee*, pp14, 16.
30. Philip M. Williams, *Hugh Gaitskell: A Political Biography*, p11.
31. *Ibid.*, p9.

2. PURPLE LOONS
Oxford, 1972–75

'Tone's come a long way since then, but he's still got the basic thrust of it all. He's developed a political realisation of the ideas, but they're still there. If he can take the people with him he can do great work, I'm telling you.'

The early Seventies were a style disaster, and not a good time to go to university if you were going to be famous later. Tony Blair's hair, a running battle zone at school, now explored his shoulders. His father says he went to Oxford to pick him up in his first year, and met a long-haired undergraduate, shirt open to the navel, a large ceramic cross round his neck and a long, black synthetic skin coat with a red lining. 'I wondered who the hell it was. Then he said, "Hi, Dad".'[1]

In his second year, Tony Blair's appearance as the lead singer in a rock band called Ugly Rumours was just as dramatic, the features graphically listed by bass guitarist Mark Ellen:

Reading from top to bottom, the long hair with the rather severe fringe – a slightly medieval look about him, a sort of Three Musketeers thing – a T-shirt that can only be described as 'hoop necked' and possibly even 'trumpet sleeved', which revealed a large acreage of rippling bare torso, and beyond that the obligatory purple loons, topped off with the Cuban-heeled cowboy boots.[2]

Adam Sharples, lead guitarist, now a Treasury civil servant, says drily: 'That certainly chimes with my memory.'

Blair chose to study law, because of his father, although he has since said that he wished he had studied history. Law was and is a tedious subject to study – involving large amounts of rote learning and offering little opportunity for flights of intellectual exploration. For no obvious reason, he also chose St John's, an all-male college, and a rather dull and conservative place, according to contemporaries, in preference to one of the more 'progressive' or radical colleges like Balliol, where his brother went. He certainly stood out. 'He looked very different. He didn't go for smashing things up, but he was lively,' says David Chater, a contemporary who is now Moscow correspondent for *Sky News*. Despite the long hair and the outrageous clothes, he was still a cautious rebel. He enjoyed attracting attention rather than offending people.

One form of attention-seeking was the aping of the *Brideshead* caricature of upper-class Oxford. This was the 'strawberries and cream' side of Blair's life there. He rowed on the river, with Chater, in a 'joke Eight'. And he was a member of the St John's Archery Club, which had little to do with bows and arrows. Nicholas Lowton, a prominent member who is now chaplain to Cheltenham Boys' College, claims it is 'the oldest dining club in Oxford'. Its main function was to hold parties, especially in the summer, although sometimes they would 'twang around in St John's Gardens . . . not after we'd drunk too much, for obvious reasons. There had been trouble with it in the past.' It was arch, not to say archaic. The members wore straw boaters and blazers; women were allowed only as guests on 'Ladies Days'.

For much of his first year, Blair went out with Suzy Parsons, generally described as one of the most beautiful women in Oxford. She was at St Clare's sixth-form college with Blair's friend Anji Hunter. He had several other girl-friends during his time at Oxford, and was usually being 'chased by several more', according to one friend.

Despite enjoying the *Brideshead* silliness, Blair was essentially a rather sensible young man. Discreet about sex, abstemious about drugs and earnest about rock 'n' roll. 'I didn't get into drugs,' he says.[3] When in his second year he was auditioned for the Ugly Rumours, he prepared for it as if he were going for a job interview, according to Mark Ellen.

Tony turned up bang on time – incredibly punctual – brandishing sheafs of paper, of lyrics that he had transcribed, and we were fantastically impressed by this, because obviously we'd told him what songs we played [although] we didn't really know what the words were, but he had got the records and he'd stayed up all night transcribing them.

The Ugly Rumours were public school rebels. The band was set up by Adam Sharples and Ellen, who knew each other from Winchester school, with drummer Jim Moon, now a merchant banker. 'We felt, looking at ourselves, that we were on the visual front a little bit tragic – yards of unconditioned hair and collective sex appeal of slightly less than zero,' says Ellen. 'What we felt we wanted was a charismatic, good-looking lead singer, and Adam suggested this guy Tony Blair. "I met this guy Tony Blair in St John's. He looks terrific. He can sing – I've seen him sing."'

So Blair was auditioned, sitting in the armchair in Sharples's room in Corpus Christi, where Sharples read Philosophy, Politics and Economics (PPE). Sharples and Ellen played acoustic guitar while Moon hit 'anything within reach in a rhythmical manner', says Ellen. And Blair sang. 'He was fantastic. He had a really good voice. It was a very high, powerful voice and he knew all the words. So we said: "Well, you're in. We're called Ugly Rumours and you can start tomorrow."' The band's name came from a Grateful Dead album of the time called *Live at the Mars Hotel*. Blair was not a Grateful Dead fan, but Sharples and Ellen were heavily into deep and meaningful gloom rock. 'If you held this album cover upside down in a mirror, the stars in the sky

spelt the words "ugly rumours", which seemed to have great
significance at the time – possibly less so now,' says Ellen.

Blair's earnestness continued. He took the whole business
seriously, Ellen says. 'I was amazed by how keen he was on
the idea of rehearsal. I think we were just a little bit looser –
"Hey, we'll just turn up and we'll be brilliant." And he was
like, "No, I think we should actually practise this and get it
right."' Ellen is the only member of the band who stayed in
the music business. He presented the *Old Grey Whistle Test*,
edited the music magazine *Q* and is now publisher of *Mojo*
magazine. His account of the band's first gig, in Corpus
Christi's oak-panelled sixteenth-century hall, is a comedy
turn in itself (BBC TV *Newsnight*, 10 June 1994). They
rehearsed – 'not very rigorously' – in the underground car
park across the road, came on stage at 8.30 and 'shuffled
into some lumpen riff'. Enter Tony Blair, stage left, in purple
loons and cut-off T-shirt.

He comes on stage giving it a bit of serious Mick Jagger, a
bit of finger wagging and punching the air. And we go into
our third song and – complete catastrophe – the drums
begin to fall off the drum riser. I can see it now in slow
motion. One by one they just fell apart and rolled off the
stage and onto the floor. And we were all absolutely frozen
with horror and embarrassment. The audience are looking
at us, and we're looking at them. And Tony just got straight
in there and dealt with it brilliantly. He grabbed the micro-
phone and said: 'We're the Ugly Rumours. Hope you're
enjoying yourself. We're playing on Saturday at the
Alternative Corpus Christi College Ball, supported by a
jazz-fusion band and a string quartet. Hope you're going to
come. Are you having a good time? I can't hear you at the
back. Corpus Christi how are you?' All that sort of stuff –
really ludicrous. He held the entire thing together, and we
were just amazed. We were running around behind him
trying to nail these drums back again. Got the kit back.
Plugged in. Got back into this appalling riff that we were

playing, and the whole thing resumed. It was brilliant, the way he dealt with it. He dealt with the hecklers at the back. He dealt with the rather worthy students in the berets who've paid their 30p admission and they're not going until they've heard a Captain Beefheart song. And he dealt with the sea of girls down at the front with the floral print dresses. You know, 95 per cent of them were probably called Amanda. And he was really funny, charming, really charismatic. I can remember standing there in the back line with my bass guitar, standing behind a sea of crash cymbals, looking at him and thinking: 'This is no ordinary junior love-god lead singer we have here. Where is this guy going to go?'

It was appropriate that Blair's recent girlfriend had been called Amanda. The band's next performance, at the Alternative Ball, was recorded by another eye witness. Blair wore 'white skin-tight trousers and strummed his bass guitar with far less dexterity than he now applies to politics'.[4]

The Ugly Rumours were not signed up by a talent-spotting record company and required to sacrifice their artistic integrity to the commercial pressures of the music industry. Despite Ellen's admiration, other comments on Blair's singing voice range from 'rough' to 'he looked great'. The band played only about half-a-dozen gigs in its brief career, and restricted itself to literal cover versions of 'Honky Tonk Woman' and 'Live With Me' by the Rolling Stones, 'Black Magic Woman' by Fleetwood Mac, 'Take It Easy' by Jackson Browne, and songs by Free and the Doobie Brothers – the last being what the band most sounded like, according to one ear-witness.

If Blair wins the next election, one of the more arresting thoughts will be that the prime minister of the United Kingdom once snarled Mick Jagger's words from 'Live With Me':

I got nasty habits.

I take tea at three.
And the meat I eat for dinner
Must be hung up for a week.
My best friend, he shoots water rats
And feeds them to his geese.
Don't you think there's a place for you
In between the sheets?

Blair also appeared on stage in comic revues and straight drama, developing from where he left off at school. He played Matt in the St John's Drama Society production of Bertolt Brecht's *Threepenny Opera* at the Oxford Playhouse in 1974. This led to an argument. Nicholas Lowton says: 'As it's set in the 1930s, I delicately pointed out that perhaps his hair had to be cut. This was not his style. There was a great scene then. He would only appear on stage if he was allowed to pop the hair under his cap.'

This was just a faint echo of the guerrilla warfare against 'those in authority' at Fettes. He still managed to provoke clashes with the St John's College authorities, however, and still used his wit to defuse them. He and a fellow law student called Marc Palley were summoned by the deans to answer the charge that women had visited their rooms outside permitted hours. A lipstick had been found in Blair's room. 'Oh, that's mine,' he replied, casually, when confronted with the evidence.[5]

However, the questioning spirit behind his rebelliousness seems to have turned into a restless search for ways to 'make a difference'. This was the other Tony Blair at Oxford. Most of the strawberries and cream brigade and the would-be rock stars knew nothing of his intellectual pursuit of moral and religious questions.

Blair the Noisy Entertainer spent his time outside St John's, in pubs and parties in other colleges, where he was a member of a number of overlapping social circles. Blair the Contemplative spent his time in college, working quite hard, reading a lot and – for a law student – quite widely. 'I was very interested in political ideas,' he says. 'I was reading everything from Tawney and William Morris through to Gramsci and Isaac Deutscher.'[6] He developed a strong relationship with a small number of people in St John's who were interested in politics and religion. Marc Palley was one of them, but the informal coterie revolved around an Australian mature student called Peter Thomson, whom Blair describes as 'spellbinding' and 'the person who most influenced me'.[7]

'Formative Influences'

Blair met Thomson through another Australian, a Rhodes scholar studying PPE called Geoff Gallop, with whom he wrote and produced sketches in a group called St John's Mummers. At the beginning of his second year, Blair produced a sketch in which Gallop, playing an Australian hick, delivered what *Cherwell* (29 November 1973) called a 'superb spoof' philosophy lecture on Wittgenstein. In Blair's first year, Gallop introduced him to Thomson, a thirty-six-year-old minister of the Australian Anglican church, reading theology at St John's.

David Gardner, now Brussels correspondent for the *Financial Times*, was another member of this 'group of friends which was very close' and whose centre of gravity was Thomson's 'tremendous enthusiasm'. For a year and a half 'long meaning-of-life sessions were very much on the agenda'. Marc Palley says: 'It's what students do, putting the world to rights, pontificating about their theories.' Two or three times a week, various people in Thomson's circle would end up, usually in his room, putting the world to rights late into the night.

There is a sense about Thomson, although he does not say so directly, that he felt he had wasted a lot of his life, and was trying to make up for lost time. He wanted to discuss –

endlessly – how moral philosophy should be put into practice. It was a 'project', to use a later word, which deeply interested Blair. Thomson says:

> I was an old retard who had arrived here from Australia, trying to become respectable. He was young, full of life, a person who had this *joie de vivre*. He was into life. He'd a keen intellect and a sense of compassion for other people. And we used to have these marvellous discussions that would go on for hours – you know, cigarettes and coffee and, because I was a bit older I had a bit more money than they did, they'd smoke all my cigarettes and drink all my coffee and we'd get into religion and politics.[8]

Other members of the circle included Olara Otunna, a Ugandan refugee who was later, briefly, Uganda's foreign minister in 1984–85 and a candidate for Secretary-General of the United Nations, and Anwal Velani, an Indian postgraduate student. 'It was no accident that most were from abroad and not products of the British class system,' says Blair. 'I could never stand the Oxford intellectual establishment. They seemed to have a poker up their backsides.'[9] However, as well as his circle of Commonwealth outsiders, Blair also hung out with products of the British public school system, however rebelliously tongue-in-cheek they were, in the rock band and the Archery Club.

Thomson was different. Relaxed, informal, garrulous, he was also a good tennis player and taught Blair: 'He hadn't played all that much, but in fact became quite good very quickly,' Thomson says.

> He used to get me up at seven in the morning. He'd say 'We've got to go and play', and I was trying to open one eye. He got quite good. But *competitive!* Oh, he wanted to win every point. But he was great. It just showed the kind of dogged determination that the bloke's got. He sets his focus in a particular way and goes for it.

It would be a mistake to see Thomson's discussions as the late-night equivalent of Christian coffee mornings. They were informal and often irreverent, although there was an underlying seriousness of purpose. Even the more private Blair at Oxford combined earnestness with detachment. Marc Palley says: 'He's got a great ability to stand back from things, and I would say when one talks about being a serious person the inference is that they take themselves seriously as well, which he didn't.' He may have taken himself seriously since then, 'but it's always with things in perspective – there's always a little bit of twinkle in the eye.'

Those who took part in Thomson's discussions were a shifting set of people, united more by left-wing politics than by religious commitment. Geoff Gallop says Thomson and he were 'both very political. I was very much an activist on the far Left, pushing a Marxist line. Tariq Ali was my guru. Peter was a Christian socialist.' Gallop was in the International Marxist Group, and a dedicated revolutionary. David Gardner says, 'I considered myself well to the left of the Labour Party'. Marc Palley was cynical about politics – and religion – but was 'liberal-Leftish anti-Establishment'. His father was the only white MP in Rhodesia to oppose Ian Smith. Thomson's theology was broad, non-institutional and politically radical. Only Otunna was an evangelical Christian. Blair's religion was nominal when he arrived at Oxford, and his politics unformed. The discussions he engaged in over Thomson's coffee and cigarettes were to change all that.

A Philosophy

According to Thomson and Gallop, there were three broad topics to which their discussions constantly returned: the relationship between theology and politics; reform or revolution (what Gallop calls 'the perpetual question'); and the concept of community. The last theme arose out of

Thomson's enthusiasm for a Scottish philosopher called John Macmurray, whom he had read at theological college. 'If you really want to understand what I'm all about,' says Blair, 'you have to take a look at a guy called John Macmurray. It's all there.'[10]

Blair's idea of community, which is perhaps his most distinctive theme as a politician, derives directly from Macmurray.

Macmurray was considered one of Britain's leading philosophers in the 1930s, when he was Grote Professor of Philosophy at London University, described in the *Spectator* as 'one of the most original minds of our time'.[11] William Temple, the Christian socialist Archbishop of Canterbury, admired him although he was not an Anglican. Because he used plain language, he was also popular, giving regular talks on BBC Radio. But his reputation did not survive the war, when he moved to Edinburgh University. Academic philosophy became dominated by linguistic analysis, an 'abstraction' Macmurray deplored. By the time Thomson came across his work, he had been relegated to a minor figure in academic theology. But Thomson was hugely excited by the central idea of Macmurray's forgotten and rather dated books, an infectious interest he took with him to Oxford:

> I was into a bloke at the time called John Macmurray. I think he was one of the most important British philosophers this century. And he was on to a concept of community. He used to say that the noblest form of human existence is friendship and that instead of being on a debit and credit ledger idea of 'If you do this for me, then I'll do that for you', we ought to develop a sense of community where people were committed to the welfare of one another.

Macmurray saw his purpose as being to challenge the starting point of modern philosophy, the idea that people are individuals first, who then choose how to relate to others. He insisted that people exist *only* in relation to others. His 'other-centred' view was not just a challenge to modern philosophy, but to liberalism. The central idea of liberalism, that individuals should be free to do whatever they like provided they do not harm others, started from an unreal assumption, according to Macmurray, because it assumed that people exist in a vacuum and only impinge on others when they choose to.

He argued that the liberal self was incomplete, because people's personalities are created by their relationships in their families and communities. Or, as Blair put it in 1993, 'We do not lose our identity in our relations with others; in part at least, we achieve our identity by those relations.'[12] Thus philosophy should start with the family as the model of society.

The effect of Macmurray's rethinking was to invert Adam Smith's dictum, 'Social and self-love are the same'. Smith said that if we follow our self-interest, we benefit the whole community. Macmurray said that by pursuing the community's interests we benefit the individuals within it, including ourselves.

Macmurray made grand claims for his philosophy, and his emphasis on doing rather than thinking (curious for a full-time, life-time academic) seemed to have more relevance than Wittgenstein to Peter Thomson's earthy and engaging quest for ways of applying morality to the real world. In fact, Macmurray's work was not the radical inversion of the assumptions of Western philosophy he claimed. The British ethical and Christian socialist thinkers of the turn of the century, such as T.H. Green and L.T. Hobhouse, also believed that altruism was the highest form of self-interest. Hobhouse's view has been summarised thus: 'The characters of men and women should be so composed that they work as earnestly and strenuously for others as for themselves, for they themselves are better for it.'[13]

What was distinctive about Macmurray was that he combined this Christian socialism with an attack on liberalism which resembled that of Conservative followers of Edmund

Burke, who emphasise the family and tradition as the bonds that hold together organic communities, and who oppose individualism and rationalism.[14] In this, Macmurray anticipated the 'communitarian' philosophy of contemporary North American thinkers such as Charles Taylor and Michael Sandel. According to Sandel, the politics of the common good enables us to 'know a good in common that we cannot know alone'. Real societies are not 'voluntary associations', he says. The shared pursuit of a common goal is not a relationship people choose, 'but an attachment they discover, not merely an attribute but a constituent of their identity'.[15]

It is precisely the combination in Macmurray of Christian socialism and a 'conservative' critique of liberalism which underpins the apparent novelty of Blair's political philosophy.

'It's a long time now since I read Macmurray,' says Blair. 'But his books are still up on the shelves. And yes, I would agree he was influential – very influential. Not in the details, but in the general concept.'[16] Macmurray's other-centred philosophy crystallised Blair's thinking:

It seemed to me a sensible explanation of the human condition. There seemed a coincidence between the philosophical theory of Christianity and left-of-centre politics. I didn't work these things out very clearly at the time, but they were influences that stayed with me. They were formative influences.[17]

Surprisingly, Macmurray did not develop his thinking from the roots of English ethical socialism, so much as in reaction to Marxism. In the 1930s he studied and translated Karl Marx's early works, which continued to influence him: 'The more a society approximates to the family pattern, the more it realises itself as a community or, as Marx called it, a *truly human* society' (Macmurray's emphasis).[18] But, while inspired by the early Marx, he rejected the later work, especially the attack on religion. Macmurray was always profoundly religious, although he was not a member of a church until late in life, when he joined the Society of Friends (Quakers). His vision of universal community was ultimately a religious one, although not of any particular religion. 'It sounds wishy-washy, but it isn't,' says Peter Thomson.

Towards the end of his life, Macmurray came to believe that politics was not the way to make a better world. He wrote: 'To create community is to make friendship the form of all personal relations. This is a religious task, which can only be performed through the transformation of the motives of our behaviour.'[19]

He wrote that 'the state is a device', necessary, to be tolerated, but not a means of enlarging and universalising community:

> If we track the state to its lair, what shall we find? Merely a collection of overworked and worried gentlemen, not at all unlike ourselves, doing their best to keep the machinery of government working as well as may be, and hard put to it to keep up appearances. They are, like ourselves, subject to the illusion of power. If we expect them to work miracles, we flatter them, and tempt them to think they are super-men . . . Those of them who are wise enough to know their limitations, and to be immune to the gross adulation of their fellows, will resign; and government will be carried on only by megalomaniacs.[20]

This was not among the lessons Blair learnt from Macmurray.

Christian Socialist

It was at this point that the debate in Thomson's Oxford circle was joined. The question was, 'How to put the idea of community into practice?' Gallop and Gardner argued for political revolution, Thomson for spiritual renewal. Thomson hoped Blair might go into the church. According to him, Blair 'wasn't really a Christian' when he met him.[21]

Blair's father Leo was and is not at all religious, while his mother Hazel's faith was undemonstrative. Despite his prep school headmaster Canon John Grove's insistence that Blair was a sincere believer, religion was 'the last thing you would have associated him with' at Fettes, according to one contemporary. Blair took part in the school's 'outside service' in the poor parts of Edinburgh, but the former school chaplain who ran the service, Ronald Selby Wright, says, 'Tony did not really have an interest in religion.'[22] Blair himself says:

> I had always believed in God but I had become slightly detached from it. I couldn't make sense of it. Peter made it relevant, practical rather than theological. Religion became less of a personal relationship with God. I began to see it in a much more social context.[23]

Blair started to go to the college Chapel, and was confirmed in the Church of England towards the end of his second year. The importance of this event in understanding him can hardly be overstated. He was prepared for confirmation by the assistant chaplain to St John's, Graham Dow, now Bishop of Willesden, who says:

> Thomson came to me and said, 'Tony Blair would like to be confirmed'. I was pleased because he was from a group that was interested in social action, rather than the more usual groups of evangelicals – of the narrowly pietistic kind – or quiet intellectuals. He was looking for something that was active, to change society. He gave the impression of someone who had just discovered something exciting and new – he didn't know it all, that's why he was such fun to talk to.

Dow says there were usually two or three candidates for

confirmation a year, and remembers the discussions he had
with Blair in his study: 'Because of who I am, I would have
been quite straight about the commitment faith demands.'
Blair 'didn't disagree' with Dow's language of a commitment
to a personal Christ and to building the Kingdom of God, but
was more interested in practical change in society. For Blair,
socialism seems to have come first, in that he left school with
compassionate, anti-Establishment leanings, and was then
animated by the connection with Christianity. Dow still has a
copy of a book Blair lent him: *What Kind of Revolution? A
Christian-Communist Dialogue*, edited by James Klugman and
Paul Oestreicher.

Blair's religious belief was private. Oxford contemporaries
who did not know him well had no idea that he was a practising Christian. Even his best friend, the atheist Marc Palley,
who knew Blair was a Christian, did not know he had been
confirmed:

> I've never been able to understand the logic of religion. It's
> not for me. We used to have long discussions, and I used to
> say it's a complete load of rubbish, baloney and gibberish.
> He wasn't a godsquadder – he was the antithesis of a
> stereotypical godsquadder – but he happened to believe.

For years afterwards, his beliefs were not well known. In
December 1991, on a visit to New York, Gordon Brown's
adviser Geoff Mulgan was surprised when, after a heavy
Saturday night, Blair was up at the crack of dawn to look for
a church. The journalist Peter Kellner expressed astonish-
ment when Blair asked where the nearest church was during
a weekend visit at about the same time. Blair was unruffled.
'It's not a sin, is it?' he asked. It was only with the election of
Christian socialist John Smith as Labour leader in 1992 that
his religion became visible, and it came as news to at least one
close friend of over a decade's standing.

Some might argue that, at a time when the motives of
politicians are distrusted as never before, it helps to be known

as a Christian. However, it is obvious that he did not ask to be confirmed at the age of twenty because he thought it might one day come in handy when running for the leadership of the Labour Party.

For one thing, it was not yet clear that Blair would choose to go into politics. Olara Otunna remembers Blair at Oxford discussing the possibility of going into the ministry: 'It was at one point very much on his mind. It was certainly one of the options that he talked about seriously.' Blair was beginning to think about the future, and was forming the idea that he wanted to do something with an explicitly ethical purpose rather than a conventional career.

However, Blair swung instead to politics as the vehicle for his moral commitment. 'It seemed a normal consequence of what we were thinking about and doing for him to go into politics and not to be restricted by becoming a priest in the church,' says Thomson. The religious commitment he shared with Blair was more a moral engagement with the secular world than a spiritual vocation. At this point, says Otunna, 'it became clearer to him that the way to make a difference, the way to be useful and to help shape the destiny of those for whom he cared, was to work through the established political process'.

This desire to 'make a difference' is interesting. It seems that Blair's early, unspecific desire to 'be something' had become more altruistic. Maybe he still wanted to attract attention, but now by 'doing something' as well.

Into Politics

Although Blair may have been tilting towards politics, it was not immediately obvious how to 'make a difference' through the established political parties. The St John's group were all left-wing, but most had no interest either in the Labour Party or student politics. They shared Henry Kissinger's view that 'student politics are the most vicious kind of politics that exist, because the stakes are so low'.

It was not just the purple bell-bottomed trousers. Mainstream politics was as deeply unfashionable as dark suits in the early Seventies. But equally, after the romance of the 1968 student rebellions, the doctrinaire and intricate Marxism into which the student Left had retreated seemed much less fun.

Against a background of economic crisis, Edward Heath and Harold Wilson seemed interchangeably uninspiring, at least after Heath's retreat from the prototype Thatcherism of 'Selsdon Man' in 1972. In the winter of 1973, war in the Middle East almost quadrupled the oil price, and Heath announced a 'three-day week' to conserve energy supplies during the coal strike. The February 1974 election confirmed the electorate's lack of enthusiasm for the two main parties, which both saw their share of the vote fall at the expense of the Liberals and Nationalists.

New thinking on the Left was still dominated by Marxism. Some strands, such as that associated with Antonio Gramsci, were increasingly liberal and pluralistic, but all started from the same texts and were bounded by the same assumptions. And the old thinking was still working its way through the Labour Party – after Europe, the main internal struggle of the time was over how many 'major monopolies' the party wanted to nationalise.

'All of us were really interested in Marx,' says Peter Thomson, but Marxism was not the answer. Gallop's sectarian advocacy of the International Marxist Group's 'correct' line 'scared the shit out of us'. Thomson recalls:

What we were all after was the attempt to transcend the party system as it existed, Labour being Labour, the Conservatives not really knowing what they were, with this early Thatcherism. To be politically involved doesn't mean you have to be a member of a political party. But the facts of life are that you've got to make a decision about political parties. It was still ill-defined, but no way were we going to go the minority track of a Marxist group. It had to be something that could be communicated to the people.

Blair says: 'I went through all the bit about reading Trotsky and attempting a Marxist analysis. But it never went very deep, and there was the self-evident wrongness of what was happening in Eastern Europe.' But, asked whether he joined the Labour Party, he says: 'Oh no, that would have been regarded as terribly right-wing. I didn't join until '75.'[24]

As with his Christianity, Blair's socialism was hidden from those who did not know him well. Many contemporaries were astonished when he emerged not just as a successful politician, but a Labour one. He may have become politically committed at Oxford, but he did not become active. He was not involved in the two closely-fought election campaigns of 1974 – he was, therefore, not even a member of the Labour Party the last time it won a General Election. Nor did he have anything to do with the university Labour Club. He did take part in a sit-in in his first year, which was part of a campaign to secure a central university student union rather than college-based unions. Later on in his time at Oxford he did go on two demos against the National Front, which organised meetings at Oxford Town Hall. He only went to the Oxford Union debating society once, dragged by a girlfriend to see Michael Heseltine give a speech. Heseltine, who was just about to discover the Conservative party conference and who had yet to swing the mace, was in his prime. Blair was impressed, but not moved.

Farewells

In the summer of 1974, at the end of Blair's second year, Gallop and Thomson left Oxford to return to Australia. Before they went, and immediately after their exams, the three of them went on a trip to Scotland, with Peter Thomson's wife Helen, who had flown out from Australia, and Geoff Gallop's girlfriend. They all squeezed into a hired Renault and drove to Edinburgh. They went past the school Blair had left three years before. 'We were driving past Fettes and Tony hit the floorboards,' says Thomson. 'There must be something about that place.' Blair did not have warm memories of his school days. For Thomson, however, Edinburgh had a different significance. In a café in the city, he wondered aloud if John Macmurray still lived there. He looked him up in the phone book, and rang him. Blair directed them through the streets he knew well to a large stone house in Mansionhouse Road.

Blair himself never got to meet the man who inspired him. They decided that, as Macmurray was now eighty-four and probably quite frail, Thomson would go in alone. Having studied Macmurray for fifteen years, the confident and talkative Australian was for once overawed. 'He was this short guy, lucid, ramrod straight. He said, "The important thing is, did you enjoy it?" I said, "I certainly did." I was a bit tongue-tied.'

If Blair and Macmurray had met, they might have had an interesting debate about the choice between religion and politics as the means to a better world. Macmurray died a year later.

After Edinburgh the five went on to Gordonstoun and then stayed in Fort William, where Thomson remembers a high-spirited game of golf on a putting green at midnight, getting eaten alive by midges: 'We'd had a few beers, I think, a few ales.' Thomson returned to his post as chaplain at Timbertop school in Australia, little knowing that he had helped shape the politics of a potential national leader. But he and Blair kept in touch. They last met when Blair visited Australia with Gordon Brown in 1990. 'Tone's come a long way since [Oxford], but he's still got the basic thrust of it all,' Thomson says. 'He's developed a political realisation of the ideas, but they're still there. If he can take the people with him he can do great work, I'm telling you.'[25] Thomson retired in 1993, at the age of fifty-seven, to a farm 3,000 feet up in the foothills of Mount Buller, North East Victoria: 'Now I watch my cattle fatten.'

Geoff Gallop, meanwhile, abandoned Marxism, and became a state MP in Western Australia in 1986, a member of the right-wing faction of the Australian Labor Party.

Back in Oxford in his final year, Blair lived with Marc Palley and three women undergraduates in what Palley calls a 'pretty damp, extremely grotty and very cold' house in Argyle Street. His academic career at Oxford is summed up, rather inconsequentially, in the 'President's Collections', a kind of end-of-term report written by the President of St John's, Sir Richard Southern, a distinguished medieval historian.

> Early 1973: 'Well organised. Apt to leave things till the last minute. But a strong interest in many things.'
> June 1973: 'Pleasing structure to work, but some weakness in content.'
> February 1974: 'Seems extraordinarily happy.'
> December 1974: 'Signs of really understanding the principles of the subject.'
> March 1975: 'Needs to be tougher in thinking through his ideas.'

Blair graduated in June 1975. According to Alexander Irvine, head of his barristers' chambers, he just failed to get a First, because 'he simply didn't exert himself'.[26] Marc Palley is sceptical: 'To be fair to you, Tony, I think that's overstating it. I think he got a good Second.'

When Blair left Oxford, then, he was definitely left-wing, and ready to see the unfashionable Labour Party as the only possible vehicle for his political interest. His beliefs were still forming, but could already be described as ethical socialist. John Macmurray was the dominant influence, but he had also read several other more familiar works of the ethical socialist canon, such as R.H. Tawney.

While many people's politics are formed primarily by their parents, this was clearly not the case with Blair and his father. Tony's prep school headmaster, Canon John Grove, says: 'Father was rather wry about it and said, "Oh, he'll soon grow out of it".' But he never did. Blair's basic beliefs have not changed since he was twenty. He is the Christian socialist son of a secular Tory.

Two weeks after he graduated, Blair's mother Hazel died at the age of fifty-two, of throat cancer. It is possible that Tony Blair invented his own socialist identity, but if he had been predisposed to the Left in politics, an explanation may well lie in her gentleness and social concern. He did not see much of his father when he was young, but his mother was always there, and they were very close. 'It was absolutely clear that she doted on Tony and that Tony adored her,' says Peter Thomson, who had stayed with the family in Durham. 'She also had a really deep social conscience and I think Tony has turned out to be the type of human being that she would have wanted him to be.'[27]

One of Blair's friends at St John's, Olara Otunna, remembers him going home at the time:

He took such trouble to care for his father who had been, I think, even more affected by this, and his younger sister Sarah, who was terribly affected by it. This was something that one could see meant a good deal. He took a great deal of trouble to make sure that the family pulled through this.

His father Leo says: 'He was very solicitous towards me, very kind. He was a very loving son. His mother adored him.'[28]

Tony Blair says that his mother's death also acted as a spur to him: 'As well as your grief for the person your own mortality comes home to you. And you suddenly realise – which often you don't as a young person – that life is finite, so if you want to get things done you had better get a move on.'[29]

Many – perhaps most – people leave university not really knowing what they want to do. When Blair started his training as a barrister in London, he had gone into law for want of any strong pull in any other direction. Becoming a barrister (again following his brother) rather than a solicitor had more appeal to the show-off in him. His days as a pop star were over. But he saw the law as a base rather than a career. The skills of persuasive public speaking are a good grounding for politics – there are more lawyers in the House of Commons than any other occupational group.

At Oxford, Blair says, 'I had no thought of going into parliament'.[30] However, Geoff Gallop says – of Blair's second year – that he 'was starting to see politics as a future, he was starting to be geared up to go into politics'. And Marc Palley says that when he moved to London with Blair, politics was 'definitely in his mind' as his vocation.

Notes

1. Martin Jacques, *Sunday Times Magazine*, 17 July 1994.
2. BBC TV, *Newsnight*, 10 June 1994.
3. *Ibid.*, 23 June 1994.
4. Mel Johnson, in a book of Corpus Christi College reminiscences, *Corpuscles*, 1993.
5. Martin Jacques, *Sunday Times Magazine*, 17 July 1994.
6. *Ibid.*
7. Keith Dovkants, *Evening Standard*, 18 July 1994; *Marxism Today*, July 1990.
8. BBC TV, *Newsnight*, 10 June 1994.
9. Martin Jacques, *Sunday Times Magazine*, 17 July 1994.
10. Quoted in *Scotland on Sunday*, 24 July 1994.
11. C.E.M. Joad, *Spectator*, undated, review of John Macmurray, *Interpreting the Universe*, 1933, supplied by Peter Thomson.
12. Tony Blair, speech in Wellingborough, 19 February 1993.
13. Norman Dennis and A.H. Halsey, *Ethical Socialism*, p63.
14. For example, Alexis de Tocqueville, *Democracy in America*, and Michael Oakeshott, *Rationalism in Politics*.

15. Michael Sandel, *Liberalism and the Limits of Justice*, pp150, 183.
16. *Scotland on Sunday*, 24 July 1994.
17. Keith Dovkants, *Evening Standard*, 18 July 1994.
18. John Macmurray, *Persons in Relation*, p155.
19. *Ibid.*, p198.
20. *Ibid.*, p200.
21. Martin Jacques, *Sunday Times Magazine*, 17 July 1994.
22. *Daily Express*, 20 May 1994.
23. Martin Jacques, *Sunday Times Magazine*, 17 July 1994.
24. *Sunday Telegraph*, 18 March 1990.
25. *Scotland on Sunday*, 24 July 1994.
26. *Ibid.*
27. Jon Sopel, *Tony Blair: The Moderniser*, p36.
28. Martin Jacques, *Sunday Times Magazine*, 17 July 1994.
29. Jon Sopel, *Tony Blair: The Moderniser*, p36.
30. *Observer*, 2 October 1994.

PART TWO

CALLAGHAN
AND FOOT

3. LABOUR LAWYER
London, 1975–80

'He has got a sort of determined, self-disciplined, slightly obsessive quality.'

It has been said of Tony Blair that he is a politician without roots. But he did not simply arrive at the top of the Labour Party from a different and more advanced planet at the end of the Eighties. He joined the party in the wake of its split over the 1975 referendum on Britain's membership of the European Economic Community. He was an active and ambitious member of the party when the Callaghan government collided first with the demands of global capital in the form of the International Monetary Fund, and then with organised labour, in the wintry guise of the public sector trades unions. He began looking for a parliamentary seat in 1980, a time of potentially terminal turmoil in the party. The idea that Blair does not have roots in the party could not be more wrong. He is not rootless, he is just young. The older politicians who surround him have been marked by public blooding in Labour's tribal warfare. His political direction was none the less forged in the red heat of the Bennite revolution in the early Eighties.

'With my class background, if all I had wanted to do was to exercise power I could and would – let's be blunt about this –

have joined another party,' Blair said after he was elected leader.[1]

When he joined, one of the most important issues dividing the Labour Party was Europe. Blair was still at Oxford when he voted in the referendum, on 5 June 1975. He voted in favour of Britain's continued membership of the EEC, along with the 67 per cent majority in the country, and most of Harold Wilson's Labour Cabinet, but probably against most of the Labour Party itself. Tony Benn had proposed the referendum, but once Labour was out of power, when the Left gained control of policy, the party promised to pull out of the EEC. On this central issue of British politics, Blair's private beliefs have been consistent – although when party policy swung against Europe he felt obliged to toe the line in public.

Blair moved into a basement flat in Earl's Court, west London, with his university friend and fellow lawyer Marc Palley. The flat, 92 Ifield Road, S.W.10, was in the Redcliffe ward of Chelsea constituency, the safe seat of Conservative Nicholas Scott. A fellow constituent was the new leader of the Conservative Party, Margaret Thatcher, elected in February in a coup of the Tory modernisers against the traditionalists. Harold Wilson, already preparing to resign the following year in favour of James Callaghan, was absorbed in a time-consuming struggle to quarantine Tony Benn in the Industry Department. Meanwhile the Labour Party was still dreaming of achieving the 'irreversible shift of wealth and power in favour of working people and their families' promised in its manifesto through ever-more unlikely programmes of state ownership and 'planning agreements'. Both government and party were oblivious to the threat from Thatcher, who asked the Conservative Party to 'put its faith in freedom and free markets, limited government and a strong national defence'.[2]

The Redcliffe branch of the Chelsea Labour Party had become inactive, and Blair arrived at the same time as two long-standing members decided to try to revive it. Sandy Pringle and Tim Bolton, then Chairman of the Chelsea

Labour Party and now a local councillor, wrote to all the members in the ward and asked them to come to a meeting in Pringle's flat.

Blair was one of the twenty people who turned up. Pringle says he was 'very encouraged to think there were all these young people around'. Pringle became branch Chairman and, at his first meeting, Blair became Secretary. Branch secretaries are automatically members of the General Committee, the all-important body which runs the constituency-wide party, and which used to choose parliamentary candidates. Thus Blair received an early initiation into the ancient rites of Labour's internal machinery. Branch and General Committee meetings were sometimes held at the Gunter Arms pub on the Fulham Road. Although they did meet in people's homes, says Pringle, they did not meet in Blair's basement flat – 'the sort of place where students would live'.

Pringle found Blair 'exceedingly bright and engaging', a 'fairly competent' Secretary, and they became quite good friends. He recognised him as a 'chap of ability', and thought his politics were like the old or Tribune Left – as distinct from the new, more Marxist-influenced Labour Left. He had 'definitely radical views in his attitude towards the establishment', and had a 'healthy disrespect' for it, says Pringle.

At about the same time as he joined the Labour Party, Blair also joined the Society of Labour Lawyers, an organisation founded in 1949 which is affiliated to the party. 'Blair, A.C.L.' is listed in the Society's membership records as 'Bar student', having started his one-year course at the Bar in September 1975.

In order to practise as barristers, students who pass the Bar exams have to get a place as a 'pupil' in a set of chambers – a group of barristers who share offices. In those days, as is still often the case, pupils were not paid by their chambers, and so the Inns of Court awarded scholarships. Before Blair's interview for a scholarship in 1976, he found himself waiting with other candidates seated in alphabetical order. He was next to Cherie

Booth, who was one of the most academically outstanding of that year's students. After Seafield Convent Grammar School in Crosby, where she was 'one of the most intelligent pupils I ever taught', according to her history teacher Margaret Oliver, she had taken the highest First in law at the London School of Economics. Like Blair, she was interested in politics, but she had joined the Labour Party three years earlier in 1972.

Tony Blair came across her again when he applied to be a pupil at the chambers of Alexander Irvine.[3] Blair had met Colin Fawcett, a QC and head of chambers, at a friend's twenty-first birthday party at Beaconsfield Golf Club. In one of those curious twists which punctuate Blair's story, his legal career began in the same deeply Conservative Home Counties town as his parliamentary career, which started in the Beaconsfield by-election six years later. Blair asked Fawcett for advice: he recommended Irvine, and agreed to 'effect an introduction'. Irvine had already taken on a pupil, and did not want another. Blair applied late, but 'he bowled me over with his enthusiasm', says Irvine. He broke his usual practice and took him on as well as the highly impressive student he had already recruited – Cherie Booth.

Alexander Irvine is now shadow Lord Chancellor – he was made a working Labour peer, as Lord Irvine of Lairg, in 1987. The youngest of his contemporaries to become a QC – a Queen's Counsel, one of the barrister elite – he is a rigorous intellectual meritocrat. He can be abrasive. According to Blair, on one of his first meetings with Irvine, he was confronted with the question: 'So, your parents were rich enough to send you to a public school then?'

Blair tried to reply tactfully: 'Well, of course you can criticise my public school education —'

'I bloody well will!' was the terse reply. (Blair told this story in an interview with Imogen Gassert, a sixth-former at Fettes, by then fully co-educational, for the school magazine, the *Fettesian*, in December 1991.)

Irvine joined the Labour Party at Glasgow University at the age of seventeen, and was a friend of John Smith's, a fellow law student there. Irvine stood unsuccessfully for parliament, in Hendon North, in the same year that Smith was first elected for the safe Labour seat of North Lanarkshire, 1970. When Blair started work in Irvine's chambers, Smith was a rising minister in the Labour government. Irvine's political contacts were to prove important in Blair's future career, although Irvine says somewhat unconvincingly that politics played no part in his decision to take Blair on, and that Blair's politics only emerged later.

In the summer of 1976 Booth confirmed Irvine's judgment by coming top in that year's Bar exams. Blair achieved an undistinguished Third class. Irvine's pupils, Booth and Blair, were now locked in competition for a permanent place – a tenancy – at his chambers. They knew that the chambers would only take on one of them at the end of their year's pupillage. But instead of driving them apart, the situation brought them closer. She says: 'I was with someone else at the time, but by the end of the pupillage I'd finished with him and started going out with Tony.'⁴ At Cherie's Christmas party in 1976, according to one account, 'during a party game which involved a certain amount of physical contact, she decided there was more to Blair than simply a professional rival'.⁵ Their relationship continued after Blair won the tenancy in 1977, and they were engaged two years later. At their wedding in 1980, Irvine proposed a toast as 'Cupid QC'. One of Blair's friends comments: 'As someone who made a speech at Tony Blair's wedding and John Smith's funeral, Derry Irvine must be a pretty important man in the Labour Party.'

Irvine says that Cherie was offered, and accepted, a tenancy elsewhere 'before the time arose for chambers to consider whether she should be offered a tenancy'. However, she would only have accepted if it had been made clear that Tony would be taken on at Irvine's chambers. She joined the chambers of George Carman, one of the most famous libel lawyers. It was a small set of chambers, which did not particularly fit her interests, because she mostly worked on family and employment law cases, and she later moved again.

Irvine says that Blair was a very good lawyer, good enough to become a QC: 'He was absolutely excellent. I have no doubt that he would have become a QC. He had a very keen sense of what was relevant. He was very good at getting to the point. He was a fast gun on paper, possessing an excellent facility with the English language.'[6]

Blair specialised in employment law, although the cases that earned the most money were commercial. One friend says: 'He is in fact basically an extremely able commercial lawyer.' His commercial work was varied, including such light relief as successfully defending the film version of *The Alternative Miss World* from the charge of 'passing off' brought by Mr and Mrs Morley, the owners of the real Miss World beauty contest company. (The film was described by a critic as a 'junket in which contestants of all shapes, sizes and sexes clad in *outré* dress or undress trod the dais'; Lord Denning, in the Appeal Court in November 1980, said he did not know 'how to put that description into English', but thought no one could possibly think it had anything to do with the real Miss World contest.)

'When I was a barrister I was a lark, sometimes in chambers to work on cases at 6.30 in the morning,' says Blair.[7] Despite the fact that most of his work was on commercial cases, Blair developed a reputation as an employment law specialist, and he acted for a number of trade unions. This prepared the ground for his future career, as employment law was soon to become a political battlefield, and union connections would be useful. Irvine's chambers also acted for the Labour Party, although Blair's first taste of political litigation came when he briefly stood in for a barrister in another set of chambers.

He was thus peripherally involved in defending the Labour Party in one of the many court actions in the Reg Prentice case, which symbolised the state of the party in the mid- to late Seventies. It was an important chapter in the mythology of betrayal that drove Labour to distraction after the defeat of 1979. Prentice was the Labour Education Secretary, then Overseas Development Minister, and MP for Newham North East. He had started on the Left of the Labour Party, but had become an increasingly unpredictable rightwinger, calling for a 'Government of National Unity'. In June 1975 he was 'deselected' by his left-wing constituency Labour Party – its General Committee voted 29-19 against him as the Labour candidate at the next election. The difficulty of carrying through this decision convinced many in the party that compulsory reselection for all MPs was necessary – a demand which was to be won in the Bennite revolution after 1979. Blair has always supported the principle, on democratic grounds, without supporting the rest of the Left's demands for ideological purification. He said in 1992:

> What is so obvious in retrospect is that where we went wrong in the early Eighties is not in introducing democratic accountability – for example, reselection. There's nothing wrong with that at all. I mean, why shouldn't people go through a process of reselection? It only ever became a problem if your local party became dominated by small cliques, whether of Left or Right, and was not representative of your local community.[8]

Two of Prentice's supporters, students Julian Lewis and Paul McCormick, challenged his deselection in the courts – at one point attempting, unsuccessfully, to have the officers of the local party imprisoned for contempt of court.[9] In October 1977, Lewis and McCormick's moral argument was destroyed when Prentice defected to the Conservative Party. (One of the witnesses called by Lewis and McCormick in their legal action was a Labour Party member called Alec Kellaway, who later joined the Social Democratic Party. It was Kellaway who made Newham North East famous for another spectacular defection in June 1994. He was by then the Liberal Democrat candidate for the parliamentary by-election there, when he re-defected to Labour on the eve of the poll, citing the party's likely new leader as one of his reasons.)

Prentice's defection was a great coup for the Labour Left, as Chris Mullin, a campaigner for automatic reselection, said:

> Roy Jenkins and Shirley Williams and all the rest of them went down there and gave speeches about what a great socialist Reg Prentice was. Then he turned round and said, 'I'm a Conservative actually, I'm not even a Liberal, I'm not a moderate, I'm a Conservative' . . . And that meant his supporters and all the rubbish they had put out in his support looked very silly indeed.[10]

However, Julian Lewis's court cases dragged on until January 1978 when, in *Lewis v Heffer* (Eric Heffer being Chairman of the Labour National Executive), Lord Denning threw out the complaint. 'I will describe it in terms of a war, for so it is', said Denning, summarising the story:

> There is a struggle for power in a parliamentary constituency. There are two factions within that party. Each is striving for the mastery of the general meeting of the local party; for it is the local general meeting which has the management of its affairs. Whichever faction gets the mastery of the local general meeting selects the parliamentary candidate for the constituency. It selects of course a man of its own way of thinking. It is a safe Labour seat. So the faction which wins will have a representative in parliament . . . In Newham North East the struggle became acute when one faction sought to replace the existing Member of Parliament, Mr Prentice, by one of its own persuasion . . . Each faction pours obloquy on the other.

The case lit up the byzantine and indefensible structures of local Labour parties. Denning's description was an accurate portrayal of the nature of Labour Party activity in that period all over the country.

There are within Newham North East a number of small branches of the Labour Party. They send delegates to the local general meeting. There are other organisations, such as trade unions, which also send delegates. The rules prescribe the number of delegates to the local general meeting . . . Some favour one faction. Others the other. They are fairly evenly divided. Each faction strives hard, therefore, to increase its own delegates and reduce those of the other faction. Each faction has done this to some extent by 'infiltration'. That is, the faction will bring in a newcomer to live in the constituency. He joins the local constituency Labour Party. He is active as a branch member and becomes a delegate for a branch. Other newcomers do the same. Just a handful of newcomers may make all the difference to the voting and to the result.

Even a passing knowledge of the case can only have helped form Blair's conviction that the Labour Party needed to reform its internal democracy.

Blair's political ambition was still unfocused. After little more than a year in the Chelsea Labour Party, he and Marc Palley moved. Palley says they discussed 'moving into an area of London which had a stronger Labour Party'. Instead, they moved to a flat in St Edmunds Terrace in Primrose Hill, in another Conservative constituency, Marylebone. Blair was not active in the Marylebone Labour Party, although his new girlfriend, Cherie Booth, was. She lived in the neighbouring Lord's-Hamilton Terrace ward and was a member of the constituency General Committee.

In 1979, Blair moved south of the Thames to Wandsworth, to 41 Bramford Road, S.W.18, by Wandsworth Bridge, the house of another lawyer friend, Charles Falconer. They had first met at school in Scotland, where Falconer went to Trinity College, Glenalmond. 'We got on very, very badly,' Falconer says. They were rivals: Falconer went out with Blair's sixth-form girlfriend Amanda Mackenzie-Stuart after Blair did. They met again towards the end of 1976, as barristers working in different offices in the same building. Falconer, a leading commercial lawyer, became a QC at the age of thirty-nine in 1991.

It was while he lived in Falconer's house that Blair began to engage in public politics, writing his second published article (the first was a staggeringly dull review of a hundred years of drama at Fettes College for the *Fettesian* centenary supplement in 1970). It was a hard-hitting and clear piece, liberal rather than socialist, on the arbitrary powers of the Immigration Service, in the *Spectator*, 18 August 1979.

Over the next two years, 'Anthony Blair' wrote eight articles for the left-wing *New Statesman* and another for the *Spectator*. (He was called Tony at Durham Chorister School, and occasionally Anthony at Fettes. As a Labour candidate in the Beaconsfield by-election in 1982 and in Sedgefield in 1983 he was Tony, and thus he has remained ever since.)

His first article in the *New Statesman* (16 November 1979) like most of those that followed, was on employment law. He was paid £45. The significance of these early writings is that he then appeared to be advocating a relatively broad definition of legally permissible secondary strike action. In one case, he supported the steel union ISTC calling steel workers in the private sector out on strike in support of their public sector colleagues. (Blair had acted for the ISTC in the case – in 1994 the union's executive was the first to nominate him for the Labour leadership, and to recommend its members to vote for him.) The Court of Appeal ruled that the private sector strike was not 'in furtherance of a trade dispute', because it was 'political'. Blair argued:

> Spreading the strike to the private steel sector will put pressure on the government to end the strike. No one seems to have dissented from that. If that is so, then of course the action in spreading the strike furthered the dispute with the BSC [British Steel Corporation].[11]

However, this indirect industrial action would have fallen

foul of the definition that he was to propose ten years later, as shadow Employment Secretary. His 1990 policy was that a second group of workers must have a '*direct* interest' in the outcome of a dispute to be allowed to strike.

Blair used quite immoderate language about the judiciary – the Court of Appeal 'massively over-reached itself' in a 'staggering' decision, he wrote. But his articles were carefully written on the points of law, and give little away of Blair's views on the heated arguments of the period over the political role of trade unionism.

When Blair moved to Falconer's house he transferred his membership to the Fairfield branch of the Battersea Labour Party, of which Falconer was already a member. After Labour lost the 1979 election Falconer remembers going with Blair to a meeting at which Alf Dubs, the new Labour MP for Battersea, reported back on the mood of the party at Westminster:

People were saying, 'What about Mr Callaghan?' Mr Callaghan was broadly quite unpopular, he was seen as a sell-out merchant etcetera, by the grassroots of the party. Having lost, all that had gone before looked a miserable failure, which in some respects it was, but not in every respect. Alf Dubs said he had been to see Callaghan, as all the new MPs do. Callaghan was depressed, he said, and bored, and Callaghan had said, 'What are you interested in?' And Dubs had said something like immigration and inner-city issues. Dubs said that Callaghan had responded by saying, 'Oh God, another immigration and inner-city issue man – what we really want is people interested in agricultural issues', and we all laughed, thinking what a dreadful fellow Callaghan was. At the same time Dubs had passed round a sheet of paper saying what he had done since he arrived in the House of Commons the month before, and it said that he had applied to join the agriculture committee of the Parliamentary Labour Party.

Blair's starting point in the politics of the Labour Party was disappointment with the governments of Harold Wilson and James Callaghan in the Seventies, and what he described in 1982 as the 'tired excuses of pragmatism from the Labour Right'.[12] There is still a trace of that now. During the leadership campaign in 1994, he criticised the last Labour government: 'In truth, government under the guidance of either main party had become too centralised, too bureaucratic and too indifferent to the fundamental rights of the citizen which no government, irrespective of their "mandate", should be able to ignore.'[13]

Callaghan inherited a weakening and directionless government which had, and still has, few friends. Although the economic crisis abated – the IMF loan secured by Denis Healey in 1976 was never actually used, inflation began to fall and living standards rose – the political crisis became acute. The trade unions destroyed the popular Social Contract, as their leaders proved unable to restrain their members' pursuit of sectional interests. Callaghan's union power base in the Labour Party collapsed in October 1978, in a wave of strikes throughout the public sector over the Winter of Discontent. Party members were further antagonised by a series of illiberal acts, most symbolically the virginity testing at Heathrow airport of Asian women claiming immigration rights on marriage.

In those days, to be a Labour Party member disappointed with the Labour government was to be left-wing. And most party members were – especially the activists who dominated General Committees. A chasm had opened up between the parliamentary leadership and party. At that time, Blair was with the party.

Falconer says 'it never occurred to me' that Blair might one day be leader of the Labour Party. 'It is quite surprising. But he has got a sort of determined, self-disciplined, slightly obsessive quality, which makes him the sort of person who will become leader of the Labour Party – or leader of a political party. He's quite skilful.' Falconer remains a close friend – many of Blair's friends are not politicians, they are lawyers and friends from Fettes and Oxford:

He's remained remarkably unchanged by the whole thing.
It happened quite quickly and therefore he remains easy to
deal with, extremely involved in, as it were, the minutiae.
Because he's got quite a lot of friends who he's kept over a
long period of time and, certainly speaking for me and my
family's relationship with him and his family, he has
remained broadly the same even though our lives have substantially diverged.

By now, Blair's life had taken a more 'Establishment' shape.

Notes

1. Tony Blair, *Vanity Fair*, March 1995.
2. Margaret Thatcher, *The Downing Street Years*, p15.
3. The chambers, 2 Crown Office Row, were headed by Michael
   Sherrard QC. In 1981 Irvine set up his own chambers with
   nine other members of these chambers, including Blair, at 1
   Harcourt Buildings, now 11 King's Bench Walk. In those days,
   individual barristers took on their own pupils, although tenancy decisions were made by the whole chambers; nowadays
   most pupils are taken on by chambers and then allocated to
   barristers.
4. *New Woman*, May 1994.
5. Martin Jacques, *Sunday Times Magazine*, 17 July 1994.
6. *Ibid.*
7. *Evening Standard*, 16 November 1993.
8. Tony Blair, interview, 8 June 1992.
9. Julian Lewis is now deputy director of research at Conservative
   Central Office. Paul McCormick is a barrister who stood as the
   Conservative candidate in Orkney and Shetland in 1992.
10. David and Maurice Kogan, *The Battle for the Labour Party*, p31.
11. *New Statesman*, 1 February 1980.
12. Tony Blair, Australian lecture, August 1982.
13. Tony Blair, speech in Cardiff, 15 July 1994.

4. ANTI-BENNITE
The Reign of Error, 1980–83

*'I'm basically a centrist in the party, and want to see it
united.'*

In the spring of 1980, Tony Blair's life changed: he and
Cherie Booth were married in the chapel of St John's
College in Oxford, the home town of Cherie's mother Gale.
Cherie's father, the actor Tony Booth, was famous for his
part as the 'Scouse git' in the television serial *Till Death Us Do
Part*. He had just given up a life of reckless drinking, woman-
ising and hell-raising. Nearly burnt to death in a fire in 1979,
he had given up alcohol and sought forgiveness from Cherie
and her younger sister Lyndsey, whom he had more or less
abandoned when they were young.

Blair underwent a more minor reformation on his wedding day: 'I had my last cigarette at 1.45pm and we married
at two. It was my wife's idea, one of the terms of the contract,
and I'm glad to say I still think I made the right bargain.'[1]

Unlike Tony, Cherie was a socialist by background and
through adversity. Cherie's father may not have been around,
but he was a famous Labour Party supporter. She and
Lyndsey had been brought up in Liverpool by Gale, who also
came from a Labour family, a working-class Roman Catholic
one. Gale gave up being an actress and took as many jobs as
she could, including one in a fish and chip shop. 'It's difficult
being a single mother now, but I think it was even more diffi-

cult then, and Gale was a tower of strength,' says Maggie
Rae, a lawyer friend with whom Cherie shared a house before
she got married. 'Cherie and Lyndsey had a difficult upbringing, in the sense that there was hardship, the family were not
well off.'[2]

Another change that occurred in 1980 was that Tony and
Cherie both began to look for seats in parliament. That story
is the subject of the next chapter. This chapter examines the
forging of Blair's political views in the period of the Bennite
revolution.

Blair was twenty-six when he and Cherie married, and that
summer they moved into their first house, 59 Mapledene
Road, E.8, in Hackney, north-east London. Cherie had been
living nearby in Maggie Rae's house, so they knew the area.
Mapledene Road is on the edge of a lattice of quiet tree-lined
streets with a mixture of 19th-century terraces and semi-
detached houses. It is an area that saw an influx of young
people buying their first houses in the early Eighties. Blair and
Booth's house was one of a row of four early Victorian three-
storey houses, just off Queensbridge Road, a wide
north-south thoroughfare through the middle of the borough
of Hackney. On the other side of Queensbridge Road is the
Holly Street Estate, which Blair once sarcastically described
as his 'favourite piece of architecture' – a sprawl of deck-
access flats at right angles to each other, crowned by a row of
four huge tower blocks. Today it is being demolished and
replaced with 'real houses' at one end, but to Queensbridge
Road it still presents a desolate face. Holly Street itself was
obliterated by the estate which bears its name, and it survives
only as the address of the four great system-built monuments
to Old Labour which loom over Mapledene Road.

This was the landscape in which Blair found himself when
the Bennite tornado tore through the Labour Party. Blair
and Booth transferred their party membership to the
Queensbridge Branch of the Hackney South Labour Party. In
some ways, they were typical of the social change that was
transforming the London Labour Party, as young professionals

moved into run-down, traditionally working-class areas just outside central London. Most of the newcomers, frustrated by the failures of the Wilson–Callaghan years, were impatient to change the party. Many were influenced by the peace movement and the women's movement outside the Labour Party, and many – though not Blair and Booth – by new Marxist ideas. When these new forces met the old guard that had run these constituency Labour parties in an unbroken but weakening line since the war, the clash nearly destroyed the party.

Blair shared with the Left the disillusionment with Labour's failure in office, although he drew sharply different conclusions from those of Tony Benn and his supporters. He saw the old working class being driven out – in the name of the working class – and felt that the few people like him were the only bridge between the old guard and the new type of activist. He was beginning to frame his distinctive argument about the need for the party to turn outward and draw people into membership.

The picture that emerges of him in this period is in some ways a surprisingly familiar one. He has been strikingly consistent in his attitude to the *party*. He was a Kinnockite before Kinnock, and an advocate of 'one member, one vote' democracy in the Labour Party long before it became possible. On the other hand, he, like Neil Kinnock, has changed his mind on some of the central *issues* of British politics. He supported unilateral nuclear disarmament. He went along with the party's policy of withdrawal from Europe, although he disagreed with it. He favoured 'enormous state guidance and intervention' in the economy, and supported trade union closed shops.

So, on policy the road he has travelled since the early 1980s is much the same road his party has taken, though he did set out down it well before most of his fellow members. Few Labour politicians – few politicians of any sort – can claim complete consistency over a decade or more. The question is whether Blair's changes of mind reflect the pragmatism of a career politician or considered shifts on the foundation of firm conviction.

The Benn Challenge

In Hackney, Blair was to devote his energy to Labour politics. It was from here that he launched his parliamentary ambitions. And it was here that he was to forge a set of political friendships which have stayed with him since, and through which he oriented himself in the charged and swirling politics of the Labour Party. His arrival coincided with Labour's national crisis.

Tony Blair and Cherie Booth attended their first meeting of their local Hackney Labour Party on 6 November 1980, according to the minutes of the Queensbridge branch. It was dominated by a debate about – of all things – the principle of one member, one vote in the party. Two rival motions were proposed for changing the system for electing the party leader, which was to be debated at a special national conference at Wembley the following January.

There were only ten members in the Labour Club on Dalston Lane, but the meeting followed all the fatuous procedure of Citrine's antique *ABC of Chairmanship*. One motion, which Blair and Booth supported, proposed that the leader should be elected not just by Labour MPs but by all the individual members of the party: 'one member, one vote'. The other was a standard wording circulated by activists of the Bennite Left, a 'model' resolution, which proposed the leader should be elected by an 'electoral college' made up of block votes divided 30/30/40 between MPs, constituency parties and trade unions.

The room may have been nearly empty, but the argument was fierce, although 'never acrimonious – quite heated debate sometimes, but none of the viciousness that characterised some of the internal Labour Party discussions of the time', according to one member. Both sides wanted to broaden the franchise beyond Labour MPs, but the Bennites wanted to give power not directly to party members, but to their representatives on constituency General Committees. One member, one vote was then a dangerously right-wing idea, associated with the Gang of Four, who were poised to set up the Social Democratic Party. In advocating it, Blair found an unexpected ally in the branch in Andrew Puddephatt, who was then firmly on the Left – he went on to lead Hackney council and is now general secretary of Liberty, the civil liberties group. He says he and Blair were 'very much on the outside of majority opinion at the time', but 'we were right and the others were wrong'. The one member, one vote motion was lost by 5 votes to 3.

The democratic choice of the Queensbridge Branch Labour Party, carried on the casting vote of the chair after a 4–4 tie, was the Bennite electoral college. This was the formula which prevailed at the special conference of the national party at Wembley on 24 January 1981, called to resolve the deadlock in the party, and which lasted until John Smith's reform in 1993.

The Left's victory on the national stage in securing the electoral college for future leadership elections was seen as a breakthrough in the war to elect the one leader who could be trusted to deliver the Left's demands, Tony Benn. But the victory had other effects. The day after the Wembley conference, the Gang of Four issued the Limehouse Declaration, and it was obvious not only that they would leave to set up a new party but that it would attract wide support from the public. The Left thought Labour's unpopularity was a temporary and necessary cost that had to be paid, and were determined to press on: the next battle would be for Benn to challenge Denis Healey for the deputy leadership, under the new system.

Blair's middle position in the party was evident in the deputy leadership election when it came in September 1981. As a rank-and-file party member, he did not have a direct vote in that election, but he told the *Guardian* later (17 May 1982) that he had preferred the compromise candidate John Silkin. When asked how he would have voted in the second round after Silkin was knocked out, he backed Denis Healey, but so reluctantly that he was unwilling even to speak his name: 'Definitely not Benn.'

This captures Blair's political position at the time. He was strongly opposed to Benn and the hard Left, but he was not a Healeyite rightwinger either. Although his left-wing Oxford friend, David Gardner, by then a journalist on the *Financial Times*, recalls: 'Tony Blair was impressed by Healey. I certainly wasn't.' In other words, his position was similar to that of the leader under whom he was to rise to the top: Neil Kinnock. Benn failed to win the deputy leadership – by less than 1 per cent of the vote in the electoral college – because Kinnock and his supporters abstained. Kinnock's abstention was a turning-point in Labour's history.

Parties Within Parties

Even before Tony Benn lost the deputy leadership election, the left-wing coalition behind him began to break up. Kinnock's peeling-off to form a 'soft' Left was reflected at the grass roots. And central to that process was a group of people who were friends of Blair's through the Hackney Labour Party.

The first, and perhaps most important, was Alan Haworth. Haworth lived with and later married Maggie Rae, a solicitor who trained as a barrister in Cherie Booth's chambers. That was how Cherie came to be living in her house at the time she and Tony Blair got married. As an ex-Communist, Rae was passionately hostile to the Trotskyist groups which increasingly dominated the Labour Left in London. Haworth, meanwhile, had been one of the 'Newham Seven', as Secretary of the Newham North East Labour Party when it voted to deselect Cabinet minister Reg Prentice. At one stage in the long and tortuous litigation over the affair, in which Blair was peripherally involved (see pp62–5), the Newham Seven had nearly gone to prison – 'which we would have quite welcomed', says Haworth, then something of a left-wing firebrand. Haworth was never a Trotskyist, although three of the Newham Seven were, and by the time he met Blair he was strongly opposed to the hard Left.

Haworth has long been an important party bureaucrat as well as a personal friend, and is now Secretary to the Parliamentary Labour Party, so he attends all meetings of the shadow Cabinet. He is one of those, like Anji Hunter, Peter Thomson and Gordon Brown, who met Blair by chance and forged long-standing bonds of mutual loyalty.

Barry Cox, Head of Current Affairs at London Weekend Television, moved in next door to Blair and Booth in Mapledene Road at the same time as they did. He became a millionaire in 1993 because LWT gave a group of managers a 'golden handcuff' share scheme to keep them during a successful bid for its franchise, and worked as fundraiser for Blair's leadership campaign. Cox and Rae jointly own the house in France where the Blair family has for a long time spent alternate summer holidays.

In Year Zero of the Bennite revolution, 1981, Glenys Thornton and John Carr moved into the Queensbridge ward. Thornton was later chair of the London Labour Party and general secretary of the Fabian Society. Carr was elected to the Greater London Council in May 1981, as a left-wing supporter of Ken Livingstone – but he too became increasingly distant from the hard Left. And Charles Clarke moved into the house that backed onto Blair's. He was a former president of the National Union of Students who had just started working for Neil Kinnock, then shadow Education Secretary, and had been elected to Hackney council in a by-election.

All except Cox were members of what could be described as the organisation which saved the Labour Party – although it nearly destroyed it first. The 'Labour Co-ordinating Committee' had come into being to mobilise the Left in the party and – less explicitly – to secure the leadership of the party for Benn. But during 1981 the LCC started to metamorphose into Benn's enemy within.

When the LCC started in 1978, under 'acting chairman' Michael Meacher, then a junior trade minister, it put itself at the head of demands for 'real' socialism in anticipation of defeat at the imminent General Election. When that defeat came, its newsletter, *Labour Activist*, called for 'a national campaign for full employment, a planned reindustrialisation programme and a reversal of Labour and Tory cuts in public expenditure' (September 1979). This meant:

> Britain should act in advance of other countries to expand her economy . . . To prevent a flood of imports that these policies might create, Britain will plan a growth of imports broadly equal to its growth of exports . . . The government should specifically make full employment its first priority. By full employment, we mean a reduction to 750,000 unemployed within two years, as a result of expansion and import planning, and to under 500,000 within two to five years.

Import controls were against the laws of the European Community, so Britain would have to leave. To these economic objectives were added the demand for unilateral nuclear disarmament, and, in order to achieve these ends in the teeth of repeated 'betrayal' by the Labour Party in parliament, the LCC argued for 'democratic accountability'.

At the 1979 Labour Party conference, the LCC demanded internal party changes. 'Twice in the active lifetime of most Labour Party members, Labour governments containing nearly all our present parliamentary leaders have gone Tory and led us to defeat.' In other words, the election defeats which followed spending cuts after the 1967 devaluation and the 1976 IMF loan. 'What this conference has to decide is if we are going to allow ourselves to be led up the same cul-de-sac for the third time running.' In order to 'make the leadership accountable to the movement', the LCC supported the automatic reselection of MPs, an electoral college to choose the leader and control of the manifesto by the National Executive.

The belief in betrayal, which explained the failure of the

Callaghan government without need for thought, was shared by many in the party who had no taste for the sectarianism which followed, or for the extremes of policy to which it drove them.

Labour's internal politics took on an absurdist quality, of high farce played with a straight face. Grown adults in the Labour Party set up something called the Rank and File Mobilising Committee. This was an attempt to bring together all the factions and cliques of the Labour Left, including the LCC and the Militant tendency. After the Wembley conference, it became the driving force behind Benn's deputy leadership campaign.

Now the LCC changed character. Two important things had changed. Before the electoral college could be set up, Labour MPs chose Michael Foot in November 1980 to replace James Callaghan as leader. Foot was a leftwinger, but acceptable to much of the middle ground in the party. He made it perfectly clear that he opposed Benn's challenge to deputy leader Denis Healey. For many in the LCC, being on the Left did not mean Benn or bust. Secondly, the success of the breakaway Social Democratic Party demonstrated the disastrous electoral effects of factional infighting.

Many in the Rank and File Mobilising Committee hailed Benn's narrow failure as a tremendous advance for the Left, and started to plan for a renewed onslaught the following year. But some of the rank and file had had enough. The LCC could no longer tolerate being in coalition with Militant, the Marxist party-within-a-party, and pulled out of the Mobilising Committee.

The LCC was run by an Executive, elected by a postal ballot of its members. In 1981 Blair's friend Alan Haworth was elected to the Executive on a manifesto which said: 'I firmly support the decision to withdraw from the Rank and File Mobilising Committee, and to seek the means of promoting Left unity which are less reliant on neo-Leninism.' Behind the Soviet-style jargon his election was a sign that something important was happening.

Haworth became Membership Secretary of the LCC and in 1982 persuaded Blair to join. The LCC had now become just the right vehicle for the backlash against Bennism. He says: 'Tony and I had a chat about how to modernise the party, how to break up the hegemony of the Stalinist Left. He mused over the possibility of starting a new organisation. I credit myself with saying that there is an organisation already.' Unlike most of the Hackney coterie, Blair clearly did not start so far out on the Left. He had to be persuaded to join the LCC in order to help fight the 'ultras' from within the caucuses of the Left.

The Hackney clique formed the core of a group within the LCC that started to organise against the hard Left in London. Charles Clarke says:

A group of us felt we needed an alternative political focus . . . We went through on a borough-by-borough basis trying to find people who we might be able to get involved. We had a planning group and Tony and Cherie came to it. They were very keen to do whatever they could, although they felt relatively ignorant of the ways of London politics.

In a mirror-image of the organisational methods of the sectarian ultra-Left, this 'faction within a faction' was brought together secretly by the LCC's Organising Secretary, Nigel Stanley, who later worked for Robin Cook and then Bryan Gould. At that time, 'very few people were prepared to come out against Benn,' recalls another member of the cabal, Jack Dromey, a Transport and General Workers Union official. Dromey's wife Harriet Harman was a radical lawyer friend of Cherie's. He was a Bennite who had come to realise that the coalition behind Benn 'was wrong and unsustainable – we had to debate and argue against the concept of the unity of the Left. There could be no unity with ultra-Leftism, there had to be an alternative, anti-sectarian Left within the party'.

Blair was not involved in the early, subterranean efforts from within the Benn camp to create the alternative Left, but he was a sympathetic ally from the centre, when some of the Bennites started to 'come over'.

By-election Circus

As the Labour candidate in the by-election campaign for the safe Conservative seat of Beaconsfield in April and May 1982 (see pp98–105), Blair was inevitably asked where he stood in the battle raging in the Labour Party. It was the first time he had had to take a political position in public. He was much better prepared than was usual for a by-election candidate at the time. Shadow Home Secretary Roy Hattersley chaired his opening news conference:

> Very often, particularly in a seat where it was hopeless, you knew that you'd got to carry the candidate, without it look-ing as if you were carrying the candidate. But with Tony, after about the first two seconds, you could tell that he could carry you. Tony just knew it all. He could work very hard.

On his own initiative, Blair had gone to party headquarters in Walworth Road and asked to be briefed on party policy. The national party's researcher on defence policy was Mike Gapes, now the MP for Ilford South.

> In those days there was no real proper organisation of any by-election. I don't remember any other by-election candidates in the early Eighties asking for briefing. He was serious and thorough. He wanted to know what the line was. He was keen, quite diffident, but very sharp. He asked all the right questions – 'What do I do if somebody asks this?'

When Blair then turned to the economic policy researcher at Walworth Road for a briefing, he found himself in the office of the former lead guitarist from the Ugly Rumours at Oxford, Adam Sharples. He and Sharples had not discussed politics at university – their talk had tended to be about whether they needed backing vocals for 'Black Magic Woman'. Now they found themselves going through the finer points of the party's Alternative Economic Strategy. 'He tackled the job of being a parliamentary candidate with the same sort of enthusiasm that he'd shown in the band,' Sharples says.

According to another Oxford friend, David Gardner, Blair was horrified to come face-to-face with the small print of the huge amount of new policy recently laid down by Tony Benn's subcommittees of the National Executive: 'Before the Beaconsfield by-election he said he'd been round to visit every office of the party, trying to find out what they thought of Europe and defence, and he was appalled.'

He was described by the *Guardian* (10 May 1982) as

highly pragmatic on the Common Market – 'come out if we must, but not as an article of socialist faith' – but firm on unilateralism. He says the older generation, accustomed to conventional warfare, has not yet awoken to the real nature of the threat, the 'warfare of the end game'.

Later that year he described both unilateralism and withdrawal from the EEC as 'really much less fundamental to a concept of socialism than is often supposed'.[3] On the question of Europe, David Gardner goes further. Blair's position at the time, according to him,

was absolutely nothing to do with suggesting withdrawal. I recall in some detail conversations we had before Beaconsfield in which the view was . . . if it becomes the case that we are obstructed from carrying out the democratically agreed socialist policy, then we confront that at the time – but that was always rather hypothetical.

However, his campaign literature was more emphatic about

the EEC than his private view. One of his Beaconsfield leaflets said: 'Above all, the EEC takes away Britain's freedom to follow the sort of economic policies we need.' That and the cost of the 'indefensible' farm policy 'are just two of the reasons for coming out. Only a Labour government will do it.' Nor did he try to downplay the party's policy of withdrawal; he told the *South Bucks Observer* (8 April 1982): 'If the voters of Beaconsfield want to protest about the government's policies on defence, the economy and the Common Market, they should vote Labour and not Liberal.'

Blair did take one clear stand on the divisions in the party. He made sure that Tony Benn did not come to the campaign, which was a rather bold thing for a by-election candidate to do at that time. The *Guardian* (10 May 1982) reported: 'At the mention of Mr Benn, he merely bows his head, says that he does not agree with him, and suggests there is now a steady move away from regarding him as the focal point for radical reform.' Blair told the *South Bucks Observer* (8 April 1982):

I'm basically a centrist in the party, and want to see it united. I do agree with some of Tony Benn's views but didn't support him for the deputy leadership. I want the internal differences in the party to be forgotten, so that we can expose the record of the government and put forward the socialist alternative.

This didn't stop the *South Bucks Observer* putting the headline 'Benn-backing barrister is Labour's choice' on its report, and Blair wrote a letter to the paper (16 April) protesting that 'alliteration is a poor substitute for accuracy', and saying 'I am emphatically not a Benn-backer'. His letter ended:

Just so as [sic] there is no further misunderstanding: I support the Labour Party's present leadership; Labour's plan for jobs; withdrawal from the EEC (certainly unless the most fundamental changes are effected); and nuclear disarmament, unilaterally if necessary; in particular I intend to campaign against Trident and American-controlled cruise missiles on our soil. I do so as a Labour Party man, not as a 'Bennite' or any other 'ite'.

What is interesting is not that he supported withdrawal from the EEC – it was party policy at the time – but that he qualified it. His public position on Europe, while still at odds with his private belief, was as far from official party policy as a by-election candidate's could be. The idea of changing the EEC to make it acceptable was explicitly ruled out in *Labour's Programme 1982* (p230): 'We do not believe a further attempt to change the nature of the Community would be worthwhile . . . Britain must therefore withdraw.' But it is curious that Blair did not attempt to focus his campaign on other issues. Instead, he chose to make Europe one of his main themes.

In this he stayed close to Michael Foot's line – anti-EEC but also anti-Benn. Closeness to the party leader turned out to be his passport upwards, not just under Foot, but under Kinnock and Smith too. Foot had been a passionate anti-Marketeer on Benn's side in the 1975 referendum, but since succeeding James Callaghan as leader he had become bitterly opposed to Benn's destructive campaign to push the party ever further to the Left. When Foot was asked why Benn had not been invited to Beaconsfield, he said it was a matter for the local organisers, and smiled: 'I think they've exercised their discretion very well.'

As for Blair's unilateralism, even John Smith – supposedly a consistent multilateralist – bowed to party policy at this time. Smith kept his political profile below sea level during the Bennite ascendancy, but his biographer Andy McSmith unearthed an interview with him in the first issue of a small left-wing magazine called *Radical Scotland* in February 1983. 'There is no great moral gulf between a unilateralist and a multilateralist if they are both genuine disarmers,' said Smith. 'What is needed is good timing so that a unilateral initiative has the maximum multilateral effect.' Not only did he accept unilateral initiatives, but he went on: 'I myself believe that Britain cannot afford to be, nor is there a good reason for being, an independent nuclear power.'[4] He may have meant that this was his ultimate objective, *if* Britain's nuclear weapons could be used as an effective multilateral bargaining chip, but it was very close to an endorsement of Labour's non-nuclear defence policy.

While Smith's idea of negotiated disarmament included one-sided moves, Blair's support for one-sided disarmament included negotiations. He wanted Britain's nuclear weapons to be included in disarmament talks, but if the talks failed he wanted to get rid of them 'unilaterally if necessary'. There was a nuance of difference between his and the moral absolutist Campaign for Nuclear Disarmament position, which was simply to get rid of nuclear weapons – regardless of international negotiations. But there is no doubt that Blair at the time was a unilateralist, and his position was exactly the same as party policy.

The Australian Papers

Tony Blair's political views of this period are preserved in most detail in a long lecture he delivered on the other side of the world in August 1982. With Cherie, he flew to Australia to visit his friends from Oxford University, Peter Thomson and Geoff Gallop. He was also returning to the country in which he had spent three years before the age of five, when his father's first job as a law lecturer was in Adelaide. Gallop now taught politics at Murdoch University in Perth, and invited Blair to give a seminar to the staff and postgraduates at his faculty. What the Australians can have made of his detailed, twenty-three-page analysis can only be guessed at. Gallop now says, tactfully, that 'they wouldn't have known all that much about the British Labour Party, but Tony spoke well, and it went down well'. It is an invaluable document.

In what we now recognise as his distinctive, disengaged style, Blair observed the antics of Left and Right in the party from a distance – in this case one of about 9,000 miles. He recognised that Tony Benn's defeat in the deputy leadership election in 1981 was a turning-point, because it split the Left. 'The Benn campaign in 1981 may, in retrospect, be seen not only as the high water mark of his own personal fortunes, but of that of the "far" Left in the party,' said Blair. 'The question of the next year is going to be whether the soft Left/hard Left split within the PLP [Parliamentary Labour Party] and the unions becomes mirrored in the constituency parties.' The constituency parties, represented by delegates who by definition were activists, were the home base of the hard Left. Eight out of ten had voted for Benn in 1981.

The central question of his lecture was: 'How can Left and Right in the party be reconciled?' Some of his prescription looks rather dated now, but the strategy was prescient. He had been ahead of Neil Kinnock on the Benn–Healey battle of 1981 – Kinnock now says he wishes he had voted for Healey rather than abstained. Now he set out the strategy for renewing the party which Kinnock was to follow after 1983 – welding the 'soft Left' together with the forward-looking Right. The Right, he declared, had to come to terms with the need for economic radicalism required by the new scale of unemployment.

> The mild tinkering with the economy proposed by the Social Democrats nowhere near measures up to the problem. A massive reconstruction of industry is needed. However, a reflation of the economy that is unplanned would lead, almost for a certainty, to inflation; and the resources required to reconstruct manufacturing industry call for enormous state guidance and intervention.

The argument should not be about *whether* to increase 'central control' of the economy, he said, but about 'containing that control and marrying it to ideas of industrial democracy'. In one of his leaflets for the Beaconsfield by-election, for example, under the heading 'Tony Blair on the Economy', he had advocated 'Price control to help fight inflation' – such were the statist assumptions of Labour policy at the time.

In the passage most mocked by later events, he went on:

> That in turn will bring any Labour government into sharp conflict with the power of capital, particularly multinational capital. The trouble with the Right of the party is that it has basked so long in the praise of the leader writers of the *Financial Times*, *Times* and *Guardian*, that it is no longer accustomed to giving them offence. It will find the experience painful but it is vital.

This was traditional left-wing rhetoric. But only two years later, Blair himself was to bask in the *Financial Times*'s description of him as one of 'the most promising newcomers'. Certainly, Blair in 1982 could not have used the phrase 'dynamic market economy' which featured so prominently in his leadership campaign.

However, he also said in Australia: 'The Labour Party sits uneasily, squashed between traditional Clause IV Part Four socialism and an acceptance of the mixed economy.' When Labour leader Hugh Gaitskell tried to rewrite Clause IV in 1959, he too described the 'mixed economy' as incompatible with the part of Labour's constitution which committed it to securing the 'common ownership of the means of production, distribution and exchange'. There is no doubt that Blair saw the need to come down on the mixed economy side of the fence. In that sense, it is possible to trace the death of Clause IV to Perth, Western Australia, in August 1982. Although it was only later that he decided that his commitment to Europe inhibited the possibilities of reflation in one country, and that multinational capital was a fact of life, not an enemy.

On trade unions, Blair was also more 'traditional' than he later became. While insisting Labour should not ignore the threat from the SDP, he thought that in the long term the new party was doomed, because 'by their disastrous embracing of the Tebbit Bill, they have isolated themselves from organised labour, a fatal mistake for any radical party'. He even described 'traditional trade union militancy' as one of 'the necessary strands of radical thought' within the Labour Party.

However, Blair's Australian lecture reserved its sharper and more profound criticisms for the Left in the party. He admitted that 'the Left has generated an enormous amount of quite necessary rethinking in the party'. But it was the Left that now needed to rethink.

The Left is keen on democracy, and rightly so. But democracy should not be seen as something abstract, something the party has within itself. The party must have a democratic relationship with the electorate. The key word is relationship. It would be absurd if the party descended into populism, merely parroting the views of 'the electorate', however those views could be gauged. Equally absurd, though, is the view that there is anything to be gained from capturing control of the Labour Party machine and leaving the voters behind.

This had been aptly demonstrated to him in the London Labour Party. By a process of caucuses within caucuses, the left-wing faction which dominated the London-wide party found itself increasingly organised through the newspaper *London Labour Briefing*, which in turn was increasingly controlled by a Trotskyist group called the Socialist Organiser Alliance. Thus the London Labour Party found itself associated with support for the Irish Republican Army, 'anti-heterosexism', opposition to the 'Falklands/Malvinas' war and, ultimately, violent revolution. Blair suggested in his Australian lecture that *Briefing* would be regarded by most Labour voters as 'incomprehensible at best and at worst as scary'. This led to what was to become later a dominant theme in Blair's politics.

> The Left's position is often inconsistent on democracy. It will advocate party democracy, yet refuse one member, one vote . . . It will talk of decentralisation yet find itself at a bizarre and remote distance from most of the opinions of those to whom 'power' is supposed to be given.

Before he had a constituency in which he could put it into practice, Blair had the idea of what the Labour Party should be like. 'A local party should grow out of a local community – the party members having roots in that community.' Blair was already formulating his view that the party needed to turn outwards and recruit far more members. Austin Mitchell MP described the actually-existing Labour Party best some years later: 'A mass party without members, an ideological crusade without an agreed ideology, a people's party cut off from the people.'[5]

As an example of the party's lack of relationship with the voters Blair cited Labour's opposition to council house sales. 'That is for perfectly sound reasons of political principle. Yet there is something mildly distasteful about owner-occupier party members preaching the virtues of public housing to council tenants.' (The four monstrous tower blocks of the Holly Street Estate were no doubt looming in his mind.) In 1982 there were relatively few people in the Labour Party who saw so clearly through the delusions of the Left.

Blair was clear what the 'agreed ideology' of the party should *not* be – it could not be Marxist. But the alternative, ethical socialism, was not developed. The Left of the Labour Party, he said, 'must look for its political philosophy to something more sensitive, more visionary, in a word more modern, than Marxism, whether in the crude vanguardist[6] form preached by Militant or in its broader libertarian form' practised by 'the group of intellectuals who left university in the late Sixties or early Seventies'.

Soft Leftie

What Blair's Australian lecture reveals is that he was already positioned on the ley-line of Labour's renewal. He was not necessarily an original thinker – one theme in his political development is the importance of mentors, such as Peter Thomson at Oxford, Alexander Irvine and later Gordon Brown. But he was a rigorous thinker, and had already thought through many of the themes that were to become central to Neil Kinnock's efforts to rebuild the party. His association with Charles Clarke in Hackney, who was already Kinnock's adviser as shadow Education Secretary, no doubt helped. Blair was already advocating what was to be Neil Kinnock's strategy – to weld the 'soft Left' and the Right of the party into a force capable of leading the party back from the brink of oblivion. However, he was doing so before the disaster of the 1983 election persuaded many in the party that it was necessary.

The lecture reveals that Blair's true position in the Labour Party was 'soft Left', a phrase he used to analyse the break-up of the Bennite coalition. If anybody doubts this, they should note that, as late as 1986, he was still a CND member. The lecture certainly reads as though it was written from the Left, damning the corruption of values close to his heart. He preferred the label 'centrist' at the time (that is how he described himself during the Beaconsfield by-election campaign), and his leftness may never have been very apparent. But the truth about the 'soft Left', in the shape of Neil Kinnock, Robin Cook, Jack Straw and others, is that, at varying speeds, their outlook became indistinguishable from the Right of the party – as represented by Roy Hattersley and John Smith.

Blair, however, had travelled a long way down that road before the 1983 election. He got his 'betrayal' in early. In this he can hardly be accused of trimming to the prevailing wind – it was more like tacking into a storm, in the belief that the wind would eventually change. But when he was elected to parliament in 1983 he already appeared, in most senses, to be on the Right. The merging of the soft Left and the young Right was consolidated in the term 'moderniser' in the late 1980s, the traditionalists in the Labour Party being the backward-lookers of both hard Left and old Right.

The labels of the early 1980s still matter in one sense. The economic radicalism of those years may have been squeezed out by the realities of a more open international economy – it is hard now to imagine a Labour leader looking forward to 'sharp conflict . . . with multinational capital'. But what remains distinctively 'soft Left' about Blair is his radicalism when it comes to change in the Labour Party. Many of the Right took the view that there was nothing much wrong with the basic structure of the party – it was just that in the early 1980s the wrong lot took control of it. What is apparent from Blair's record in 1980–83 is a sense of his fundamental re-appraisal of the task of the Labour Party – a rethinking more complete than Neil Kinnock was able, or John Smith inclined, to undertake.

Notes

1. *Evening Standard*, 16 November 1993.
2. *Daily Mail*, 16 January 1995.
3. Tony Blair, Australian lecture, August 1982. The text of Blair's speech was transcribed and updated sometime between October 1982 and April 1983.
4. Andy McSmith, *John Smith*, pp110–11.
5. Austin Mitchell, *Beyond the Blue Horizon*, p85.
6. 'Vanguardism' is the belief that the more advanced sections of the working class – the vanguard – must take control of the trade unions and the mass party of the working class and use that control to radicalise the rest. In other words, as Blair put it in his lecture, 'capturing control of the Labour Party machine and leaving the voters behind'.

5 . The Race for a Seat

Hackney, Beaconsfield, the North East, 1980–83

'I suppose you just look at the world around you. Think things are wrong. Want to change them.'

Tony Blair started looking for a parliamentary seat as soon as he and Cherie moved into Mapledene Road, Hackney. But he had been thinking about it for some time. His Australian friend from St John's College, Geoff Gallop, returned to Oxford in 1977, to study for a doctorate at Nuffield College. He was thinking about a political career in Australia, and when he and Blair met, 'we would talk about what we were going to do when we got elected'.

Blair's unfocused desire at university to 'make a difference' had become specific. But why did he want to be a politician? He was asked this question in one of the earliest profiles of him, by Martyn Harris in the *Sunday Telegraph*, 18 March 1990. His answer was curiously evasive, as if he were slightly embarrassed by his early idealism: 'I was interested in politics, and in trade union law. I decided this was what I wanted to do.'

'But what did you want to do exactly?' asked Harris.

'Well, get into government. Actually run something.'

'Why?'

'Well, I suppose you could go into all the slightly twee motives. I suppose you just look at the world around you. Think things are wrong. Want to change them.'

Blair's first experience was daunting. In December 1980, he was one of seventeen who applied to be the Labour candidate in Middlesbrough, near his boyhood home of Durham. To be considered, he had to be nominated, by a branch of the party or by a local affiliated union or society. He got one nomination, from a branch of the electricians' union, but failed to make the shortlist. Stuart Bell, a fellow barrister, was the successful candidate, and is now a member of Labour's Trade and Industry team. He says: 'I met Tony Blair for the first time in the office of Tom Burlison, who said, "I've got this young lad here looking for a seat."' Blair was certainly in the right place. Burlison was a significant power-broker in Labour politics in the North, as the Regional Secretary of the General and Municipal Workers Union (now called the GMB). But Bell had already secured that union's backing. In fact, Bell had the seat sewn up. Blair may have been nominated by the electricians' union, the EETPU, but Bell says: 'The EETPU did a deal with me that they would nominate him but vote for me.' A fitting initiation in the parliamentary selection game.

Burlison says: 'My thinking was that [Tony] had to serve his apprenticeship in the Movement. He was quite a charismatic character, but he was young, pretty fresh-looking. I didn't think he was going to get a Northern seat.'

Back in Hackney, Blair threw himself into the fight against the Bennites. He first organised to win a position at the lowest level of Labour's scorched grass roots. A member of the branch for just four months, he tried to oust the then hard-Left Branch Secretary, Mike Davis, at the annual general meeting on 5 February 1981. The 'coup' involved persuading the old-style local councillor, Miles Leggett, to ask some of 'the old ladies' from the council estate to come to the meeting. Friends of Blair's also called on members beforehand, urging them to come to vote for him, because he was 'such a nice man'. It is most unusual to have house-to-house canvassing for such a humble position in the Labour Party. But it was necessary: at the meeting, Blair was elected Secretary, by just 17 votes to 15 for Mike Davis. Someone who was there saw a 'glint in his eye; I realised that here was a very ambitious man'. He also made no secret of his desire to become an MP, at a time when it was often considered improper to be so open about your intentions. Another member remembers: 'You were supposed to want to be a good comrade – if others urged you to put yourself forward, you would do it reluctantly, for the good of The Cause.'

At that moment, however, the Labour Party did not seem to be a good bet for an ambitious would-be politician. On the day Blair was elected Branch Secretary, Labour's former deputy leader, George Brown, was one of many to sign a *Guardian* advertisement in support of the Limehouse Declaration. The Declaration, by Shirley Williams, Roy Jenkins, William Rodgers and David Owen, only set up a 'Council for Social Democracy'. But the launch of a new party had become inevitable, and the Social Democratic Party was born at the beginning of March.

For Blair the *Guardian* advertisement was particularly significant because the MP for Hackney South was George Brown's younger brother Ron. Blair's father-in-law, Tony Booth, says in his autobiography that he heckled George Brown when he, Booth, was on the platform at a Labour Party celebrities rally early in 1964. Brown had proudly declared that he had found his brother Ron a seat, at which Booth shouted: 'Nepotism, nepotism!' That seat, Shoreditch and Finsbury, later became part of the constituency into which Booth's daughter moved.

It is possible that Blair might have thought at some stage of succeeding Brown, then fifty-nine, although it would have quickly become obvious to Blair that he was out of tune with the Bennite vanguard then sweeping to power in the constituency party. Brown himself says he saw Blair as a possible successor in time: 'He followed me quite closely. He supported my views on Europe – he was very supportive of Europe. He was a sensible man, very able.'

However, some members of the Queensbridge branch were

not prepared to wait for Brown to retire. They thought he was unacceptably right-wing, sympathetic to the Gang of Four, and wanted to deselect him. Their first move was to demand that he repudiate the SDP. The minutes of the meeting of the Queensbridge branch on 2 April 1981 are in Tony Blair's handwriting: Item 4, correspondence, notes the receipt of a letter from the MP, Ron Brown. Skating over the intense controversy, Blair recorded drily: 'It was felt by some members that the letter did not reject in sufficiently personal terms the Social Democratic Party.'

The party's new automatic reselection procedure now began to operate, and Blair was an active member of the group of Brown's supporters who organised to defend him. In the atmosphere of the time, it was an awkward task. As Chairman of the London Group of Labour MPs in 1981, Ron Brown was in the front line of the battle against the left-wing insurgency in the capital. Ken Livingstone described him as a 'particular problem' who 'did everything possible to sour relations between Labour MPs and the GLC'.[1]

By the autumn, many Labour MPs realised that they would not be reselected, or simply decided that the Bennite tide could not be turned. Brown says:

> My brother and I disagreed on not very much. But there were two things. One was on Denis Healey. He used to like him, and they got on very well. I used to say to George, 'He's a *viper* – watch out for him.' And my brother I'm sure is sitting up in heaven reading what Healey said about him in his book, and thinking, 'My little brother was right; what a shit Healey is.' The other thing was that my brother was quite clear straight away after Callaghan gave up, that it was no good sticking with the Labour Party. I said 'Not yet', I held out a bit longer.

With Blair's help, Brown was successfully reselected. He then almost immediately defected to the SDP, in October 1981. John Lloyd, the *Financial Times* writer and later editor of the *New Statesman*, was also a member of the Hackney South Labour Party and, like Blair, on the General Committee. He thinks Brown's defection hurt Blair:

> For people like Tony and me and the others who were Ron loyalists it was an absolute smack in the face. It would have been wonderful if he had fought on for what he believed in. But actually to say then, 'I've got a magic carpet called the SDP,' was awful. So the Left clearly said, 'We always told you, this guy is a traitor,' and what could we say?

This drama, a less extreme variation of the Reg Prentice story, was being played out in Labour parties throughout the country.

Brown lost the seat at the following election, and he is still bitter. 'It's ruined my life, but at least we've proved the point. I'm not saying I'm happy about it, but now they're all like I am.' Blair himself was never tempted by the SDP. He would not have disagreed with the SDP on policy, with the exception of proportional representation. But he thought they were wrong to leave. He believed the Labour Party had to change. He was hostile to Tony Benn because he thought Benn advocated precisely the wrong sort of change. But too many of the SDP, and Ron Brown was a good example, seemed to want to go back to the Labour Party as it had been.

It was with feeling that Blair invited former SDP members to return to the party after his election as leader: 'Of course I welcome back those people who left the Labour Party in the early 1980s for reasons that were understandable at the time. The Labour Party went through a bad period then.'[2]

In one small acknowledgement of his would-be patron, Blair took up one of Ron Brown's campaigns when he became an MP: in 1987 he pressed the government to tighten up the controls on flammable foam-filled furniture, which Brown had pursued as adviser to the furniture workers' union.

Despite Blair's closeness to Brown, John Lloyd, who was

firmly on the right wing of the Labour Party and an open admirer of Denis Healey, regarded Blair as something of a 'trendy leftie'. They often disagreed over the tactics of fighting the hard Left on the General Committee. Blair was a coalition-builder, always appealing to party unity, while Lloyd's instinct was to confront what he saw as leftist nonsense: 'Blair would always say, "This is alright, we can soften it", while I would say, "No, it's rubbish, we've got to throw it out."'

If a Labour rightwinger like Lloyd regarded Blair as a trendy leftie, the Bennites thought he was suspiciously rightwing. A friend of Blair's who supported Benn in 1981 remembers:

> When I first met Tony he was definitely not identified as a trendy leftie at all. I remember those of us who were trendy-leftie thinking he was quite right-wing. Nor was Cherie a trendy leftie, although she was definitely more of a feminist than him. The image that I had of him was of a very earnest, very serious person.

Blair was centrist, but his contacts in the party were on the Right. In 1981 the head of his legal chambers, Alexander Irvine, introduced Blair to John Smith, his friend from university, then shadow Trade Secretary. Blair wrote a paper for Smith on legal aspects of privatisation.[3] This was a time when Smith was lying low, waiting to see if the Bennite flood would ebb, and busying himself with his legal practice in Scotland. It was extraordinary for a member of the shadow Cabinet, but Smith made only two speeches in the Commons in 1981 after February, and then did not speak at all in Commons debates for thirteen months until the end of 1982, when he was appointed shadow Energy Secretary.[4]

In the autumn of 1981 Blair was again nominated but not shortlisted for a northern seat, Teesside Thornaby, most of which became Stockton South in the boundary changes two years later. The vacancy was created by another defection to the SDP of a sitting MP, in this case Ian Wrigglesworth. He was, like Blair, a graduate of the Redcliffe branch of Chelsea Labour Party. Although Wrigglesworth had local roots, he was bitterly resented as an outsider, and the local party was determined not to have 'another carpet-bagger'. To them, Blair was just a 'Southern smoothie'. The successful candidate, Frank Griffiths, confirms Blair's centre-Left position. He recalls Blair protesting, 'in a friendly but firm way', to a group of members in Teesside Thornaby that he was on the Left of the party because he was a supporter of *Tribune*. This was just before the newspaper – which Michael Foot had edited in the Fifties – was captured by the Bennites. In fact, Blair was lucky to be unsuccessful here, because Wrigglesworth held Stockton South in 1983. He lost it in 1987, and is now chairman of the Northern Confederation of British Industry and a Liberal Democrat. Blair also spoke to various Labour Party branches and affiliates in the next door seat – Stockton North – but failed even to be nominated.

Blair himself thought he was not left-wing enough to be chosen as a parliamentary candidate. Sandy Pringle, Blair's first Labour Party mentor from Earl's Court, remembers meeting him and Cherie Booth at a Greater London Labour Party conference in early 1982. Pringle knew that Blair was looking for a constituency and said: 'Any luck, Tony?'

'Not so far,' said Blair.

'You've got to wear all the right badges.'

With which, says Pringle, 'Blair ruefully agreed'. Blair certainly thought his refusal to subscribe to the entire Bennite wish list was an obstacle to getting a candidacy.

Blair's next attempt to become a Labour candidate was more modest. The man who was to lead the Labour Party in just twelve years' time now aspired to be a Hackney borough councillor in the 1982 local elections in London. It was a time of conflict between Labour councils and central government, and within Labour councils between Right and Left. When Ken Livingstone seized control of the Greater London Council he inspired the Left with the rhetoric of confrontation with the Conservative government. 'The 1982 elections must be fought on the strategy of opposition to, not administration of, Tory policies,' wrote Livingstone's ally Jeremy Corbyn, now the MP for Islington North.[5]

Labour-controlled Hackney was one of the targets of the Left's 'Target 82' campaign. Blair wanted to be a councillor for his own safe Labour Queensbridge ward. Of a shortlist of five, he came fourth, and was thus saved the character-forming experience of serving on the new hard-Left Hackney council. In fifth place came Miles Leggett, the sitting councillor who had helped Blair become Branch Secretary the previous year. Blair's friend Barry Cox comments bitterly: 'Leggett was despised by the Trots and the Bennites, because he was the sort who believed in trying to help the people he represented.'

No voting figures are recorded in the minutes, only the fact that there were twenty-eight members present. What the minutes also fail to record is that Blair himself was not actually present. Instead, Cherie Booth argued for him. A court case kept him away, but there was a strong feeling at the meeting that he should have been there if he wanted to be considered seriously. 'I don't know that he would have been selected anyway,' says Mike Davis, the ousted Branch Secretary. Blair had been a member there for little more than a year, and 'we weren't sure where he was coming from'. However, it soon became clearer where he was going. Two months later, Blair was the surprise choice as the candidate for the by-election in the safe Conservative constituency of Beaconsfield.

Beaconsfield

The death of the Powellite Conservative MP Ronald Bell was reported in the Press as an opportunity for the Liberal-SDP Alliance to continue its spectacular by-electoral progress. A swing as great as that which delivered Crosby to Shirley Williams in November 1981 would have given Beaconsfield, the eighteenth safest Conservative seat, to the Alliance.

The question of who would be the Labour candidate was of little interest. Blair took advice from John Smith, through Alexander Irvine, and Tom Pendry, the centre-Left Labour spokesman on overseas development (and a friend of his father-in-law Tony Booth), and put himself forward.[6] The *Slough Express* on 26 March 1982, a week before Labour's selection conference, named only three of the shortlist of four: John Hurley, Jean Swaffield and Valerie Price.

Hurley, who was then the leader of Slough Borough Council, believes however that Blair was the choice of the party 'organisation'. He remembers that there were two questions asked at the selection conference which seemed to him to be aimed at putting Blair in a good light. One was about a research paper on housing which he, as the leader of an urban council, 'might have been expected' to know about – and did not – but, he thinks, Blair did. As a disappointed candidate, he may be over-estimating the forces arrayed against him. The state of Labour's national organisation at that time was such that 'fixing' a by-election candidate may have been beyond it, although Blair did use planted questions in Sedgefield the following year.

In any case, there can be no doubt that Blair was selected on merit. Doug Vangen, the present Chair of Beaconsfield Labour Party, was at the selection conference. He recalls Blair as 'like a breath of fresh air' and 'outstanding'. He came across as sincere and honest, in contrast to people who 'just trot out the party handout'.

Cherie Blair – as she called herself for the purposes of the by-election – joined energetically in the campaign. In one of his election leaflets, she wrote 'A message from Cherie Blair', a socialist feminist pitch sold in a Tory-MP's-supportive-wife style:

As a member for ten years I believe only the Labour Party

shows real concern for the welfare of women today. At a time of economic recession, women are often the first casualties, not only in terms of employment – and unemployment – but also because the burden of public spending cuts falls most heavily on them . . . I know Tony would do a good and caring job of work for this constituency and I hope you will vote for him on May 27.

In addition to this early experience of reconciling the role of politician's wife with her own political identity, Cherie also asked her father, Tony Booth, to add some showbusiness autograph-chasing to the campaign, with Pat Phoenix. As Elsie Tanner, Phoenix, whom Booth later married, was a *Coronation Street* megastar and drew larger crowds than the candidate himself.

Blair was chosen as the Labour candidate on 1 April 1982. The next day, Argentina invaded the Falkland Islands. On 3 April, an emergency sitting of the House of Commons approved the sending of a task force, after the Labour leader Michael Foot demanded action. Three weeks later, British forces recaptured South Georgia. On 1 May, the task force bombarded the Falklands. With the by-election to be held on 27 May, the campaign was dominated by news of the war, which helped reconnect Margaret Thatcher with popular opinion, and which punctured at least three of the wheels of the Alliance bandwagon.

Blair was caught in Labour's national dilemma. 'I supported sending the task force,' he told the *Sunday Telegraph* (9 May 1982). 'At the same time I want a negotiated settlement and I believe that given the starkness of the military options we need to compromise on certain things. I don't think that ultimately the wishes of the Falkland islanders must determine our position.' The *Guardian* (12 May 1982) described Blair's comments as 'a careful analysis of the British military options', while the *Daily Telegraph* (14 May), whose reporter Godfrey Barker hounded Blair during the campaign, alleged that his position on the Falklands was 'victory to the

Argentines'. What Blair actually said was: 'There are limitations to our military ability,' and 'there must be proportionality between lives lost and the cause at issue'. The weakness in his position – which was that of the Labour front bench – was that 'the cause at issue' was territorial gain by aggression. He appeared to be willing to allow a dictator keep what he had wrongly seized. Even the *Guardian*'s friendly paraphrase of Blair's views impaled him on this hook: 'A promise of self-determination for the Falklanders could lead to a full-scale war, he said. Nor was he convinced about such an abstract purpose as preventing the aggressor from retaining his spoils.'

Cutting Teeth

However, the campaign gave Blair the chance to be noticed by almost the entire leadership of the Labour Party. Party leader Michael Foot was impressed by candidate Blair, and delivered an endorsement to BBC TV's *Newsnight*, dog-eared from use ever since, as he stepped out of a fish-and-chip supper at the Stag and Hounds pub in Beaconsfield: 'We're very proud of everything he's been saying here and, whatever the result, we believe he's going to have a very big future in British politics.' It wasn't the kind of thing he said about every Labour by-election candidate – famously, he refused to endorse Peter Tatchell in Bermondsey early the following year. But it was also a warmer endorsement than that bestowed on the leadership-approved Ossie O'Brien in Darlington.

The Beaconsfield campaign saw a surprisingly large number of senior Labour politicians – excluding Tony Benn – pass through this quintessentially Conservative exurb. Shadow Chancellor Peter Shore came to denounce the new monetarists in the Cabinet – Margaret Thatcher, Geoffrey Howe, Leon Brittan, Patrick Jenkin. 'What is the one thing these people have in common? – they're all lawyers,' said

Shore at his most condemnatory. Barrister Blair sat beside him, expressionless, on the platform.

Denis Healey, Stan Orme, Merlyn Rees and Gwyneth Dunwoody were also scheduled for the final fortnight, prompting the headline in the *Slough Observer* (14 May 1982): 'Labour moderates are backing Blair.' Michael Foot and Roy Hattersley, on the left and 'moderate' wings of the party respectively, teased each other about Blair's intra-party loyalties. Foot says that when he remarked to Hattersley, 'What a good candidate we've got down there,' Hattersley claimed Blair as a supporter of his. To which Foot replied: 'Oh? He seemed all right to me.'

John Smith also came to the campaign, and Beaconsfield was where Blair first met Neil Kinnock. Three Labour leaders present and future came together at the by-election to bless a fourth. Like the others, Kinnock was impressed:

> There he was in the silvan lanes of Beaconsfield, nicely received by people because he was a pleasant, articulate but not over-smart man from London. He fought a great rearguard action because he was active, because he was accessible, because he was charming, and when he did hustings with other candidates he attracted people. He wasn't in any sense precocious or flashy, and he was fighting it out of duty – and curiosity, I think, to see what it was like. He couldn't have picked a better place to cut his teeth – right down to the gums as the result turned out – but it was a creditable performance in very difficult circumstances.

The *Telegraph*'s Godfrey Barker described Blair as 'too nice and too unguarded to be a politician'. Blair told a news conference that he supported the industrial action taken by health service workers. Barker pointed out that the health service action could endanger life.

Mr Blair began a *mauvais quart d'heure* such as no Labour

candidate has known in any by-election one can recall. 'Of course it is the case that people may suffer as a result,' he responded blandly. 'It is not the fault of those taking industrial action that they are doing so.'[7]

Barker's account is no doubt an exaggeration, but Blair was described as 'rattled' by the *Daily Express*, which also gleefully reported this incident.

The *Sunday Express* on 23 May thought him trendy enough: 'Mr Blair, with his unexceptionally fashionable views (in Labour terms) on everything from the Common Market to disarmament, is cutting little ice.'

On one issue, though, Blair's views were not left-fashionable, and that was on law and order. In one of his election leaflets, Blair described the rise in crime rates as a 'tragedy' and, in an early rehearsal of one of his themes, welcomed a government measure: 'The decision to put police "back on the beat" is a welcome move back to closer contact with the public and in the right direction to help reduce crime.'

However, the by-election campaign, and especially the last week, was utterly dominated by daily reports from General Galtieri's crime wave in the South Atlantic (the theft of a small British colony). On Friday the week before polling day, British troops landed at San Carlos bay on the Falkland Islands. The following Tuesday, HMS *Coventry* was lost and SS *Atlantic Conveyor* was hit by an Exocet missile, with thirty-one killed. The Conservative candidate, Tim Smith, who in 1994 resigned as a junior minister in the 'cash for questions' scandal, was filmed listening anxiously to the news on the radio. He drove around the constituency clutching a letter from the Prime Minister: 'I hope that the electorate will demonstrate their support for the Government's resolute response to the crisis in the South Atlantic, and for our policies at home.'

Two days later, the voters of Beaconsfield responded to Margaret Thatcher's call. The Liberal-SDP Alliance candidate, Paul Tyler (now the Liberal Democrat MP for Cornwall North), came an ordinary second. (In a bitter footnote to Blair's Hackney years, his MP Ron Brown, now in the SDP, came to Beaconsfield to campaign for Tyler.) Blair's final leaflet of the campaign was headed, unconvincingly, 'Why Conservatives are voting for Tony Blair.'

In the BBC's studio on the night of the by-election, Peter Shore, flanked by Norman Tebbit and Cyril Smith, echoed Michael Foot's endorsement of Blair: 'He really is a most entertaining, attractive and obviously first-rate candidate, and we'd very much like to have him in the Parliamentary Labour Party.'

At the count, Blair had already prepared his press release, which started by congratulating Tim Smith. He stood on the balcony with the other candidates as the result was announced, smiling broadly but still stiff and embarrassed, with a huge red rosette which looked like a comedy production prop. The result was a poor one for the Labour Party, its share of the vote halving from 20 to 10 per cent, as it dropped from second to third place behind the Liberal. According to the *South Bucks Observer* Blair 'could not hide his disappointment at losing his deposit' (the requirement was then to obtain 12.5 per cent of the vote – it was reduced to 5 per cent in 1985). His 3,886 votes seemed an unpromising first test of his appeal to his fellow-citizens.

Blair had impressed a pantheon of leading Labour politicians, but he still had no prospect of getting into parliament. The *Daily Telegraph* (18 May 1982) had reported the following exchange in Beaconsfield: '"I suppose you're hoping for a nice safe seat like Dagenham after losing your deposit here," a colleague solicitously inquired. "I haven't thought about it," replied Mr Blair disarmingly.' Bryan Gould had already been selected as the candidate for Dagenham in January 1982, and there were now few safe seats left which had not chosen their candidates.

Blair points to the timing and positioning of his start on the road of political advancement as evidence that he was not a

career politician, although sometimes, as in the *Spectator* (1
October 1994), he protests too much:

> Believe me, fighting the '82 Beaconsfield by-election for
> Labour was hardly seen as a smart career move. Michael
> Foot was struggling with the problems of leadership, Tony
> Benn was in charge of policy, Arthur Scargill was leading
> the trade unions, and we were in the middle of the
> Falklands war.

This last is a dash of added colour, as the war had not
started when he decided to put himself forward. But his general point seems obvious. Nevertheless, it was not obvious to
most Labour members and supporters in 1980 that the party
was facing extinction. For them, the electorate simply had to
be given the chance to deliver a verdict on Margaret Thatcher
and unemployment. It is unlikely that anyone applying for
Labour seats at that time would have done so on the basis that
the party would still be in opposition in 1995. Blair himself
was certain that Labour would survive and recover, as he said
in his Australian lecture.

The Year of Living Restlessly

Returning to Hackney politics from the spacious lawns of the
Home Counties, Blair threw himself into a period of campaigning, thinking and writing about politics. It seemed the
Beaconsfield by-election had come too late to be a stepping-
stone to a safe Labour seat. He was invited by the
Beaconsfield Labour Party to fight the seat again at the
General Election, and was inclined to accept. His wife Cherie
had meanwhile been selected as the Labour candidate for the
safe Conservative constituency of Thanet West.

He asked the advice of his head of chambers, Alexander
Irvine, who says: 'I advised him that sometimes amazing

things can happen in politics, and persuaded him to ride his luck.'[8] Blair said No to Beaconsfield, but his only hope seemed to be that the review of constituency boundaries, delayed since 1981 by court action by the Labour Party, might come into effect before the election and shake the political kaleidoscope.

Meanwhile, Blair pursued two issues in speaking engagements and in articles – the 'Tebbit Bill', which proposed new trade union law, and the question of judge-made law constraining Labour local councils.

The Tebbit Bill, which became the Employment Act 1982, weakened the closed shop and allowed the selective dismissal of strikers. Blair opposed it, as a barrister specialising in employment law. He had seen it coming. In the *New Statesman*, 21 August 1981, he wrote a short article warning that a European Court of Human Rights decision would undermine the closed shop. The court ruled in favour of four British Rail workers dismissed for failing to join the 'appropriate' union. The new Employment Secretary, Norman Tebbit, later confirmed that 'my position on the closed shop had been strengthened by the findings'.[9] Without explicitly defending the closed shop, Blair identified precisely the hook on which he was nearly impaled eight years later as shadow Employment Secretary. The court's decision, he said, 'dodges the true issue – does the right to join a union imply the right not to join a union?' Then, his implied answer was No. In 1989 his unequivocal answer was Yes. But in his campaign against the Tebbit Bill, Blair focused more on the possible victimisation of trade unionists or strikers than the erosion of the rights of unions to force people to join.

Blair's campaign against judge-made law also continued an earlier theme. He attacked his own profession for doing the Conservatives' work for them in *Labour Weekly* (5 February 1982). In an article headed, 'When the judges step into politics', he condemned the law lords' ruling against the GLC's 'Fare's Fair' policy of subsidising public transport. The judges had invented the concept of 'fiduciary duty' which required councils not to put up local taxes – then the rates – 'unreasonably'. This mattered because of the archaic local government law which held councillors personally liable if they breached their 'fiduciary duty'. The Queensbridge Labour Party minutes for 10 June 1982 contain a gem of historical irony. Tony Blair moved, and Cherie Booth seconded, a motion for that year's party conference, condemning the courts' interference in politics. It was carried by 11 votes to 0.

> Conference reaffirms its belief that democratically elected local authorities should be answerable to their electorate and that political decisions should not be subject to the interference of the courts.
>
> Conference calls upon the next Labour government to introduce legislation which will:
> (a) abolish the judge-invented doctrine of fiduciary duty (which means that the duty to ratepayers takes precedence over manifesto pledges), and
> (b) restrict councillors' liability to surcharge or disqualification to cases of serious crime.

Of the eleven people present, who could have imagined that, when they called upon 'the next Labour government', such a government could be led by the proposer of the motion? Blair took the motion to the General Committee of the constituency party. He was no longer Secretary of the Queensbridge branch, but was still a member of the General Committee as a delegate from the Transport and General Workers Union (its white-collar section cannot have had many self-employed barristers on its books). A similar motion was sent to the 1982 party conference by the Society of Labour Lawyers and several other constituency parties. As Composite 66, it was then carried, and so became (and still is) Labour Party policy. If Blair becomes Prime Minister, we look forward to a delegation from Queensbridge Branch Labour Party presenting him with a demand from himself to reform the law.

The Battle Against Militant

The Labour Party conference in Blackpool in 1982, as well as passing Blair's Composite 66, also marked the moment when Michael Foot began to assert control over the party. His most significant victory was to win the conference's backing for action against the Militant tendency. Blair's description of the sect in his Australian lecture, delivered a few weeks later, is one of the clearest:

> Militant is an avowedly Trotskyist group, whose links go back to the Revolutionary Socialist League in the 1960s. It has sixty-four full-time workers, including thirty-four at a regional level. Militant say that they only 'sell the *Militant* paper'. The Centre and Right say it is much more than just a group selling a paper; it is, in effect, a secret conspiracy, a party within the party. Following a report by the General Secretary and National Agent into Militant, the NEC [National Executive Committee] voted narrowly to establish a Register of all groups in the party. To qualify, the group has to show it abides by Labour's constitution. The constitution in effect outlaws parties within the party. Thus it is plain, since the report expressly said that Militant was a party within a party, that Militant will not be permitted to register.

It was this decision of Labour's National Executive which was approved by the Blackpool conference. The reason Blair knew so much about it was because Labour's National Executive had just taken legal advice from Alexander Irvine on how to deal with the tendency. Michael Foot explains that Blair 'was the liaison between the Executive and our official lawyers, but he knew everything that was going on, and why it was so important that we get it right . . . What we wanted to make sure was we didn't offend against natural justice.' The point of the whole exercise was to start expelling members of the Militant tendency, but this was a legal minefield, and it was suspected that Militant might take court action. Foot and Jim Mortimer, the party's general secretary, were surprised to be advised that Militant might have a good case in law. Blair advised that the Register would be a watertight and fair way to kick the Trotskyists out. Foot says:

> At the conference in Blackpool when we set the whole thing in motion, when I moved the resolution, and Jim Mortimer wound up, we carried it then, but all that was based on his advice, you know. I don't want to say that he determined it, but we took full account of what he said.

However, the idea of expelling people for their politics was difficult for the Left of the party to accept, with its folk-memory of right-wing purges in the 1930s and 1950s. At that Labour conference, nine out of ten constituency parties voted against setting up the Register, only to be overwhelmed by the block votes of the unions.

Once the Register was set up, the Left was divided. The 'soft' Left faction to which Blair belonged was in a quandary. The Labour Co-ordinating Committee (LCC) supported conference decisions, and it was sympathetic to Foot's leadership, but it was opposed to expulsions.

Blair's friend on the LCC Executive, Alan Haworth, argued that Militant members should not be expelled for their views, but because they were secretly members of a different political party. Foot had the same debate with the editors of *Militant* when they were summoned to the National Executive: 'They said it was just like the Bevanites. I said it was nothing like the Bevanites. The Bevanites were an open conspiracy as I called it.'

The LCC could not fudge its view of the Register, because it was one of the groups which was asked to comply with it. In October, the LCC Executive voted by 7 votes to 2 to recommend that they should co-operate with the Register. However, as a democratic group, the LCC's position would have to be decided by its members at its annual meeting in Newcastle, on 21 November 1982.

It was a crunch moment for the LCC, and Haworth knew that the vote might be close. Any member of the LCC may attend and vote at its annual meeting, so it was important to mobilise. He asked Tony Blair and Cherie Booth to go with him and Maggie Rae to Newcastle to 'vote against the Trots' – although it should be said that their leading opponent, Tony Benn's chief organiser Jon Lansman, was not actually a Trotskyist.

The meeting was on a Sunday, so the two couples stayed in a hotel on the moors above Alston for the weekend. Haworth remembers it because they had lobster, and because the landlord's mother was very old and kept trying to come into the dining room. The landlord kicked the door behind him as he served gin and tonic; it appeared sinister, but he later explained. Maggie Rae didn't want to go to the meeting the next day, and wanted to see Durham Cathedral instead. But Alan Haworth insisted. On Sunday, all four of them went to the meeting.

There were 150 people in the Rutherford Hall of Newcastle Polytechnic. The Register was the first issue to be discussed, and the debate did not appear to be going the Executive's way. Haworth sat next to Blair, and was surprised when he suddenly got up:

> That was the first time I heard him make a speech impromptu, unrehearsed, without notes. I wanted to make an intervention, because the debate was going ultra-lefty. He said, 'Oh, this is shit.' When he went forward to speak, I was worried that he might be embarrassing or counterproductive. I tended to think he was a bit naive, inexperienced. But it was brilliant, just perfect. He was confident and courageous.

Blair knew what he thought about Militant, and was used to getting a hostile reception for his views from Labour audiences. He thought it was one reason why he had made so little headway in his search for a parliamentary seat. But this was the first time he realised he could hold and sway people. The Executive's line prevailed – by just 72 votes to 61.

The LCC decision to co-operate with the Register left Militant isolated, and the tendency's only defence was now to go to the capitalist courts. The next month, the Labour Party's National Executive would meet to declare that Militant was a separate party, which meant that the members of the 'Editorial Board' of the newspaper could be expelled. Militant tried to get an injunction to stop them. Blair appeared in court as Alexander Irvine's junior counsel to defend the Labour Party, and Militant's application was thrown out. The five members of Militant were in due course expelled from the party.

However, the battle against Militant had only just started and the Labour Party was still heading for disaster in the looming General Election. In December 1982 some Conservative MPs were already urging Margaret Thatcher to call a June election. The government still had a year and a half to run, but it was becoming increasingly likely that she would go to the country in 1983. The Bermondsey by-election in February was a disaster for Labour. The local party chose Peter Tatchell as its candidate, who advocated 'militant forms of extra-parliamentary opposition'. In this the party openly defied Foot, who said in the Commons that Tatchell was 'not an endorsed member of the Labour Party [he meant candidate] and, so far as I am concerned, never will be'.[10] Tatchell lost the formerly safe Labour seat to the Liberal Simon Hughes by nearly 10,000 votes. The pressure for a June election increased.

Only legal action by the Labour Party against the new constituency boundaries stood in the way. But the case collapsed in the House of Lords, and there was a scramble of Labour candidates for a reduced number of safe seats. The party had refused to select candidates for the new constituencies while it was challenging them in the courts. However, the late shake-out of candidates did not yield any openings for Tony Blair – instead, a growing caravan of displaced Labour MPs chased the last few vacancies. As Blair's thirtieth birthday approached, he was depressed because he had not found a seat: 'I'd been getting fairly desperate to fight the election, and I could see everything disappearing.'[11] He was resigned to fighting the election campaign as the – supportive – husband of the candidate in Thanet North.

In April, Blair's hopes were unexpectedly raised. Right next door to his childhood home of Durham, the boundary commissioners had recreated the constituency of Sedgefield. The number of seats in County Durham had not changed, so all the existing MPs had expected to end up with a safe seat when the music stopped. But Ernie Armstrong, the MP for North-East Durham, upset the game of musical chairs when he opted for North-West Durham instead of shuffling south to Sedgefield. This left David Watkins, MP for Consett in north Durham, without a seat, and, of course, a vacancy in Sedgefield, a south Durham seat. It was suspected that Armstrong had been trying to create a vacancy for his daughter, Hilary (she eventually succeeded him as the MP for North-West Durham in 1987). Thus was a seat for life created for someone. However, Blair had no contacts in Sedgefield, and by the end of April a few tentative enquiries established that it looked as though the local Labour Party there had been stitched up by the hard-Left MP, Les Huckfield. His own Nuneaton seat in the Midlands had been turned into a Conservative one by boundary changes. Blair's hopes fell again.

On 28 April, a week before his thirtieth birthday, Blair was the political gooseberry at a Labour Party rally in Margate Town Hall, at which Cherie, her father Tony Booth and Tony Benn all spoke. Reg Ward, the Chairman of Thanet North Labour Party, remembers Blair as 'hyperactive', and says he had to remind him that he was 'the candidate's husband, not the candidate'. For the rally, the hall was packed and, in a vibrant echo of a Labour era which was about to pass, Benn spoke brilliantly. According to the next day's *Isle of Thanet Gazette*, 'Miss Booth said she was delighted to be sharing a platform with the two Tonys who have inspired her in her quest for socialism'. What the third Tony thought of this is not recorded. Blair argued with Benn about Militant in the car on the way back to London. All his disagreements with Benn could be summed up in this one issue. Benn's toleration of Militant was of a piece with the myth of betrayal, the idea that Labour had lost the 1979 election because it did not offer enough 'real' socialism. Benn may not have agreed with Militant, but he thought they were 'real' socialists.[12]

The members of the Hackney circle confirm that Cherie Booth's politics were close to Blair's, although noticeably to the left of his. However, her acknowledgement of Benn's 'inspiration' may have been no more than Blair's confession that 'I do agree with some of Tony Benn's views', offered in the spirit of party unity in the Beaconsfield by-election campaign. That she was hostile to Benn's version of party democracy was confirmed later, when she stood and won a place on the LCC Executive in the winter of 1983. Her manifesto said, in language identical to that of her husband: 'The Labour Party must be more than just a party of activists. It must be part of the community and have a democratic relationship with the community as a whole.'

A week after the Margate rally at which she and Tony Benn spoke, Cherie threw a surprise party for Tony Blair's birthday. He was just thirty, but was gloomy about his future. That weekend Margaret Thatcher retreated to the Prime Minister's country house at Chequers to consider the implications of that week's local elections. On Monday, 9 May, she announced that the General Election would be on 9 June. Blair decided to go up to Sedgefield anyway, in Alexander Irvine's words, to 'ride his luck'. Cherie said: 'He went up North one day, and he never came back.'

Notes

1. Ken Livingstone, *If Voting Changed Anything, They'd Abolish It*, p177.
2. Tony Blair, *Guardian*, 6 October 1994.
3. Keith Dovkants, *Evening Standard*, 18 July 1994.
4. Andy McSmith, *John Smith*, p99.
5. *London Labour Briefing*, December 1980.
6. Tom Pendry was one of the MPs who followed Neil Kinnock in abstaining in the Benn–Healey deputy leadership contest in 1981.
7. *Daily Telegraph*, 19 May 1982.
8. Jon Sopel, *Tony Blair: The Moderniser*, p58.
9. Norman Tebbit, *Upwardly Mobile*, p233.
10. Mervyn Jones, *Michael Foot*, pp480–81.
11. BBC TV, *Newsnight*, 21 November 1988.
12. Tony Benn was not so impressed by his discussion with Blair that he recorded it in his diaries. I am grateful to Ruth Winstone for checking the original entry.

6 . AFTER EXTRA TIME
Sedgefield, 1983

'If there was a moment when history should have noticed him, it was then.'

On the day the Labour Party nearly destroyed itself, its future leader knocked on the door of a small terraced house in the former pit village of Trimdon, in County Durham. It was Wednesday, 11 May 1983. In London, Michael Foot chaired the meeting to draw up Labour's manifesto. Rather than re-open deep divisions over policy, it was decided to reprint in full a 'campaign document' published two months earlier, with a new foreword by Foot. Only the shadow Chancellor Peter Shore spoke up in the meeting for a short manifesto – from which things could be left out. Neil Kinnock, the shadow Education Secretary, had made his unhappiness clear in a letter to Foot the day before. But, in the manifesto meeting itself, the doubters sat on their hands. Chief doubter Gerald Kaufman privately called it 'the longest suicide note in history'.

Up in Durham, staying with friends, Tony Blair made the telephone call that would change his life. To be chosen as a candidate, he first needed to be nominated. 'He phoned me up and asked if he could come and see me because I was the Secretary of the Trimdon Village branch,' says John Burton. 'He got a list of secretaries from the Secretary of the

constituency party and noticed that Trimdon hadn't nominated anybody. I said, "Well, the best time will be tonight
because there are five of us having our post-election meeting."' Burton and his fellow councillor Terry Ward had just
been re-elected to Sedgefield District Council in the local
elections the week before, 'and we were going to send a
thank-you letter out, so we were having a meeting and a few
drinks in the house'.

At 9pm, Blair's car pulled up outside 9 Front Street South,
Trimdon. He later said he nearly did not get out of the car; he
nearly just drove back. One of the five Labour Party members
in Burton's house that night, Paul Trippett, recalls:

> We were less than a month away from an election, he didn't
> have a nomination, he was going to a branch that didn't
> have an inclination to nominate anybody particularly, going
> to a stranger's house to meet some people, and he said he
> just thought, 'What am I doing here?' He sat for a minute
> or two, and then he thought, 'I've come all this way, I
> might as well go in.'

He knocked on the door and Burton asked him to come in
and sit down. The most important item of business for that
night's meeting was the football match on the television, the
European Cup Winners' Cup Final between Aberdeen and
Real Madrid. 'So he said he quite liked football,' says
Burton. 'Whether he was being polite or not I don't know.
We had some beer and some wine and he came in and sat
down.'

Trippett says: 'He sat there, watched the match, took part
in the conversation guys have when the match is on, you
know, "Good shot", "Bad cross", so he was one of the guys.'
The game, tied at 1–1, went into extra time, so Blair had to
wait another half an hour. Aberdeen scored another goal to
win. Then they asked him why they should nominate him.

Peter Brookes, another of the five, says they gave him a bit
of a grilling: 'Why on earth should we give a nomination to

this bloke who's just arrived and spoiled the football? We don't know him from Adam. He talks posh and he comes from London. Why on earth should we consider him at all?'

Terry Ward, a left-wing health service union activist, was the most aggressive. 'Terry gave him a bit of a hassling about the health service, and Tony acquitted himself very well,' says Trippett. Ward was impressed, but not persuaded. He wanted a 'proper socialist' of the hard Left.

Burton, a local councillor who was on the right wing of the party, recalls Blair's 'ideas for change, for broadening the base of the party, which he was talking about then – and things like Europe, where he wasn't in line with party policy because he said we should play a more important part in Europe. He believed the future lay in Europe.' Blair did not bowl them over, but they liked him. Brookes, a social worker, says:

> He was very open and honest. We actually felt when we were talking, 'This guy is sincere. He means what he is say- ing.' You thought, 'He really wants this.' He was saying things like how much he did want to get into politics, to get a parliamentary seat because he thought he could make a contribution to the future of society. He didn't really need to do that in terms of his personal situation because he was a very successful barrister doing industrial law. And he was sharing this with us, 'I don't need this for the money', sort of thing.

The fifth member there was Simon Hoban, the branch's youth officer. He was favourably impressed, but said little. Trippett, a joiner for Sedgefield District Council with a dry sense of humour, was lukewarm:

> He gave us this spiel about standing in Beaconsfield and he had this letter off Foot saying that people of the calibre of Tony should be in the House. That letter swung a lot of us straight away, because we had a great affection for Michael

Foot, because he was a leftwinger – we didn't know what Tony's views were at that time, but we thought he must have some radical views, or Foot wouldn't have written this letter. He wasn't too bad with the questions. Nothing out of the ordinary. He came across, he was a young lad, good looking, well spoken, personable. I wasn't bothered one way or the other. So I thought, 'Yeah, if you want to, we'll go for it.'

It was John Burton more than the others who thought there was something special about their visitor. Inevitably, there were other calculations. After Blair had gone, Trippett turned to Burton and said: 'What are we going to do?'

'I think we've agreed we'll get him the nomination from the branch.'

There was a pause. Trippett asked: 'John, how about you standing?'

Burton deflected the question, and the two resumed the conversation later in the kitchen, out of earshot of Terry Ward, Burton's fellow councillor. Burton's problem was that the leader of the council, Warren McCourt, was one of those interested in the seat. According to Trippett,

> Burton said, 'No, I think it would be easier getting an out-sider elected than myself. The worry that I've got is that if I stand and don't win, and I stand against the leader of the district council I might be ostracised in the branch.' So John obviously had given it some thought, he had the answer ready when I asked him.

Burton admits: 'I might have been interested.' But he says that if Blair had not rung him that day, he and his friends would probably not have played an active part in the selection. He confirms that he thought it would be easier to get Tony Blair elected than himself. 'It's whether you're a prophet in your own land. As soon as I met Tony, anyway, I knew that he was the chap and not myself. That he was better able to take the party forward and change the party than I would be.'

Nine days later, Blair would be the Labour candidate for one of the safest seats in the country. Four of the five people in Burton's house that night – Terry Ward dropped out – became, with Phil Wilson who had been away that week, the 'Famous Five' who worked to get Blair selected and then elected. Burton, Brookes, Trippett and Wilson are still the core of the 'Sedgefield posse' which provides Blair with such a strong base. They had just run a local election campaign, to re-elect Burton and Ward to Sedgefield council against presumptuous SDP opposition, and were looking for something else to do.

They were aware that the hard Left was organising for Les Huckfield, but what they did not know was that he did not have nearly as strong a grip on the delegates to the selection conference as most people assumed. Sedgefield was a new constituency, and the local Labour Party was assembled from bits of old parties with very different outlooks and loyalties, so its politics were fluid.

Despite not being bothered 'one way or the other', Paul Trippett took the next day off from his job to drive Blair round to visit some of the delegates to the selection conference:

I stayed in the car, I just pointed out where they lived and what they were called, and Tony went in, because I thought, 'If this guy wants it, he's going to have to do a bit of work himself, I'm not going to spoon-feed him.' And what he was actually doing, he was very clever. He was going in to see them, and he wasn't saying, 'Vote for me'. What he was saying was, 'I would like to be on the shortlist first. If I get on the shortlist and you've already decided to support somebody, and if your person goes out, would you then transfer your vote to me?' That was his line, because by this time a lot of people had made their minds up. I think people took notice of that. Here was a sensible, quiet young man who wanted a chance – that was part of his appeal then, and it's part of his appeal now.

Meanwhile, Burton, as Secretary, hurriedly convened a meeting of the Trimdon Village Branch of Sedgefield Labour Party for that Saturday. Unless Blair received a nomination from a branch or affiliated body, his name could not be on the shortlist, and the selection conference could not vote for him.

The 'Famous Five' threw themselves into the campaign. Blair moved into John Burton's house, Peter Brookes lent him his car, and Paul Trippett took more time off work.

Nowadays, Trimdon branch has 200 members. That Saturday morning in the village's Community College there were just fifteen – as well as eight or nine would-be candidates. John Burton says:

> Tony said that of all the times, ever – then, before and since – he has never been as nervous as he was that day. He thinks he made the worst speech of his life, and was really worried. His speech was five minutes, I think, and question and answer. He was quite convinced he wouldn't get the nomination.

Burton's memory of Blair's speech is that it was 'perfectly all right – he was just nervous'. As well he might be. Sedgefield was the last constituency Labour Party in the country to choose a candidate. At each stage in the process, Blair was lucky.

The chairman of the branch, George 'Mick' Terrans, just happened to be the chairman of the new constituency party as well. 'He was the big politician in the area,' says Burton. Despite being formally pledged, as a retired miner, to his union's candidate, he liked Blair instantly, and gave him an unobtrusive boost. Terrans commented that all the applicants except Blair had already been nominated by other branches or affiliates. Burton says: 'I moved as Tony Blair didn't have a nomination that we give our nomination to him, and there was a 12–3 vote for that, which was a little bit naughty. He allowed that.' (As chairman, Terrans should have asked the meeting to vote on each applicant in turn.)

The next day, Sunday 15 May, Burton visited George Ferguson, Secretary of the Sedgefield Constituency Labour Party, who wrote a carbon-copied letter. 'I hereby acknowledge receipt of your nomination in respect of: Anthony Charles Lynton Blair.' The selection conference was to be held on Friday, 20 May. The Blair campaign, having taxied around the obstacles of party procedure, was airborne.

The Trimdon Posse

Of course, sudden as Tony Blair's arrival at John Burton's house was, it was not just a stroke of luck. Blair had been scouring the North East for a seat for two-and-a-half years. And he had known about the possible vacancy in Sedgefield for several weeks before he contacted Burton. Giles Radice, the MP for Chester-le-Street (most of which was absorbed into his new seat of Durham North), took an interest in the battle for Sedgefield, and had already met Blair:

> I first met him at a Fabian meeting in Hackney, and I remember him as bright, nice. He'd just been the candidate in Beaconsfield. Then John Lloyd, who is a mutual friend of ours, said that he was trying to get this seat, very much at the last moment, in the North East, and could I be of any assistance? I met him at supper with the Lloyds, in London, and I was very impressed by him, I must say.

Radice spoke to Joe Mills, the regional baron of the Transport and General Workers Union in the North. He was also that year's Chairman of the Northern Region Labour Party. Before he went to John Burton's house, Blair went to visit him, says Mills:

Tony arrived at my office one morning, looking for support for the Sedgefield seat. He'd been round seeing people. He came in, said he was from London, but had originated from the North, and was interested in having this seat. I explained to him that at that time the Transport and General Workers Union had a sponsored candidate called Les Huckfield in the field, and I was expected to support this gentleman. We talked at length, Tony and I, about what his philosophy was, and what I was impressed about was the fact that he was very keen on the one member, one vote issue which I was promoting in the early Eighties, much against a lot of the other people in the party. And I thought, 'Well, this is a fella we could support.'

The Northern region of the TGWU was always right-wing in Labour Party terms, and Mills had no intention of supporting Huckfield. 'I was really passionately opposed to Les Huckfield and did everything I could to stop him,' he says. Huckfield 'turned up at my office with a Northern Region TGWU tie on – I don't where he got that from. He was in my office, with the chap who was bringing him round, Alan Meale' (Meale is now the MP for Mansfield and Parliamentary Private Secretary to John Prescott).

Huckfield asked Mills to write a letter to the Sedgefield Labour Party endorsing him, says Mills: 'I remember bringing my secretary into my office and saying to her to take down, "Les Huckfield is a sponsored member of the TGWU." He said, "Is that it?" And I told him, "I'm not recommending you, that's all I'm bound to do as an official of the union."'

Blair was (and is) a member of the TGWU (he was, after all, a TGWU delegate on the General Committee of the Hackney South Labour Party) and had spoken at a TGWU weekend school in Durham in June 1982.[1] Weekend schools were a useful network for rightwingers in a union dominated at national level by the Left. The TGWU did not actually have many branches affiliated to the Sedgefield Labour Party, but with Mills's help Blair managed to get one of them to nominate him. The Trimdon party branch nomination turned out not to be the single thread by which his hopes hung, but it was the more important. Blair went into the selection process with just two nominations, while Huckfield had several. But, as John Burton says, one nomination can be as good as a hundred, because it means you can be considered for the shortlist.

Tom Burlison, Mills's equivalent in the other big general union, the General and Municipal, was also keen to help Blair, whom he had met when he went for Middlesbrough in 1980. Burlison asked his political officer, Nick Brown, to look at Sedgefield. Brown, who had himself just been chosen as the candidate for Newcastle East, checked, but all 'his' union delegates in Sedgefield were 'left-wing people who couldn't be influenced', he says. For many years afterwards, it was assumed that, because Blair's selection was unexpected, it must have been fixed by 'the unions'. The truth is that their main contribution was to fail to help his opponent.

Before he went up North, Blair had also contacted the local party secretary, George Ferguson, but he, a procedural stickler, had refused to disclose the names and addresses of the secretaries of nominating bodies until the selection process began formally. Meanwhile, Les Huckfield was already organising in the constituency, using the connections of the Left's networks.

Once a junior industry minister (1976–79) on the Right of the Labour Party, Huckfield had transformed himself into a more-Bennite-than-Benn member of the party's National Executive. His move across the spectrum was rapid. According to Michael Crick in his book, *Militant*, Huckfield was hostile to the tendency as late as 1978, the year he joined the National Executive – the Left's power base. At that time he was still suggesting to ministerial colleagues that Militant full-timers should be investigated to see if they were claiming state benefits. But by September 1982, he was the only Labour MP to attend a Militant conference in Wembley stadium to protest against the 'witch-hunt'.[2]

At the height of the Left's advance in April 1980, Huckfield argued successfully on the National Executive for a ban on all car imports. This was too much even for Tony Benn, who doubted its feasibility and tried to amend the proposal. When he failed, however, Benn ended up voting for it, and it was carried by 10 votes to 6.[3] Most Labour politicians do not know – or care to remember – that it was once official party policy to prohibit all imports of motor cars. Such socialist autarky was to no avail – Huckfield was replaced on the National Executive by John Evans in 1982.

Huckfield had been the MP for Nuneaton since 1967, but, after the boundary changes, it looked as though the seat would fall to the Conservatives at the coming election (it did). He first challenged a fellow MP, Roger Stott, for the candidacy in Wigan, a redrawn safe Labour seat which included most of Stott's former West Houghton constituency. It was a bad-tempered contest, and on 24 April 1983, Huckfield lost the vote at the selection conference in Wigan Old Grammar School assembly hall by 113 to 100. The Wigan Labour Party Chairman, Jim Maloney, recalls that Huckfield was furious when he was told the result in a side room. 'If you think you've heard the last of me, you're mistaken,' he is reported to have said. Myth has it that Huckfield got in his car at 8.45pm and drove straight to Sedgefield.

Huckfield had thus been lobbying his cause in Sedgefield for two weeks by the time Blair arrived. By 7 May, Huckfield was already being treated by some in the Sedgefield party as the candidate. At a meeting organised by the National Union of Mineworkers as part of its campaign against the closure of Fishburn coke works, the Labour Party was embarrassed by the fact that the Conservative and Alliance candidates for Sedgefield accepted invitations to speak. Tongue-in-cheek, BBC TV's *Newsnight* filmed the meeting for a report on 'the constituency with no Labour candidate'. In the meeting the chairman proposed a stand-in from the audience – Les Huckfield. As he took his seat on the platform, followed by

Newsnight's camera, there was a ripple of dissension in the hall. George Ferguson, scrupulous as ever, pointedly did not attend the meeting, and said: 'It could be construed that we're pre-empting who is to be the prospective parliamentary candidate. Personally I don't think it would be right to put anyone in that chair.'

As Blair and his 'Famous Five' supporters canvassed delegates to the selection conference, it became clear that many of them shared Ferguson's dislike of Huckfield's pre-emption. But opposition to Huckfield was split between several others – hence Blair's tactic of asking people for their second-preference votes. The 'Five' were mostly inexperienced. Only John Burton was a delegate to the selection conference. But he was well-known and widely liked – a centre forward for Bishop Auckland amateur football team, a PE teacher, banjo player in a folk band and, of course, a Labour district councillor. 'Lo and behold!' says Burton. 'Some of the delegates I'd been to school with. Some of the delegates I'd played football with, and some of the delegates I was related to.'

Phil Wilson, returning to Sedgefield the week after Blair's arrival, was quickly swept up in the venture. He had only joined the Labour Party – because of his support for the Campaign for Nuclear Disarmament – in March 1983, and was already active in his civil service union, CPSA. He had been away at the union's conference in Brighton, proposing a constitutional amendment which he later discovered had been drafted by Cherie Booth, who had done some legal work for the union. As soon as he met Blair, with Burton, he knew 'there was something about him', he says. According to Wilson, Burton took him aside and said: 'We've got to support him, you know, he's Cabinet material.' They did so.

The campaign was exhilarating. 'It was a happy time, it was all new to all of us. And to Tony himself. We were treading new ground, we were having to work things out,' says Paul Trippett. Trippett had been a member of the Militant tendency, become disillusioned, and left the Labour Party. He had only rejoined the party the month before, to work for the re-election of Councillor John Burton, his former teacher. His initial motive for throwing himself into the campaign to get Blair chosen as the candidate was simply that it was a challenge. As he says, he had not been particularly impressed by Blair on that first night, although he quickly came to admire him. He was motivated by the urgency of the campaign: 'Politics is extremely, mind-numbingly boring. I need to be doing something.' He had been galvanised by the SDP threat in the local elections:

> It stimulates you. The SDP was formed and they just looked at the Labour Party and said, 'It has sat on its back-side for too long'. And I think we had sat back as a Labour Party in the North East. We took people for granted – the old guard had. It stung us a bit. Anyway, we won that, and we were still in the euphoria of the victory, and then this guy knocks on the door and asks for a nomination, we decide to give him it, and then it has to be done. Unlike council politics, where you debate things for weeks on end, and there's resolutions and everything, this was *politics*, moving, and it was exciting.

Tony Blair's curriculum vitae for the selection is a badly-typed two-page document (opposite). John Burton got a friend to type it who was not a typist – 'you can see she wasn't a typist!' – after Blair got the branch's nomination. It was copied from Blair's handwritten version, and is full of errors and misreadings.

Like all good CVs, it is selective. It starts with Michael Foot's endorsement of 'Tony Glair', obviously quoted from memory, as the wording is quite wrong (Foot was actually more effusive, see p101). It omits any reference to his private schools. In July 1990, he was asked by *Marxism Today*, 'What do you blame your parents for?' and answered, 'Thinking that sending me to public school was a good career move!' (He later adopted a different line in the *Independent*, 2 July

NAME : TONY BLAIR

AGE : 30 years .

TRADE UNION : Transport & General Workers Union

PREVIOUS PARLIAMENTARY EXPERIENCE

I stood, during the Falklands war, in the Beaconsfield by-election,
a Tory seat with a majority of 23,000. I lost, (unsurprisingly) but
gained valuable experience. Michael Foot speaking on BBC Newsnight
on 26th May 1982 said,
    "In my view Tony Glair will make a major contribution to
British Politics in the months and years ahead".

BACKGROUND

I lived in County Durham from 1958 to 1975, first in Durham City
and then from 1963 to 1975 on a new housing estate at High Shincliffe.
From 1972 -75 I attended Oxford University (St.John's College) where
Iread Law. I graduated in 1975 with a B.A. (Hons) in Law.
1975/6 I was a student at the Inns of Court School in London, passing
my professional exams in the summer of 1976.
1976/7 I was pupip to Alexander Irvine Q.C. At the end of my
pupillage, at the age of 24 years, I was awarded a full place in
Chanbers as a practising barrister. Since 1977 I have worked as a
practising barrister in those chambers.

NATURE OF WORK

I specialise in trade union and industrial law, which, in effect, has
meant living and working in London. I also work for several major
County Councils and in the area of civil liberties. In addition I
have represented the Labour Party. The unions I have worked for
include: T.G.W.U.; I.S.T.C.; N.U.R.; G.M.B.A.T.U.; T.S.S.A.;
A.U.E.W.; N.A.L.G.O.
Amongst the major cases in which I have been involved over the past
few years are:
    - Defending the Labour Party in court action against the Reg Prentice
      and his supporters
    - Defending the Labour Party in the action against it by Militant
    - Defending ILEA in its decision to peg school meal prices at 35p
    - Several cases arising aout of redundancies by the British Steel
      Corporation, inclusing winning the unfair dismissal claim of
      the 30 Birmingham steelworkers
    - I have, in particular, worked in cases where trade unionists
      have been selected for redundancy, espesially in the TGWU and ISTC.
    - Most recently, I acted for the Port Talbot steelworkers, in their
      case against the BSC.

PUBLICATIONS AND LECTURES

Amongst the papers I have written for are - The Guardian, New Statesman,
Spectator, Labour Weekly. These articles habe concerned trade union
law, civil liberties, and_race_relations. I have lectured regularly in
Trade Union law over the years, giving the 1982 Society of Labour
Congress lecture on the Tebbit Act.
In addition I as a discussion leader at the TGWU weekend in Durham
City in June 1982, speaking on the Labour Party, and I was invited and
gave a lecture on the Labour Party and its future in Perth, Western
Australia to Murdoch and W.A. Universities, later published in
Australia.

PARTY OFFICES
I have held offices in three London constituencies, and been a member
of each G.C. I am at present a TGWU delegate on Hackney South G.C.
(a labour seat with a sitting SDP defector).
I am a member of the Executive of the Society of Labour Lawyers
concentrating particularly on trade union and logal government law.
MEMBERSHIP OF OTHER ORGANISATIONS
C.N.D.; N.C.C.L. ; L.C.C.

FAMILY
I am married to Cherie Booth, who was born and bred in Liverpool.
Cherie is now a barrister (having come top. in the professional exams
in 1976 for the whole country). She specialises in child care and
adoption work. Cherie's father is the actor, Anthony Booth of 'Till
Death Do Us Part' fame. Anthony and Pat Phoenix, from 'Coronation
Stree', both came and canvassed for me when I previously stood for
Parliament and would be happy to do so again.
Cherie and I , as yet, have no children.

SHORT STATEMENT OF VIEWS AND INTENT
I have always wanted to come back to the North East to represent the
community here. I would, of course, live in the constituency if
selected, and I would be a full-time M.P. Cherie's work, unlike mine,
could transfer to the North.
I believe an M.P. has two tasks: to know and work with the Community
he or she represents;and to put the best possible case for that
community in Westminster.
I believe in a united Labour Party offering radical solutions within
a framework that people understand and that touches their everyday lives.
I support Party policy as determined by Party conference. When
arguments do take place, they should take place within the Party, not
on the media; and in a spirit of democracy. That means not only the
right to express your views, but the right to have them listened to.

1994: 'I have never found my educational background a problem with ordinary voters. I have only ever found it a problem
with middle-class journalists.' And, perhaps he should have
added, Labour Party selectors.) Nor would you get the
impression from his description of his work as a barrister that
he ever indulged in corporate litigation, or represented
employers. And the suggestion that Cherie's work 'could
transfer to the North' was never acted on.

The CV confirms that Blair was a member of the
Campaign for Nuclear Disarmament, despite his denial in
September 1994. Unilateral nuclear disarmament was never
prominent in his recorded views, although he had been
explicit about his support for the policy as a candidate in the
Beaconsfield by-election.

The CV may have been scrappy, but its 'Short Statement
of Views and Intent' prefigures one aspect of the later, glossier
Blair – it is notably bland and abstract: 'I believe in a united

Labour Party offering radical solutions within a framework
that people understand and that touches their everyday lives.'

This was the document that the Executive Committee of
the Sedgefield Labour Party had before it when it met in
Spennymoor Town Hall on Wednesday 18 May – just a week
after Blair's arrival – to draw up a shortlist of candidates.
Spennymoor was the largest town in the Sedgefield constituency, and the Trades Council there was the power base of
the hard Left. There were sixteen applicants who filled in
yellow nomination forms. They included David Watkins, the
displaced MP for Consett, Joel Barnett, another displaced
MP and former Cabinet minister, Hilary Armstrong, Sid
Weighell, the recently-retired railway union leader, and Ben
Pimlott, now a professor and biographer of Harold Wilson –
as well as Blair and Huckfield.

The Executive Committee, a small body dominated by the
Left, decided on a shortlist of six, which was designed to
favour Huckfield.

Blair's name was not on the list.

As the General Election campaign was already underway,
the selection procedure had been compressed. So the next
day, the larger and more politically mixed General Committee
of the constituency party met, again in Spennymoor Town
Hall, to approve the shortlist. John Burton went to the meeting with one objective – to add Blair's name. This was the
decisive meeting, because it was the General Committee that
would meet again the following day to choose the candidate.
Fewer people would turn up for the shortlisting meeting on
Thursday night, but, if there were a majority for adding Blair
to the shortlist, then he would be well placed for the selection
meeting on Friday, at which there would be a full turnout.

Burton recalls:

They went through the whole list, everybody who had a
nomination to see if they should be added to the shortlist.
Barnett – No. Then they came to Blair. I got up and said,
'I've got this letter from Michael Foot saying he wants him

in the House as soon as possible'. Nobody understood that it's a fairly standard letter, and it went down well.

Blair was waiting with Burton's wife Lily, Peter and Christine Brookes, Phil Wilson and Paul Trippett in the Red Lion in Trimdon. When John Burton returned from the General Committee meeting he paused on the threshold, looking downcast. 'What happened?' asked Peter Brookes, his heart sinking.

'You're not going to believe this,' said Burton. 'They only added one name to the shortlist. And that was Tony Blair.' As Burton recalls, 'Wheee! The place went up with joy.' Blair's name had been added to the list by one vote. (The official constituency party records have been lost: Burton recalls that the tellers disagreed, one saying the vote was 42–41, the other 41–40; but both agreed Blair had won, so demands for a recount were ignored.)

The next day, Blair went back to Durham Cathedral, in whose precincts he had lived and gone to school, to pray. He did not know that John Burton, a church warden of St Mary Magdalene on the Green in Trimdon, had let himself into the church late the previous night to do the same. Burton's wife Lily recalls wondering where on earth her husband had gone.

On Friday night, 119 delegates attended the selection meeting at Spennymoor Town Hall. All seven of the expanded shortlist spoke for ten minutes and took five minutes of questions. Les Huckfield might have realised that it was going horribly wrong when he found himself pushed on the defensive in answer to questions from the floor. Blair and Burton may have been inexperienced, but they were not innocent.

Burton has kept the scribbled notes of the questions which he planted among friendly delegates. One, on the back of an envelope, has 'Roger Stott' written at the top – it was presumably suggested by Stott, Huckfield's adversary in Wigan: 'Don't you think Mr Huckfield it counts strongly against you that you deserted Nuneaton when it became a marginal seat, allowing the opp. parties to say Labour couldn't win because the sitting MP had defected?' Three other questions, headed 'Joe Mills', are on two scraps of paper. The sharpest was: 'The TGWU supported the Register of groups. How can Huckfield continue to oppose it. You advocated strict adherence to party conf[erence decisions].' Huckfield's defence of Militant (at whom the Register was aimed) did him no good. TGWU Northern region boss Joe Mills explains:

> We had ensured that people going to the selection conference would expose Huckfield's credentials. The ordinary people in the Durham area were opposed to Tony Benn's policies. We had to get Huckfield to come over quite clearly as supporting the same policies as Benn – to ensure Huckfield could be seen for what he was.

In Sedgefield, a local anti-Marxist tradition survived. The former MP for Sedgefield in its pre-1974 incarnation, David Reed, says the outlook of the party then had been 'middle to Right' on the spectrum of Labour politics. He recalls a debate in a Miners Welfare Hall in which he engaged a couple of Young Communists in argument, to vigorous applause. In 1983, even left-wing delegates had no time for Militant if Michael Foot and the party conference were against them.

Huckfield's assiduous organising among the local hyperactivists of the hard Left had given a misleading impression of his strength. The roots of County Durham's ethical socialism went deeper.

Blair spoke last. 'He was brilliant, excellent – energetic and alive with ideas,' says Burton. He remembers that Blair mentioned Europe in his speech, because one of the delegates teased him about it:

> Ron Mahon, who was one of the officers from NUPE regional office, walked up when Tony said about playing a part in Europe and said, 'Your lad's just lost it.' And I said, 'I don't think so. The party's changing on Europe.' And of course it was changing.

When it came to the voting, Blair won fewer than a third of the votes on the first round. But he was in the lead. 'It's going to happen,' thought Burton. 'It's really going to happen.' Huckfield came a poor second, and a grassroots activist from Durham, Pat McIntyre, beat Sedgefield council leader Warren McCourt. Bill Giffin of the Fire Brigades Union, Frank Robson, a farmer and Darlington councillor, and Reg Race, another hard-Left displaced MP, failed to win significant numbers of votes. Blair led in each round of voting, but there were five votes before he finally overcame Huckfield. The records may be lost, but John Burton wrote down the votes in his green book, in which as a councillor he wrote down all the details of cases he dealt with.

	Round				
	1st	2nd	3rd	4th	5th
Pat McIntyre	17	18	20	29	
Bill Giffin	8	5			
Tony Blair	39	53	51	58	73
Warren McCourt	15	14	16		
Les Huckfield	27	27	32	32	46
Frank Robson	5				
Reg Race	8	2			

'I do believe it was the women who gave Tony the vote,' says George Ferguson, Secretary of the Sedgefield Labour Party. He says that after the final round the Chairman, Mick Terrans, forgot to announce the figures: 'We brought them all out on the stage to hear the result. And Mick Terrans said, "We've got a new MP, let's give him our congratulations." I had to nudge him to say, "Who is it?" He said, "Oh, Tony Blair."'

John Burton recalls that the result wasn't immediately clear, but remembers it slightly differently. 'Terrans started to say, "We've got to organise for the General Election now, less than three weeks away", and then something about having a "bright young chap" as the candidate, and the penny dropped.'

The news spread fast and far. Blair telephoned Cherie at the home of her Thanet North party chairman, Reg Ward. At about midnight that night, in a hotel in Scotland, shadow Home Secretary Roy Hattersley was woken by a hammering on his door. He was due to make an election campaign speech the next day. When he opened the door he found Mary Goudie in a dressing gown. 'Not at all what I'm used to,' he says. She was working for the Labour Party as his 'minder', but she is also the wife of James Goudie, a barrister with whom Blair shared a room in his chambers.

'What's the matter?' said Hattersley.

'Have you heard about Blair?' she said.

Hattersley couldn't remember who Blair was at that moment, so he said: 'Come in, come in.'

'Young Blair's done this extraordinary thing,' she said. 'He hadn't been shortlisted, and he's gone round and knocked on all the doors. And he's got it.'

'From then on,' says Hattersley, 'whenever anybody said to me that Blair wasn't strong and tough, I always thought of Mary Goudie beating on my door at midnight that Friday night. If there was a moment when history should have noticed him, it was then.'

However, it was the middle of a General Election campaign, and history had other things on its mind. That day shadow Foreign Secretary Denis Healey appeared to disagree with Labour's defence policy, and opened up a gap between himself and Michael Foot. It was not clear that the Labour Party would survive.

It was not the first time the Sedgefield constituency had chosen an unexpected, young candidate. In 1970, when Blair, aged sixteen, lived just down the road on the outskirts of Durham (although he was away in Scotland at boarding school), there was a minor political drama in Sedgefield. Its Labour MP of twenty years, Joe Slater, retired. A miner and NUM official, he had risen, through being parliamentary private secretary to Hugh Gaitskell and then Harold Wilson in opposition, to the less-than-dizzying height of Assistant Postmaster General in government. Everyone assumed Slater would be succeeded by his old agent, Harry Smith.

However, a twenty-four-year-old local journalist, David Reed, was annoyed that the Sedgefield nomination appeared to be 'fixed'. He was in some ways a prototype Blair, and describes himself as 'social democratically minded'. He spent three months meeting all the branches and affiliated organisations he could. He won the candidature narrowly on the second ballot, and in the General Election in June 1970 was elected the youngest Labour MP – just as Blair would be thirteen years later.

Once he was selected, Tony Blair and the Trimdon posse threw themselves into the local General Election campaign. Cherie Booth came with her father Tony Booth and Pat Phoenix, who campaigned for Blair as promised.

Blair's election address, which later became controversial, was produced in haste, with only twenty days to polling day when he was chosen as the candidate. In his address, Blair said: 'We'll negotiate withdrawal from the EEC which has drained our natural resources and destroyed jobs.' At the selection conference, he had declared himself a pro-European, which he had not done in Beaconsfield. It is, then, slightly curious that he should have so enthusiastically endorsed the party's anti-European stance in public.

When he referred to his selection conference speech as evidence of his consistency on the issue of Europe during the leadership campaign, Home Secretary Michael Howard wrote to *The Times*, quoting Blair's 1983 leaflet and saying:

Election addresses give candidates the chance to highlight policies of particular personal importance . . . Roy Hattersley, someone whose support for Community membership has never been in doubt, chose not to mention the party's commitment to withdrawal in *his* 1983 election address. Why did Tony Blair not do the same?[4]

The explanation cannot simply be that he used pre-prepared party material. The leaflet was based on standard material, but included, among other things, a reference to the planned closure of Fishburn coke works in the constituency. It is more likely that, although it was not so important to toe the party line as in a by-election campaign, Blair felt that – having made his point inside the party – he should maintain party unity in public. He said in his Sedgefield CV: 'I support party policy as determined by party conference. When arguments do take place, they should take place within the party, not on the media.'

Howard – also elected to parliament in 1983, and about to enter a long and competitive relationship with his fellow barrister – is right to suggest that it would have been possible simply to have left the 'withdrawal from the EEC' sentence out. Blair's acceptance of the party line does not sit easily with his later incarnation as a 'conviction politician'. But Howard's lawyerly argument will not bear the weight he places on it. The EEC sentence appears in a long list summarising party policies, headed, ironically, 'Labour's Sensible Answers'. On the back of the address was Blair's 'A Personal Message', in which – in contrast to his Beaconsfield literature – he did not mention Europe. The only substantive paragraph here is:

> The Tories say there is no money to create new jobs. But they spend billions of pounds on dangerous nuclear weapons. They spend billions on keeping people on the dole. They encourage the rich to invest billions abroad each year. This isn't sense – it's insanity!

It is, all the same, a paradox that Blair entered parliament on a ticket of loyalty to a party which he has been trying to change ever since.

The 1983 General Election

The Labour manifesto, agreed on the day Blair knocked on John Burton's door, promised a non-nuclear defence policy; withdrawal from Europe; a rise in public spending, paid for by borrowing, including a 50 per cent rise in local council spending; the return of privatised industries to public ownership and 'public investment' in others; a Price Commission which could freeze or cut prices; and the reversal of council house sales.

It would have been a difficult programme to sell at the best of times. But the Labour campaign in 1983 was publicly described by Roy Hattersley as a 'shambles'. A shambles was originally a board on which meat scraps and offal would be displayed for sale. The grisly metaphor was appropriate. Professor David Butler wrote, 'It is difficult to think of any campaign fought by a major party since the war that was more inept,' and thought, after the turmoil since 1979, it was the beginning of the end: 'Future historians may well see the period as a crucial stage in the decline and fall of the Labour Party.'[5]

Future historians may now see the period differently. But there is no denying that on 9 June 1983, the party nearly carried out its suicide threat. Margaret Thatcher inspired adulation and loathing in roughly equal measure, but, as has often been observed, she benefited from a divided opposition. Labour gained only 28 per cent of the national vote, and just avoided getting fewer votes than the Liberal-SDP Alliance on 26 per cent. But in Sedgefield, the future leader of the Labour Party was elected with a majority of 8,281 votes. He had squeezed into parliament not at the last minute but during extra time. His father, Leo, came to the count – intensely proud of him, despite their political differences. Nearly 300 miles away, in Thanet North, his wife was pushed into third place by the Alliance and only just saved her deposit.

Afterwards, Blair wrote to thank all the people in Trimdon who had helped him. Peter Brookes is the only one who still

has his letter, dated 20 June 1983: 'There was one thing that
I really wanted to do, and I have been given the chance by you
to do it. I only hope your faith in me will be repaid.'

Tony Blair was asked by his school magazine in December
1991: 'What makes a Fettesian become a Labour MP?' His
reply: 'A catalogue of errors and mistakes.' Actually it was
luck, and a lot of hard work. John Burton was clearly the
most important person in securing the seat for Blair. After the
election, when they were in a car together, Blair turned to him
and said: 'I'll say this once, and I won't say it again. I can
never, ever repay you for what you've done for me.' Burton is
quite open about living his political ambitions through Blair.
Since retiring as a teacher at the beginning of 1994, he now
works as Blair's assistant in the constituency. He is still one of
Blair's closest confidants – one of the half-dozen or so, for
example, who knew about the decision to try to rewrite
Clause IV before Blair announced it in his first party conference speech as leader.

Blair's luck was not just in scraping into parliament at the
last possible moment, but in being elected for Sedgefield. It is
a place which has given him roots. In his first speech in the
Commons, Blair said: 'The constituency of Sedgefield is
made up of [real] communities. The local Labour Party
grows out of, and is part of, local life. That is its strength.' It
was true enough. And it was going to become more true.

Paul Trippett remembers celebrating Blair's election with
Phil Wilson in the Red Lion until 4am. 'Then I had to get up
to go to work on the Friday. I was tired. I felt empty, I just felt
nothing. But then that weekend we all talked about it with
Tony, about how we would make it the best constituency in
the country, and it started again.'

Notes

1. Tony Blair, Sedgefield CV, see pp127–8.
2. Michael Crick, *Militant*, p180.
3. *Labour Weekly* 2 May 1980.
4. *The Times*, 7 July 1994.
5. David Butler and Dennis Kavanagh, *The British General Election of 1983*, pp64, 274.

PART THREE

THE KINNOCK YEARS

7 . NEW KID
Backbencher, 1983–84

'Remember how you felt on that dreadful morning of 10 June. Just remember how you felt then, and think to yourselves, "June the Ninth, 1983: never, ever again will we experience that".'   Neil Kinnock, October 1983

On arriving in the House of Commons, did Tony Blair survey the wreckage of the Labour Party and think, 'It shouldn't take me too long to rise to the top of this pile'? As he had predicted in his Australian lecture the previous August, 'the present electoral system . . . will provide Labour with a solid 200-seat base'. In fact the party received a terrible shock, returning just 209 MPs – Blair was one of only thirty-two new members – and facing a Conservative majority of 144.

At the age of thirty, he was the youngest member of the Parliamentary Labour Party, a bloodied rump army. The Labour Left was ruined, but could not see it. Its leader, Tony Benn, had lost his Bristol seat, but in his battle-delirium he welcomed heroic defeat as moral victory – 'eight and a half million votes for socialism'.

For Blair, defeat was defeat – moral, philosophical and overwhelming – and as far as he was concerned the weight of the landslide required the party almost to start again. Over the next four years it was often unclear whether the party had either the unity or the will to continue. Blair sometimes gloomily predicted that he had become an MP at just the wrong time, although he never seemed genuinely likely to abandon his vocation.

In his first speech in the House of Commons on 6 July 1983, Blair made one point that the divided party could still agree on – that mass unemployment was unacceptable. As is customary in a 'maiden' speech, he described his constituency and recalled its political traditions. He quoted from the first speeches of his predecessors. David Reed – who had also been the youngest Labour MP of his time – and Joe Slater had been optimistic.[1] But 'the speech most appropriate to my constituency now is not the speech made in 1970 or even the speech made in 1950'. Instead he quoted from John Leslie, the new MP for Sedgefield in 1935, in a well-chosen extract from another age of dole queues:

> Everyone will agree that it is nothing short of a tragedy that thousands of children are thrown on to the labour market every year with no possible prospect of continuous employment, with the result that thousands drift into blind alley jobs and drift out again. They have no proper training, they feel that they are not wanted and the future seems hopeless.

Blair attacked the government for being 'complacent or uncaring' about the return of mass unemployment, breaking with the convention that maiden speeches should not be 'controversial' – although he denied that the facts of deprivation and unhappiness were controversial, because they were beyond argument. He said that, without work, his constituents 'not only suffer the indignity of enforced idleness – they wonder how they can afford to get married, to start a family, and to have access to all the benefits of society that they should be able to take for granted'.

This was not the conventional language of the Labour Party of 1983. This emphasis on the desire of real people to settle down, start a family and get on in life was only really reclaimed for Labour by Blair as leader a decade later. But he spoke the Eighties language too. He attacked that year's Budget for benefiting only those on three times average earnings, which contradicted the 'myth that the Conservative Party is the party of lower taxation for the people'. And he spoke the older language of ethical socialism in a passage of some power, in which he explained how the moral – and not exclusively Christian – beliefs of his early adulthood had sought political expression:

> I am a socialist not through reading a textbook that has caught my intellectual fancy, nor through unthinking tradition, but because I believe that, at its best, socialism corresponds most closely to an existence that is both rational and moral. It stands for co-operation, not confrontation; for fellowship, not fear. It stands for equality, not because it wants people to be the same but because only through equality in our economic circumstances can our individuality develop properly. British democracy rests ultimately on the shared perception by all the people that they participate in the benefits of the common weal.

It was an eloquent and confident personal credo, which stands well as a summary of his political beliefs at the start of his steady and largely unobtrusive rise to the top of the Labour Party.

It is instructive to compare Blair's maiden speech with the new version of Clause IV of Labour's constitution adopted twelve years later. The language of his 1983 speech was dated even then – few people actually talk of the 'common weal' – and he speaks differently now. 'Equality', specifically 'equality in our economic circumstances', and the Christian socialist word 'fellowship' reek of R.H. Tawney and other dusty books. 'Equality' only appears in the new Clause IV as the less distinctive 'equality of opportunity'. But the ideas in 1983 were also simpler. The philosophical mantra of John Macmurray – translated in the new Clause IV as 'by the strength of our common endeavour we achieve more than we achieve alone' – is missing, despite supposedly being such a persistent influence from Oxford days. The rights and duties which arise from Macmurray's work are also absent – to be rediscovered, if not reinvented, later.

Kinnockite

Before he spoke in the House of Commons, however, his first business as a new Labour MP was to take a position in the leadership election, which started on the Sunday after the General Election, when Michael Foot announced his resignation. Four candidates immediately emerged: Neil Kinnock, Roy Hattersley, Peter Shore and Eric Heffer. Bryan Gould, returning to the House after an absence of four years, threw himself into Shore's campaign:

> The first time I really registered Tony as a person was when we held a meeting in one of those 'W' rooms, down off Westminster Hall, and it was a fairly small meeting I'm sorry to say. Peter's candidature didn't really get off the ground. But one of the people who did turn up – there weren't more than a dozen or so – was Tony Blair. And I immediately thought, 'Well here's a bright young new member, this is rather encouraging'. But I spoke briefly to Tony afterwards and it became clear that he was going to all the meetings. He obviously thought the House of Commons was like going up to university – you went to Buddhists and you went to the communists and you picked up their literature and you decided which of the clubs you'd join.

Even so, Blair did not bother to sample the excitements on offer from the campaign of Eric Heffer, standing as the candidate of the Bennite Left.

Gould supported Shore principally because they were both

firmly opposed to membership of the European Community, and Gould confirms that it was plain that Blair did not share that view. In fact, the tide of opinion in the party was turning. During the leadership election campaign, Neil Kinnock argued that Britain had been in the Community for over ten years, and that the Labour Party would have to accept that it was no longer practical to come out. Kinnock was the front-runner for the leadership from the moment Foot resigned – in fact, Foot's resignation had been timed deliberately to assist him.[2] Blair backed the 'dream ticket' of Kinnock for leader, Hattersley for deputy.

Over the next nine years, Blair was to develop a close relationship with Kinnock – to the point where, when Kinnock resigned in 1992, Blair was a possible contender for the deputy leadership of the party. Blair describes himself as 'a political soulmate' of Kinnock's, although it was John Smith and Roy Hattersley who were his first patrons, and he was initially only one of a group of talented backbenchers whom the new leader promoted.[3] By the end of his leadership, Kinnock and Blair were bound together in the common 'project' of party modernisation, with Blair always at its leading edge.

In 1982, he had already set out in his Australian lecture the course Kinnock would follow as leader – detaching the soft from the hard Left, in alliance with the Right. But the scale of the disaster of the 1983 election – the gulf between the public and Labour's policies – made him think again about the party's fundamental beliefs as well as internal tactics. In his lecture, Blair had said that Labour could defeat the Conservatives 'without altering its policies at all. Its policies indeed already recognise, if sometimes unconsciously, the changes that have taken place in our social and economic attitudes'. Now he revised that view. His lawyer friend Charles Falconer, with whom he shared a house in 1979, observes:

I think there was a real sea-change in Tony's attitude to

things after '83. Because I think the '83 defeat is seminal. Obviously he was aware of the shortcomings of the position in 1983, but it was quite a stunning defeat in '83, not because it was unexpected but because it was large. Tony Blair in the early 1980s was less radical than now. Now he realises that the Labour Party needs to re-create itself; then he was defensive of many things in the party. His position now is much more destructive of the Labour Party as we know it, which I say is a good thing. Tony in the period after the '83 election became aware that here was a party that could not *begin* to cope with what was happening politically. Without change, he came to believe at that period, and always said it since '83, without fundamental change in the Labour Party, we would never win.

Blair could not express such a stark view in public, although in his first television appearance his direction was clear. 'The image of the Labour Party has got to be more dynamic, more modern . . . Over 50 per cent of the population are owner-occupiers – that means a change in attitude that we've got to catch up to,' he said. He was one of two 'typical new Labour MPs' interviewed in a Westminster pub for BBC TV's *Newsnight* on 22 June 1983. The other was Margaret Beckett – not technically new, but a 'retread' who, as Margaret Jackson, had been MP for Lincoln and a Labour minister in the Seventies. Although he looked younger, the contours of his face more rounded, his smile more lippy, he sounded exactly as he does now. In a time-traveller's preview of a future leadership contest, Beckett offered a backward-looking and rather half-hearted defence of Labour's election campaign: 'The basic themes we were putting forward will be seen to be relevant.' She too sounded exactly as she does now.

(The programme also showed prescience in its choice of other guests. The presenter, Peter Snow, then talked to two new Alliance MPs, an abundantly curly-haired Liberal called Paddy Ashdown and the one MP who was even younger than

Blair, twenty-three-year-old Charles Kennedy of the SDP, later leader and president respectively of the merged Liberal Democrats. Only the Conservative contingent failed to live up to their part in foretelling the future: David Heathcoat-Amory is a junior minister and Christopher Chope lost his seat in 1992.)

As Blair developed his analysis of what had gone wrong, he had to judge how much of it he could safely express. An early, bruising experience is part of the Blair mythology. Soon after the election, the hard Left in Spennymoor in his constituency organised a 'public meeting' – the sort of meeting no normal member of the public would ever attend – to build on the Great Leap Forward for socialism which the 1983 election represented.

Blair agreed to speak, and describes the meeting – a little dramatically – as 'the greatest humiliation I have ever experienced'. He argued that the party had to change, that it had lost touch with society, and that many of the changes in society were for the better. Although his emerging Sedgefield fan club was there, the mood was hostile. In the version told by Blair's agent John Burton, the left-wing MP Dennis Skinner spoke after Blair, and savaged him for 'betraying socialist principles'. As Skinner was speaking, Les Huckfield, Blair's rival for the Sedgefield seat and no longer an MP, walked in. '*There* is a man true to his socialist principles,' declared Skinner, pointing, to loud applause.

After the meeting, Blair told John Burton: 'Maybe I was wrong, I shouldn't have said those things.'

He replied: 'You must never stop saying those things. You mustn't move towards the party. The party must move towards you.'[4]

This is a moral fable which has been lovingly retouched in the memory. Skinner remembers it differently, pointing out that he would never have praised Les Huckfield, a former rightwinger and ministerial rival to his ally Bob Cryer. Nor does he remember attacking Blair personally, although he would certainly have disagreed with him.

However, it is not as if Blair's public position was outrageously revisionist – under Foot, Kinnock and Smith he was always found to be nestling just on the 'modernising' side of the party leader. But in 1983 backing the leader was not necessarily a soft option. Neil Kinnock's middle position between Left and Right of the party was an isolated redoubt that had to be fought for. Much of the reformation that took place over the Kinnock years now appears obvious and inevitable. The shock of near oblivion in the 1983 election convinced many that the party had to change, but – apart from on Europe – the party's instinctive reaction to change of any sort was to suspect betrayal. Many of those who elected Kinnock were the kind of socialists, identified by Richard Crossman, who were 'always looking around for someone to betray them'.

Looking back, the task of rebuilding the party seemed to take a long time. Although Foot had moved against Militant in 1982, for example, it was not until Kinnock's 1985 conference speech that the battle was really won, and two supporters of the tendency were still Labour MPs until they were expelled from the party in 1991. When Blair was first allocated an office as a new MP he had to share with one of them, Dave Nellist. They must have made a surreal combination.

After a few months Blair found more palatable company.

Two Bright Boys

Blair and Gordon Brown shared a windowless office in the Palace of Westminster until Brown was elected to the shadow Cabinet in 1987. He and Brown got to know each other soon after Blair noticed Brown's debut in the House on 27 July 1983. Brown's 'maiden' speech does not read well now – it is a wall of statistics about poverty and the meanness of the social security system – but (like Blair's) it was delivered with confidence and authority and (unlike Blair's) some wit. He recalled what the then Minister for Social Security, Rhodes Boyson, a gothic item of mill-town splendour, had written five years earlier about the ease of gaining self-employed work: 'To become a window cleaner little equipment is needed – a bucket, a leather or two and a ladder.' Brown commented: 'When the Prime Minister talked regularly during the election about ladders of opportunity, I had not realised that the next Conservative government would have something quite so specific in mind.' To 'On your bike' Brown now added 'Up your ladder' as a Conservative solution to unemployment.

Brown's underlying message was very different from his message now. The implication then was that the most urgent priority of socialism was to increase social security benefits. Since 1992, that has been relegated to the status of a political residual. As Blair put it in a speech that Brown helped write in the leadership election campaign, 'a large social security budget is not a sign of socialist success, but a necessary consequence of economic failure'.[5]

Brown, only two years older than Blair, was an established politician when he entered the House of Commons. He was Chairman of the Scottish Labour Party, had written and edited books about Scottish politics, had first stood for parliament in 1979 – in John Smith's home constituency, South Edinburgh – and had been an elected student politician at Edinburgh University in the early 1970s, when Blair was at Oxford. The politics of the Scottish Labour Party were different from the rest of the country, and especially London, but Brown and Blair found they agreed to a surprising extent on what was wrong with the party. The Bennite new Left was less successful in Scotland, because it met resistance from the strong traditions of the old Labour Left. In this respect, Scotland was similar to Sedgefield. Brown was an anti-Bennite leader of the mainstream Left in Scotland, which fought against such excesses as a motion of censure on the party leader, Michael Foot, passed by the Executive of the Scottish party.

Significantly, Brown had already worked on proposals for expanding the membership base of the party as a means of

countering the Bennite threat. In an attempt to outflank
activist-led General Committees, he tried to formulate plans
for one member, one vote democracy in the party which
would bring in trade unionists who contributed to party funds
as Labour Party members. This early prototype of John
Smith's reforms did not get beyond some Scottish Labour
Party internal papers, but it showed a prescient understanding of the technical and political obstacles to widening the
party's franchise.

Whereas Blair could equally have supported Kinnock or
Hattersley for the leadership in 1983, Brown was a purer
Kinnockite. When Brown became an MP he joined the centre-Left Tribune Group, of which Kinnock was the leading
member. So Brown naturally found himself on Kinnock's
leadership campaign committee. (While the *Tribune* newspaper had fallen to the Bennites, the Tribune name was kept
by what now became the centre grouping of MPs, and the
hard Left contingent broke away to form the Campaign
Group.)

Blair was in the centre-Left LCC, the Labour Co-
ordinating Committee, which organised at the grass roots but
never operated as a faction in parliament. Paul Convery, then
the Secretary of the LCC, recalls the only meeting of the
faction's MPs just before the party conference in September
1984. Blair was there, along with Harriet Harman and Robin
Cook (who was also a leading Tribunite). 'Tony Blair said he
had no intention of working in any formal organisation of
MPs and didn't see any value in it. The core of his case was
that he saw correct argument and merit as the way to move
the party, rather than factional organisation,' says Convery.
Blair's lofty attitude did not last long. The next year, 1985,
Gordon Brown persuaded Blair to join the Tribune Group,
partly because it was an instrument of Kinnock's tactic of
detaching the soft Left from the hard Left, but partly because
it would be an effective route to the shadow Cabinet.

Blair's political partnership with Gordon Brown was to
endure. From the start, Brown was the senior partner, better

versed in the ways of the Labour Party, and – as a former
television reporter and editor – in the ways of the media. He
also expounded with some authority a compelling and damning analysis of the state of the party at the time. Blair's friend
Charles Falconer is one of several witnesses who attest to
Blair's awe of Brown. He says Blair was 'mammothly dazzled
by Brown's power. I don't think he ever thought at that stage
that he would be leader of the party. People always regarded
Brown as the obvious man.'

However, the relationship was not wholly unequal. Blair
perhaps had a better 'feel' for the voters, and was more in
touch with people who were not in politics. Blair had won his
Sedgefield seat by direct personal canvassing, and by charming influential allies, rather than simply by fixing and
deal-making. And he knew little about the media. He
watched, admiringly, as Brown made the headlines, often
with leaked government documents. 'While the rest of us
were dying to get our names on page eight of the *Guardian*, he
was hitting the front page,' says one envious colleague. Blair,
meanwhile, could not even get Labour Party bodies to publish his Great Thoughts. The Fabian Society rejected his draft
for a pamphlet on the subject of 'community' soon after the
1983 election.

Although they were Kinnockites, Blair and Brown had
their first taste of political advancement through the patronage of the Right of the Labour Party. John Smith had already
spotted their talent. He knew Brown directly as the candidate
in his home South Edinburgh constituency in the mid-1970s,
and Blair through his friend Alexander Irvine, head of Blair's
chambers.

As soon as Blair came into the House, Smith was
recommending him. The Labour MP Tam Dalyell, still inde-
fatigably pursuing conspiracy theories about the sinking of the
Belgrano in the Falklands war, sought out Smith's opinion
on a point of international law:

John said, 'I can't do this, my mind is on all sorts of other things, but if you want to ask a lawyer, go and search out Tony Blair, who has worked for me and Derry Irvine, who is an absolutely brilliant lawyer,' he said, 'a better *lawyer* than I am, in these matters, and ask him for an opinion.' Now, I explained this problem to Tony Blair as an educated layman would. All I can say is, the following day, he produced a two-page handwritten synopsis of the major legal points, and it was extremely skilfully done. I said to John, 'You were quite right, he is a brilliant lawyer, only an extremely clever mind could have done that.' And I've always said that he had an extremely elegant, sharp mind.

(Dalyell nevertheless voted for John Prescott for the leadership of the party in 1994.)

New MPs who want to be promoted to the 'front bench', where they face government ministers across the despatch box, need to attract attention in debates and learn about legislation and procedure. The usual way of doing this is to get on to a committee scrutinising Bills line by line. As a member of a committee, a backbencher is more likely to be 'called' by the Speaker in the Chamber.

As the new shadow Employment Secretary, John Smith chose the Labour backbenchers on the committee examining the latest chapter of Conservative trade union law. From the new intake, he chose Brown and Blair. Outside parliament, Blair had opposed the 'Tebbit Bill', which became the 1982 Employment Act, in *New Statesman* articles and talks. Inside parliament, he now had the chance to oppose the next Bill, brought in by Norman Tebbit's successor as Employment Secretary, Tom King. This brought in legal requirements for ballots – for union leaders, political funds and before strikes.

In Blair's first speech on the subject, on 8 November 1983, he clashed with King and with a new Conservative MP, a fellow barrister called Michael Howard. Unlike his 'maiden' speech, Blair's first engagement in the wordfight of British politics was not exceptional, and contained no hints of future promise. His argument against the Bill's provisions for pre-strike ballots was narrow and legalistic – as might be expected from someone who did not disagree with them in principle. Where he did stray into questions of principle he gave up hostages to fortune – and the ransom has been demanded by Howard ever since.

Six years later, Howard and Blair faced each other from the front benches over yet another Employment Bill. By then, Labour had accepted the central principles of the 1983 legislation, and Howard reminded Blair of his description of it as 'shabby, scandalous and a disgrace'.

Blair attacked the government, too cleverly, for 'state intervention', saying the issue 'is not whether elections are good or bad, but whether it is right for the state to intervene and dictate to trade unions how they should conduct their affairs'. But that was not the point. What mattered, then as now, was whether union members need to be protected, and whether there is a wider public interest in unions' internal affairs. The Bill may have been biased, because it required unions to ballot on political donations, but imposed no equivalent obligation on companies. But he went too far when he declared that the Bill 'has nothing to do with democracy – it has everything to do with interfering with the rights of British trade unionists to organise freely in the association of their own choice'.

If Blair did not make an immediate mark in House of Commons debates, he had fallen among people, like Smith and Brown, who could teach him how to. He found himself a member of an effective team. Alan Clark, then a junior minister at the Employment Department, recounts the 'ghastly' experience of a committee session on the Bill in December 1983 in his *Diaries*: 'Labour has a very tough team. Little John Smith, rotund, bespectacled, Edinburgh lawyer. Been around for ages . . . And two bright boys called Brown and Blair.'

New Man

In January 1984, Tony Blair and Cherie Booth's first son
Euan was born, as coyly advertised in his CV for the
Sedgefield seat eight months before: 'Cherie and I, as yet,
have no children.' Nicholas and Kathryn followed at approxi-
mately two-year intervals. In a minor symbol of generational
shift, Blair was there:

> I attended the births of Euan and Kathryn, and only
> missed the arrival of Nicholas because he was early. I was in
> the constituency and had to race through the night to get
> back to London. Euan took ages, a day more or less, and
> had to be induced. Kathryn was a Caesarean and all over in
> 45 minutes. You feel pretty useless. But I'm pleased I was
> there. It's good for your partner, I think, and you're hum-
> bled by what she goes through.[6]

That year, the family also bought 'Myrobella', a large old
house tucked behind a terrace of old miners' cottages in
Trimdon Station, the centre of his new political universe.
There are actually four Trimdons, within a few miles of each
other: Trimdon Village, Trimdon Grange, Trimdon Colliery
(where there is no longer a colliery) and Trimdon Station
(where there is no longer a station). The family began a life
based in London, but with roots in the constituency. In 1986
they moved 'up' in London from Hackney to Islington, the
modern equivalent of Hugh Gaitskell's liberal Hampstead.
Charles Falconer, a friend of the family, says: 'They've got a
life firmly based in London – quite sensibly. They go to
Sedgefield a lot, but they live as a family together, rather than
living these etiolated lives that a lot of politicians live.' Cherie
continued to be active in the Labour Party – she was elected
to the Executive of the LCC, increasingly now a Kinnockite
pressure group, at the end of 1983, and was re-elected for
another year in December 1984.

The LCC was increasingly becoming a platform for centre-

Left activists to become better known in the party as a step up into parliament. Eight of Cherie's fellow members of the Executive later became MPs – Peter Hain, Kate Hoey, Mike Gapes, John Denham, Mike Connarty and Barbara Roche – or Euro-MPs – Wayne David and Anita Pollack. Cherie, however, after two years on the Executive, decided that one politician in the family was enough, and her priorities are now 'family and work – politics comes third', according to friend and Islington neighbour Margaret Hodge, MP for Barking.

During her time on the LCC Executive, Cherie took sides in at least one significant debate. The testing issue for the Left in 1984–85 was the miners' strike. Some on the Executive remember her as one of those most opposed to the strike. The argument was not about the justice of the miners' cause, but the fact that they had been called out without a ballot. The clarity of her stance is to her credit, as many in the Labour Party were trapped in hand-wringing equivocation, including the leader. Neil Kinnock later felt the strike was a 'lost year' in the modernisation of Labour.

Tony Blair's view was the same as Cherie's, but he was not required to adopt a public position on the strike. He confined himself to expressing his concern that the police were exceeding their powers, when Kent miners were stopped at the Dartford Tunnel on their way to picket other pits. But the damage the strike inflicted on the Labour cause, as he saw it, clarified the change of views on picketing and secondary strike action from those he had expressed in his *New Statesman* articles in 1979–81. As shadow Employment Secretary four years after the strike he was determined to lay to rest the ghosts of 'mass' and 'flying' pickets.

On the LCC, however, Cherie was better known as the daughter of actor Tony Booth than as the wife of Tony Blair. She once said: 'I started life as the daughter of someone, now I am the wife of someone and I'll probably end up as the mother of someone.'[7] Now she was just starting on the role of 'wife of someone'. After only seventeen months in parliament, Tony Blair was summoned to the Leader's Office.

Notes

1. See p134.
2. Robert Harris, *The Making of Neil Kinnock*, pp213–14.
3. Martin Jacques, *Sunday Times Magazine*, 17 July 1994.
4. *Ibid.*
5. Tony Blair, speech in Southampton, 13 July 1994.
6. *Evening Standard*, 16 November 1993.
7. *Sunday Telegraph*, 2 October 1994.

8. UP YOUR LADDER
Treasury Team, 1984–87

'I believe in politics that if you calculate too much, you miscalculate.'

In November 1984, the Leader of the Opposition asked Blair to come to his room. 'Tony was absolutely shivering,' recalls Charles Clarke, Neil Kinnock's Chief of Staff. 'He had no idea what it was. What had he done? The idea that he might be on the front bench was absolutely beyond him. It was the first time he'd been called to see the leader. And he was knocked absolutely flat.'

Kinnock says he said to Blair: 'I'd like you to go on the front bench.' There was a long silence, and he said: 'Don't you want to go on the front bench?'

'Yes. Yes, I do,' said Blair.

'Well, listen, I want you to be in our team and that's that.'

'I want to be in the team, too.'

'What's the matter then?' Kinnock asked.

'I'm a bit surprised.'

About one-third of Labour MPs were on the front bench, members of the 'shadow government', and assigned to cover government ministers and departments.

After less than a year and a half in the Commons, Blair joined shadow Chancellor Roy Hattersley's team as its most junior member. Peter Riddell in the *Financial Times* described him as one of 'the most promising newcomers', and his was hailed as 'the fastest promotion since David Owen's in 1968'.[1] (After he became leader, Blair caused some resentment when he was not prepared to provide the same fast track for any of the 1992 intake.)

Although Kinnock promoted him, he was Hattersley's protégé – Hattersley had been impressed when he first met Blair during the Beaconsfield by-election campaign the year before he was elected. Apart from Blair's intelligence and capacity for hard work, one detail had stuck in Hattersley's mind: 'Tony's one of the most polite people I've ever met. It's a very minor qualification, but I think I've probably done fifty by-elections and only two candidates sent me letters afterwards. And Tony was one of them.'

Hattersley also secured promotion for Stuart Bell, another of his favourites in the 1983 intake. Bell, who beat Blair for the Middlesbrough seat, joined the Northern Ireland team. Bell recalls Blair saying to him in wonderment: 'Only eighteen months ago I was still looking for a seat.'

Gordon Brown, meanwhile, declined the offer of a frontbench job. He says that he felt he could learn more and attack the government more effectively from the back benches, although it has also been suggested that he was offered a shadow Scottish Office post, and did not want to be typecast as a Scottish politician. Brown joined John Smith's trade and industry team the following year.

Blair was clearly ambitious, but avoided giving the impression of being self-promoting. Hattersley says he shared Kinnock's restless insistence on the need to win power: 'One of his abiding features when he was a very young Member was that he was always saying that there's no point in doing things if we didn't win. From his earliest time here the importance of winning has been one of his cardinal beliefs.' Kinnock is contemptuous of those of his colleagues who regard the business of opposition as an end in itself and talk of their front-bench positions as jobs. 'Jobs they ain't,' he snarls.

Blair cannot have been an MP for long before he made some calculations about the future. He has said, believably, that he never thought Labour would win the 1987 election. But he might have expected to be in the shadow Cabinet (as he was) by the election after that, which he must have thought Labour could win. It is unlikely that his ambition was calculated beyond that, although most politicians might daydream about becoming Prime Minister while pretending to listen intently to dull speeches in meetings at which they do not really want to be. He used a curious yardstick when discussing how long the government intended to tolerate mass unemployment in the 1986 Budget debate: 'I think of the time when someone of my generation will be the average age of the members of the Cabinet. That is a long way off, in the year 2010, but I wonder if it is contemplated that we should carry 4 million unemployed until that time.'[2] If 2010 was his target date for the Cabinet, he seems on course to beat it.

However, there is no evidence of a Heseltinian back-of-envelope timetable for advancement to Number 10. Blair says now:

> I believe in politics that if you calculate too much, you miscalculate. Therefore there is no point in worrying. If it happens, it happens, and if it doesn't, well, there's lots more to life. People who become obsessive about political ambition usually are either (a) dangerous or (b) they fail.[3]

It is perhaps too early to judge whether Michael Heseltine's career will finally bear out Blair's dictum.

One consequence of his early promotion is that he hardly took part in the Main Event of the House of Commons, Prime Minister's Questions – until he became Leader of the Opposition. Apart from the party leaders, of course, the occasion is considered to be primarily one for backbenchers. Margaret Thatcher was at her peak: 'It was the clear sense of an identifiable project for the Tory party that I did admire. It is absolutely essential in politics. That is what keeps you going.'[4] Her admirer, Tony Blair, speaking in 1994, was an inexperienced MP when he first clashed with her ten years earlier. In March 1984, he asked for a freedom of information law. Sarah Tisdall had just been imprisoned for six months for leaking to the *Guardian* a memo on the concealment of the deployment of cruise missiles to Greenham Common. Thatcher cuffed him away. The government, she said, had to be able to 'trust those in the civil service who have charge of secret documents to keep those documents to themselves'.

His third question, however, in October 1984, produced a memorable answer. He asked how she squared Chancellor Nigel Lawson's statement that 'unemployment is not an economic problem but only a human or social one' with her recent endorsement of the 1944 Employment White Paper. Her government was generally considered to have abandoned 'full employment' – a cross-party goal launched by the White Paper which, as Blair said, 'puts the battle for jobs at the heart of economic policy'.

She claimed that the White Paper had 'a great deal in common with the policies the government are pursuing —' before being interrupted by disbelieving Labour MPs. 'I have a copy in my handbag,' she declared. And she quoted from it: 'Without a rising standard of industrial efficiency we cannot achieve a high level of employment combined with a rising standard of living.' Thus was Blair partly responsible for making Thatcher's handbag famous.

Roy Hattersley was impressed with his new recruit:

He was just as good as I expected him to be. He was hugely industrious and could always do it. If he had to do hideous things in the House of Commons, like wind up on the third day of the Finance Bill, he would always do it well. You knew there were only five people in the House, and I was one of them. One of the others was that man who was Financial Secretary and was going to be prime minister – John Moore. And John Moore would make a hideously embarrassing speech, declaiming to the House. Tony would make a complete little rounded speech that you'd be pleased to read in *Hansard*.

In 1985, having made an early impact in the House, he also started to become better known in the party and on the media. He remained in touch with the grass-roots Left through the LCC, in which Cherie was active, as it developed first as a source of 'critical support' for Kinnock's leadership, and then as a 'moderniser' faction arguing the case for heretical rethinking of policy, and for one member, one vote democracy in the party.

In the spring of 1985, LCC Secretary Paul Convery organised a series of fringe meetings at regional Labour Party conferences, and remembers Blair speaking at the Southern Region:

> We were pushing the themes of modernisation of the party apparatus, of developing it as a campaigning organisation, of building the membership. He spoke without notes to a meeting of about twelve people, most of whom seemed to come from Thanet North, where Cherie had been the candidate. It was a very, very interesting speech. I was struck by the themes, very much what he is saying now – the need for morality, a strong moral base. And I was struck by the style, the reflective style. I thought two things: 'I've never heard anybody speak like this,' and 'Jolly posh chap, this.'

Blair first appeared on *Question Time* on 16 May 1985. Just to be invited into this television arena is a great step for a rising politician. Blair beat Gordon Brown to it by three years. On the programme, he went first, articulate and confident, opening with one of his theme tunes, Bipartisan Reasonableness: 'If I could begin on a positive point and say what areas of the new public order legislation one could agree with – there are measures to tighten up the laws against racism and measures to tighten up the law against football hooliganism . . .'

It was the day the Liberal-SDP Alliance pushed the Conservatives into third place in a Gallup poll. Sir Peter Parker, aged sixty, claimed the Alliance was the force of the future. Unfortunately for him, another representative of the force on the programme was the seventy-one-year-old Baroness Seear, while a bright frontbencher who had just turned thirty-two spoke for the defunct Labour Party. Parker teased him as one of the 'tired young men from the Labour Party'.

Blair returned the back-handed compliment by accepting that Labour and the Alliance desired the same ends:

> If you can accept that there is virtually a consensus against this government, the choice for the country is whether they want the politics of the Alliance, which is all words and aspirations, or whether they want the Labour Party, which has the policies to translate those aspirations into reality.

Blair's private view, in fact, was that the Labour Party's policies were far from ready to meet anything quite so testing as reality.

Blair's main energies in this period were directed to developing his reputation in the Commons. Although its importance is sometimes over-rated, performance in the House is still an essential test for a politician aspiring to highest office. After tackling the Prime Minister, he tussled with the Chancellor of the Exchequer, Nigel Lawson, whose intellectual clarity he admired. In January 1985, as a junior Treasury spokesperson Blair invited Lawson to reject the 'ludicrous dogma that government intervention is always wrong and market forces are always right', which inspired a typically magisterial put-down: 'Nobody is always right, not even the honourable gentleman . . . Experience shows that, on the whole, it is easier for markets to correct mistakes, even though they make them, than it is for interventionist governments to do so.'[5]

The Chancellor airily patronised him on another occasion, saying, 'The difference between the two sides of the House is that the Opposition discuss problems, but we solve them' – a point not lost on his opponent.[6] It was not until 1987 that Blair was finally getting anywhere near even in his clashes with Lawson. On 29 April, shortly before the election was called, the Chancellor tried to downplay a Treasury study which showed that tax cuts did not create jobs. When Blair commended the study as 'excellent', Lawson intervened to say: 'Has the honourable gentleman read it?'

'I have read it,' Blair replied crisply, and chided him: 'It is wrong of the right honourable gentleman to commission a report and then dismiss it simply because he does not like the findings.'

Although Blair attacked free-market 'dogma', Lawson feels, like many Conservatives, that his opponent was engaged in lawyerly dispute rather than ideological disagreement:

> I was always slightly surprised that he was in the Labour Party at all. He is quite definitely the least socialist leader the Labour Party has ever had. Someone like John Smith was a moderate socialist, on the Right of the party, instinctively, in his bones. I don't feel Tony Blair is – I don't want to cause trouble for him – but I don't feel he is a socialist.

Premonitions

Shadowing the Treasury during Lawson's zenith gave Blair an early taste of an issue of enduring political significance – European monetary integration. It was part of the founding ambition of the creators of the European Community to achieve 'economic and monetary union'. Put simply, the authors of this vision wanted all tariffs and other barriers to trade abolished, leading in time to the establishment of one money across Europe, replacing national currencies.

This stage would be arrived at by gradually linking the currencies closer together in the Exchange Rate Mechanism.

Britain's Labour government refused to join the ERM when it was set up in 1979, and for a long time monetary union seemed a distant goal. But when Jacques Delors became European Commission President in 1985, he drove the vision forward at a time when the ERM had become a stable, low-inflation club.

This forced politicians to think about the reality of greater European integration – and nowhere was the controversy more divisive than in Britain. This was the economic and political question which would destroy first Lawson, then Geoffrey Howe and then Thatcher herself. And the consequences of Britain's entry to the ERM in 1990 have still not played themselves out.

At the beginning of 1986 Blair had to take a position on what was then for most people the relatively obscure question of the ERM. The bulk of the Labour Party still regarded the European Community with suspicion as a capitalist club. It was one they no longer wanted to leave but still wanted to change fundamentally. They voted against the Single European Act later that year not because it was creeping federalism – the reason why Margaret Thatcher later regretted it – but because it cleared the ground for market forces without adequate social protection.

On 29 January 1986 Blair gave Labour's reasons for opposing a Liberal-SDP Alliance motion that Britain should join the ERM 'forthwith'. Some commentators had urged Britain's entry the previous autumn. Lawson later revealed that both he as Chancellor and Howe as Foreign Secretary had favoured entry in November 1985, but had been overruled by the Prime Minister.[7] They had come to the conclusion that it was a defence against inflation and financial instability.

In the debate, Blair intervened in Roy Jenkins's speech to say:

Suppose we had joined in October or November last year and the best rate we could have achieved was 3.60 or perhaps 3.50 Deutschmarks to the pound. Considering the pressure on the pound last week, is it not the case that we would have been raising interest rates?

This was an accurate point, to which Jenkins replied that there is never the 'perfect opportunity' – also true. Nearly seven years later, having joined at 2.95 Deutschmarks to the pound, the Blair scenario came to pass – the pound came under pressure and interest rates went up. But in the intervening period, the Labour Party, and Blair, changed policy.

Blair started by arguing against the ERM in practice, not against the principle. 'The balance of advantage still lies against our joining,' he said. It was

> essentially a means to an end, and for it to succeed there must be a clear and common area of agreement between members on economic policy and objectives. We are not convinced that policy objectives that are currently pursued in the European Monetary System converge sufficiently with those which we would want to be pursued domestically.

Again, precisely the arguments that would be used against joining the Exchange Rate Mechanism four years later.

However, he then went beyond the 'balance of advantage' line to use what would now be blunt Euro-sceptical language against the *principle* of joining the ERM (then often referred to as the European Monetary System, or EMS, of which it was technically only part): 'The EMS is essentially a Deutschmark bloc. It could be said that we would be putting Herr Pohl of the Bundesbank in 11 Downing Street.'

He elaborated the point about lack of 'convergence' of economic interests in a way which was later to be used by Labour critics against the leadership's change of line:

> In many ways it is easier to understand the case for the government, rather than the opposition parties, wanting

us to join the EMS. Joining the EMS implies a fiscal and monetary policy convergence. The fiscal and monetary policies of the German Bundesbank are tight.[8]

Blair went on to say: 'The exchange rate is important, but is a residuary [sic], not a fundamental.' Meaning that membership of the ERM could not itself be an instrument of economic policy, because the pound's value on the foreign exchanges would simply reflect the 'fundamentals' – the soundness – of the British economy. Surprisingly, this was the orthodox economic theory espoused by Thatcher and her adviser Alan Walters, and initially by Lawson. But Lawson had come round to the view that ERM membership, by tying Britain to the conservative German central bank, would give people confidence that inflation would be lower in future, which would itself help dampen inflationary pressures.

Blair's argument appeared to be at the same time one of timing and one of principle. He complained that the Alliance was suggesting immediate entry, at a time when the pound was sinking, but also pointed to the difficulty of *ever* pursuing the separate interests of British economic policy under the constraints of the ERM. He seemed to imply that, in time, the economic policies of the ERM countries *might* converge with 'those which we would want to be pursued domestically'. But he also seemed to say that economic policy should *always* be decided by national politics, and not by the Bundesbank – he stressed that Labour and the Alliance would always want to pursue a more expansionist policy than either the Conservatives or the Bundesbank.

Although his attitude to them was inconsistent, Blair had at least identified the fundamental and difficult issues. As Bryan Gould, who was to take the opposite view, remarks, 'You get the impression with Tony that there is a brain being engaged, somehow.' But Blair, for all his professed interest in economics, would never have been, as Lawson was, an economists' Chancellor of the Exchequer. Gould also commented, cruelly, 'Whatever is Labour Party orthodoxy, Tony believes that.'

Since he voted 'Yes' to Europe in the referendum in 1975, Blair's attitude to Europe reflected the tensions which pulled at the party's policy. He publicly supported withdrawal in 1982–83, while privately stating his objections. In 1986 he attacked the ERM and the Single European Act, but was now edging towards the historic switch of 1988–89 when Labour would become 'more pro-European' than the Conservatives. In 1986, his – and his party's – position resembles an artist's impression of the missing evolutionary link. It has some of the features of its ancestors, but also a clearly discernible new outline. However, evolution is a slow process, and it was incomplete, on Europe and other issues, when the party next presented itself to the British people in 1987.

The 1987 General Election

Europe was one policy which had been 'modernised' more than most by the time of the 1987 election. The party went in to that campaign with essentially the same policies on defence and the economy as it had had in 1983. Much of the prescriptive detail was cleared away, but the economic policy was still basically what Gordon Brown later repudiated as TSB – 'tax, spend and borrow'. With a substantial amount of renationalisation thrown in.

In the run-up to the 1987 election, another central character entered the Blair story. Peter Mandelson was appointed Labour Party director of communications in October 1985. He had grown restless at London Weekend Television, where he worked on *Weekend World*. The grandson of wartime Home Secretary Herbert Morrison, he had been a parliamentary researcher and a Lambeth councillor, and was now keen to get back into politics. In the labels of the time, he was a rightwinger, having worked for Roy Hattersley's leadership campaign in 1983. He was not Neil Kinnock's first choice for the post, but he was a friend of the leader's aide, Charles

Clarke, and was appointed as the compromise candidate by a deadlocked National Executive. Along with campaigns co-ordinator Bryan Gould, he was the architect of Labour's highly professional 1987 election campaign.

Blair would of course have risen through the shadow ministerial ranks and become better known to the public without Mandelson's help. But, certainly after the 1987 election, Mandelson became increasingly important in advising him, and helped present him as one of the most persuasive public faces of the 'new model party' which Kinnock then tried to construct.

Until 1987, however, Blair was widely unknown – Gordon Brown was much more successful at getting himself noticed. Blair attracted a little media coverage for a long-running attack during 1985 on the secrecy with which the Bank of England used public money to bale out Johnson Matthey Bankers – but outside the House of Commons he was just one of several anonymous, if obviously rising, middle-ranking frontbenchers.

Not everyone was impressed. His friend from Hackney South Labour Party, John Lloyd, became editor of the *New Statesman* in August 1986, and wrote that it was important that 'Labour has a stronger shadow Treasury team'. Damning shadow Chancellor Roy Hattersley with faint praise, he turned to the rest of his team:

> Oonagh MacDonald has so far battled hard without too much effect and Terry Davis shows little signs of battling at all. Tony Blair, the bright young barrister who is the junior member of the team, has taken pains to bone up on his subject, but his eagerness does not amount to weight.[9]

Blair was furious, and telephoned Lloyd to say so. 'You're saying I'm lightweight.' Lloyd was taken aback, and said he had meant that he was inexperienced. 'That is not what it says,' retorted Blair. He must have been especially hurt to be bracketed with MacDonald and Davis, of whom Blair shared

Lloyd's low opinion. According to one colleague, Blair used to come out of Treasury team meetings saying they were 'absolutely dreadful'.

Blair was gloomy about Labour's prospects in the 1987 General Election. After losing the Greenwich by-election to the SDP in February, Labour was in third place in the opinion polls. Blair thought the party might end up being overtaken by the Liberal-SDP Alliance, which had nearly happened in 1983. That it did not is one reason for his admiration of Peter Mandelson, who ran Labour's most professional and innovative campaign.

Blair himself had a low-profile election. Some friends remember him spending much of the time in his Sedgefield constituency – hardly a marginal seat. His name does not feature once in the log of BBC TV news and current affairs programmes throughout the campaign. To make matters worse, his only significant public outing was an embarrassment to him.

At a Labour news conference on 31 May, he and Gordon Brown attacked Conservative housing and education policies. As Regional Affairs spokesperson, Brown was busy, touring the country and always in demand on regional television. Blair's lack of experience showed when he said that the Conservative plans to increase private rented housing bore Margaret Thatcher's personal 'thumb mark' and were the product of 'an unchecked and unbalanced mind'. Shadow Home Secretary Gerald Kaufman, chairing the news conference, quickly insisted that Blair was not questioning Thatcher's mental stability, but attacking the 'ethos of Thatcherism'.

The timing of Blair's remark, which might otherwise have passed unnoticed, was unfortunate because it came on a day when Labour politicians appeared uncertain of how to tackle their dominant opponent. Bryan Gould had said that morning, 'There is one campaign issue which encompasses all others – the personality of Mrs Thatcher', while other leading Labour politicians were reported to be privately worried that concentrating their fire on her might be seen as 'over the top' by floating voters.

After she had gone, of course, Blair revised his opinion of Thatcher's 'unchecked and unbalanced mind'. Although 'she came to confuse the notion of knowing your own mind with refusing to listen to anyone else', he admitted that he admired her firmness and clarity.[10]

The 1987 General Election can be summarised simply. Labour won the campaign and the Conservatives won the votes. The soaring seagulls, the stirring Brahms and the ruthless management of television coverage contrasted sharply not just with the 1983 campaign but – less sharply – with the Conservative campaign. That contrast for a moment led Thatcher to uncharacteristically 'wobbly' behaviour, but she need not have worried.

On 11 June 1987, Blair increased his majority in Sedgefield from 8,281 to 13,058. But nationally, the result was another ghastly blow for the Labour Party. The Conservatives still had a majority of 102, and Labour's share of the vote had increased by just 3.2 points to 31.5 per cent. This time there were no excuses. The party had presented a fundamentally unpopular programme to the British people almost as well as it could plausibly be presented. Only now did the party really begin to face up to the huge amount of policy change that would be needed. Between 1983 and 1987, only the policy on Europe and some of the more ornate elements of the seige economy had changed. Between 1987 and 1992, Neil Kinnock would ensure that policies on defence, public ownership and trade unions would go – the last would be Blair's responsibility – as part of a complete policy review.

Notes

1. Andrew Roth, *Parliamentary Profiles*. 'Promotion' does not include to the whips' office.

2. *Hansard*, 20 March 1986, col 503.
3. *The Times Magazine*, 1 October 1994.
4. *The Times*, 6 July 1994.
5. *Hansard*, 24 January 1985, col 1114.
6. *Ibid.*, 13 February 1986, col 1081.
7. Nigel Lawson, *The View from No 11*, pp483–508.
8. The Bundesbank is of course not responsible for tax policy – the meaning of 'fiscal' being a curious Blair blind spot – although the conduct of monetary policy has implications for taxes.
9. *New Statesman*, 22 August 1986.
10. *The Times*, 6 July 1994.

9. CITY SLICKER
Shadow Trade and Industry Minister and Shadow Energy Secretary, 1987–89

'The resources required to reconstruct manufacturing industry call for enormous state guidance and intervention . . . That in turn will bring any Labour government into sharp conflict with the power of capital, particularly multinational capital.'

After the General Election, Blair made his first assault on that plateau of political ambition, the shadow Cabinet. The annual election, in which all Labour MPs vote, is the unlit gateway to that ambition. It was an acutely timed move. There is always a clear-out of old faces just after a General Election, and it was soon but not too soon, when he might have got a derisory vote.

He asked the advice of Bryan Gould, the star of the General Election campaign, who was expected to do well in the shadow Cabinet elections:

In '87 he asked me – it's a nice quality in Tony, he wasn't interested in my view, but it was his way of canvassing support – he asked me whether I thought he was too young and too inexperienced to have a go at the shadow Cabinet. And I said, 'I think you're entirely up to having a go. I mean, don't be disappointed if you don't get in the first time, but have a go.'

Blair was aware that he needed allies and organisation. Merit is all very well, but the most important thing for an aspirant shadow Cabinet minister is to get on a 'slate' – a list of approved candidates organised by one of the rival ideological factions.

At that time, there were three slates, organised by the Right, the Tribune Group and the hard-Left Campaign Group. Although very few MPs voted blindly for a whole slate, endorsement by one of these groups was a big help. Shadow Defence Secretary Denzil Davies was the only member of the shadow Cabinet who was not on a slate. Once, in the 1950s, the Tribune Group had been a small left-wing caucus. Now it was no longer in any meaningful sense 'left wing' on Labour's internal spectrum – it had become a 'ladder of opportunity' up which able, centrist frontbenchers could climb into the shadow Cabinet. After 1983, the Tribune Group expanded to include about half of all Labour MPs.

Blair was a prime example of the new Tribunites, who had followed in Gordon Brown's footsteps. Brown had been a member of the group since he became an MP; Blair only joined the Tribune Group in 1985. As when he joined the LCC in Hackney, he was a centrist joining a left-wing faction as it moved towards him. This meant he was eligible to take part in the vote that mattered – the ballot among members of the Tribune Group to decide who should be on the Tribune slate.

Despite Blair's distaste for machine politics and his protestation in 1984 that he was not interested in 'factional organisation', he had to use the system if he were to advance his career. Nick Brown, his ally in the Northern Labour Party, former GMB union political officer and now the MP for Newcastle East, ran a 'syndicate' for the Tribune ballot. This syndicate in a faction was effectively a party-within-a-party-within-a-party, and it helped get both Gordon Brown and Tony Blair endorsed as 'official' Tribune Group candidates for the shadow Cabinet.

So Blair won a place on the Tribune slate, and stood for the shadow Cabinet. In the election of fifteen members, he came seventeenth, with seventy-one votes. It was a very good result for a first attempt, but not so good as to prompt envy.

Many people claim to have been the first to see Blair's future leadership potential. One of the more credible is Giles Radice, a neighbouring MP in County Durham who lost his place on the shadow Cabinet in those elections. He claims to have said to Blair: 'Look Tony, you are the man of the future. I don't think we can win with Neil. I think that you are the guy, and I'm going to do what I can to get you on the shadow Cabinet as quickly as possible.' (The next year Radice did not stand again, and some of his Northern Region support must have switched to Blair, helping to elect him.)

Bryan Gould, who topped the shadow Cabinet poll, failed to win the post he wanted: shadow Chancellor. Roy Hattersley, vacating the Treasury portfolio for Home Affairs, ensured the succession of John Smith – like him, he was a pro-European and an older rightwinger. Instead Gould took the second most important economic post, as shadow Trade and Industry Secretary, and Blair was appointed his deputy, responsible for the City of London and consumer affairs. The two had worked together for a year in Hattersley's Treasury team – Gould having been brought in as shadow Chief Secretary to the Treasury, in addition to the important election job of campaigns co-ordinator.

Gordon Brown, elected to the shadow Cabinet at *his* first attempt, took Gould's place as shadow Chief Secretary under John Smith. Although Smith and Gould were embarking on a personal and policy feud (which would culminate in a leadership contest five years later), Gould's apparent role as Blair's patron was of no ideological significance. Gould was a party moderniser but a Euro-sceptic, before either term acquired its later connotations. Brown pursued a career strategy of sticking as closely as possible to John Smith, while Blair's strategy resembled that of the junior Social Security minister of the time, John Major, of openness to all strands of opinion within the party.

With Brown in the shadow Cabinet as Smith's deputy, the 'seniority gap' between Blair and Brown was as wide as ever, although not quite as wide as it looked. The City brief was 'seen as the principal job outside the shadow Cabinet at that point', according to Gould. 'The brightest people were given the job and if they proved themselves in that, it was the obvious launching pad.' Others included Gould himself and Mo Mowlam. A reason for this was the opportunity for media coverage, Gould says:

> One of the good things about doing the City job is that you can actually get yourself a lot of attention on the financial pages, particularly in the Sundays. There was a period when I and then Tony found ourselves on the front page of the *Observer* every second week because we would do something about Lloyd's or Barlow Clowes.

By coincidence, Blair's promotion brought him up against the next generation of Conservative leaders. As Gould's deputy, he faced Kenneth Clarke, deputy and Commons understudy to David Young, the Trade and Industry Secretary who was in the House of Lords. Blair's first parliamentary job, though, was to finish the business of opposing the Finance Bill, which had been postponed from before the election. As a result he found himself briefly facing John Major, the new Chief Secretary to the Treasury, and Norman Lamont, the Financial Secretary, who was responsible for getting the Bill through. Blair – always courteous in the House – complimented Lamont warmly, thanking him on 20 July for what was 'the most detailed explanation that I have ever heard on the Third Reading of a Finance Bill'. Lamont reciprocated on BBC TV's *Newsnight* the following year (21 November 1988):

He's a very effective parliamentary performer. He doesn't speak for the sake of speaking . . . He asks very pointed questions. I did once take the Finance Bill through committee when he was my opposite number and I was very impressed (a) by how much he'd done his homework, and (b) by his ability to think quickly on his feet.

Much later, when Blair became leader, it was Lamont who warned: 'The Conservative government faces a monumental challenge from the new and fresh leadership of Tony Blair. It can hardly be over-estimated. Blair has moved the Labour Party sharply to the centre.'[1] He may then have had other reasons for talking up the threat from the new Leader of the Opposition, of course, as the Lamont–Major partnership proved less than enduring.

Cultural Revolutionary

In China the intellectuals had to be despatched forcibly to the countryside for re-education. Neil Kinnock attempted something much more difficult. He had to persuade the Labour Party to go voluntarily. The policy review launched at the Labour conference in Brighton in September 1987 was a unique attempt to re-educate an entire political party.

Fate has an off-beat sense of humour: the idea for the policy review came from a memo by Adam Sharples – Blair's lead guitarist from the Ugly Rumours at Oxford. He had moved from Labour Party headquarters to the public sector union NUPE, where he worked for Tom Sawyer, Tony Benn's successor in the chair of the Labour National Executive's main policy committee.

Sawyer was the most Kinnockite of union leaders. He had come from the Left, but had been humbled by his attachment to democracy – NUPE had balloted its members in 1981 on Labour's deputy leadership, and they had backed Denis

Healey over Tony Benn. Since then Sawyer was relentless in trying to reconnect Labour politics with what his members – and the wider electorate – actually wanted. That was the gist of Adam Sharples's blueprint for the policy review, which Neil Kinnock took up, and which was approved at the September meeting of the National Executive. The memo said:

> Our policy must be responsive to the concerns of the voters – particularly those we need to win over. This is not to say we should abandon our programme in favour of a collection of 'popular' policies. But policy development cannot be divorced from communication of that policy.[2]

The choice facing the Labour Party was a stark one. Its vote in the 1987 General Election was so low that it was fruitless to argue – although the hard Left did – that the policies should be presented with more conviction. Even if that could have increased Labour's vote slightly, it would not be enough. The party either had to change its policies radically, or it had to do a deal with the third party, the Alliance. In the short term, the second option would have been a curious strategy because the two parties of the Alliance had just begun a disastrous merger which would split both parties and cause a temporary crisis of identity.

Many in the Labour Party, however, were persuaded that a pact between the opposition parties was the only long-term hope for power. A pact would mean Labour would have to accept the case for reform of the electoral system – a central demand of the Liberal-SDP Alliance. But that was a price many were happy to pay. Fifteen motions to the Labour conference in 1987 advocated proportional representation, or PR. Blair's view, set out in the *New Statesman* (4 September 1987) has not changed since, despite some behind-the-hand hints:

> Labour's new enthusiasts for PR put their case not primarily on grounds of constitutional principle, but as a

strategy for power. The implications of their case are fundamental: that Labour cannot ever again win a majority of seats in parliament; *and* that what cannot be achieved through the front door of majority government can be bundled in by the back door of coalitions and electoral pacts. This view rests on dangerous delusions.

One delusion, said Blair, was the notion of an 'anti-Thatcher' majority. Under proportional representation, 'there is no guarantee that the 1987 election would have produced a Labour-led coalition'. This was irrelevant, because electoral reform would have to come *after* a successful Labour-led pact at a General Election. (In any case, proportional representation would at least have guaranteed a Conservative–Alliance coalition rather than an unchecked Conservative government.)

But Blair's central argument was a powerful one, which turned to the need for fundamental change in the Labour Party:

The real question for the Labour Party is *why* it is not achieving sufficient electoral support. It must face this question irrespective of whether we retain the present electoral system or change it, whether we stand for election alone or in a pact. The campaign for PR is just the latest excuse for avoiding decisive choices about the party's future.

A coalition still has to decide its economic policy, its industrial policy, what it intends to do about defence or foreign affairs or trade union law . . . There is no decision that would be justifiable for Labour to make in order to win power in a coalition that it should not be making anyway for itself.

Some of the Labour Party conference resolutions betray a comforting view that electoral reform legitimises self-indulgence: we can become a true socialist movement without the need, as Colne Valley Labour Party puts it, 'to appeal to the wavering middle ground'. In practical terms, this is the most dangerous delusion of all.

Blair has pursued this political argument consistently, taking exactly the same line after the 1992 election. He has always set out to win over the 'wavering middle ground' voters directly, rather than to do a deal with the centre party which supposedly represents them. What he fought shy of then, and still to some extent now, is setting out in any detail the policies required to do that.

Blair offered his analysis of Labour's electoral failure in an article in *The Times*, 1 July 1987. In a typically abstract and philosophical way, he argued that the programme just announced by Margaret Thatcher's second government reflected 'an extreme view of individual responsibility'. He explained:

> The large majority of the measures in the Queen's Speech are predicated on the basis that individual choice does not in any way depend on social opportunity; the further people are from the institutions of society, the better they will be. Thus, Mrs Thatcher's answer to education problems is to allow schools to leave the system . . . The answer to concern over pensions is to take out private insurance. The NHS is inviolate only because of its place in the public affections. But if it did not exist, this government would never have invented it. No intellectual energy, no political impetus is given to improving what we do as a society rather than as individuals.

His purpose in this article was to do what he tried to do on a grander scale in his leadership election campaign seven years later. First he set out what he saw as the fundamental philosophical divide between Labour and the Conservatives, and only then did he draw policy conclusions from these first principles. He thus avoided an overt challenge to Labour policies, or even any criticism of his party at all, except to say,

'The government has been able to challenge the post-war consensus because it was weak and people were tired of it. Labour has failed to recognise this and shift its ground.'

Putting that fault right was the purpose of the policy review.

Kinnock's determination to win was often underestimated. No one thought he would abandon the non-nuclear defence policy, but he had already decided to do so. He drove the plan for the policy review through a sullen and uncertain conference, and it was his energy more than anything which drove the process forward over the next two years.

In the end his determination was too great; he insisted so relentlessly on the need to win that he gave the impression of forgetting what he wanted to win for.

Blair was never going to make the same mistake – not out of calculation, although there must have been some of that, but simply through the different process by which he had arrived at his convictions. The contrast between Kinnock and Blair was epitomised in their first television appearances as MPs. The ethical basis of Kinnock's socialism had once been the moral absolutism of opposing the evils of capitalism and nuclear weapons, which he expressed in an interview on a windswept Welsh hillside in 1970. Blair's was not just a kinder, gentler ethical socialism, but one focused more on end states – fellowship or community – and more rooted in real life, as he said in his *Newsnight* appearance in a pub in 1983 (see p146). Certainly there was sentimentality and nostalgia in Blair's vision of community, but it was based on those glimpses of a better life in actually existing communities. Kinnock's romanticism, with which the Labour Party was suffused, was always postulating socialism as the holy city on a distant hill.

Curiously, for Blair is the Christian socialist and Kinnock the non-believer, Kinnock's roots were in a socialism of Original Sin, holy war and salvation. The world was tainted by the wickedness of capitalism, and only those who had a change of heart – preferably through the heroism of workers in struggle – could be saved. Whereas Blair was a relativist, seeing good and bad in everyone, Kinnock had been a fundamentalist. If profit and nuclear weapons were morally wrong, then most of the electorate were condemned. It was his past moral absolutism combined with his insistence on winning which opened the way for Kinnock's changes of mind to be seen as opportunist, rather than the product of sincere reflection.

The 1987 party conference suspected opportunism, but could not put its finger on the leader's intentions. Blair was a member of the supporting chorus whose role was to help smooth the leader's path. On the day of Kinnock's speech, 29 September, Blair urged the party to have the self-confidence to review its policies in another article in *The Times*. He cleverly warned against 'capitulation to the old ideas of the Tories'. He took privatisation as an example – one which touched the conference's raw nerve. Labour had spent the summer reeling before the 'bourgeois triumphalism' of Thatcherism, as commentators hailed a third election victory as proof that Margaret Thatcher had remade the nation's psyche in her own image. Blair took issue with the idea – which the Labour Party half-believed – that she was now invincible, because privatisation had turned Britain into a nation of share-owners:

The notion that we have thereby created a generation of stock market investors is fatuous. All that has been shown is that if something is given away, it will be gratefully received. Of course, if Labour promises to take the gift back, it will not excite popularity among the beneficiaries. None of this means that privatisation is right, or means that public ownership is wrong.

This sweetly persuasive, pragmatic approach contrasted with that of his front-bench boss. The next day, Bryan Gould was unexpectedly heckled in his speech to the conference, precisely because delegates thought he wanted to accept privatisation and ditch public ownership. The previous week he had said: 'The idea of owning shares is catching on, and as socialists we should support it as one means of taking power from the hands of the few and spreading it more widely.'[3] The jeers and shouts of 'You are a disgrace' came at exactly the wrong time for the leadership. The conference was debating a motion to renationalise British Telecom, extend public ownership generally and reaffirm Clause IV. Kinnock did not want it passed.

Kinnock feared that with the Old Testament orthodoxy of Clause IV dragged into it, Gould's provocative revisionism was counter-productive. It was time for a loyal emissary from the leader's camp to be sent out to try to reverse the impression Gould had given. As the vote was being counted, Blair appeared on BBC TV's live coverage outside the Brighton conference hall: 'The issue is not whether we throw overboard public ownership or Clause IV. The issue is how you implement those things in practice in a modern world today.'

Vivian White, the BBC's reporter, put to him that there were some people who wanted to reinterpret Clause IV – knowing that Blair was one of them. Blair was adamant. 'It's not even a question of reinterpreting it. It's a question of giving effect to it.'

In this disingenuous deflection, Blair was making a serious point, much as he would when he eventually asked for Clause IV to be rewritten in 1994. By trying to focus the attention of a suspicious party on what it would mean to 'give effect' to Clause IV, he hoped to open up a debate which would be bound to lead to reinterpretation and rewriting. But he recognised that to start with the demand for revision, before the debate had even begun, would only end in failure. It would be several years before he would feel able to 'say what we mean and mean what we say'.

So, in order to win support for the policy review, Blair continued to assert to Vivian White that black was white. He defended the review as a thoroughgoing and fundamental reaffirmation of all Labour's existing policies: 'I think once the policy review starts taking place, people will realise there's no revision, there's no scrapping, there's no bonfire of commitments. What there is, is a more practical assessment of how you translate your principles into practice.' Of course, in private, destruction and rebuilding were his twin themes. Blair even hinted at it in a *New Statesman* article (4 September), when he wrote of Labour's need for 'profound changes in ideas and organisation', and observed: 'The key to Mrs Thatcher's political success has been in destroying and re-creating contours of electoral support.'

Chocolate Soldier

There were three important changes that Neil Kinnock had in mind for the policy review. Trade union law, nuclear defence – and public ownership. As spokesperson on the City, Blair was to have a continuing role in trying to rid the party of the perception that it wanted simply to take back everything the Conservatives had sold off.

Immediately after the election, he had hinted at an important new direction for policy, which he would try to develop – largely without success – during the policy review. Labour had missed a trick in responding to privatisation, he said: 'The most credible argument in favour of privatisation – competition – was discarded. A really radical policy would have addressed the interests of consumers. Instead, the only protection is a government quango.'[4]

It was an argument he took up in his first appearance in the House of Commons as City spokesperson, asking how the takeover by British Airways of British Caledonian fitted with the government's policy of 'efficiency through competition'.[5] However, the implication that Labour should favour competition where possible in the public services was not followed through.

In May 1988 the Swiss company Nestlé launched a

takeover of British confectioner Rowntree. This brought into sharper focus Blair's evolving views on 'the power of capital, particularly multinational capital' with which he had once expected a Labour government to be in 'sharp conflict'. The question Blair and his party faced was when the British government should intervene in the working of the market. Blair's response to the Nestlé bid exposed him as something of an economic nationalist.

He had already clashed with trade minister Kenneth Clarke on competition policy. Blair was sceptical about big corporate takeovers, and pointed to the well-known academic evidence of poor performance by merged companies, and the fact that hostile takeovers are rare in Germany and Japan. This was a respectable argument, although it gave the impression that he was suspicious of the 'dynamic market economy' which he later embraced. His view of takeovers by *foreign* companies was even more 'conservative'. Clarke caricatured his position: 'That no foreigner should be encouraged to invest in this country and that no Englishman should be encouraged to invest abroad.'[6]

Blair did nothing to contradict this impression in a spontaneous exchange in the debate on Rowntree on 8 June. He listed other companies 'at risk' from foreign hostile takeover. A Conservative MP interjected: 'So what?'

'I will tell the honourable gentleman so what,' Blair retorted. 'If the entire structure for decision-making within United Kingdom industry passes outside United Kingdom control . . . there will be no guarantee that we will control our industrial future.'[7] This nationalist reflex is interesting because it is at odds with Gordon Brown's 'New Economics', expounded as party policy since 1992, in which the location of ownership and control is now seen as largely irrelevant. The sale of the Rover Group to BMW (in 1994) revealed the cross-cutting instincts of the Labour Party. Despite Labour's more relaxed attitude to European economic integration, the party was fiercely opposed to the German takeover of Britain's only big car-maker. It would

seem that Blair, like most of the party, still leans towards the
Old Economics.

Bonfire of Commitments

Labour's instincts on competition and markets made the shift
away from public ownership difficult. The other changes that
Neil Kinnock wanted to achieve touched equally deep emotions in the party.

As one of Kinnock's increasingly trusted favourites, Blair
was now appointed to the 'People at Work' policy review
group, one of seven set up after the policy review was
approved by the 1987 conference. It was a vital committee,
dealing with trade union law. However, in two years, Michael
Meacher, the shadow Employment Secretary responsible for
it, was unable to produce what Kinnock wanted from it – a
decisive break from what might be called Scargillism. But, by
planting Blair on the group, Kinnock ensured that it would,
eventually, deliver the right result.

The third issue – which touched different but equally jan-
gling nerves – was defence policy. This was the change Blair
was least involved in. Since his early support for unilateral
nuclear disarmament in 1982–83, it had hardly featured in his
public profile.

As with his private views on Clause IV, his views on defence
could not be revealed on television, but they could be gauged
indirectly. In his constituency, the Sedgefield posse could say
things that he could not. They were a sounding board for
Blair's political ideas, and propagandists for the policy review.
The following year, in October 1988, John Burton, Phil
Wilson and Paul Trippett were interviewed for a *Guardian*
survey of Labour Party grass-roots opinion. Trippett, the former Militant member, was now a blunt realist:

Round here we are desperate, desperate to win the next

election. Most political parties, when they get a drubbing at an election, start to change some policies. All parties do it when they've had three drubbings. It's unbelievable to think that some people can still say nothing's gone wrong.

Wilson said:

Some people in the party say that the [policy] review, by taking notice of opinion polls and what voters outside the party think, means we'll end up with lowest common denominator politics. But people like that believe Labour will win in spite of the working class, not because of it. I haven't got that kind of contempt for working people.

More specifically, all three said that the non-nuclear defence policy had to go, including Wilson, who had joined the party because he supported the Campaign for Nuclear Disarmament. Burton said: 'I'd like to believe that everyone in the party believes nuclear weapons are morally wrong. But I don't think it's worth losing three elections in a row. There is so much good we can do the working class in education, health and jobs.'

Blair's support for CND had also lapsed. He was last claimed as a member in May 1986, when his name appeared on an advertisement by parliamentary Labour CND in *Sanity*, the CND magazine. In June 1988 Neil Kinnock said, 'There is now no need for a something-for-nothing unilateralism.'[8] And a defence policy motion symbolically including the word 'multilateral' as well as 'unilateral' was only narrowly defeated at the 1988 Labour conference.

The world was changing. After the Reykjavik summit in 1986 between the Soviet Union's new leader Mikhail Gorbachev and Ronald Reagan there was a gradual thaw of frozen certainties, and by the end of 1988 there was a sense in the air that change might be possible.[9] No one knew what Kinnock would do. Not even shadow Foreign Secretary Gerald Kaufman, a convinced multilateralist himself, who was about to start work on the second and critical phase of the policy review group concerned with defence.

Onwards and Upwards

Tony Blair worked hard in 1987–88 to build up his support among Labour MPs for his second attempt to be elected to the shadow Cabinet. He had 'Leadership Approved' stamped on his forehead at a time when the parliamentary party was rediscovering the joys of loyalty. After his appointment to the employment policy review group, another mark of Kinnock's favour was his mission to investigate the October 1987 stock market crash on behalf of the shadow Cabinet. 'I'm a one-man committee,' he told the *Times* Diary, 'with a double brief – to suggest regulation to reduce volatility and to find out if there are ways to reduce speculation.'[10]

Bryan Gould saw it as a sign that Kinnock wanted Blair in his shadow Cabinet: 'At that point there were always about two or three people who were recognised as coming up strongly and wanting places in the shadow Cabinet, and Neil was good at promoting them, and this would have been his attempt to give Tony a leg up.'

Kinnock agrees, but also praises Blair's 'forensic skill' in writing reports: 'One of the good things is they were never long. He would get to the point in a language everybody could understand and profit from.'

Blair also acquired a useful platform outside the Commons as his articles for *The Times* became an irregular column, more or less fortnightly, until August 1988. This was a good way to get noticed by his parliamentary colleagues. On 24 November 1987 he wrote in favour of televising the House of Commons: 'Politics works through publicity and television is the best form of publicity.' He set out his early views on sound-bite politics, and demonstrated a sound grasp of media handling:

Our news today is instant, hostile to subtlety or qualification. If you can't sum it up in a sentence, or even a phrase, forget it. Combine two ideas or sentiments together and mass communication will not repeat them, it will choose between them. To avoid misinterpretation, strip down a policy or opinion to one key clear line before the media does it for you. Think in headlines.

He was perfectly capable of making these observations for himself, but they coincide precisely with the Peter Mandelson guide to political communications. 'These are very depressing reflections because they bear heavily on the quality of our democracy,' Blair wrote, going on to offer a manifesto of political evasion: 'The truth becomes almost impossible to communicate because total frankness, relayed in the shorthand of the mass media, becomes simply a weapon in the hands of opponents.'

Electric Avenue

At the age of thirty-five, Tony Blair had been an MP for just five years. In that time he had risen faster than any contemporary with the exception of his friend and ally Gordon Brown, who was already in the shadow Cabinet as deputy to the shadow Chancellor, John Smith. But now Blair was poised to join him.

In May 1988, Blair employed a new adviser. Anji Hunter, who had been a friend since they met as teenage rebels while they were both at school, had worked for him since the 1987 election in vacations, while she studied for a degree at Brighton Polytechnic. She had not really been political until she became, at the age of thirty, a student again. She was now married, with two small children, and had finally decided to complete her disrupted education. She got a First in History and English. A week after her finals, she started working for

Blair full-time. She joined him just as his star was about to rise further. She has been one of his closest political confidants throughout his time in the shadow Cabinet.

Over that summer Blair had the chance to shine with the financial scandal of the Barlow Clowes affair. He had just arrived in the Members' Lobby on his return from a trip to Japan, when he was intercepted by a new Labour whip, Alun Michael. Some of Michael's South Wales constituents had lost money with an investment group. He says:

> Tony came in with his suitcase still in his hand, and I told him there was something I thought he should know about. We had about a five-minute chat, and he looked slightly glazed. I was convinced he hadn't taken it in. But then ten minutes later I got a call from him, saying he'd been thinking about it. The thing that impressed me was that he immediately analysed the situation, came to a conclusion and checked it back, and had gone to the heart of the matter.

Bryan Gould was happy to let his deputy take the limelight in his fight on behalf of pensioners who had lost their life savings through a failure of government regulation. 'Bryan gave Barlow Clowes to Tony and let him get on with it. A lot of shadow Cabinet people wouldn't do that,' says Nigel Stanley, Gould's political adviser. Blair's ability to grasp the important facts of a complicated situation was not in doubt, but he showed political sharpness too, embarrassing the government with the evidence that it should have known all along that Barlow Clowes was a dubious investment group. The publicity he attracted was well-timed.

In November, Blair was elected to the shadow Cabinet at his second attempt, coming ninth, while Brown maintained the political differential by coming top of the poll. Brown had stood in for John Smith when he had his first heart attack in September, and had been universally acclaimed for a 'penetrating assault' on Chancellor Nigel Lawson during a debate on the economy. The Chancellor had decided to discontinue some economic forecasts: 'Most of us say that the proper answer is not to discard the forecasts of the Chancellor but to keep the forecasts and discard the Chancellor.'[11] It was a parliamentary triumph in which Brown's accomplished skill contrasted with Blair's brittle performance.

Blair heard the result of the shadow Cabinet elections as he was waiting to be interviewed by Emma Udwin for LBC radio, and said he had to call his wife first. Soon afterwards, he blinked modestly in the limelight: 'I'm still young. I've had some good breaks. I've been very lucky, but I'm acutely conscious of the fact that the history of politics is littered with the P45s of those who were supposed to be rising stars and ended up being shooting stars.'[12]

Joining the shadow Cabinet meant that 'we started getting a lot more media attention', says his wife Cherie, although not everybody knew what Blair was famous for. 'At a rock concert someone came up and said, "You're in that band, aren't you?" I thought it was funny, but Tony was quite put out.'[13]

Neil Kinnock wanted to make him shadow Employment Secretary, feeling that Michael Meacher had not been bold enough in revamping this important area of policy. But Meacher still had powerful backing on the Left and even centre-Left. Kinnock says:

All shadow Cabinet allocation is a jigsaw. And I wanted the jigsaw to come out in a particular way a year before that happened. But because of the disposition of forces in the party I couldn't quite make the jigsaw come out the way I wanted so I had to put a piece to one side.

So Blair became shadow Energy Secretary instead for a year. He was described by *Private Eye* as 'the bright-eyed, innocent energy spokesman wheeled in by Kinnock to replace John Prescott'.[14] He was given a substantial parliamentary job – that of fighting electricity privatisation against Cecil

Parkinson. This was a bigger test of the same issue he had faced at trade and industry – the Labour Party's changing stance on public ownership.

Blair started as a traditionalist in his first debate as a member of the shadow Cabinet, on the electricity industry, on 12 December 1988: 'We are proud that we took the industry into public ownership. When we come to power, it will be reinstated as a public service for the people of this country, and will not be run for private profit.' This clear pledge to renationalise the electricity industry was absolute, underpinned by 'the stupidity, indeed the impossibility, of an energy policy determined by the interests of the private sector'.[15]

However, Blair followed what was becoming a regular pattern. The Labour front bench would oppose privatisation, promising to renationalise, but then they would decide that there were more important things to do with the money, and the restoration of public ownership would recede into 'when resources allow' limbo, until – in most cases – privatisation was finally, grudgingly accepted. By the time of the 1992 manifesto, Labour's ambitions for the electricity industry were limited to a pledge to assert 'public control' rather than ownership, and only of the National Grid – the cables and pylons.

In the meantime, Blair took full advantage of the contrast between him and his government counterpart. Cecil Parkinson had been close to Margaret Thatcher's throne, but his career was now in genteel decline. He lacked the edge and quick wits to exploit his far greater experience. The privatisation of electricity was also a policy full of holes. It would raise money – but allow Blair to argue that the one-off gain to the taxpayer would be used irresponsibly to pay for tax cuts. Despite the rhetoric of promoting competition, the consumer would only be protected by regulation. And it would expose decades of dishonest accounting for nuclear power.

'The Secretary of State says that he is introducing real competition,' said Blair, in an early encounter. 'He kept on mentioning competition during his speech, as if the more he mentioned it the more real it became.' Every time Parkinson intervened, Blair left him limping. He derided the 'sheer, breathtaking irrelevance' of the obsession with privatisation, against the 'real agenda for a modern energy policy' – energy conservation.[16]

'Beautiful Person'

Blair's new interest in energy conservation was not wholly spontaneous. In the run-up to the European elections in June 1989, the nation, and especially southern England, went a distinct shade of political Green. Towards the end of the long Lawson boom, the Conservative protest vote was worried about traffic, air quality, dirty beaches and global warming. The merged Social and Liberal Democrats, initially called just the Democrats, were languishing fourth in the opinion polls behind the Green Party.

Fiona Reynolds, then the Assistant Director of the Council for the Preservation of Rural England, lobbied Blair on the subject of electricity privatisation from a Green perspective. She says he was 'quite different' from conventional Labour politicians, for whom the energy portfolio meant coal and jobs. 'He was not a born-again Green, but he was looking around him and saying, "Where can I build some alliances?" And he saw that Green issues had to figure.'

Blair's new Green credentials provided just the excuse that was needed to groom him as one of Labour's front-line faces. Having played no part in the 1987 General Election campaign, he appeared in party political broadcasts on 3 May and 12 June 1989, just before the county and European elections respectively. The double campaign was pivotal to the party's strategic plan for the General Election, then at least two years away. The plan was drawn up by Philip Gould, co-convenor of a group of volunteers in the advertising and marketing industries known as the Shadow Communications Agency, which ran Labour's opinion research, advertising and broadcasts under Peter Mandelson.

Blair – in a well-cut blue suit in the broadcasts – was one of 'the beautiful people' about whom John Prescott regularly complained. Although a multitude of other Labour politicians appeared in the broadcasts, only Blair and Harriet Harman appeared in both. Such favouritism caused resentment among the Debrett's tendency of the parliamentary Labour Party, endlessly fussing over seniority and precedence, serving one's time and earning respect in the Chamber.

What would have infuriated them the more was that Blair did not speak on his energy brief in either broadcast. In May, he talked about homelessness and the poll tax. In June, he talked about Green issues. He did not even talk about the environmental impact of energy policy, complaining variously about water and air pollution, the disposal of toxic waste and the government's refusal to adopt a more stringent Europe-wide health warning on cigarettes. All of these (apart from the last) were Jack Cunningham's responsibility as shadow Environment Secretary.

However, the traditionalists could not accuse Blair of being simply the creation of the image makers. He paid attention to the detail of parliamentary business, fighting the electricity privatisation Bill with diligence and some creativity. During the committee stage, when the Bill was debated in detail, Blair's oldest child, Euan, then five, was not sleeping: 'It was a hellish time, getting up two or three times in the night to settle him, then going to work next morning.'[17] However, the way he fought the Bill was one of the reasons given for voting for him six years later by Chris Mullin, Tony Benn's chief organiser in the early 1980s. Writing in *Tribune* (8 July 1994), which he once edited, Mullin praised his strategic thinking:

As shadow Energy Secretary, for example, faced with the privatisation of electricity, instead of wasting hundreds of hours on irrelevant trench warfare, he identified the half-dozen or so key issues and arranged for them to be debated at a time when the outside world was still awake.

Mullin was the only member of the left-wing Campaign Group to vote for Blair in 1994.

Fiona Reynolds supports this view:

He was very unlike anyone I'd ever worked with on a Bill before. Normally what happens is that the government dictates the agenda. He drafted amendments which triggered the key debates and set the timetable. He ensured that each committee session had one point for debate, and one only.

Successful lobbying from the Green pressure groups won an amendment to the Bill in the House of Lords requiring the electricity industry to promote energy efficiency for the sake of the environment. Cecil Parkinson had the amendment thrown out again in the Commons, but became irritated when his young opposite number tried to intervene in his speech on 20 July 1989: 'This is not the Old Bailey,' he snapped. 'The honourable gentleman is not Rumpole and I am not in the dock. He will have an opportunity to make his speech in a moment.'

The government's arguments for privatising the nuclear electricity industry were particularly thin, and Blair had considerable sport with Parkinson four days later when he abandoned the plan to sell the older Magnox nuclear power stations. 'Well, Mr Speaker – here we have it,' he exclaimed delightedly, '. . . renationalised before they are even privatised.'

By the time of the Labour Party conference in October 1989, his arguments were vindicated as it became clearer that investors would not buy Nuclear Electric at any price. It was a confident Tony Blair who addressed a Labour conference for the first time. Even after six years of Kinnockite modernisation, shadow Cabinet members who were not also on the National Executive still had to speak 'from the floor', and were allowed three minutes (this had applied in government, as when Chancellor Denis Healey had to defend the spending cuts required by the International Monetary Fund against three minutes of barracking in 1976). But three minutes was all Blair needed.

Blair the tyro populist attacked electricity privatisation: 'We do not want it postponed, we do not want it delayed, we do not want it put off, we want it abandoned here, now and forever. (*Applause*.)' And Blair the environmentalist deployed alliteration and inversion in his cause:

> In place of that tired Tory agenda for the Eighties – privatisation, pollution, price rises – we give the country a new vision for the Nineties where conserving energy is as important as producing it . . . Under Labour the environment will govern our energy policy, not energy policy govern our environment.

That was the last that was heard of Blair the Green, however. While declaring boldly 'there will be no more nuclear power stations under Labour', he had already alienated more committed environmentalists by accepting the specious argument that there would be an 'energy shortage' if a Labour government did not complete nuclear power stations under construction, including Sizewell B. This argument, which did not take account of the scope for saving energy, was close to the heart of 'Nuclear' Jack Cunningham, MP for Copeland (which includes the Sellafield nuclear reprocessing plant) and then shadow Environment Secretary.

Nor has the environment been part of Blair's political outlook since. There was one sentence on it, for example, in his twenty-page leadership manifesto in 1994. And the 'energy shortage' argument was back when Cunningham finally gained control of Labour energy policy as part of the trade and industry brief to which Blair appointed him. The possibility of a Labour government building more nuclear power stations 'cannot be ruled out', Cunningham said in January 1995.[18]

Nevertheless, Blair's one-year tenure of the energy brief was topped out when, in November, the government abandoned the sale of Nuclear Electric.

The Bottom of the Locker

The collapse of the government's nuclear privatisation plans was not, however, adequate cover for the obvious illogic of Labour's position on public ownership. After getting his fingers burnt at the Labour conference in 1987, Bryan Gould was wary of going back into the kitchen. He appears to have misunderstood, though, the reasons why Neil Kinnock had been displeased with his call to 'leapfrog Thatcherism' on the issue of share ownership. Kinnock had only been annoyed at the timing of his revisionist remarks, and was now worried that the issue was being allowed to slide in Gould's policy review group, on 'A Productive and Competitive Economy'. Towards the end of the two-year policy review in the spring of 1989, Kinnock feared that Gould had conceded too much to conservative forces in the trade unions on the question of public ownership. Most importantly, British Telecom was still lined up for renationalisation – quite unnecessarily in Kinnock's view.

As the shadow minister responsible for the biggest privatisation at the time, electricity, Blair was forced to take sides in the dispute between Kinnock and Gould. Just as the review group's report was completed, Gould was surprised to find Blair in his office as a member of a delegation from Kinnock, along with Gordon Brown and John Eatwell, the leader's economic policy adviser. According to Gould, they told him they were unhappy with the final draft of his policy document. Gould told them it was the result of 'a pretty carefully worked-out compromise' and says he 'sent them away'.

Later that year Gould was moved to Environment, and Brown was given his Trade and Industry brief. Kinnock defends his intervention:

The discussions – I wouldn't call them real antagonisms – came from a need that I and others felt to sharpen [our] approach, and not to convey the impression that at the bottom of our lockers somewhere we still had this idea of wholesale recapturing of the denationalised industries.

The 'discussions' came too late to avoid giving that impression. Gould's contribution to the final policy review document, *Meet the Challenge, Make the Change*, did promise 'wholesale recapturing' – although not yet:

The speed with which we act on our commitment to return privatised enterprises to the community will necessarily depend . . . on the constraints of finance and legislative time. We are confident, however, that we can make real progress and in reasonable time.

This was a curious conclusion to emerge from a group headed by Gould, who at the start of the policy review had said, 'We have no interest in treating the Tory privatisation programme as a video we wish to play in reverse.'[19] More damagingly, from Kinnock's point of view, the pledge to re-nationalise British Telecom had survived. Because the Conservatives had sold only 51 per cent of its shares, it would have been relatively cheap to buy back the 2 per cent needed for absolute control. The Conservatives were to solve this problem by selling off the rest of the government's stake, but Kinnock thought the wrong signals were still being sent.

As the two-year policy review turned into an annual rolling revision, the bottom of that particular locker was never really cleared out. One problem was that the government kept filling it up with new, even more essential services, such as the water industry. Even Blair's modernising platform for the leadership had a faint, irrepressible echo of 'wholesale recapturing' built into it. 'Most people would not regard it as a sensible expenditure of money . . . unless you had a very great deal of money to spend,' he said in 1994, 'that you renationalise the water industry as opposed to, say, spending the money on health or education.'[20] He had not abandoned renationalisation because it would be the wrong way to achieve socialist objectives, but simply because it would cost too much.

It was not until the rewriting of Clause IV that the Labour Party's formal attachment to 'wholesale' public ownership was finally broken. However, in 1989 Blair soon found himself trouble-shooting a different piece of unfinished policy review business, one that had haunted Labour since the Winter of Discontent in 1978–79.

Notes

1. *Daily Mail*, 8 November 1994.
2. Colin Hughes and Patrick Wintour, *Labour Rebuilt*, p42.
3. *Channel Four News*, 25 September 1987.
4. Tony Blair, *The Times*, 1 July 1987.
5. *Hansard*, 16 July 1987, col 1279.
6. *Ibid.*, 11 May 1988, col 310.
7. *Hansard*, 8 June 1988, col 892.
8. BBC TV, *This Week Next Week*, 5 June 1988.
9. Colin Hughes and Patrick Wintour, *Labour Rebuilt*, p111.
10. *The Times*, 2 December 1987.
11. *Independent*, 26 October 1988.
12. BBC TV, *Newsnight*, 21 November 1988.
13. *New Woman*, May 1994.
14. HP Sauce, *Private Eye*, 26 May 1989.
15. *Hansard*, 12 December 1988, cols 681, 687.
16. *Hansard*, 12 December 1988, cols 682, 688.
17. *Evening Standard*, 16 November 1993.
18. BBC TV, *North of Westminster*, quoted in the *New Statesman and Society*, 24 February 1995.
19. Colin Hughes and Patrick Wintour, *Labour Rebuilt*, p131.
20. Tony Blair, *Financial Times*, 11 June 1994.

10 . OPEN SHOP

Shadow Employment Secretary, 1989–92

'Neil Kinnock was aghast with pride and admiration at the way Tony carried that off.'

In October 1989, Neil Kinnock put in place the piece of his shadow Cabinet jigsaw left over from the previous year. Tony Blair's reward for embarrassing the government over electricity privatisation was to come fourth in the shadow Cabinet elections, behind Gordon Brown, John Smith and Robin Cook. Kinnock promoted Brown to shadow Trade and Industry Secretary and Blair to shadow Employment Secretary. Blair was closing the gap on Brown.

In his first shadow Cabinet post, Blair had a substantial but straightforward task – to deal with a big privatisation Bill which required sound judgment and safe hands. It raised questions about public ownership, but ideology was secondary. Now he was given responsibility for changing party policy in one of the central areas of ideological renewal – trade union law.

Ever since the unions, led in Cabinet by James Callaghan, sabotaged *In Place of Strife*, Barbara Castle's White Paper, in 1969, the Labour Party had appeared unable to resist the sectional interests of organised labour. The strife returned, most signally in the public sector unions' discontent of the winter of 1978/9. It was clear that there was something rotten in the relationship between the unions and a Labour government, a flaw rooted in the dual entity of the Labour Party itself and its institutional expression, trade union block votes in the party.

In Kinnock's first parliament as leader, he was unable to shift the party's policy on trade union law, and found the party trapped between ill-chosen disputes such as the miners' strike and the *Stockport Messenger* lockout, and a government determined to extract every possible vote from wave after wave of new laws against unpopular unions.

Kinnock's description of Michael Meacher as 'weak as water' reflected his judgment of Meacher's period in the employment brief and in the chair of the policy review group covering trade union law. The group's title, 'People At Work', was applied ironically to the apparent inactivity of its membership. In May 1988, Meacher's was the only first-stage report from the seven policy review group reports to be rejected. And the group's final rewritten report, produced in May 1989, started to unravel as soon as it was finished.

Over the summer of 1989 it became clear that there was a serious gap in the review group's work. It had proposed no sanction on unions for breaking the law. The report rejected the sequestration of unions' assets – a means of enforcing the law which had been developed by the courts, rather than invented by the Conservative government. The courts' powers of sequestration had been extended and used against the miners, the print union NGA and, most controversially at the time, the seafarers' union in its dispute with P&O Ferries.

Blair, as a member of the 'People At Work' group, and Charles Clarke, Neil Kinnock's Chief of Staff, organised a rescue operation. With three weeks to go before the 1989 Labour Party conference, Alexander Irvine, the head of Blair's legal chambers and now a Labour spokesman in the House of Lords, was called in to devise a scheme. He proposed setting up specialist 'Labour Courts', like the Family

Division of the High Court. The idea was sold to Ron Todd, the TGWU General Secretary, as a means of preventing ignorant and prejudiced High Court judges who knew nothing about industrial relations imposing draconian sanctions on unions trying to stay within the law. According to Charles Clarke,

> Meacher was saying to me, 'The unions won't have this', and I said, 'Look, the TUC will have it, the T and G will have it, the GMB will have it, NUPE will have it' – because I knew they would. There was a thing in his mind which was 'The Unions', which he couldn't deal with.

Just before the Labour conference Meacher was forced to put his name to a 'clarifying statement' adding the Labour Courts idea to his review group's report. Usually when someone issues a clarifying statement you know they are in trouble. And Meacher was. Weeks later, Meacher became shadow Social Security Secretary, while Blair knew he had to move quickly to reconstruct the policy before it received any further scrutiny. He cannot have suspected that the way he handled another gap in Labour's policy would propel him into the category of possible future leaders of the party.

On 21 November 1989, television coverage of the House of Commons began. The next day, Blair, who had long supported it, and Charles Kennedy, another child of the television generation, appeared with Rhodes Boyson, an anti-television television natural, to review the experiment, on an earlier innovation, breakfast television.

Blair may have had second thoughts a week later, when viewers of the new BBC TV *Westminster* programme on 29 November saw him fall victim to one of the finest parliamentary ambushes recently sprung. There he was, speaking confidently in a debate against his opposite number, Norman Fowler, on the subject of the latest draft of the Social Charter, just published by the European Commission. Six months earlier, he said, Margaret Thatcher had condemned the first draft as 'more like a Socialist Charter', and he expounded enthusiastically on why Labour supported the charter and all the rights it would give the British people. But the latest draft of the Charter contained some new words. Timothy Raison, the former Conservative minister, intervened to ask a question:

> Will the honourable gentleman tell us the Labour Party's view of one right in the charter – the right concerning professional organisations and trade unions: 'Every employer and every worker shall have the freedom to join or not to join such organisations without any personal or occupational damage being thereby suffered by him'? That would put an end to the closed shop. Is that the Labour Party's position?

It was not. The party's new policy document had a whole section headed, 'The right to join a union', but said nothing at all about the right not to join. It said nothing about closed shops, which required 2 million workers to join specified unions in order to get or keep jobs covered by them, and which the government was preparing to abolish.

Raison had hit on precisely the issue that Blair feared. Within days of taking his new post, he had seen the new draft of the Social Charter and spotted the problem. He had talked to union leaders, but they had refused to accept that it was a problem for them. Blair was forced to stall: 'If it has that meaning, it also has the meaning that one has the right to be a member of a trade union. How the government would justify their position on GCHQ, I do not know' – a statement which drew a predictable response from the opposite benches.

As the words of the charter, 'the freedom to join or not to join', echoed around the Chamber, his own words from the *New Statesman*, 21 August 1981, had come back to haunt him, when he said a judgment of the European Court of Human Rights 'dodges the true issue – does the right to join a union imply the right not to join a union?'

As Blair tried to carry on with his speech, Norman Fowler seized his opening, and asked whether Blair would support the government if it abolished the pre-entry closed shop. 'I will take lessons from the right honourable gentleman on the pre-entry closed shop when he is prepared to restore rights to trade unionists at GCHQ,' replied Blair. The Conservative benches were delighted, and mayhem ensued when Blair refused to give way again. 'If I may say so,' he said, 'I have given way a darn sight more than the Secretary of State.'

After the debate, 'Blair came down to the Shadow Cabinet room, and was quite clear about what needed to be done, and then followed it through', according to Neil Stewart, then in Neil Kinnock's office.

Kinnock was obviously supportive, and recalls that he told Blair: 'Whenever you're asked, "Is this Kinnock's view?" say, "Yes". If there are any awkward bits, well, we'll find a way of dealing with that. And that's what he did.'

However, the initiative for ending support for the closed shop came from Blair. Charles Clarke, also in the leader's office, says, 'In fact, Tony moved faster on that than I think Neil might have done.'

This was another occasion when he went to see deputy leader Roy Hattersley for advice. Not that he needed it: it was clear to him what he had to do. Having made the Social Charter – which later became the Social Chapter of the Maastricht Treaty – central to its case for Europe, the Labour Party could not reject a part of it. Especially as the principle of the closed shop was hard enough to defend. But Blair was careful to cover all the bases. 'I think this is the second thing, after his selection, which demonstrates his steel,' says Hattersley.

At the beginning of December, Blair appeared in another Labour Party political broadcast. It was unintentionally sinister, as some creative mind had decided to make a feature of the front bench's 'shadow' titles. Blair walked out of darkness towards the camera, as the voice-over announced: 'Tony Blair is shadow Minister for Employment.' It was an apposite image, for Blair was indeed about to walk 'out of the shadows'.

Armed with the leadership's backing, Blair went back to the trade union leaders. According to one of them, his approach was quite different from other Labour politicians, who assumed that deals had to be done and negotiations entered into. His approach was not, 'Will you back me?' but, 'I am going to do it and you know it's right, don't you?' Blair's public embarrassment in the House of Commons paradoxically helped his cause – it was a vivid demonstration of what he had insisted, that the unions and the party had to choose between the Social Charter or the closed shop. Most of the trade union leaders knew it was a change that had to be made, but were not prepared to say so in public. Their unwillingness was the kind of attitude which intensely frustrated Kinnock – who was 'aghast with pride and admiration at the way Tony carried that off', according to Jack Dromey, national secretary of the Transport and General Workers Union.

Within a week, Blair had spoken to, and neutralised opposition from, all the relevant unions – except the one most opposed, the NGA print union. Blair says he tried to speak to the union's leader, Tony Dubbins. Dubbins insists there was no contact. At a news conference on the Social Charter on 6 December, Blair said he accepted it 'in its entirety'. On 12 December he told the *Financial Times* Labour would not 'pick and choose' from it. These hints prepared the ground for a seven-page statement to his Sedgefield Labour Party on Sunday 17 December 1989, followed by a 'media roadblock' the next day. It was difficult to get through the day without hearing or seeing him, from breakfast television through to *Newsnight*.

His case was simple. Labour supported the Social Charter, and one of the fundamental social rights contained in it was the right not to join a union. He accepted that, in order to win the right *to* join, which he attacked the government for failing to guarantee.

The NGA and its leader, Tony Dubbins, were beside themselves. The NGA depended on the closed shop more than most unions, and had been bruised by long and bitter disputes. It had failed to defend its closed shops – by illegal mass picketing – at the *Stockport Messenger* after the 1983 election, and at News International which moved overnight from Fleet Street to Wapping. Dubbins was furious enough with the change in party policy, but could not believe that he had not been consulted. The day after the announcement, he demanded that Blair come to the union head office in Bedford to explain himself. Blair went, and was subjected to a one-sided screaming match. The meeting is described by one present as 'extraordinary'. The verbal violence was an expression of Dubbins' powerlessness, however. The deed had been done, and there was nothing he could do.

Stewart, who followed Blair's progress from Kinnock's office, says: 'He faced Dubbins down. That shapes my judgment. It's about managing people – you should be leading people, but with just a hint that you know what you want of people. The question that matters is what happens if people cross him.'

Blair had been nervous about how his move would be received by the rest of the party, but the storm passed quickly.

His name was reviled in his absence at the next meeting of the National Executive, for the 'undemocratic' way in which the policy change had been sprung on unsuspecting party and union members. *Private Eye* reported that 'Tony Blair, the smarty-pants in charge of Labour's shadow employment team', was 'savaged' at a meeting of the Parliamentary Labour Party.[1]

But at the shadow Cabinet, he found himself supported – surprisingly enough – by John Prescott. It was a significant hint of mutual respect to come. A former shadow Employment Secretary himself, Prescott had already thought through the problem. He claims credit for having moved the party from its historic attachment to the idea that trade disputes should be settled without involving the law, to a model of industrial relations based on legal rights. One such right was that to join a union: 'That implies the right not to join,' Prescott said simply.

'He was the only other member of the shadow Cabinet who understood it,' says Mike Craven, then Prescott's assistant.

There was some – but surprisingly little – grumbling at Blair's coup from the lower levels of the party and the unions. More significant was the private grumbling of the Conservative Party. Norman Fowler had brought forward his Employment Bill to that week in December, and was disappointed to discover that, with one bound, his opponent was free. Blair taunted Conservative MPs in the House of Commons: 'There they were, all togged up in their party best, and they put their hands into the magician's hat, hoping to pull out a nice white, bright, sprightly, lively rabbit, but instead find that they are holding a very dead fox.'[2]

The closed shop had never been a high profile political issue, for the simple reason that for more than ten years the supposedly virulently anti-trade-union Conservative government allowed it to continue. Most closed shops existed for the convenience of employers, and to prevent 'free riders' – that is, workers who refused to join trade unions but who benefited from conditions negotiated by them. Philosophically, however, they had always been difficult to justify, as the starkness of the Social Charter principle made all too clear. It might have been preferable, from Labour's point of view, to start from the principle of 'freedom to join or not to join' and then deal separately with the free-rider problem by allowing workers who do not want to join the union to make some other kind of contribution. But Blair did not have time for that luxury. Once the government finally brought itself to abolish the closed shop altogether, it would have been disastrous for the Labour Party to be seen as defending an illiberal principle.

It was the relic of an old form of industrial relations, which was in decline but which inevitably appealed to the party's instinct for archaic forms of solidarity. In some ways, this skirmish prefigures the later fight to change Clause IV, in that Blair was resolved to eradicate an issue that opponents could use to attack the party. The fact that both relics appeared to serve only the party's sense of nostalgia reinforced his determination to 'eliminate the negatives'.

The Next Leader of the Labour Party

Neil Kinnock's favour immediately began to shine more fiercely on Blair. Harriet Harman recalls the moment, around January 1990, when she realised that Kinnock regarded Blair as a possible successor:

> Neil said, 'Here comes the next leader of the Labour Party,' when he came into a room, and I laughed because I thought he was joking – I didn't mean that it was ridiculous, but I didn't realise he was serious – and I looked at him and I realised he was completely serious. At that point I thought, 'I wonder.'

We have to remember the depths of obscurity from which Blair rose in just four years. At the end of 1989 and beginning of 1990, an academic survey of Labour Party members was conducted by Patrick Seyd and Paul Whiteley. Blair was not even on the list of thirteen Labour politicians asked about – Harman and Gordon Brown both were. So was Bryan Gould.[3] As one who had basked in the leader's approval in earlier years, he recognised what was happening:

> When I was very much Neil Kinnock's blue-eyed boy, which would have been around '86, '87, and through to '88, when major debates took place in the shadow Cabinet, which wasn't all that often, I would signal that I wanted to speak and Neil would almost always bring me in at the

end, before he wound up. He knew, or hoped, as was usually the case around that time, that I would say something pretty helpful to him, and he could then bounce off that into the wind-up of the discussion. But I noticed in more recent years that Tony fulfilled this role, from '90 onwards, say. Tony, as befits someone called on to do that, would usually say something of pretty mind-blowing banality, but supporting the leadership on whatever it was.

The closed shop episode was the significant moment at which Blair started to close the seniority gap between him and Gordon Brown. Kinnock identified the two of them early on as leaders of the future. He admired Gould, but in 1988 and 1989 he seemed to tilt more towards Brown as his successor. He went through a period of post-electoral depression at the beginning of 1988, during which he jokingly said to Brown: 'Be on hand. The party may need you.' But now Kinnock thought it was Blair rather than Brown who demonstrated the boldness the party needed – the closed shop episode was vital in forming that view. Blair had delivered modernisation.

At the same time, Brown, newly appointed shadow Trade and Industry Secretary, also had unfinished policy review business to attend to. This was the matter which had prompted his visit to Bryan Gould's office with Blair and John Eatwell – Kinnock had now put Brown in Gould's job to get rid of the commitment to renationalise British Telecom. The way he set about his task compared unfavourably with Blair's swift strike. One source says:

> He would vacillate and vacillate. He said, 'What are the unions going to say?' Kinnock's office said, 'We'll tell you what the unions are going to say.' And Gordon just wouldn't focus, wouldn't do it, wouldn't take a risk, thought the unions would be against it.

In some ways, Brown fell victim to high expectations. When he first topped the shadow Cabinet poll in 1988, his political modesty was mixed with a genuine foreboding, a shrewd awareness that he might have peaked too early. If Kinnock and those around him expected much of him, it was of the 'showdown with old Labour' kind. Instead, as shadow Trade and Industry Secretary, Brown preferred to immerse himself in the hardest task of all – rethinking left-of-centre economics.

By this time, Blair had obviously demonstrated ability and loyalty to the leader. Certainly Kinnock recalls no time at which Blair even privately expressed dissent in the slightest about the direction in which he was taking the party – or the pace. But when Blair was given the chance to change party policy, he moved with a speed that took Kinnock aback.

Blair did not actually start to overtake Brown for another two years, but it was the turn of that year, 1990, when he could start to entertain serious leadership ambitions, and the balance between the 'two bright boys' began to tilt.

On the same day that Blair ditched the closed shop, 17 December 1989, another significant event occurred in the Blair story. The party's director of communications, Peter Mandelson, was selected as Labour candidate for the safe seat of Hartlepool, next door to Sedgefield. Blair's close friend in Sedgefield, John Burton, was interested in the Hartlepool seat but, having in a sense 'stood aside' for Blair in Sedgefield, he now stood aside for Mandelson. Why? 'Because Tony wanted Peter. He would have supported me, but I knew he wanted Peter. I realised Peter would be a great asset.'

Mandelson stayed at the Blairs' house in Trimdon while he tried to become the candidate. Blair's tacit support was useful to Mandelson, although his main backer was Tom Burlison, the GMB union regional secretary. Mandelson won the selection easily in a weak field. He left his job at Labour headquarters the following summer. Neil Kinnock was displeased that he should abandon his post, although Mandelson remained an informal adviser to the leader. But he also began to play a more important role as an adviser to Blair. At the

same time that the leader identified Blair as a future successor, one of Kinnock's most influential aides moved in next
door to him.

Looking to the Future

The new year also brought Blair face-to-face with an old
sparring partner, when on 3 January 1990 Michael Howard
became the first of the 1983 intake to enter the Cabinet, as
Employment Secretary. He was a more skilful opponent than
either Cecil Parkinson or Norman Fowler, and would get the
better of Blair more often than most observers noticed. They
were both barristers, both sharp. It was only Howard's somewhat self-satisfied manner that prevented his earning more
credit from their two-and-a-half-year tussle.

It was a period during which Blair's confidence as a parlia-
mentarian developed, as his speeches gained in assurance
and flair. For much of the time, though, his engagements
with Howard were a ritual, which would go something like
this: In an opposition debate on unemployment, Blair would
attack Howard for cutting the training budget. Howard would
pretend not to be making cuts, and then attack Blair for not
promising to restore them. Blair would respond by saying the
'training revolution' would be paid for by a levy on companies
which did not provide training. Howard would seize theatri-
cally on this, describe it as a 'jobs tax', and turn forensic in his
pursuit of its appearance and disappearance in successive
Labour policy documents. Blair would then denounce
Howard for not caring about the unemployed. Finally,
Howard would retaliate by saying Labour's plan for a minimum wage would destroy up to 2 million jobs.

As they applied their legal minds to dissecting routinely
each other's arguments, both were polite and avoided personal attacks, preserving courtroom niceties. One of Blair's
distinguishing features as a politician is his absolute

aversion to personal insult. Some of those who have drafted speeches for him have been surprised to discover that he takes out some of what they think are their best lines for this reason.

The worst Blair would say about Howard was that he had been 'biting the wrong mushroom', such was his distorted vision of the paradise of Britain, overflowing with jobs and training opportunities.[4] Or that he should be called the Secretary of State for Interviews, as that was all he was offering the unemployed: 'In-depth advisory interviews,' he quoted from an official document, 'subsequent advisory interviews . . . special advisory interviews . . .'[5]

One of Howard's better counter-strikes was to compare Blair with 'Private Fraser in *Dad's Army*, whose response to every situation is to cry out, "We're doomed – doomed, I tell you."'[6]

Sketchwriter Matthew Parris captured their parliamentary relationship in its mature phase, when Howard produced yet another batch of proposed changes to trade union law in July 1991. A Green Paper was published on giving individuals the right to obtain injunctions to prevent strikes in public services, among a host of minor measures. Parris described them as 'clinker from the coals which once made a blaze before which Mrs Thatcher warmed her hands through three elections'.[7] Howard certainly gave the impression that the point of his measures was to embarrass the Labour Party, long after the real imbalances seen by Conservatives in trade union law had been righted. Conservative MPs, welcoming an old theme like a familiar security blanket, cheered Howard on. Parris described his opponent's dilemma:

What could Blair say? He was surrounded by TUC dinosaurs from mining constituencies. To please them with a thundering rehearsal of the glories of unreconstructed trade unionism would play straight into the hands of Tory Central Office. A quieter response would disappoint his own side.

Mr Blair pitched it just right. With the lightest of touches and complete self-confidence he sauntered through the green paper, grinning. He tweaked this, prodded that, inspected the teeth of a clause or two – and pronounced that it did not pass muster. It was all got up for the hustings. He gave examples, seemingly very learned examples, with the winning assurance of a likeable young swell.

His own side barely understood what he was saying, but loved it. Later, Mr Howard painstakingly picked it apart. But Mr Blair won the moment, and that matters in the Chamber. A certain swagger helps, and a public school education provides it. Class still counts for something in the parliamentary Labour Party.[8]

In their first clash, in January 1990, Blair had struck a similar pose. With the closed shop a dead issue, Blair could safely condemn the rest of the Bill which Howard had inherited from Norman Fowler as a leftover from the 'industrial cold war', and accuse the Conservatives of adopting an adversarial approach to industrial relations.[9]

However, Blair was aware that there were still plenty of leftovers from earlier battles on his side. When Howard asked for the definition of secondary strike action that would be allowed under Labour, Blair tartly told him that they were debating the government's Bill, not Labour policy documents. Hardly an adequate response, but it had the appearance of an effective put-down.

Howard was striking the right target. He knew that Blair was uncomfortable with the policy he had inherited from Michael Meacher, and the definitions of secondary action and secondary picketing were the main defect. Labour had accepted pre-strike ballots, the most important reform. But Kinnock and Blair, with the memory of the 1984–85 miners' strike burned into their minds, still saw the spectre of Scargill escaping through Meacher's form of words. They could see a re-run of that strike, with miners' flying pickets asking the power workers, lorry drivers, railway workers and dockers to come out in support. The Meacher document would allow sympathetic strikes if workers were balloted and had a 'genuine interest in the outcome of a dispute'. Howard pressed Blair for a definition of 'genuine interest', which was quite capable of including all the groups of workers whose support the miners had tried to win. What was worse, Meacher's document said nothing at all about picketing.

Blair's revamp appeared in *Looking to the Future* in May 1990, a revised overall policy document on which the next manifesto would be based. 'Genuine interest' was replaced by 'direct interest between two groups of workers of an occupational or professional nature'. This appears hardly less broad, and Blair's new text gave as an example 'where the outcome of the primary dispute will necessarily *or probably* affect the terms and conditions of the other employer's employees' (emphasis added). Workers at coal power stations could have argued that the outcome of the miners' strike would *probably* affect their terms and conditions. But if secondary strikes are sometimes described as 'indirect' industrial action, then requiring a 'direct' interest had the appearance of ruling out most secondary action.

In any case, the change allowed Blair to assert that the policy had been tightened up. In fact, he now claimed he was simply restoring the spirit of the original Conservative legislation in 1980, before it was distorted by wicked judges – precisely the kind of chutzpah of which Meacher, a person of Puritan virtue, was not capable.

On picketing, Blair backed the restriction to six pickets, but said he would allow secondary picketing – completely banned by the Conservative government – 'where the second employer is directly assisting the first employer to frustrate the dispute'. Again, definition is a matter of interpretation, but it allowed Blair to insist that the type of mass picketing and flying pickets that occurred during the miners' strike 'cannot be allowed to happen again – that's why we want to lay this whole area to rest'.[10]

These word-plays may seem rather small beer and sandwiches, but Blair was pushing the limits of the possible. This was demonstrated by a last-minute reverse when the May meeting of the National Executive rejected Blair's draft on picketing by 12–11 in the morning, and then approved it by 16–2 in the afternoon. In the interim, seafarers' leader Sam McCluskie left the meeting, thinking he had defeated Blair's text. Although he was a Kinnock loyalist, his union had had its assets seized by the courts earlier in the year in the P&O dispute, over the issue of picketing.

During lunchtime, Kinnock and his aides scrambled a rescue operation to twist arms and call in favours. For all Blair's skilful persuasion, obviously not all the furniture had been nailed to the floor. Blair was 'very frustrated, but he kept his nerve', according to Kinnock, who had to do the talking. 'The only way to bring it about was to take advantage of one or two absences and to use some tortuous language. So that's how it was done. But I was playing poker, and it came out right in the end.' That decisive vote in the afternoon, to 'clarify' the morning's decision, did indeed 'lay this whole area to rest'. Conservatives still hurl general accusations that Labour would take Britain back to the bad old days of strikes and disruption – but the specifics of Labour policy on trade union law have not been heard of since. He had eliminated another negative.

Partly by accident, partly by design and partly by patronage, Blair had by now put together most of the qualifications for highest office in the party. (Few yet noticed, however, apart from Giles Radice and Neil Kinnock.) Blair was English, by accent and constituency, when the party needed to break out of its Celtic strongholds; he was good on television; he was respected in the House of Commons; he had shown some steel by – in the American phrase – 'speaking the truth to power', taking on trade union vested interests in the party. But he had never spoken to a Labour Party conference from the platform. On 1 October 1990 in Blackpool, he had his chance.

It was an upbeat time for the party. Margaret Thatcher's government had suffered six months of catastrophic unpopularity since the riots provoked by the new poll tax in England and Wales in April. Nigel Lawson's resignation the previous year had exposed deep divisions over Europe, and now Michael Heseltine stalked the studios, unable to foresee where circumstances might lead him. Labour had completed its policy review and looked forward with some excitement to the next election. The shift in the party's attitude to trade union law was one of the important and symbolic changes. Here was Blair's chance to identify himself with the 'new politics' in his allotted ten minutes.

As he walked out to the podium, he was, of course, nervous. The conference platform – one of the most striking in recent years – was dominated by a tilted row of four huge photographs of 'real people'. The theme was 'Looking to the Future', echoing the party's 1945 manifesto, *Let Us Face the Future*. In front of Blair lay row upon row of real activists in the Victorian heaviness of the Winter Gardens.

Blair's speech was shouted and too fast, and went straight into a series of sloganised pledges designed to draw applause. 'One of our first acts as an incoming Labour government will be to restore the trade union rights of GCHQ workers – in full.' He promised the right to join a union (he omitted to mention the right not to join); to better maternity leave; to stricter enforcement of health and safety law; and to a minimum wage. After each burst of applause, he called, as if offering them for sale on a market stall: 'New rights.'

Then he launched into Brownesque ideas for the 'training revolution'. He promised: 'Not workfare by the back door, but opportunity by the front. Not some scheme designed for the unemployment statistics, but training, real training.' Expecting applause, he looked up and declared: '*That* is the programme Labour puts forward.'

No one clapped. He quickly looked down at his notes. Disaster struck. He could not find his place.

'And that is why it is so essential —' he stopped, shuffling the papers on the rostrum, 'that we realise – that the training programme – that Labour has, is a training programme that embraces a new agenda for Britain.' Watching the videotape now, the humiliation Blair felt is excruciatingly obvious, but to most delegates at the time it was simply a weak patch in an otherwise excellent speech. By now Blair realised that he had lost a page, and would have to improvise a passage to link to his peroration. He regained his fluency, despite looking desperately lost, coming up with some more lines of 'pretty mind-blowing banality' (Bryan Gould's phrase) with which he no doubt padded out his impromptu speeches to small gatherings of Fabians and others.

After eighty seconds that must have felt like eighty years, he was back on his text, attacking the Conservatives for their approach to industrial relations. 'It is *they* who are unable to escape the politics of conflict and grasp the potential for partnership. It is *they* who embrace the agenda of the Seventies, because they've no answer to the problems of the Nineties.' The delegates applauded happily.

Tim Walsh, an economist who was an external adviser to Blair on employment policy, recalls that 'afterwards back in the Press room at conference a number of party workers were gloating over his mishap – he does seem to evoke either great affection or great distrust among party activists'.

Many of the trade union delegates viewed him with suspicion too, after his apparent embracing of 'Tory anti-union legislation'. They hankered for the simplicities and certainties voiced by John Prescott, who had been Michael Meacher's predecessor as shadow Employment Secretary, and who had said the previous year: 'We shall repeal all of it. There's no little bits you can keep of it. There is nothing you can keep of this legislation . . . It has all got to go.'[11]

Joe Mills, Blair's patron from the Northern Region of the Transport and General Workers Union, recalls being told: 'There's your fella. That's the guy you actually supported as the Member of Parliament for Sedgefield, causing all these

1. Tony Blair aged about two, with brother Bill.

2. Hazel Blair, Tony's mother, with daughter Sarah.

3. Bill, Sarah and Tony Blair, aged about seven, one and four, when the family lived in Adelaide, Australia.

4. Leo Blair, Tony's father - law lecturer, barrister and aspiring Conservative politician.

5. Tony Booth, Tony Blair's father-in-law, as the *Militant*-reading socialist son-in-law of working-class Tory bigot Alf Garnett, in *Till Death Us Do Part*.

6. 'Blair Two' at Durham Chorister School.

7. ABOVE: Blair (*left*) as Captain Stanhope in a production of R.C. Sherriff's First World War play *Journey's End* at Fettes College, 1971.

8. 'He was into Led Zeppelin and Cream': Amanda Mackenzie-Stuart, Blair's sixth-form girlfriend at Fettes.

9. The strawberries-and-cream brigade: Blair at St John's College, Oxford.

10. Alexander Irvine, Lord Irvine of Lairg, head of Blair's legal chambers. The Blairs spend holidays at his house on the Kintyre peninsula, Scotland.

11. 'Too nice and too unguarded to be a politician' (*Daily Telegraph*): the by-election candidate in Beaconsfield samples cheap beer at 30p a pint, 1982.

12. With Cherie, her father Tony Booth and his late wife Pat Phoenix, during the General Election campaign in Sedgefield, 1983.

13. With four of the 'Famous Five' who helped him win the Labour candidature in Sedgefield, on the day after his election as leader, July 1994; (*l-r*) Phil Wilson, John Burton, Paul Trippett and Peter Brookes.

14. 'Two bright boys': with Gordon Brown at a press conference, February 1992.

15. With John Smith, who had decided to delay his move against the trade union block vote, at the Labour conference in Blackpool, October 1992.

16. At John Smith's funeral in Edinburgh, May 1994, with David Blunkett, Roy Hattersley, Glenys Kinnock, Gerald Kaufman and Neil Kinnock.

17. The Smile:
    Spitting Image
    puppet.

18. 'Principle liberated from particular policy prescriptions' (he really said it, at
    a Fabian Society conference, 18 June 1994): cartoon by Steve Bell for the
    Guardian, 21 June 1994.

19. New Leader: with Cherie on his election as Labour leader, 21 July 1994.

20. Handing on the flame: with Neil Kinnock on the balcony of Church House, outside his leadership victory party, 21 July 1994.

21. 'Personal Political Secretary': Anji Hunter, the teenage rebel Blair met when they were both at school in Scotland.

22. The launch of Blair's tour of the country to campaign for a new Clause IV, with the shadow Cabinet's Big Three, Gordon Brown, John Prescott and Robin Cook, 26 January 1995.

23. 'Common endeavour': with deputy leader John Prescott at a photocall after putting the finishing touches to the new wording of Clause IV at Blair's Islington home, 12 March 1995.

24. Blair unveils the new Clause IV with Tom Sawyer, Labour Party General Secretary, at John Smith House, London, 13 March 1995.

25. 'I would love to be a judge': Cherie Booth on becoming a QC, 25 April 1995.

26. Blair triumphant at the Clause IV Special Conference, Westminster,
    29 April 1995.

27. With Cherie: 'I'm very proud of him. I think he's got a lot to offer, and I really want him to succeed.'

28. 'Strong family' man: with Euan, Kathryn and Nicky at 'Myrobella', their
Sedgefield home.

29. With Kathryn on the swing, 'Myrobella', 1992.

problems. We told you that would happen.' It was banter, but 'they weren't very happy about it', says Mills.

Just four years later, Blair would be addressing a Labour conference in the same Winter Gardens – as leader.

It's Time for Change

No sooner was the 1990 Labour conference over than it was forgotten. That weekend Chancellor John Major and Foreign Secretary Douglas Hurd finally prevailed over a weakened Margaret Thatcher, and the pound joined the European Exchange Rate Mechanism. Seven weeks later, she was gone. The following year, Blair was to say that 'he viewed the biggest Tory mistake of recent times as the deposing of Margaret Thatcher. A vital sense of direction (even if admittedly in the wrong direction) was lost.'[12] It was a peculiar judgement, as he had once described her mind as 'unbalanced', and its purpose was probably to stir trouble in a divided Conservative Party.

In November 1990 Thatcher was succeeded by her Chancellor, a man with 'a quiet, dull grey, low cunning that is all his own' – a soubriquet of Nick Brown's that Blair had described as 'a compliment' in a knockabout debate on the Public Expenditure White Paper in February that year.[13]

As soon as Major became Prime Minister, government and opposition were locked in the Sumo embrace of the 'Long Campaign'. The Conservatives bounced back in the opinion polls, although Labour remained ahead. Major constantly looked for the moment he could call the election, and Labour constantly forced him to postpone it. Labour appeared confident and professional, but the truth was that its strategy was running on autopilot. The strategy had been designed to fight Thatcher, and was never satisfactorily changed to deal with a leader who was at the same time her extension and her opposite.

The Labour Party was in limbo. After the two-year policy review ended in 1989, all that was left was a defensive clearing-up exercise, aimed at filleting out the remaining embarrassments that had slipped through the net. Revealingly, it was Gordon Brown's adviser, Geoff Mulgan, who later criticised this as the 'default strategy', based on 'the conviction that Labour should position itself to benefit by default from the government's inevitable loss of popularity'.[14] The creative process of rethinking the party's positive appeal – which had hardly even begun by 1989 – was thus abruptly stifled.

Charles Clarke, Kinnock's Chief of Staff who oversaw much of the review, admits:

> It was a negative process, which was its great weakness, but it was a simple process of going through the different policy areas eliminating the negatives and finding the positives. We actually had a piece of paper on which we listed all the negatives to run through, and that way we could try to stimulate the positives.

The positives, however, remained stubbornly unstimulated.

As shadow Employment Secretary, Blair had got rid of one specific negative, support for the closed shop, and had revised industrial relations policy more generally to eliminate actual and imagined horrors. But despite claiming to offer 'new rights' at the workplace, Blair made only a modest contribution to the 'positives' side of Charles Clarke's piece of paper. He and Brown may have had private reservations about the 'default' strategy, but publicly they were bound to it.

New 'rights' to maternity leave, protection from unfair dismissal, union recognition and a minimum wage were not election winners. As one commentator said of the 1987 election, Labour's commitment to social issues 'resembled an airline with a safety problem marketing itself on the quality of its in-flight meals'.[15] Unless people believe that Labour can deliver a strong economy, neither the NHS nor new rights at work will persuade them to vote Labour.

Full Employment Dropped

On the central ground of economic policy, Blair had two contributions to make. Neither was successful, although in both cases he shared responsibility with the leading figures in the party. Neil Kinnock described 'education and training' as the commanding heights of a modern economy, and yet his shadow Employment Secretary failed to put forward either a large or a detailed training programme. And, while Blair was in the Employment post, Labour played down the goal of full employment – a goal which could have been a symbol of the party's confidence that it could deliver a strong economy.

For many years, the main job of the opposition employment spokesperson had been to sound outraged on television when the monthly unemployment figures were published. It was a role in which Labour's 'Mr Angry', John Prescott, had excelled in the mid-Eighties. As unemployment fell during the end of the Lawson boom, from 1986 to 1990, that role fell into neglect, but when unemployment started to rise again in early 1990, Blair's response was muted.

He had already made some effort to understand the history of full employment. Early in his parliamentary career he had goaded Margaret Thatcher into pulling from her handbag a copy of the 1944 Employment White Paper – which did not actually use the phrase, but is associated with it – to claim that she agreed with parts of it (see p160). Just after the 1987 election, he told the House of Commons that he had been reading the debates on the Education Act 1944, which brought in free education for all. He said: 'I link that with the Employment White Paper published the same year, which said that the responsibility and duty of government was to ensure full employment to the extent that they could.' That last qualification is important, both as a summary of the message of the 1944 White Paper, which was more cautious than is commonly thought, and as an indication of Blair's own carefulness.

Blair's self-improving study of 1944 *Hansard*s also induced a nostalgia for an era of political consensus:

> I noticed that the tone of the speeches was very different from the tone of the speeches that we hear now. Honourable Members on both sides realised that the country had tremendous problems and that it was in the interests of everyone to deal with those problems . . . It is extraordinary that, forty years on, we are debating not how we achieve those things [free education and full employment], but whether it is desirable for the state even to attempt to achieve them.[16]

What *was* extraordinary was that, two years later, the Labour Party, with Blair as shadow Employment Secretary, itself abandoned the goal of full employment. It was a goal which had only just been reaffirmed in the final policy review document, *Meet the Challenge, Make the Change*, approved by the 1989 party conference:

> Our objective is a fully-employed economy in which everyone of working age has the opportunity to take paid work . . . It is a long time since full employment was the objective of government, so long that as a goal it may seem unrealistic. However, as we explain in this report, it is a goal that can be achieved.

However, in the weeks after the party conference in 1989, Neil Kinnock and his economic adviser John Eatwell, with shadow Chancellor John Smith and *his* 'economic adviser' Gordon Brown, executed an about-turn on the issue of Britain's membership of the European Exchange Rate

Mechanism. Hardly anyone noticed, because Nigel Lawson had just resigned. But certain consequences flowed from this fundamental change in Labour policy.

Once Labour advocated ERM membership, it meant that the overriding objective of its macroeconomic policy in government would be to maintain the value of the pound against the Deutschmark. Critics in the party, such as Bryan Gould, who had been moved to the non-economic post of shadow Environment Secretary, said this meant interest rates and government borrowing would have to be decided by the pound's exchange rate, and could not be set to achieve other objectives, such as 'full employment'.

Brown and Eatwell argued, and Smith agreed, that this was a false trade-off. They concluded that it was not possible simply to cut interest rates and print money to reflate the economy and create lasting jobs. This would suck in imports, cause inflation and lead to unemployment later. Apart from emergency measures to help the people who had been unemployed for a long time, the main ways to create lasting jobs were to raise the skills of the workforce and to encourage long-term investment.

However, instead of arguing that ERM membership was the best way of moving towards 'full employment' in the long term, they, and Blair, ditched the phrase. It vanished from the party's 1990 policy document, *Looking to the Future*, where the goal was downgraded to the 'highest possible levels of skilled and rewarding employment'.

Blair's role in the historic switch in Labour's economic policy was subordinate: as ERM membership gradually became the party orthodoxy, his personal view remained indistinguishable from the party line. Despite being Bryan Gould's deputy from 1987 to 1988, Gordon Brown was his guiding influence. But Blair understood that joining the ERM was not merely a matter of being a 'good European', having argued in 1986 that it 'would be putting Herr Pohl of the Bundesbank in 11 Downing Street'. He now believed that sharing some monetary sovereignty with the Bundesbank was necessary for

Labour's anti-inflationary credibility. As Lawson's inflationary 'blip' threatened to run out of control, dropping full employment must have seemed a price worth paying.

Kinnock refuses to accept that the phrase was dropped *because* of the ERM commitment, but now admits that his caution may have gone too far:

> After '87 I managed to get people to distance themselves more because what I'd found right through that period was that people wouldn't distinguish between full employment as we'd known it from about 1949 to about 1977, and what full employment would mean in a differently structured economy. I'm perfectly prepared to use the term 'full employment' . . . but I didn't want to be tied to a specific figure or to a phrase capable of misinterpretation that was in danger of being a slogan. Nobody else can bear responsibility for it. It was part of trying to disentangle real, achievable policy purposes from sentiment. Perhaps I overdid it, I don't know.

Blair showed some signs at the time of thinking that Kinnock had overdone it, although he must have been 'in the loop' when the decision was taken to drop the term from policy documents. In November 1991, when Blair was asked in an interview if he was 'aiming for full employment as it was understood in the Fifties and Sixties', he said, 'Yes, that principle still holds good.'[17] And just before the 1992 election, he said that full employment was achievable and 'must be the objective of any civilised government'.[18] This was excitedly reported in the *Independent* by political editor Anthony Bevins as, 'Labour returns to aim of full employment', although Blair was, and remains, rather wary of the phrase.

Blair and Bevins jousted about full employment, not only during the election but for years afterwards as well. During the 1994 leadership contest Bevins interviewed him for the *Observer*. 'We didn't dump the commitment to full employment,' Blair insisted.

'Yes you did,' said Bevins.

'You and I have discussed this a million times; I don't accept it,' replied Blair, who reminded Bevins of the 1992 interview. 'Before the last election, I actually raised the aspiration of full employment . . . so, far from having any responsibility for dumping it –'

'You brought it back.'

'I articulated it,' said Blair carefully. Bevins then suggested that a genuine commitment to full employment meant at least a million jobs being created. Blair rejected the idea of a target, promoted at the time by John Prescott: 'I just don't think it's very helpful to put –'

'I don't care what you think is helpful,' Bevins interrupted. 'You say you want to eliminate the scars [of long-term and youth unemployment]. That means a million jobs.'

'Well, the main thing is to start getting your programme into place, your unemployment down,' Blair persisted. 'Caution in targets doesn't relax in the least the objective. It stems from a desire not ever to get into a situation where we're misleading people.'[19]

There was, in any case, no reference to full employment in Labour's 1992 manifesto, which merely said, 'We are determined to make a swift reduction in unemployment', and suggested that long-term progress depended on Europe-wide co-ordination: 'Unemployment must be tackled by the European Community as a whole.'

At the launch of the manifesto, Kinnock explained the omission: 'We want to achieve, as any responsible government would want to achieve, full employment. What we refuse to do is to give the impression that there is some magical lever to be pulled that can secure that . . . We will not mislead the unemployed.' But Kinnock's caution risked confusing the electorate, because the aspiration to full employment remains a good symbol of the party's values. John Prescott's leadership campaign two years later was to show that there was life in the old slogan yet.

Blair's caution served to underscore the party's lack of confidence in the means by which it planned to build a strong economy. The 'Training Revolution' was certainly more than a slogan, but it lacked the resources and mechanisms to be wholly credible. It looked like sloganising too, when it became the slightly more upmarket 'skills revolution' by the time of the election. Blair then extravagantly described it as 'our greatest single priority'.[20] Unfortunately for him, it was not the greatest single priority of John Smith's pre-election shadow Budget.

The Conservative mechanism for raising standards, National Vocational Qualifications, was described by the National Institute for Economic and Social Research as little more than 'certifying a semi-literate underclass'. But Blair's response failed to turn the argument decisively against the government. Most of the resources to pay for training were supposed to come from a levy paid by companies which did not spend at least 0.5 per cent of their wages bill on their own training. But Gordon Brown in particular was sensitive to the Conservative charge that this was a 'tax on jobs', and so the policy was never pressed with confidence and vigour. Selling a policy with which he broadly agreed in principle, but in the specifics of which he had no confidence, was Blair's peculiar skill, although it could hardly repair Labour's strategic weaknesses.

By the time of the election, the Labour Treasury team allowed him to promise to spend £300 million on higher-level skills. Some insiders felt this was a presentation-led policy, designed to look modern rather than dealing with the more pressing problem, which was with semi-skilled workers. But the real difficulty was that Blair was arguing for both a huge increase in the amount of training and in the quality of it, without credible institutions and incentives to ensure either.

Team Player

As the preparations for an election intensified, Blair increasingly took a leading role. The Labour campaign strategy was designed to build up the 'Economic Team' around a leader who was distrusted by the voters Labour needed. For all his strengths as a party manager, it was accepted – even by Kinnock himself – that he had to be seen as surrounded by solid, reassuring competence.

The 'team' were John Smith, Tony Blair, Margaret Beckett and Gordon Brown. They were introduced to the nation in a party political broadcast on 18 April 1991. It was a fourfold example of a film genre known in America as the 'biopic'. This is a thirty- or sixty-second biographical commercial, usually screened at the beginning of election campaigns, to define a candidate in the minds of the voters. The Economic Team broadcast was made by Hugh Hudson, director of *Chariots of Fire* and 'Kinnock – The Movie' (the 'biopic' of the Labour leader in the 1987 election, probably the most celebrated British political broadcast).

Over pictures of Blair, in a leather jacket, picking up his daughter Kathryn on a bridge in front of a sunny Durham cathedral, the voice-over said: 'Age thirty-seven. The youngest member of the shadow Cabinet. MP for Sedgefield, Durham. Born in Edinburgh, son of a law lecturer . . .' This was followed by a burst of opportunity chat from Blair:

> There is an immense wealth of talent and potential, and we don't use it, and the reason that we don't use it is that we don't give people the opportunity to develop their own personality, to build their own character, to realise just exactly what they could be – because they could be anything they want to be, provided they get the opportunities. Now, you can't do everything for people, you can't run their lives for them, you can't make all their choices for them. But you can at least give them access to the type of opportunities that I enjoyed, and that many people don't enjoy.

It was a significant marker, because it demonstrated his fluency as a mass politician and because it picked up the theme, 'Opportunity Britain', which the communications agency under Philip Gould had devised for that year's campaign, which was expected to be a General Election year. Blair was interviewed for the broadcast by journalist Fiona Millar, who lives with Alastair Campbell, then the political editor of the *Daily Mirror*, now Blair's press secretary. Her enthusiastic 'Mmmms' punctuate Blair's message, delivered with a taut urgency that seemed to cut through the stasis of Labour politics in that period. There seemed to be genuine frustration in his voice when he said: 'The Tories have had twelve *years* in which to do something about training and education.'

Blair was the star of the Labour Party's public opinion research. Although still little-known, he came across better than any of his colleagues in television clips which were regularly tested on groups of floating voters. Researchers recall only one occasion on which he failed to score highly, when he talked about the problems of having a home in London and another in his constituency, which sounded as if he were complaining about owning two houses.

It is no coincidence that the Economic Team were also the Leadership Team after the 1992 election. Smith and Beckett were the leadership ticket, and Brown and Blair – once they ruled themselves out of the running – were their lieutenants. John Smith had built himself a commanding position in the party by 1991. Blair consistently told friends in this period that he thought Labour would lose the coming election, because it had failed to change enough. The implication of that, however, is that he must have thought that Smith would inherit the leadership. Having switched tracks with barely a click between Foot and Kinnock, he was now switching to Smith. This caused Kinnock some frustration, according to his Chief of Staff, Charles Clarke: 'He thought they were too loyal to John. And, yes, there were a number of occasions around then when Tony and Gordon agreed with Neil, but wouldn't say so.'[21]

There were occasional rumours of attempts to encourage

Smith to oust Kinnock as leader early in 1991. Smith did not deny that he would be a candidate 'if for one reason or another there arose a vacancy for leader of the party'.[22] But he vehemently refused even to discuss the idea of challenging Kinnock. There were many people in the party, even some who admired Kinnock as much as Blair did, who were tempted by the thought of changing leader – as the Conservatives had just done – but knew that it was not practical under the party's long-drawn-out election procedures.

By the time of the 1991 Labour Party conference, in Brighton, Blair himself was increasingly being talked about as a leadership candidate some time in the future. His speech to the conference rehearsed some of the themes and phrases which were to become the building blocks of his leadership platform. 'Using the power of all for the good of each', he intoned:

> This is modern socialism; its means ever changing, its purpose ever constant, founded on the belief that we are more than buyers and sellers in some impersonal marketplace, not merely individuals stranded in helpless isolation, but human beings, part of a community with obligations to one another as well as ourselves.

Condemning the government's record on unemployment, he developed the idea of 'social cohesion' with something of a hint of his later slogan, 'tough on crime and tough on the causes of crime'. He used a similar two-part device: 'No one but a fool would excuse the rioting that disfigured our inner cities a few weeks ago. But no one but a Tory would ignore the social despair in which such evil breeds.'

It was a good speech. It embarrassingly outshone those of the 'big five' – Neil Kinnock, Roy Hattersley, John Smith, Gerald Kaufman and Gordon Brown – who had been earmarked by party officials for prominence in the important run-up to the General Election. Blair had learnt the lessons of that eighty-second gap in his 1990 speech.

The Wager

In the five years between the 1987 and 1992 elections the speed and economy of Blair's rise was remarkable. No time was wasted, no years were spent treading water. Starting as an able junior frontbencher, in Year One he made his first attempt at the shadow Cabinet and was rewarded with one of the best positions outside it. In Year Two he was elected to the shadow Cabinet and given a junior post. In Year Three he was given one of the important economic posts, and in a single act of political courage and judgment pulled off a coup against the closed shop which made his reputation. In Year Four he became part of the leadership team and was blooded as a conference speaker. In Year Five he gave a hint of broader themes of social cohesion, and came out of the 1992 election as a serious contender for the deputy leadership of the party.

Some interested observers were even willing to put money on Blair as a future leader. 'How much will you give me for Tony Blair to be Prime Minister by the end of the century?' asked George Elliott of the Sedgefield bookmaker Billy Day in 1991. Elliott, the owner of a local taxi company, regularly ferries Blair and his family to and from the airport and station. He says Day, a former Middlesbrough footballer, replied: 'Don't be silly, man.' When Elliott persisted the next time they met, he offered 500–1, and Elliott bet £10. He says:

> I thought, 'What a good-looking man, to be an MP, which we're not used to in the Labour Party.' He dresses smart and everything, and he comes over well on television. Well, I have racehorses myself, you see, and I'm a betting man, so I just thought, 'There's an opportunity for a good sport.' I used to listen to Tony a lot, and he came over very well, I thought, 'Well, if we're ever going to have a chance, there's the man to do it.'

Ever since then Elliott has plagued Day's life, as it looks

ever more likely that he might collect his £5,000. 'He's a really lovely fella, Tony, and I think his turn's right now.'

Notes

1. HP Sauce, *Private Eye*, 2 February 1990.
2. *Hansard*, 29 January 1990, col 55.
3. Patrick Seyd and Paul Whiteley, *Labour's Grass Roots*, pp153, 246.
4. *Hansard*, 21 March 1991, col 504.
5. *Ibid.*, 5 June 1991, col 345.
6. *Ibid.*, 4 November 1991, col 204.
7. Matthew Parris, *The Times*, 25 July 1991.
8. *Ibid.*
9. *Hansard*, 29 January 1990, col 50.
10. Tony Blair, BBC TV, *On The Record*, 27 May 1990.
11. *Labour and Trade Union Review*, December 1989.
12. Tony Blair, interview in *The Fettesian*, December 1991.
13. *Hansard*, 13 February 1990, cols 230–31.
14. Geoff Mulgan, *Tribune*, 1 May 1992.
15. Martin Harrop, 'Political Marketing', *Parliamentary Affairs*, 1990, p281.
16. *Hansard*, 8 July 1987, col 439.
17. Tony Blair, BBC TV, *On The Record*, 17 November 1991.
18. *Ibid.*, 1 March 1992.
19. *Observer*, 10 July 1994.
20. *Financial Times*, 27 January 1992.
21. Jon Sopel, *Tony Blair: The Moderniser*, p124.
22. *Daily Record*, 14 January 1991.

11. 'MODS'

The Modernisers and the 1992 Election Campaign

'The task of social or collective action today is not to abolish capital, as part of some war for supremacy between management and labour, but rather to enhance the power of individual employees.'

The year 1992 was the crucial one in Tony Blair's rise. By the start of it, he was one of the 'Leadership Team', but he was still Gordon Brown's younger brother. Brown and Blair, in that order, were the leading modernisers in the Kinnock team. By the end of the year, they were the leading modernisers in John Smith's team, but their positions had reversed – although not everyone had noticed.

In order to understand Blair's rise, it is necessary to explain the rise of 'the modernisers'.

For years, argument in the Labour Party took the form of Right versus Left: Gaitskellites versus Bevanites, Jenkinsites versus Wilsonites, social democrats versus Bennites. But in the late Eighties a new division came to overlay the traditional ideological one, using terms entirely favourable to one side. The 'modernisers' were different from the Right and the centre-Left whence they came. Although they paid homage to the values of the past, they did not respect the traditions of either wing of the party. They wanted a kind of party that has not existed – or at least succeeded – in Britain: a mass left-of-centre party independent of but sympathetic to the trade unions.

You can tell a lot about Blair from the date he joined the
Labour Party: 1975. His first formative experiences were of
the failure of the old Right (Callaghan) and then of the unre-
ality of the new Left (Benn).

The modernisers were never a coherent faction, but in the
year or so before the 1992 election, Gordon Brown and Tony
Blair put themselves at the forefront of an increasingly well-
defined body of ideas – a new politics growing within the
shell of the old Labour Party. Under Neil Kinnock's leadership, parts of the old husk had fallen off, but the new party
was not yet fully formed. The idea of 'modernisation' was a
conscious attempt to fill the ideological vacuum on the Left.
As such it was rather narrowly based. It did not arise from a
social movement outside the party, or from the grass roots or
the unions within it. It was synthesised by the parliamentary
leadership, drawing on such intellectual forces as the Left
could muster.

Nor was modernisation a coherent ideology – although
under Blair as leader it could become one. It was as much a
process as a prescription. Blair's insistence on a mass membership as the basis of a relationship with the electorate was a
way of kicking the party in a certain direction, destination
unknown.

The term 'moderniser' started to be used during the policy
review of 1987–89, and was used to define the Kinnockite
alliance of 'soft' Left and Right. It reflected not just a recognition of the extent to which the Labour Party needed to change,
but also support for a particular kind of change – the model
being that of a continental European social democratic party.
Other international models were also important – although
the main inspiration, the Clinton campaign, came later. Blair
visited the United States in 1986, and in 1990 Blair and Brown
also visited Australia, to see how Bob Hawke's Labor government had won its three election victories.

But the European model was probably the dominant one.
'We should go out of our way to build common cause with
other parties around the world in searching out the way

forward,' wrote Blair just after the 1992 election defeat. He pointed out that the French and Australian socialists had held on to power, and 'adapted in government, though not without huge internal tensions', while the Left in Germany, America and Britain had been in 'long and painful' opposition. In other words, there was no single model, merely a self-assembly kit of clues. 'There are great movements of history at work here,' Blair wrote, in his vacuo-Olympian style – the plain conclusion from his survey is precisely the opposite.[1]

For the modernisers, the Labour Party could no longer be the political wing of the trade union movement, in an economy of conflict between labour and capital. Blair said: 'The trade union movement is a tremendously important, integral part of British society *but* it's important that Labour speaks for the whole community' (emphasis added).[2] They felt that the policy review had hardly even started the task of rethinking British socialism. Despite the removal by the vanload of unpopular policies, the policies that remained were not ready to withstand the rigours of an election campaign. And, after Roy Hattersley's early efforts faded, the review hardly involved the asking of any philosophical questions.

What Kind of Socialism?

The modernisers sought to redefine socialism – a process topped out when Blair restyled it 'social-ism' during his leadership campaign. For a long time Blair has borrowed the language of *Marxism Today* to describe the new politics as a 'project' (usually with an 'agenda'). *Marxism Today* was one of the trading posts of the new ideas – its editor and intellectual entrepreneur, Martin Jacques (now deputy editor of the *Independent*) met Blair in 1991. Blair rang him to suggest an article. Jacques's inclination was to say No straight away, 'but there was something in it that held me off,' he says. He and Blair met, and have been friendly ever since. 'The challenge

for socialists is to re-establish the agenda for public action
without the old failings of collectivism,' Blair wrote in the
magazine in October 1991.

The language was abstract and off-putting, but it was an
important article. The idea was simple, derived from the
ethical socialism he had talked about at Oxford. Socialism is
about people's fulfilment in fellowship with others. Or, as he
now put it, 'the use of the power of society to protect and
enhance the individual'. This meant 'a new over-arching
concept of the public interest standing up for the individual
against . . . vested interests'. This was 'in truth the implicit governing philosophy of today's Labour Party'. Of course it was
no such thing – the modernisers' 'project' was to make it so.

What was new and significant was his acceptance that the
state could become a 'vested interest in itself, every bit as
capable of oppressing individuals as wealth and capital'. He
wrote:

> In the latter part of the 19th century, and the early part of
> this century . . . democratic socialists equated the public
> interest with public ownership. So that, though their moti-
> vation and values were, and remain, correct, and though
> they correctly analysed the shortcomings of the early capi-
> talist system, they had no developed analysis of the
> limitations of public ownership through the state as a
> means of helping the individual.

Since then, capitalism had

> drastically altered with the advent of a modern sophisti-
> cated market – the state became large and powerful . . .
> [and] the majority of people became taxpayers funding the
> activities of the state and therefore anxious as to how their
> money was used.

Although there remained a role for public ownership, 'The
public interest demands action by government to ensure a

fully competitive market to prevent monopoly and to encourage choice.' Public ownership was not necessarily in the
interest of either consumers or workers: 'The task of social or
collective action today is not to abolish capital, as part of
some war for supremacy between management and labour,
but rather to enhance the power of individual employees.'

It is impossible to disentangle the influence of Gordon
Brown – such a sentence could have been written by either of
them. On economic issues their partnership was so close – or
Blair's deference so total – as to give them a joint personality.
Theirs was a double message: overtly against public ownership, covertly against another 'vested interest' – not
mentioned – the trade unions. 'Thatcherism enjoyed far
greater popularity as an attack on the vested interests of the
collective than it ever did as a positive political philosophy in
its own right,' wrote Blair. During the 1992 election campaign, he was styled 'Labour's Employment Secretary', as
the Labour front bench tried to rid themselves of their shadows. As such, he made it clear, on the eve of the poll, that
Labour could not be beholden to the sectional interests of
trade unions:

> I've said it so many times, I'm even amazed that people still
> ask me the question, that there'll be no special favours
> whatever, that there'll be no inside track, we will treat
> everyone fairly, but no sectional interest has any particular
> purchase on a Labour government.[3]

What is surprising, looking back, is how Blair appeared to
be the most extreme of leading modernisers while saying such
unspecific things. It was always the implication carried off
from his words which pointed to dramatic change, rather
than the words themselves. His post-election analysis, set out
in *Fabian Review*, 9 May 1992, for example: 'The lesson in
my view is clear . . . to continue and intensify the process of
change. This must happen at the level of both ideas and
organisation.'

As always, he was keener to establish the principle than to set out specifics. Indeed he said, 'in some areas I confess quite frankly, and I don't apologise for it, I don't know what the answers are in terms of actual policy conclusions'.[4] But the broad principle, that Labour must be the party that stands up for the individual against 'vested interests', had implications which were to become more open after the election than when he first outlined the theme in *Marxism Today* the year before.

The vested interests theme was a rather artificial and unspecific device which served an important purpose in the development of Blair's political thought. It allowed him finally to break with 'Labourism' while using rhetoric that sounded distinctively left of centre. In his Australian lecture in 1982, for example, he had talked of 'the broad Labour movement', and regarded the Labour Party's base in the trade unions as its bulwark against the SDP threat.

But the vested interests theme was also an attempt to breathe new life into the older ethical socialist tradition which Blair had encountered at Oxford. Since the war, the idea that the purpose of politics was to build a more moral society had been sidetracked – Labour had come to regard the state as the 'provider' of a better life, rather than as a means towards people discovering it for themselves.

Blair's acceptance that the state itself could be a vested interest contained – as ever – radical implications. Public ownership was itself nothing to do with socialism. The public interest could equally be served by government action to encourage competition and curb monopolies. Labour ought to be on the side of the consumer rather than that of public sector trade unions.

To many people in and out of the Labour Party, if Blair's views had been spelt out in this way, it would have confirmed that he was not, or was no longer, a socialist. This was mainly because Labour had been so closely identified for so long with a particular definition of socialism. Blair claimed to be trying to go back to first principles. But the socialist principles

he identified actually contained few guides to distinctive political action. Most Conservatives affect to be opposed to vested
interests and in favour of competition. Hence Blair's need to
emphasise other vested interests – privatised monopolies, big
business, the banks and the Common Agricultural Policy.

The Long Campaign

The run-up to the 1992 General Election was one of the
longest ever known in British politics. As soon as he became
Prime Minister in November 1990, John Major was anxious
for a mandate to call his own. Unfortunately for him, it was
too risky to call a post-Gulf War 'khaki' election, because the
Labour Party had supported the government. In May 1991
Labour won the Monmouth by-election and pushed him on
to the autumn. But by September 1991 the Labour lead in
the opinion polls – probably largely illusory as it turned out –
pushed him into the new year and up against the five-year
deadline.

During this long preamble, there were three battlegrounds:
the ground on which the Labour Party was preparing to fight;
the ground on which Brown and Blair wanted to fight; and
the ground on which they actually ended up fighting.

Despite all the agonising of the policy review, the ground
which Labour had prepared – although prepared is too considered a word for the accidental process by which priorities
were set – was still essentially old-fashioned. Since the previous election, the party had junked three important unpopular
policies. The non-nuclear defence policy, most nationalisation
and, thanks to Blair, the restoration of 'irresponsible' trade
union power had all gone. But this emphasised what was left,
which was mainly what Americans call 'tax and spend'.

For all Labour's attempts to grope its way towards a programme that dealt with the central problem of employment,
the party found it had blocked itself in by the pledges to raise

the state pension and child benefit. Blair and Brown considered the special status accorded to those two expensive promises to be a mistake. And in deciding how to pay for them Labour made another mistake, although it may have appeared entirely logical at the time.

For decades there has been an anomaly in the tax system. National Insurance contributions – a tax which supposedly pays for social security benefits – are not charged on earnings above a relatively low amount – £20,280 a year in 1992. The result was that some higher earners were taxed less heavily than lower earners. Labour promised to abolish this limit, and levy National Insurance on all earnings – a tax rise that would pay for most of its programme.

With hindsight, there could hardly have been a worse political miscalculation. Millions of middle-income earners would have been caught. Not surprisingly, they were susceptible to Conservative claims that all taxpayers would pay £1,250 a year more in taxes under Labour. And for what? A promise to recycle most of the money in cash benefits to different groups of voters – pensioners, and families with children.

The ground on which Brown and Blair wanted to fight the 1992 election was 'the economy, stupid', as the Clintonistas would shortly say. Not only did the pensions and child benefits pledges – approved in the Lawson boom years – have a musty feel by the time of the election, they had next to nothing to do with a programme for economic recovery. What was worse, worthy as they were, they drained the bulk of the resources a Labour government might have had at its disposal in order to pay for its economic recovery package.

Brown and Blair had been developing the priorities of the modernisers' programme during the party's frozen period, 1989–92: education, training and a jobs programme aimed at the long-term unemployed. In January 1992, when the Conservative 'tax bombshell' campaign started, they were dismayed by the prospect of Labour sustaining the damage of that assault while unable to reap any political benefit from the spending increases to which they *were* committed. It was

notable that Labour's campaign did not give great prominence to the pensions and child benefit promises. Labour
made one party political broadcast about child benefit and
one particularly crass one on pensions, which featured jolly
pensioners chuckling over what they would do with their
windfall gain of £5 a week.

When it came to doing something about their priorities,
however, Brown and Blair were in an awkward position. The
spending pledges owed their origin to John Smith's policy
review group in 1989, when Brown was shadow Chief
Secretary responsible for public spending issues. They were
codified by Margaret Beckett, his successor in that job, as
'Beckett's Law' in 1990, which was that they were the only
two spending promises that would definitely appear in the
manifesto. They were very much the property of the
Economic Team. The team member least implicated in the
policy was Blair, but loyalty ensured that his and Brown's
disquiet was only aired in Smith's room.

In any case, Brown and Blair had not thought out a better
way of dealing with pensioners in poverty, and were only just
beginning to develop the argument that money spent on getting parents into work is a better way of dealing with children
in poverty than simply raising child benefit for all. At the
time they only argued that the bottom of a recession was not
the right time to honour promises agreed during a boom.

Neil Kinnock, meanwhile, had separately identified the
problem of the National Insurance ceiling. He recognised the
symbolism of bringing in higher taxes at a level as low as
£20,280. Although it was well above average earnings, it
could be seen, as Bryan Gould pointed out after the election,
as a 'cap on aspirations'. On 14 January, at what was to
become a notorious dinner with journalists in Luigi's restaurant in London's Covent Garden, he floated the idea of
phasing in the National Insurance change.

Shadow Chancellor John Smith was not pleased. His view
was that phasing in would not have solved the problem, only
postponed it. It also drew journalists' attention to a weakness

in Labour's policy – while under fire from the Conservatives. With two months to go before an election campaign, Kinnock provoked Smith into defending the policy instead of dealing with the problem.

The Luigi's dinner effectively ensured that the spending priorities and the 'cap on aspirations' tax rise would stay in Smith's shadow Budget, announced when the election was called in March. Smith acknowledged the validity of the modernisers' arguments, however, when he became leader, by setting up the Commission on Social Justice. The Commission's unwritten brief was to 'do something' about the pensions and child benefits hook on which the party had dangled for so long.

In the election campaign, Blair and Gordon Brown felt pushed aside. Resentments swirled as Labour politicians manoeuvred behind the scenes of the public campaign to ready themselves for victory or defeat. Blair and Brown, as John Smith loyalists, found themselves eclipsed by Smith's older loyalties to his right-wing Labour allies. Roy Hattersley and Jack Cunningham flanked the shadow Chancellor as the heavyweights of Kinnock's ballast. Instead of the 'Economic Team', the leader was bolstered by the 'Right Team', as the leaders of the old Solidarity faction asserted their control – Hattersley because his long-serving adviser, David Hill, was now the party's director of communications, and Cunningham because he was campaigns co-ordinator, a shadow Cabinet post invented in 1985 for Robin Cook.

Blair and Brown wanted Brown to be campaigns co-ordinator, as he effectively became in 1995, and some who are close to them believe the election result might have been different if he had been – although policy commitments and Neil Kinnock's character would actually have given him little space to move history onto a different course.

With Cunningham and Hill as media planners, and while Peter Mandelson was occupied as the candidate in Hartlepool, Blair and Brown were not on television during the campaign as much as they thought they ought to be. In

the heated pre-election atmosphere, Brown fell victim to the
suspicions of his colleagues because he had set up his own
'secret' campaign headquarters in an office near Waterloo. In
fact, the office had been planned as the election base of the
Economic Team, led by John Smith, but at the last minute
Smith's staff moved into a union office next door to Labour
Party headquarters in Walworth Road. His deputy, Margaret
Beckett, went with him, while Blair never really based himself
there when MPs had to move out of their Westminster offices
at the start of the campaign. Brown's large staff of seven
(compared to Blair's two) also contributed to the appearance
of a personal power base. This fuelled speculation after the
election that Brown had designs on the party leadership, in
competition with Smith – speculation that was damaging to
Brown and counter to his consistent strategy of loyalty to his
powerful patron. Blair, as ever, floated free from any suspicion
of intrigue – partly because he was not seen as a threat. But
his leadership ambitions were about to become more
apparent.

Minimum Wage, Maximum Trouble

During the election campaign itself, Blair's worst moments
came when he had to defend one of the few 'positive' economic policies that the modernisers possessed – the minimum
wage. But it was a policy about which he always appeared
defensive – and he defended it as a lawyer defends a client.

Labour had reversed its position on the minimum wage in
1986, upsetting traditionalists of both Labour Left and Right.
Both preferred that such things should be decided by that
mantra of the Seventies, 'free collective bargaining'. To the
old Left, the low-paid should be organised in unions, not
paid a minimum wage decided and enforced by the capitalist
state. To the old Right, it was a threat to differentials.

Eric Hammond, former General Secretary of the

electricians' union EETPU, now merged with the engineers, tells in his autobiography of how he clashed with Blair and John Edmonds, the leader of the general GMB union, which represents many unskilled workers, at the 1990 Labour conference:

> BBC Television asked me to join a panel reviewing the day's conference with John Edmonds and Tony Blair. Instead of dealing with the day's events, I launched into an attack on the national minimum wage. It upset Mr Edmonds and caused Tony Blair to have a long discussion with me afterwards. I don't think he had fully understood our objections. As he stormed out of the studio, Edmonds said to me with all the pomposity he can muster, 'Thank you very much for that.' Blair obviously had not thought through the effects of the policy on skilled people like ours.[5]

Edmonds says: 'I was a lot ruder than that. I think Tony was nonplussed. I got angry, and no doubt pompous. As I remember it, Hammond left first, with me throwing swear-words at his departing back.'

With the help of the Trades Union Congress, Blair managed to stifle the objections of other unions. Gavin Laird, the AEEU General Secretary, continued to express a 'personal view' against the minimum wage, but his union toed the TUC line in the pre-election period.

The minimum wage was nevertheless a difficult policy to defend, and Howard hammered away at a single, simple proposition: If employers are forced to pay some of their workers more, they will employ fewer of them. Howard claims, with some justification, to have won their two-year-long argument:

> He was very uncomfortable on that issue. Either it is so low that it doesn't make a difference, or it is so high that it costs jobs. If it means that employers are going to have to pay more than they would otherwise pay, there will be some

employers who will not be able to afford to pay that, and they won't offer the jobs.

In May 1991, Howard quoted gleefully from a Fabian Society pamphlet by Fred Bayliss, a former chairman of the Labour government's Pay Board and a *supporter* of the minimum wage. This said that different computer models of the economy 'suggest upper bounds of about 250,000 and 880,000 for the employment effect'. For 'employment effect' read 'job losses'.

Even Bayliss's first figure – a quarter of a million job losses – was bad enough. With friends like that, Blair did not need Conservatives. He did not accept that the minimum wage would cost *any* jobs, of course, although Howard quoted some of Blair's unhappy phraseology, in a letter to the *Independent* (27 June 1991), to make it sound as if he did: 'I have not accepted that the minimum wage would cost jobs . . . I have simply accepted that econometric models indicate a potential jobs impact.'

Howard mocked Blair's refusal to accept City economists' forecasts of the effect on jobs: 'It may be that the shadow Secretary of State for Employment sees himself as essentially a provincial figure, a man of the people, keeping his distance from the City circuit, distrustful perhaps of its estimates in these matters.' Howard offered to help him, by quoting the view of a hotel proprietor in Sedgefield that 'Labour's plan would be nothing short of disastrous'.[6]

Bayliss's higher figure, of 880,000 jobs lost, was the worst-case estimate of the impact of Labour's higher long-term target for the minimum wage. Blair quickly abandoned the long-term goal, in effect, saying it would be implemented 'when, and only when, prudent' – in other words, never.[7] The long-term target did not appear in the 1992 manifesto, only the initial rate of £3.40 an hour.

Blair's retreat did not stop Howard continuing to make the most outlandish use of the Treasury's computer model of the economy. At one point an exasperated Blair snapped primly: 'The right honourable and learned gentleman takes the biscuit.' Howard's estimate of 2 million job losses was based on 'the assumption that everyone in the workforce, including the Governor of the Bank of England, will get a 25 per cent pay increase as a result of the minimum wage policy. Are not these assumptions absurd?'

However, Blair's speech in this, one of the fullest debates in the House of Commons on the subject, in July 1991, was muted on the moral case for the policy:

> Of course the minimum wage must be implemented carefully and of course we cannot set it at too excessive a level, but we will start the process of having a minimum wage. We shall take care, but we shall introduce it, because it is fair and right and because a society that treats its most vulnerable badly is a society not worthy of the name.[8]

The BBC's industrial correspondent, John Fryer, spoke to Blair several times on the subject, as shadow Employment Secretary. Fryer thought his arguments were unconvincing – although put with obvious skill – and his evidence weak, and asked him why he did not just abandon the policy: 'Although he never moved off it privately, when you looked into the whites of his eyes you detected a lack of true conviction.'

During the election campaign, on 17 March 1992, Blair was challenged on BBC *Election Call*. 'My business is threatened by the minimum wage,' boiled Joyce Elliott. 'I run a small daycare nursery in Hereford. I have created twelve jobs, but I'm really going to be caught in a trap and it is very worrying.'

Blair's answers were perfectly reasonable, although they did not engage directly with her complaint: 'The reason why we believe a minimum wage is necessary is in order to ensure that all employers compete on the quality of the workforce, on the basis of the skills and talents of the workforce, and not on the basis of low pay.' This betrayed the gap between the rhetoric of the 'skills revolution' and people's perceptions of everyday work situations, and Elliott's passion gave her the apparent upper hand.

'It's no use Mr Blair talking about business, business, Europe and so on, we want to know how we are going to survive, that is the question,' she said.

'Yes, but as I've been explaining to you, the evidence is that it will not have the adverse effect that you say it will, because of course all other employers —'

'Of course it will do, I'm sorry,' interrupted his caller.

'All other businesses providing the same service will be subject to the same legislation,' continued Blair, sounding like a doctor reassuring a patient as he amputated the wrong leg, 'So they're not going to be able to undercut you.'

The nursery owner was finally faded out, indignantly protesting, 'I'm talking about *my* business and thousands of businesses like mine . . .' (On the same programme, Blair actually got away with a much more blatant evasion on the question of privatisation receipts not being available to a Labour government to plug the hole in the public finances. He simply ignored the quietly-spoken reasoned arguments of the caller.)

Blair had sounded defensive, and failed to turn the issue into one of basic social justice. But he had negotiated the difficult waters of a live phone-in without making a 'gaffe' – the crudest journalistic test of modern politicians.

The next day, Blair blew his top. Shadow Transport Secretary John Prescott, having been kept off the Labour headquarters 'Key Campaigners' list, had managed to book himself to appear on Sky TV's rival to the BBC's *Election Call*. Asked about the minimum wage, he went as far as admitting that it would lose some jobs: 'I think you have to accept there may be some shake-out in some of the jobs in certain areas, but generally it will be beneficial to the community.'

All Blair's defensive obfuscation – refusing to accept the blindingly obvious – had been cut through by Plain Speaking John. It did not matter who was right, although the evidence favoured Prescott – the politics were that Prescott had committed the ultimate sin of saying something out of line on somebody else's subject.

The BBC's correspondent, John Fryer, spotted the discrepancy between Prescott and Blair and spoke to Blair on his mobile phone in Darlington to ask him to come to the BBC studio in Newcastle to comment on the *News*. 'I'm not having it, John,' said Blair, according to one account of the conversation. 'I'm the spokesman on employment. There's no way you're going to run that story. I can't get up to Newcastle to the studios to defend it. And if you can't pull this story, you'd better let me speak to someone who can.' Blair was in a strong position, because during election campaigns BBC rules are stricter and more cautious than usual – it might have seemed 'unfair' to broadcast that story without an official Labour spokesperson. Blair had not refused to appear, but was merely 'unable' to get to a studio. The Prescott story was not broadcast.

Later in the campaign, Prescott finally got on to the mainstream media – he was the guest on BBC *Election Call* on 30 March. By now he had been coached in the correct line on the minimum wage: 'A dynamic economy does have adjustments and changes, I can't ignore that.' That phrase 'dynamic economy' is a giveaway clue as to the source of the new, improved Prescott.

The Fourth Defeat

Blair was unusual in that he did not expect Labour to win the 1992 election. According to his barrister friend Charles Falconer, he thought that 'the change' had not come about sufficiently by then. Blair disagreed with his assistant James Purnell, who bet him a bottle of champagne that Labour would win – a debt which was never collected. This may have been partly fashionable pessimism, as Blair has a tendency to describe any adverse situation as hopeless and any setback as the end of his political career. But it also reflected a political judgment which was different from the conventional wisdom. The fact that nearly everyone thought Labour *was* going to win or, rather, form a government in a hung parliament, was one of the reasons for the party's pre-election paralysis. Although the Conservatives recovered after the Fall of Thatcher, Labour held a small lead in the opinion polls most of the time.

Labour's election campaign was professional and largely gaffe-free, but it was curiously lifeless. The party appeared to be drifting into a hung parliament in which it would form a minority government. Even Labour's strongest issue, the National Health Service, was not as strong as it looked. The surreal squabble in the media compound over Labour's propaganda use of a girl's ear operation – the so-called War of Jennifer's Ear – didn't help, but the NHS alone was never going to win the election. And Labour went into the election with no policy on electoral reform – while the leader said, to a *Granada 500* live studio audience hooting derision, that he had a view but he was not going to tell them what it was.

Blair's pessimism about the outcome of the election was briefly disturbed during the last few days of the campaign. The polls on Wednesday the week before polling day put Labour up to 7 percentage points ahead, and at the weekend he visited Redruth in Cornwall, where he was puzzled by Labour's highly optimistic canvass returns. For a few days he might have allowed himself to dream of a ministerial Rover. But early in the week of polling day he and Neil Kinnock spoke at a rally in Kinnock's constituency. The Labour leader already felt that the election was slipping away, and Blair returned to his long-held view that the party had not done enough to win.

On Tuesday that week, Labour's strategy meeting was 'extremely jumpy', according to the playwright David Hare, observing it for his play, *The Absence of War*:

Philip Gould reads out the overnight figures and reports

that John Major's personal popularity is suddenly up. Although he emphasises that this figure is for Major, and not for his party, his voice suddenly trails out as he remarks that he doesn't like Labour being at 38.7 per cent after all the . . .[9]

The next day, the day before the election, the party was taken aback by the ferocity of the Conservative newspapers. The *Sun* carried nine pages headed 'Nightmare on Kinnock Street'. The *Express* and the *Mail* ran similar attacks.

Most people in the party remained confident. On polling day, John Smith left home in Edinburgh saying that when he came back he would be Chancellor of the Exchequer. He had agreed a statement at the Treasury about exchange rate policy, to be issued after the polls closed.[10]

On the night of 9 April 1992, Kinnock and Blair's pessimism was quickly confirmed. Just after 11 o'clock, the result in Basildon was announced. This was an important marginal seat, with a large working-class Conservative electorate. The swing to Labour was miserably small, and David Amess held the seat. 'That's it,' said Kinnock, watching television with his wife Glenys. His dream was over.

Blair, in Sedgefield, increased his majority again, to 14,859. But the Conservative candidate – Nicholas Jopling, the son of former Conservative Chief Whip Michael Jopling – also increased his share of the vote, by 1 per cent. It was the Liberal Democrat who lost out.

It was not much consolation at the time, but Labour did better than it deserved to. The party's share of the vote rose just 3.5 percentage points to 35 per cent – to only just over one-third of the total. Although Labour was 7.6 points behind the Conservatives, John Major's majority was only twenty-one seats. Labour benefited from out-of-date constituency boundaries and ran a particularly efficient campaign in marginal seats. But the Conservatives had fought a poor campaign in the middle of an economic recession. For Blair, this confirmed his view that Labour still had a lot to do, and no time to lose.

Notes

1. Tony Blair, *Fabian Review*, 9 May 1992.
2. Tony Blair, interview, 8 June 1992.
3. BBC TV, *Newsnight*, 7 April 1992.
4. BBC TV, *On The Record*, 10 May 1992.
5. Eric Hammond, *Maverick*, p168.
6. *Hansard*, 12 March 1992, col 996.
7. Tony Blair, Letter to the *Financial Times*, 12 June 1991.
8. *Hansard*, 9 July 1991, cols 799, 826.
9. David Hare, *Asking Around*, p219.
10. James Naughtie, 'A Political Life Observed', in *John Smith: Life and Soul of the Party*, edited by Gordon Brown and James Naughtie, p54.

PART FOUR

THE SMITH
YEARS

12. THE OVERTAKING OF GORDON BROWN
Aftermath of the Fourth Defeat, 1992

'After the '92 election, the Cabinet Secretary Robin Butler said, "Who's going to be the leader after next?" and I said, "Tony Blair." I think the argument was always going to be, "Who's going to win the election for Labour?"'

Neil Kinnock conceded defeat at five o'clock in the morning of 10 April 1992, on the steps of Labour headquarters in south London. With Glenys by his side, he said:

I naturally feel a strong sense of disappointment. Not for myself, for I am fortunate, very fortunate, in my personal life. But I feel dismay, sorrow, for so many people in our country who do not share this personal good fortune. They deserve better than they got on the ninth of April, 1992.

Bryan Gould, standing next to Glenys, looked stern. He would later that day be planning for the next campaign – his own, for the leadership of the Labour Party. He knew that John Smith was already the favourite to succeed Kinnock, but he hoped that a good start to his campaign would shift the balance. And he knew that Kinnock himself was favourable towards him. Kinnock did not think Gould could win, but hoped he would become deputy leader.

For some of the party's leading figures, a fourth defeat was too much. They had allowed themselves to believe they would be in government. Few could bear to take part in the public post mortem. But, later on the morning of 10 April, Blair offered his morning-after analysis from Sedgefield on BBC TV's *Election '92*:

> Our obvious sense of disappointment must be balanced by a sense of achievement, that we took so many seats in different parts of the country. But it was too much to do – so it now appears – to come from where we were in 1987 to actually win an overall majority.

He had already made up his mind that if Labour lost, then it was time to speak out. He was nearly thirty-nine. He had been in parliament for almost a decade. He had risen close to the top in the Labour Party, but that was no use if the party stayed in opposition. He had a pretty clear idea of what the Labour Party was doing wrong, and a rough idea of what a new Labour Party should be like. And he felt that if the party could not make the change – another change, perhaps as great as the change it had made since 1983 – then there was no point in staying. He had the cautiousness of ambition, but – unlike Gordon Brown – the impatience of a man who knew that he could always give up politics. His wife earned enough to keep the family, and he could return to law.

He also knew that he had to strike instantly. He wrote at the time:

> The great danger with the Labour Party is that it loses – and it's like a bucket of cold water thrown over it. It gets a real shock and it says, 'We'd better do something about this situation.' Then it dries out, and the sun comes out, and it says, 'Oh, this isn't so bad.' It's happened every single election.

Of course, the question of the party's direction was closely related to its choice of a new leader. Peter Sissons asked if Neil Kinnock should go. 'That is not even on the agenda at the moment,' replied Blair, knowing that the leadership election had already begun. 'He has our tremendous respect and gratitude and support.'

Just as in 1983 – and later in 1994 – there was never any serious doubt as to who would win the leadership election. The real questions were: What direction would John Smith take, who would be his deputy, and who, eventually, would succeed him? These were questions that exhausted Labour politicians now turned to. Blair discussed them with Gordon Brown and the Newcastle MP Nick Brown on a walk through the Durham countryside from his house in Trimdon on the Saturday after the election.

Gordon Brown's position was so strong that he was having to discourage speculation that he might run against John Smith for the leadership. It was certainly assumed – not least by Blair – that Brown would be Smith's successor. But just two years later, Blair and Brown's eleven-year friendship reached its most testing moment, when support for Blair turned out to be overwhelming. How did that happen?

If Blair thought that Labour would lose the 1992 election, he must also have realised that Smith would be the new leader, and would want a deputy. No doubt he realised what Gordon Brown now realised, which was that Brown could not be deputy leader because the Southern floating voter would not want two Scots as a leadership team. This was not a very good reason for excluding him, but seems to have been accepted by all those close to these decisions, including Brown himself.

That weekend's *Observer* reported that 'Mr Smith is thought to favour Margaret Beckett . . . as his deputy leader'. But on Sunday she told colleagues and journalists that she would not run for deputy leader, and even 'suggested to Mr Smith that other contenders, such as Mr Blair or Mr Brown, might be more appropriate running mates for him', according to the *Daily Telegraph* (13 April). This possibility had already occurred to Mr Blair, who was in Sedgefield, and on the telephone almost every waking moment.

Meanwhile, at lunchtime, Bryan Gould entered the lists on BBC TV's *On The Record*. Although he did not formally declare, because Kinnock had not yet resigned, it was obvious that he intended to run for the leadership. It was also obvious that Smith would not willingly have Gould as his deputy – the two had been personal rivals for too long, and the political differences between them over Europe were too great. Nor would Smith favour John Prescott, also a Euro-sceptic and an opponent of Britain's membership of the European Exchange Rate Mechanism.

With Margaret Beckett out of contention, Blair had to decide whether or not to put himself forward. He hesitated long and hard.

John Smith, for his part, sounded Blair out. If he could not persuade Beckett to change her mind, sources close to Smith suggest that he preferred Blair. This raised in an early form the acute problem of Blair's relationship with Gordon Brown.

The phone bills mounted. Peter Mandelson and Harriet Harman urged Blair to stand. Kinnock and Hattersley urged him not to. Mandelson and Harman wanted to advance the modernisers' 'project'. If he did not stand, what guarantee was there that Smith would not take the party back to traditionalism – or at least to a less aggressive modernism? Suppose he and Brown secured the shadow Home Secretaryship and the shadow Chancellorship respectively, but lost all the policy battles?

Kinnock and Hattersley's motives for arguing against his standing were different. Kinnock wanted Bryan Gould to get the deputy leadership. Despite his disappointment with Gould over public ownership in the policy review, and his wariness of his Euro-scepticism, he thought that Gould – like Blair – was intelligent, articulate, 'English' (Gould is actually from New Zealand), and essentially a moderniser. Kinnock says 'there was never any kind of rift of any description' between him and Gould: 'He's a thoughtful, articulate and dynamic fellow – a man I like very much. Stories of "Bryan Gould alienated from Kinnock", "stranded", "demoted" were all bloody rubbish.'

Kinnock's view was that Gould could win, but that it was too early for Blair. Robin Cook, who had been Kinnock's campaign manager and who was now Smith's, hoped to persuade Gould to go for the deputy leadership. Smith seems to have gone through a revolving series of options in these few days, because at one point he was receptive to the idea of Gould standing for deputy in return for Gould not challenging him for leader.[1] Gordon Brown, expecting to become shadow Chancellor, tried to persuade the Kinnocracy that Gould, who was opposed to membership of the European Exchange Rate Mechanism, would be the wrong deputy to impose on Smith.

If Kinnock did not want Blair to stand because he thought Gould had a better chance, Hattersley's reason for dissuading his protégé was more personal:

I urged him not to stand for deputy because I believed he should be leader of the Labour Party one day . . . I believed he was John's natural successor, more than Gordon. I then assumed that John was going to be leader for two parliaments and we would almost certainly win the coming election, and there was nothing to be gained for him being just deputy. Everybody who's been deputy leader knows it's a rotten job and everybody tells their friends not to do it. Everybody told me not to do it. And I didn't take their advice. Tony did take mine. I think he was very torn.

Cherie wanted him to stand. She never wavered in her ambition for her husband, and appears to have seen his chances more clearly than he. Still he hesitated. There were more telephone conversations, backwards and forwards.

The most important influence on Blair's decision was Gordon Brown. A few of those who were close to the hesitating Hamlet suggest that Brown could not accept the idea of Blair overtaking him to the deputy leadership, and tried to discourage him for that reason. One insider emphatically rejects the idea that Brown saw Blair as a rival:

> Remember where we were. Nobody thought that John Smith represented continuity of the modernising project. He represented something different. The modernising project, therefore, was in the custody, no longer of Neil, but of Tony and Gordon. The question was, who was going to be best placed to do what. I have seen this perhaps at closer quarters than anybody. There wasn't any rivalry. I do think I would have spotted it if either of them had been seeking an advantage relative to the other. It was all seamless. One thing that was very irritating to a lot of other people was that they were a pair of twins, and there was no one else in the family.

Nevertheless, Blair, having considered John Smith's tentative overtures, told him that if one of the twins should run for the deputy leadership, 'We have decided that it should be Gordon.' Because all parties to these intricate negotiations agreed that the leadership ticket could not consist of two Scots, Blair was effectively saying that neither would run.

But Blair was under pressure from some of his closest advisers to break with Brown and put himself forward anyway. An extraordinary letter to the *Guardian* on the Monday after the General Election revealed some of the hidden thinking of the modernisers. It was written by Colin Byrne, who had resigned as Labour's chief press officer the previous autumn. The letter exposed some of the private resentments of the modernisers against John Smith, but it also revealed a tilt against Brown, whose loyalty to Smith was paramount. It was particularly interesting because Byrne was engaged to Kinnock's press secretary, Julie Hall, and had shared a house with her and Peter Mandelson, the new MP for Hartlepool.

John Smith may be a very nice man . . . But what is his record, or that of a handful of centrally-placed right-wing shadow Cabinet members and trade union leaders who are about to emerge as his campaign managers and backers, on the radical reforms Labour has made to its policies and practices – and must go on making if it is not to tread water, sink and die?

What did the Right ever do about Militant during the bitter years up to Neil Kinnock taking over? What did they do about reforming the party's relationship with the trades unions and its industrial relations policies? What did they do about Europe? The answer, as I saw for myself during those years of crucial policy review and National Executive Committee meetings, was usually to sit on their hands and let the Kinnocks and the Blairs take the flak.

The use of Blair's name without the other half of the couplet, 'Brown and —', was highly significant, as Smith's biographer Andy McSmith comments, to anyone who follows the 'Kremlinology of the Labour Party'.[2] It was also somewhat propagandist, as Blair was not even a member of the National Executive until later that year. Byrne was reflecting his admiration for Blair's role in private meetings of shadow Cabinet members. But how much did Byrne's rage against Smith represent the views of Blair, or of Mandelson?

Blair, Brown and Mandelson all knew about the letter the day before, and all three tried to persuade Byrne to withdraw it, even after he had faxed it to the *Guardian*. 'They believed I was being emotional and not acting in the interests of the party,' says an unrepentant Byrne. Mandelson, who was and is now again a close friend of Byrne's, did not speak to him for three months afterwards. But this was not because Mandelson disagreed with the contents of the letter, only with their being made public.

While the tone and personal nature of the letter was the freelance emotion of a Kinnock-loyalist, there is no doubt that all three – and Kinnock himself – viewed the prospect of

Smith's succession with varying degrees of disquiet. Blair was of course personally close to Smith and would never, for example, have attributed to him any weakness in the battle against Militant. After all, it was through Smith that he and Alexander Irvine came to defend the party against Militant in 1982. Blair did disagree with Smith over the need for change in the party, and those disagreements were to become sharper over the next two years, but they remained amicable.

There was one other, vitally important, aspect to Blair's dilemma. If he stood for the deputy leadership, could he win? That was at the heart of his discussions with Gordon Brown and Nick Brown in Trimdon on the Saturday after the election. As the former fixer for the GMB union's Northern Region, Nick Brown was an expert on the old politics of union block votes. His view was pessimistic.

Many of the union leaders who would influence the block votes in the largest part of the electoral college (40 per cent) were unsympathetic to his policy changes on trade union law, even if they respected him. Besides, the two largest unions, the Transport and General Workers Union and the GMB, had already reached an understanding that 'the ticket' was Smith–Beckett. Blair's popularity among party members, who had 30 per cent of the votes, was untested. Among Labour MPs, who had the other 30 per cent, what mattered was Smith's endorsement, open or hinted.

It became clearer each day that the most important factor in all the calculations was whether Smith could persuade Margaret Beckett to change her mind and enter the race. It is possible that Smith did not really want either Blair or Brown as his deputy, because they would have been in too powerful a position underneath him, and speculation about their eventual succession would have been destabilising. Beckett was the best solution from Smith's point of view. She was not seen as a future leader, and would therefore not be seen as a threat to him; she was loyal; she was competent; and she was a woman.

Nick Brown was despatched to see her, in order to sound

her out on behalf of Blair and Gordon Brown. He made an appointment to meet her at her office in the House of Commons at 10.30 on Tuesday morning. As he arrived, a few minutes early, he met John Smith coming out. Smith asked Nick Brown to come into his office and told him: 'Margaret has decided to stand, and I think this is a very good idea.' Blair had hesitated too long. It would now be an act of open defiance to put his name forward.

On Wednesday 15 April, Beckett held a press conference to reverse her position: 'On Sunday I said I was not stepping forward and that I was at the back of the queue, rather than the front, but I have been moved to the front.' One union leader suggests that, surprised that John Smith wanted her as his deputy, she had ruled herself out simply in order to test her support. John Prescott and Ann Clwyd also announced they would stand. Prescott says he decided to run because he thought Beckett had pulled out. In Sedgefield, Blair announced that he would not be a candidate.

The day before, bookmakers at Sedgefield racecourse had been offering odds of 10/1 against his becoming leader, a bet which some enthusiastic local people had taken (Smith was 1/6 odds-on favourite, with Gould at 6/1 against). Now he backed the Smith–Beckett ticket in an interview on BBC TV's *Look North*:

John and Margaret offer tremendous intellectual leadership, which is very important; they've got immense political experience – both were ministers in the previous Labour government; and, most important of all, they will carry on the process of changing and reforming the Labour Party to make sure that our ideas and organisation fit the age we live in.

Which is about as good an example of political irony – in the proper sense of the word – as can be found. To many of the modernisers, the description of Margaret Beckett as an intellectual leader is frankly sarcastic; 'the previous Labour government' is code for 'tainted by the failures of office' – containing at least an implication that experience could have been balanced by youthful vigour; while the last point was an attempt to chain the leadership ticket to the modernisers' project. There is a hint in Blair at moments like these of cheeking the masters at Fettes. He was showing off to those in the know, while pledging loyalty to 'Those in Authority' in the party.

Those five days after the General Election remain one of the most vital episodes of Blair's career so far. It is difficult to judge whether he should have stood or not. The one thing that was certainly a mistake was to hesitate, because it allowed Smith and Beckett to decide the question. Charles Falconer, Blair's friend from the Seventies, says: 'I'm not sure that Tony thought being deputy was necessarily a good thing. Though now he will probably regret not having run.' Blair did affect to believe that the deputy leadership of the Labour Party was a peculiar non-job. But his intense ambition would not quite let the matter go.

As events turned out, it did not matter. But if he had become deputy leader he would have emerged more strongly as the leadership candidate of the future, the modernisation of the party would have been pushed forward more vigorously, and he would not have become isolated in the way that he did, which would have mattered had Smith lived. On the other hand, his relationship with Gordon Brown would have come under strain two years before it needed to. Friends say that the experience taught him not to hesitate when his moment came, and that when Smith died Blair was firm in his resolve.

The most important effect of Blair's hesitation over the deputy leadership might have been to change the balance of power between him and Gordon Brown. Most people who are close to Blair think he genuinely deferred to Gordon Brown until the 1992 election. But now the relationship started to change. In the inner circles in which Blair consulted, he emerged as the bolder and more impatient of the two. He appeared keen to put himself forward and stand up for what he believed, whereas Brown seemed unwilling to take risks. It was a pattern which would develop more strongly over the next two years, as Blair put on political weight rapidly.

Blair's private regrets were outweighed in public by the fact that he would have more time to see his children. Cherie said: 'When it came to whether or not he was going to run for the deputy leader's job, Euan said he was glad that Daddy has chosen to spend more time at home.'[3]

The Smith Campaign

John Smith was not a 'moderniser'. But he knew that Blair and Brown were an important source of new ideas for Labour's future, and they had a central place in his leadership campaign team. (They had no formal role, although Brown was Margaret Beckett's campaign manager for the deputy leadership.) Smith had no past record of enthusiasm for internal party reforms, but was quite clear that one member, one vote had to come. In the immediate aftermath of defeat, the logic of change was inescapable. In any case, Bryan Gould launched his leadership bid saying that if he were elected, it would be the last time a leader was elected by block votes, and Smith was forced to respond. Blair and Brown seized the chance to define the climate of party opinion.

The debate was quickly framed by commentators in terms of 'modernisation' versus 'one more heave'. But no one publicly argued for 'one more heave' – the opposition to the modernisers came from the 'traditionalists', whose analysis of Labour's defeat was diametrically opposed to Blair's. They argued that Labour lost because it had changed too much, not that it had changed too little. However, the argument of left-wing traditionalists such as John Prescott was based on an unconvincing reading of history. He argued that the modernisers were 'the people, with their emphasis on image, that helped Labour lose the last two elections. Therefore, Labour should restate its ideological beliefs with conviction.'[4] But what were those beliefs? The principles on which the party fought the 1983 election? Or perhaps the 1979 election – safety first with Uncle Jim Callaghan? It seemed that what the traditionalists really wanted was to refight the 1945 election. However, Prescott has always been less of a traditionalist than he seems, because he has always argued, like Blair, for 'traditional values in a modern setting'.

The strength of the 'modernisers' was that theirs were the most coherent ideas in the Labour Party, and John Smith became a sort of honorary moderniser for the purposes of the leadership campaign. Although Blair and Brown did not contribute as much as they claimed to Smith's manifesto for the leadership contest, *Pathways to Victory* – Robin Cook was the principal author – it was undoubtedly a 'moderniser' document.

Bryan Gould, having made a flying start, lost ground quickly. Although he had no realistic chance of winning the leadership, he could perhaps have become deputy leader. Cook tried to persuade John Smith to endorse him, and even when Smith plumped instead for Beckett, Gould still had strong support in the party. But, having entered himself for both posts, he ignored the advice of his campaign manager, David Blunkett, to withdraw from the leadership race and concentrate on fighting for the deputy leadership. Thus he exchanged the Gould–Gould leadership ticket for a one-way air ticket to New Zealand. As the campaign progressed, Gould increasingly played to the 'traditionalist' gallery, calculating that his only hope was to swing the block votes of the conservative unions, alarmed by the threat from the modernisers to their power in the party.

On 18 July 1992 John Smith and Margaret Beckett were elected leader and deputy leader of the Labour Party. The following morning, the *Sunday Times* colour magazine devoted five pages to a profile by Barbara Amiel of the 'leader in waiting', Tony Blair. Its appearance was no coincidence, nor was it idle mischief-making by the Conservative press. It was the longest and most prominent profile article of him yet, and was overwhelmingly favourable. The introduction read: 'Yesterday Labour elected a new leader. Some feel the party should have skipped a generation and gone for Tony Blair. At the very least they believe he should have stood for the deputy leadership.' There is no proof of Peter Mandelson's influence, but those views were the same as his. The same day's *Sunday Express* ran a story by Fiona Millar, who lives with Alastair Campbell, Blair's future press secretary, reporting that John Major and many of his Cabinet suspect Blair 'will one day be the man to take them on'.

Private Eye commented waspishly that Blair was

> the latest in a long line of bright young-ish things from the Labour Party front bench to be named sorrowfully as the 'leader Labour missed' . . . Those who have had this treatment in the past include Eric Varley, Richard Marsh, Robert Kilroy-Silk, Brian Walden, Alf Robens, Wilfred Fienburgh, Gerry Reynolds, Tony Crosland, David Owen, Shirley Williams, Roy Jenkins and others too obscure to recall. What they have in common is that they mostly belong to the Tory-minded wing of the Labour Party.[5]

Blair's name will not now be added to that list, although accusations of Tory-mindedness will no doubt continue.

Five days after John Smith was elected leader, on a modernising platform (with 91 per cent of the vote), Gordon Brown came top, and Blair second, in the shadow Cabinet elections. Both were rewarded with the posts they wanted: Brown became shadow Chancellor; Blair was appointed shadow Home Secretary. The modernisers had won everything but the leadership.

Home Affairs

At the time of the shadow Cabinet reshuffle in July 1992, Blair consulted his mentor, Roy Hattersley, the outgoing deputy leader and shadow Home Secretary. 'He came and talked to me about what job he ought to do, because he very much wanted to do the Home Affairs job,' says Hattersley.

> I told him to take it. It's a rotten job in government. It's a pretty good job in opposition. What you want in opposition is a lot of parliamentary work. Also, what you want in opposition is something that looked like it meant seniority – the shadow of the Home Secretary. In government you're waiting for somebody to break out of prison every day. In opposition you're hoping that somebody will break out of prison so you can complain about it.

Again, Blair was not asking advice so much as canvassing support. He had fixed on the post for some time. It was natural: Brown would be shadow Chancellor, and he would take one of the other shadow great offices of state. He was interested in being at some stage either shadow Foreign Secretary or the real thing in a John Smith government. World statesman he was not, but his passing knowledge of American, Australian and continental European politics was a more than adequate qualification in the modern Labour Party.

However, the shadow Foreign Secretary would have to hold together a divided party through the long process of ratifying the Maastricht Treaty, while the shadow Home Secretary was staring a great political opportunity in the face. Blair had seen that the traditional role for that post – complaining about prison escapes – did not begin to exploit its potential.

The next two years were to see Blair transformed from deft Labour politician to potential Prime Minister. At the time of the leadership election in 1994, Blair told one member of the shadow Cabinet that he had 'learned as much in the last two years as he learned in the previous ten'.

It was not until the start of 1993, however, that Blair deployed the 'sound-bite and fury' with which to seize that opportunity. When he took the post in July 1992, there was surprisingly little evidence in his record as a politician of economic affairs that his views on crime and the family were in any way special. He had expressed concern about crime and welcomed more 'bobbies on the beat' in the Beaconsfield by-election in 1982. He had talked of the aspiration of his constituents 'to get married, to start a family', in Sedgefield in 1983. More recently, in his 1991 and 1992 conference speeches, he had talked about 'social cohesion'. It was also possible to deduce that his insistence on renewing a real relationship with the electorate would mean adjusting the party's attitudes on social issues. That was the point of his drive to broaden the party membership, including that of his own party in Sedgefield, as he said in June 1992:

> I find now when I go to my local branch meetings, not only is there a very much bigger attendance, but the questions that people ask me will be wholly different. If they're younger people they might ask me about the environment. If they're elderly people they'll ask about law and order and crime. The political agenda, the politics, of the local party gets driven in a different direction because of the activities and participation of ordinary people.[6]

In private discussions with friends, Blair has always expressed the sort of views he expresses now on crime and the family. However, it could not be guessed that he was about to bring about a category shift in the Labour Party's stance on social issues, a shift which invites comparison with its change on Europe.

Into the Overtaking Lane

Three factors shifted the balance of power between Gordon Brown and Tony Blair. The first was Brown's promotion to shadow Chancellor. The second was Blair's own performance as shadow Home Secretary. Blair emerged as the better communicator of the two, while Brown seemed to become if anything more inarticulate. And the third was Blair's greater prominence in the battle for 'one member, one vote' in party decision-making.

Gordon Brown's accession to the shadow Chancellorship was logical, but it was to be his undoing. He was running into treacle, defending Labour's adherence to the European Exchange Rate Mechanism up to the moment when the pound was devalued in September 1992. When the pound was devalued, Brown's reputation went down with it. And he pursued rigidly the line of 'No New Taxes'. Both policies were arguably right if Labour was to win, but they perplexed party members. Blair recognised the need for political breadth, while Brown seems to have been cautiously following John Smith's route to the top. It was widely assumed that the economic portfolios were always the commanding heights of parliamentary power and, therefore, that the shadow Chancellor was automatically the effective deputy leader. This was not necessarily true.

Brown's problem was that he was a Roundhead, with Bryan Gould playing the role of the Cavalier, wrong but romantic. Brown argued austerely and consistently that Labour could not afford to be the party of devaluation. The party was already seen by the voters and the markets as unreliable on inflation, and it was generally accepted then that devaluation would be inflationary.

Gould was surely wrong to see devaluation in itself as an instrument of policy, and to promise a hedonistic utopia of easy money liberated from control by 'the bankers', as British exports undercut the world. As shadow Chancellor before the 1992 election, however, Smith seemed to make the opposite mistake of allowing membership of the European Exchange Rate Mechanism to be seen as his only instrument of policy. He argued consistently that the real priority was to strengthen the economy so that it would be able to sustain ERM membership, but failed to give substance to the necessary programme to achieve it. The party, having plumped for the ERM partly because Margaret Thatcher was against it, allowed the tactic to be a substitute for policy.

When it became clear, after the 1992 election, that Britain would struggle to stay in the ERM, Brown as shadow Chancellor took the hardest line in resisting calls for devaluation or the softer option, 'realignment within the ERM'. Even Neil Kinnock, in one of his last acts as leader, argued for realignment in a letter to the *Financial Times*.[7] There was only one reason why he could not openly advocate devaluation, as his adviser Neil Stewart explained bluntly at the time: 'It's a dickhead says it before the Tories.'

Brown was in good company among economists, and thought that 'realignment' was wishful economics. What realigners wanted was for the Deutschmark alone to go up in value. But the French insisted on the franc going up with it, in which case realignment effectively meant devaluation of the pound. But for John Smith the politics of distancing Labour from the government's disastrous policy grew more urgent, and he became increasingly irritated with Brown's rigid line. In the days before devaluation was forced on the government in September 1992, a public rift opened when Brown ruled realignment out and Smith ruled it in. The two of them clashed fiercely in private.

When devaluation happened, Bryan Gould was able to say: 'I told you so.' But, as usual in politics, this was an arid satisfaction. John Smith stood by his aboriginal pro-Europeanism, and persuaded the shadow Cabinet and National Executive that the pound's ejection from the ERM strengthened rather than weakened the argument for a single currency. A single currency would, he said, 'guarantee an end to intra-European currency speculation'.[8] This was too much for Gould, who

delivered his resignation letter to the reception of the Imperial
Hotel in Blackpool on the first day of the Labour conference.

It was Gordon Brown who was the lightning conductor
for discontent in the party. Perhaps because no one could
doubt Smith's European credentials, as one who had defied
the party whips to vote to go into the European Community
in 1971, Smith was able to take a relatively relaxed and
pragmatic attitude to Britain's new-found freedom outside
the ERM. It was Brown who had to insist that this could not
mean a return to a policy of expansion fuelled by government borrowing. This was when his communication skills
were found wanting. Thus, for the greater good of the party,
he unwittingly sacrificed his prospects of becoming leader
on the altar of monetary rectitude (as had Denis Healey,
who at least had the satisfaction of holding government
office).

Soon afterwards, in November 1992, Brown dropped the
tax and spending plans of the 1992 election campaign. He
later promised a Labour government would not 'tax for its
own sake' and that 'we only tax if it increases opportunity for
individuals or for the community as a whole'. He went further, saying that 'if we can cut tax when it is prudent to do
so . . . we will'.[9] And he refused to say directly that the better-
off would have to pay higher taxes under Labour. Party
members found Brown's line on tax even more baffling than
his adherence to the ERM.

Barbara Castle expressed their dismay: 'I think it's absurd
for Labour to be fighting on negatives like, "We won't tax and
we won't even spend, unless it will lead to opportunity."
That's what they said, which has beggared every question
under the sun.'[10] As the best woman Prime Minister the
Labour Party never had, for many party members Castle con-
jured up a golden age when being left-wing was simple. Now
Brown's case was complicated, and made all the more difficult to understand by the dense, epigrammatic language in
which he expressed it.

Satirists confirmed Brown's decline. Even before the 1992

election Rory Bremner growled, 'What the people of this country want is lists, long lists, short lists, depressing statistics, disturbing industry results and gloomy surveys.'[11] By November 1992, Matthew Parris was reflecting mainstream opinion, mocking Brown's reply to Chancellor Norman Lamont's Autumn Statement in similar terms:

> It was a tragedy, he said. Millions faced:
> - cuts
> - joblessness
> - starvation.
>   . . . Pencil poised, I waited to continue:
> - impetigo
> - beri-beri
> - rickets . . .
>   But he omitted these, predicting:
> - tragedy
> - disaster
> - catastrophe
>   . . . and sat down.[12]

At the time of the 1994 leadership election, some assumed that Blair owed his victory to the abolition of block votes for internal elections in 1993. In fact this change turned out not to make the difference. If there had been a sudden vacancy for the leadership at the end of 1992, Blair might have won, even under the old block-vote system.

There is no doubt that in 1992 Neil Kinnock and those around him – the Kinnocracy – were firmly of the view that after John Smith, Blair rather than Brown would be the next leader. Kinnock's Chief of Staff, Charles Clarke, says:

> I remember after the '92 election, Robin Butler [the Cabinet Secretary] said, 'Who's going to be the leader after next?' and I said, 'Tony Blair.' Not who I thought should be: who *would* be. I think the argument was always going to be, 'Who's going to win the election for Labour?'

Blair might not have insisted on standing for the leadership at the end of 1992, of course, as he would then have been more likely to defer to Brown. That was about to change. In January 1993, Blair suddenly became a force to be reckoned with.

Notes

1. Andy McSmith, *John Smith*, pp267-8.
2. *Ibid.*, p288.
3. *Sunday Times Magazine*, 19 July 1992.
4. *Guardian*, 31 December 1992.
5. HP Sauce, *Private Eye*, 31 July 1992.
6. Tony Blair, interview, 8 June 1992.
7. *Financial Times*, 15 July 1992.
8. Labour Party National Executive Committee statement on 'Europe: Our Economic Future', 23 September 1992.
9. Gordon Brown, 'New Economics' speech, 17 February 1993.
10. BBC TV, *On The Record*, 26 September 1993.
11. BBC TV, *On The Record*, 23 February 1992.
12. Matthew Parris, *The Times*, 13 November 1992.

13. LESSONS FROM AMERICA
The Clinton Campaign, 1992

'We had to start with reality, which is that we'd lost so many of the previous elections, and I think Governor Clinton's greatest insight was: it wasn't the voters' fault; there was something wrong with the party that we did need to change.'

Inevitably, after the loss of the 1992 election, jaded Labour eyes were cast enviously at the other side of the Atlantic, where the left-of-centre was at last gaining ground. Two of Tony Blair's closest associates paid particular attention to the Clinton campaign.

Philip Gould, a former advertising executive who played a central behind-the-scenes role in Labour's 1992 election campaign, flew to Little Rock, Arkansas, to work in the Clinton campaign 'War Room'. He stayed in America until election day, 3 November 1992, and learned some of the lessons of a successful campaign. It was the first time the Democrats had won the presidency since 1976, when Jimmy Carter triumphed.

The first lesson was 'rapid response'. Gould helped the head of the Clinton campaign team, James Carville, put together a television commercial rebutting a Bush campaign attack within twenty-four hours. The Bush team had copied a Conservative party political broadcast, alleging the precise amounts of extra tax people would have to pay if their opponents were elected. Gould knew from bitter experience that such charges had to be challenged immediately. Carville, whose slogan was 'Speed Kills Bush', knew it too, but Gould helped provide an additional line of attack. For a day, Carville's description of the Bush commercial as 'an imported copycat campaign based on lies and distortions' was a minor story in America.

'The biggest difference between us and the Labour Party was that we responded. They never did, and they got beat,' says Carville.[1] Actually, the biggest difference was that if George Bush were known for one thing, it was his 'Read My Lips: No New Taxes' pledge in the 1988 election. As he had broken that promise, he was not in a strong position to attack Clinton on tax – a lesson which may not be lost on British Conservatives.

Peter Mandelson, who had worked with Gould in Labour's 1987 election campaign, also drew an immediate political lesson from Clinton's success:

> People in America decided to take Clinton on trust when he said that he wouldn't spend or tax more than people could afford, and that what the taxes went on would definitely improve their lives and be used to generate growth and prosperity in the future. The Labour Party can do that, but of course you have to decide where you're going to hit people in taxation terms. And if you hit too low, if you hit too many people, you're going to lose.[2]

That was a more or less direct criticism of John Smith's shadow Budget, which hit people earning more than £22,000 a year, and which would have meant that one in six taxpayers paid more. Clinton's plan to raise taxes only on those earning more than $200,000 a year hit fewer than one in a hundred American taxpayers. Gordon Brown as shadow Chancellor seemed to have taken the same point when, a week after the American elections, he quietly ditched the policy of tax rises, saying that they were inappropriate in a lengthening recession.

However, the level of taxes was not the only aspect of winning the trust of the American voter. Clinton ran as a 'New Democrat'. It is no coincidence that Blair – advised by Peter Mandelson and Philip Gould – will run at the next election as 'New Labour'. The modernisers learned much from Clinton's broader political strategy.

Blair and Brown visited Clinton's advisers in January 1993. By then, most of the people who ran the Clinton campaign were part of the 'Transition Team' preparing to take over the White House. Much of the trip was arranged by the sharp Political Secretary at the British Embassy in Washington, Jonathan Powell. A Clinton enthusiast, he had followed the campaign closely and reported back to a sceptical Foreign Office in London that he thought Clinton would win. Blair and Brown were entertained at an Embassy lunch hosted by First Secretary Christopher Meyer, later to become John Major's press secretary. Powell, later to become Blair's Chief of Staff, tried to explain their visitors' significance to an American journalist: 'These guys are the two most able politicians in the Labour Party.' He turned to BBC producer Tom Restrick, who was filming Blair and Brown's visit, for confirmation. Restrick agreed. He also ended up working for Blair during his leadership campaign.

The Washington trip was controversial, because the question of what lessons to draw from Clinton's victory had already stoked the bitter moderniser-traditionalist argument in the Labour Party. A few days earlier, John Prescott, the leading 'traditionalist' in the shadow Cabinet, had launched a pre-emptive strike. He claimed there were some in the party 'who are obsessed with image', who were 'about to draw exactly the wrong conclusions from Bill Clinton's victory'. Their real aim, he said, 'is to turn Labour into a social democratic party – proportional representation, homage to Maastricht, divorce from the unions'.[3] The link between Clinton, proportional representation and the Maastricht

Treaty was tenuous, to say the least. But divorce, or at least amicable separation, from the unions as 'vested' interests – on that, Blair's views certainly chimed with Clinton's attack on 'special interests'. For Clinton's campaign team, the main reason for supporting the North American Free Trade Agreement seemed to be because the unions were against it.

Clare Short, an even more outspoken 'traditionalist' on the Labour National Executive, saw 'Clintonisation' as a conspiracy to sell out the deepest values of the party. By the time Blair and Brown went to America, she was seething:

> The secret, infiltrating so-called modernisers of the Labour Party have been creating myths about why Clinton won, in order to try and reshape the Labour Party in the way they want it to go. I think they have very little understanding of Labour's traditions, of its strengths. They look at the polls to find out what the weaknesses are. They're willing to rip lots of things up without realising they'd have nothing left.[4]

One of Clinton's most striking pledges was to 'End welfare as we know it' by putting a two-year time limit on the receipt of welfare benefits. Short saw Brown and Blair's doubts about Labour's spending pledges on pensions and child benefit in this light. It was a harsh, uncaring light which convinced her that Brown's abandonment of Labour's 1992 tax policy was a betrayal in the fight against poverty, because it meant ditching the spending pledges designed to help the poor:

> The hint we get on this is, 'Dump the poor'. That appears to be what they are saying. 'Labour is seen as the party of the poor. You can't get the mainstream. Dump the poor.' That would destroy the party. People like me don't want to belong to a party that does that.

The American connection also fuelled her suspicions because of its association with opinion-poll-driven, money-led politics. Blair and Brown were both already suspect because

---

they were familiar with American politics. Blair also had a bizarre family connection. His father-in-law, Tony Booth, tells the story in his autobiography, *Stroll On*:

> As I was then twenty-one, I told my parents that I was going to try my luck in the theatre. My father said to me, 'If you walk out of that door, you'll never walk back again. We don't want anything to do with the theatre. The last time a Booth was in the theatre was a disaster as far as our family was concerned. My great-great-grandfather's brother was the father of the actor John Wilkes Booth, who assassinated President Lincoln!'

Blair's own previous experience of American politics was largely gained on a visit in 1986. But in 1984, he had watched the re-nomination of Ronald Reagan on television:

> I'll never forget a Republican convention in 1984 just before the presidential election. Someone took the platform and said: 'When did you ever hear the Democrats say "No" to anyone?' It was an absolutely defining criticism of the Democrats. They were surrounded by self-interest groups that they never ever said 'No' to. In the end you had the Republicans representing the country with the Democrats representing this rainbow coalition of interests. Whether Clinton succeeds or fails, his strength was to break free of that.[5]

It was after that election – in which Walter Mondale was the 'Old' Democrat candidate for the presidency – that Bill Clinton, the Governor of Arkansas, set up the Democratic Leadership Council with other prominent Democrats. The DLC was a realist faction within the party, and it became the ideological power base of the Clinton campaign. One of its aims was to give the Democratic party a 'populist' message, one that reflected the values of the majority: this meant rejecting the idea that the party should represent a series of interest groups. And it meant, in a grandiose American phrase revived by the Clinton campaign, 'speaking the truth to power' in the Democratic party.

Al From, the director of the DLC, explained the faction's central purpose when Blair and Brown visited him at the offices of the Transition Team on Vermont Avenue:

> What we wanted to do in the Democratic Leadership Council was re-establish the Democratic party as the party of opportunity for all – the party of upward mobility. When I was a kid, way back in the 1940s and 50s, if you wanted to get ahead in the country you were a Democrat. In the 1980s, if you thought about wanting to get ahead, you probably looked at the Republican party. We had to change that.

Bill Clinton succeeded in making that change – perhaps only temporarily – by campaigning on behalf of 'the forgotten middle class, who work hard and play by the rules'. Blair's equivalent, in a country where nearly two-thirds of people still describe themselves as working class, is 'middle-income Britain', and he says he wants to reward those 'who work hard and do well'.[6]

From's origins were on the right wing of the Democratic party, but in the Clinton campaign he teamed up with pollster Stanley Greenberg, a former academic of the intellectual Left. They embodied two strands of thinking similar to those of the 'modernising' coalition in the British Labour Party – the creative Right and the realist Left. Greenberg moved away from the traditional Left in the mid-Eighties when, as a social scientist, he carried out a study of the Detroit suburb McComb county, Michigan. This was classic 'Reagan Democrats' territory: the blue-collar workers who had defected from Carter to Reagan in 1980. They are the sociological cousins of Britain's Basildon voters. Greenberg came to the conclusion that the Democratic party had lost touch with its own people. But it was not until the end of the Cold War, says Greenberg, that people like him and From could work together, as their differences over the nuclear arms race faded in importance.

By the time of the 1992 election, when nearly half the American population lived in suburbs, both of them saw McComb county as the locus of the Democrats' problem. In the Reagan–Bush years, the Republicans were the party of the suburbs.[7]

Al From, observing the British election campaign from the DLC, noticed that John Major started his campaign in an out-of-town DIY centre – a 'suburban hardware store', From called it. And he noticed the snobbishness of the response to it: 'The press over there and certainly the Labour Party chided him for that. He knew exactly what he was doing. He went where the votes were.'

The DLC saw its task as forcing the Democratic party to come to terms with social change, a process called 'reality therapy'. For Paul Begala, Carville's partner in the political consulting business and a strategist and speechwriter for Clinton, it was simple: 'We had to start with reality, which is that we'd lost so many of the previous elections, and I think Governor Clinton's greatest insight was: it wasn't the voters' fault; there was something wrong with the party that we *did* need to change.'

It was clear to Blair and Brown that they were talking the same language. But the 'Clintonistas' had expanded the vocabulary.

'My advice to Governor Clinton was not to get into a debate over how many times he had raised taxes [in Arkansas], but to talk about the fact that he was for ending welfare as we know it,' said Al From. But the link between welfare and taxes was not in fact the connection that Clare Short feared – that benefits would be cut in order to compete with Conservative tax cuts. Al From went on:

You're not going to convince the American people, or the British people, in my view, by arguing, 'We're only going to raise taxes by this much not that much.' What you have to

show is that you are identified with the values of the majority of the people, the middle class of the countries. If you
do that, then people say, 'Well, they're going to spend our
taxes wisely.'

This was the point picked up by Peter Mandelson. And the
values of the majority – in America and in Britain – are
socially conservative.

Begala explained how Clinton took up the ideas of 'communitarian' philosophers through the DLC:

He had worked for years on a set of ideas as a governor that
put personal responsibility back at the centre of an activist
communitarian philosophy, requiring responsibility in
exchange for opportunity. And that applies to a host of
issues. It applies to crime, where he was a Democrat who's
very tough on crime. It applies to welfare reform where he
supported child care, medical care, job training skills for
people on welfare – but then after two years you had to get
off. You had to demand that sort of responsibility of
people. That was a revolutionary breakthrough for a
Democrat.

Apart from that telling phrase, 'tough on crime', this was
not new to Blair and Brown, but it was put with a clarity
bordering on aggression that would have reinforced their own
thoughts.

The American adventure seemed to give Blair in particular
a sense of perspective. He seemed suddenly to have seen the
larger picture. He instantly acquired a language in which to
express his 'social moralism'. And he felt able to translate his
political themes into what he called 'a radical, populist, anti-
elite, anti-establishment message'.[8] Apart from the new
moralistic rhetoric on social issues, since January 1993 his
speeches have been scattered with Clintonomics. He attacked
'trickle-down' (the idea that the wealth of the rich will trickle
down to the rest), and repeated Clinton clichés about

'change', that meant 'most people having six or seven jobs in a lifetime instead of just one', and that 'unemployment is not just about why you lost your last job, but why you cannot find a new one'.[9] However, there is more to the Clinton connection than a few plagiarised sound-bites.

Some of the lessons from America were similar to those Blair and Brown had learnt on their trip to Australia two years before: eight years after Blair gave his lecture in Perth. This time they met Bob Hawke, the Prime Minister, and Paul Keating, the Treasurer who later ousted him. In between Blair's visits, the Australian Labor Party had completely reinvented itself. On the day the 1983 general election was called, the party had ditched its leader Bill Hayden. He had been the architect of many of the changes, but lacked electoral appeal, and under Hawke the party went on to win three consecutive victories. One commentator described the 'New Model' Labor Party as 'assertively pragmatic, anti-utopian and non-socialist'.[10] One of Hawke's sayings was: 'In politics, winning is not everything, but it is the beginning of everything.'[11]

By the time of Blair's 1990 visit, Hawke and Keating were pushing a programme of privatisation and deregulation similar to that of the British Conservative government. It was described as 'market socialism', and was obstinately opposed within the Labor Party. On the other hand they maintained an Accord – a social contract – between government, employers and unions, which aimed at consensus and social solidarity.

'An Imported Copycat Campaign'?

Blair insists, with some justification, that he has not simply transplanted an ideology from a different political culture. He has used the similarities between the ideas of the modernisers on both sides of the Atlantic in order to apply some of the New Democrats' vivid, populist language to a body of ideas which he had already largely developed.

The strategic lesson of Clinton's election victory was a banal but important one – that all politics is a battle for the middle ground. The idea that, if a party listens to the siren voices of the soft centre, its core supporters will become disaffected is a durable one in the Labour Party. But Blair was elected in 1983, when Michael Foot was welcomed rapturously by CND members and committed socialists in safe Labour areas – while habitual Labour voters deserted in huge numbers. Clinton's campaign manager James Carville put it most graphically: 'Whenever I hear a campaign talk about a need to energise its base, that's a campaign that is going down the toilet.'[12]

Clinton proved that a successful campaign for the middle ground *also* appeals to its natural supporters. British elections have shown the same thing. Parties that win elections win votes in the middle ground as well as in their heartlands. In 1979 and 1983 Labour lost votes not just in the middle ground but also from among its core supporters.[13]

Blair had long argued against Labour being the party of the dispossessed, a view expressed passionately in May 1993:

We play the Tory game when we say we've got to speak up for the underclass rather than the broad majority of people in this country. It's not just an electoral fact that you will lose an election if you allow yourself to be painted into that corner, though you will. It is also that it is false. Because the aspirations that I know from my own constituency unite the majority of people in that constituency, are infinitely more important than trying to divide people up into groups and saying Labour's task is to take those who are on social security benefit and represent those people. They don't want that and they don't need it. What we have got to do is to show how, by giving those people opportunity, we actually assist the whole of society to prosper.[14]

Clinton's victory showed how a broad-based electoral coalition could be built. The sting in the tail, of course, is that the Clinton administration started a slow slide into disarray almost from the day of his inauguration. Asked about the Democrats' huge defeat in the 1994 mid-term elections, Blair implied that the President had lacked the determination to pursue 'New Democrat' policies in office: 'You don't run on one basis and govern on another.'

The trouble is that Clinton ran on two bases at once, and fell between them in office. His campaign appealed to traditional, liberal Democrats and at the same time convinced middle-ground voters that he really was 'a different kind of Democrat'. But, in power, he was unable to deliver either the 'New Democrat' goods (welfare reform) *or* the liberal goods (universal health care).

Blair's response to Clinton's failure was weak and unconvincing: 'We have got to be quite clear about our priorities as New Labour, what we're going to do, what we're going to achieve, and how you deliver those specific objectives.'[15]

But, as Blair and Brown returned on the overnight flight from America, these problems lay far ahead. The two central themes which travelled back from the United States with them were 'social moralism' and resistance to sectional interests. Both had been part of the modernisers' project before the American trip. But, on their return, they became central, as the struggle intensified to distance the party from the trade unions, and Blair unleashed ten words on crime that were to change his world.

Notes

1. Mary Matalin and James Carville, *All's Fair*, p378.
2. BBC TV, *On The Record*, 17 January 1993.
3. *Guardian*, 31 December 1992.

4. Unsourced quotations in this chapter are from interviews in November 1992 and January 1993 for BBC TV, *On The Record*.

5. Keith Dovkants, *Evening Standard*, 18 July 1994.

6. Asked how they would describe themselves 'if you had to choose' between working class and middle class, 62 per cent said working class and 34 per cent middle class in 1987: Anthony Heath and others, *Understanding Political Change*, p75.

7. William Schneider, 'The Suburban Century Begins', *The Atlantic Monthly*, July 1992.

8. Tony Blair, BBC TV, *On The Record*, 17 January 1993.

9. All examples from Tony Blair's acceptance speech on election as leader, 21 July 1994.

10. Graeme Duncan, *The Australian Labor Party: A Model for Others?*, Fabian Society pamphlet 535, October 1989.

11. Bob Hawke, *The Hawke Memoirs*, p110.

12. Mary Matalin and James Carville, *All's Fair*, p207.

13. Anthony Heath, Roger Jowell and John Curtice, *How Britain Votes*, p158.

14. Tony Blair, untransmitted BBC TV discussion with Roy Hattersley, Kenneth Galbraith and Ben Pimlott, 26 May 1993.

15. Tony Blair, BBC TV, *Breakfast with Frost*, 18 December 1994.

14. SOCIAL MORALIST
Shadow Home Secretary, 1992–94

*'It is the duty of the statesman to create for the citizen
the best possible opportunity of living a good life. This
is not to degrade morality, but to moralise politics.'*
Aristotle, *Ethics*†

'I think it's important that we are *tough on crime and tough on the causes of crime* too.' Those were Blair's opening words when he was asked if Labour should take a new firm line on crime, on BBC Radio 4, *The World This Weekend*, 10 January 1993. Terrible things had become commonplace, he went on to say, and not just in inner-city areas:

Friday nights made absolutely impossible for people; old people afraid to live within their own home, never mind go out on the streets; young people often intimidated by other young people: these things are wholly unacceptable, and those that commit these types of offences should be detected and caught and punished, if necessary severely. But I think that what we have got to do is recognise that there are two sides to this, there's the side of personal responsibility, which we must enforce against those that are committing crime, but then there's also some of the deeper and underlying causes, which we've also got to address.

His interviewer Nick Clarke accused him of trying to have his cake and eat it, talking about personal responsibility while saying society was to blame.

That would be a cop-out. That's not what I'm saying. I'm not saying that society's to blame, that you can use social conditions as an excuse. Indeed . . . there have been situations of poverty and unemployment where people haven't been committing criminal offences. But I do think it's just a statement of the obvious that in circumstances where people are without hope or opportunity, when the sense of community itself breaks down, and people don't have respect for others, they don't have any standards or decency underpinning their conduct, then you are more likely to get criminal offences occurring. So society, if you like, has not merely a duty, it is in its interest, to try and create the conditions in which people get a chance in life. But the other side of that, and this is maybe where the left-of-centre parties have not faced up to things the way they should, is: where people are given chances, they're expected to take them, and they're expected to take responsibility for their own individual actions.

Nick Clarke was interested in how far personal responsibility went. Would this mean locking up people as young as twelve, as some police officers had suggested?

Obviously there will be a category of people who society requires protection from, and they are going to have to be locked up – some of them. Now, on the other hand, if you simply get to the stage where you've locked up the kid, in a sense you've lost. And the reoffending rate for those that then come out of these institutions is very, very high indeed. But if for example you were to intervene at a much earlier stage with penalties and punishments *within* the community, then I think that you would have a better chance of deterring them from going further up the

scale . . . I do not believe that dealing with them once
they've become persistent young offenders is the crux of
the issue, the issue is trying to deter them from ever getting
into that position.

Unexpectedly, Nick Clarke found he now had only one
test of 'firmness' left. Was Blair prepared to see the prison
population rise?

You've got to be prepared to punish those that have committed criminal offences, and, where necessary, that will
mean custody. But let's be quite clear, the objective of any
sensible Home Secretary is not to increase the prison population. And you see that is why I say to you that you've got
to try to deal with both aspects of this problem . . . The
Tories have given up on crime. The best that they can hope
for now is to get a few headlines in the newspapers. What
we need is a proper national strategy for crime that's both
tough on crime and tough on the causes of crime.

Thus ended a perfectly formed, revolutionary interview,
from which Blair's first and last words would reverberate over
the next eighteen months, helping to carry him to the leadership of the Labour Party.

The phrase itself came from Gordon Brown, although he
denies it. Sources close to both of them confirmed this to the
author at the time. It is an example of a distinctively
Brownian device, the 'varied repetition'. 'Full and fulfilling
employment' is the simplest example from Brown's own
repertoire. (The quintessential Brown is the 'inverted repetition', such as: 'Our aim is not increased opportunities to tax –
we will not tax unless we can increase opportunities.')[1] The
phrase is also Blairist in structure, based as it is on the 'false
choice', as in, 'We need to get away from the approach that
says it's either all society's fault or it's all a matter of individual responsibility.'[2]

A few months later, Brown must have swallowed hard

when a shadow Cabinet meeting discussed the problem of getting Labour's message across on economic policy. John Smith teased his shadow Chancellor with a twinkle and a smile: 'Why can't you come up with a slogan like Tony's?' Blair looked embarrassed, but said nothing.

The phrase was even borrowed abroad. It was used by Rudolf Scharping, leader of the German Social Democrats, in his unsuccessful campaign for the October 1994 General Election.

Thus Brown's greatest contribution to his friend's election to the leadership may have been to provide him with the material to convince the party that he was someone who could beat the Conservatives.

If the phrase itself was Brown's, the thinking behind the slogan was joint intellectual property, brought into focus by their visit to the Clinton team. Blair's *The World This Weekend* interview came just three days after they returned from America. One of the ways in which Bill Clinton was 'a different kind of Democrat' was that he was 'tough on crime'. In America, of course, toughness goes further than in Britain. For one thing, it means unhesitating support for the death penalty. Clinton returned to Arkansas during the election campaign to sign the famous death warrant in January 1992 for Rickey Rector, who was severely brain damaged. Rector had shot a police officer and then himself, after which he had a frontal lobotomy. One American commercial in the 1990 mid-term elections went so far as to feature the candidate walking past a gallery of blown-up photographs of all the people he had had put to death. In America, being tough on crime is also often code for being anti-black.

None of that was relevant to Blair and Brown. However, they were interested in the way Clinton's 'modernising' faction set about redressing the perception that Democrats wanted to absolve criminals of personal responsibility. 'The Right has won public support through its willingness to emphasise moral accountability in the fight against crime – an accountability too many on the Left felt uncomfortable in publicly espousing,' wrote Ed Kilgore in December 1992. Kilgore was a policy analyst with the Democratic Leadership Council, Clinton's ideological power base. He urged 'tactics and strategies that not only work against crime and the conditions that breed it, but that restitch the fabric that holds our communities together'.[3]

Those words were an uncanny preview of the themes Blair was about to develop throughout 1993. A month or two later Blair could have written or spoken them without alteration. In the Clinton campaign, Blair suddenly saw how his long-standing ethical socialist convictions could animate an aggressive political strategy.

The question of personal responsibility for crime was part of a larger theme, expressed in forthright language by Paul Begala, Clinton's strategist and speech writer: 'There had been a drift in the past toward a notion that the larger community owed the individual something, and yet there was no reciprocal obligation. That was wrong. It was destructive of the social order.' In America, these ideas were associated with a new school of political philosophy called 'communitarianism'.

Communitarian ideas were not new – the American communitarians had rediscovered the work of, among others, the Scottish philosopher John Macmurray, whose work had inspired Blair at Oxford University in the early 1970s. American philosophers such as Michael Sandel came again to Macmurray's central idea, that the isolated individual of liberal philosophy was incomplete (see pp41–4). Blair had at last found a populist language in which to express the ethical socialist ideas which had formed his political convictions.

Social Morality

Labour has always been seen as a liberal party, but especially so since the great reforms of the 1964-70 government under

Home Secretary Roy Jenkins. The abolition of hanging, the easing of divorce and abortion, the legalisation of male homosexuality: all marked Labour out as anti-authoritarian. Race equality law identified the party with regulations to enforce liberal ideas. But those reforms were also associated with social and political changes which eventually led to Labour being seen as out of touch with public opinion and 'soft' on crime.

Public attitudes, especially to sex equality and divorce, did become more liberal, but the Labour Party found itself carried away far beyond public opinion. By the middle to late Eighties, the myths of the 'loony Left' caricatured liberal attitudes to sex and race. On crime, Labour was seen as hostile to the police, because of the stance of some sections of the Left in control of a few local councils. On the family, the party was sometimes seen as favouring lone motherhood over two-parent families, because of feminist arguments against the family as an oppressive institution of the patriarchy.

Blair frequently refers back to an earlier period of Labour's history. 'Some of the strongest speeches you will ever read about crime were made by members of the post-war 1945 government.'[4] In fact, law and order was hardly a prominent issue of the time. The Criminal Justice Bill of 1948 was notable mainly because it abolished birching, and is mentioned little in accounts of the period, with one major exception – its treatment of the issue of hanging. Sidney Silverman, a Labour backbencher, proposed an amendment to suspend hanging for a trial period. Most of the Cabinet, including the Home Secretary James Chuter Ede, were opposed to the amendment, although Aneurin Bevan supported it. The amendment was narrowly passed in the House of Commons – in the only serious backbench rebellion of the 1945–51 government. However, the House of Lords struck it out, and the government used the whips to prevent Labour backbenchers from reinstating it. So ended the possibility of a major reform of the criminal justice system. It is significant

that Blair finds more to commend in the era of Attlee and Ede
than that of Wilson and Jenkins.

Blair holds to a liberal line, however, against the death
penalty and in favour of racial equality, equality for homo-
sexuals and a woman's right to choose on abortion. He
argued to equalise the age of consent at sixteen for hetero-
sexuals and gay men in February 1994 (the Commons in the
end only voted to bring the gay age of consent down from
twenty-one to eighteen). He set out his views on abortion in
his *Times* column on 19 January 1988. The Commons was
about to vote on the Private Member's Bill introduced by
David Alton, to restrict abortion to eighteen weeks (from
twenty-eight weeks) unless the woman's life was threatened or
the foetus had a 'disability incompatible with life'. 'Personally,
I have found this an agonising decision,' he wrote. 'Both my
constituents and probably my constituency party would wish
me to support the Bill.' Sedgefield has a sizeable Roman
Catholic population, dating from Irish immigration to the
coalfields around the turn of the century. His parish priest –
whose church he sometimes attends, Cherie being a Roman
Catholic – had also lobbied him. But he concluded:

> The inescapable consequence of the Alton Bill is that a
> woman will be made, under threat of criminal penalties, to
> carry and give birth to a child, perhaps severely disabled,
> that she does not want. I do not say she is right, in those
> circumstances, to have an abortion. But I cannot in con-
> science, as a legislator, say that I can take that decision for
> her.

The article demonstrated his ability to be direct but not
confrontational with people who disagreed with him.

Although Blair appears straightforwardly liberal on some
issues, he accepts some of the Right's case that Sixties liberalism undermined personal responsibility.

The themes of Blair's new argument, developed with
increasing force during 1993, were simple. First, society has

a responsibility to give people the hope of a better life. Secondly, in return, they have a responsibility to give something back to the community and to obey its rules. And thirdly, because mutual obligations originate in family responsibilities, the family must be strengthened.

The first part was standard Labour Party doctrine – Blair stated it conventionally in his 1992 conference speech, his first as shadow Home Secretary:

> When young men and women seek but do not find any reflection of their hopes in the society around them, when the Tories create a creed of acquisition and place it alongside a culture without opportunity, when communities disintegrate and people within them feel they have no chance to improve and nothing to strive for, then it takes not a degree in social science, merely a modicum of common sense, to see that in the soil of alienation, crime will take root.

The second part, personal responsibility, was entirely new to parts of the Labour Party. Blair's innovation was to go beyond the standard line to talk about being tough on crime, punishment, and even to hint at imposing obligations on the unemployed to take up 'opportunities' offered to them. At the time, those seeking more specifics were met with the exasperated response: 'You don't understand – no one in the Labour Party has used the word "punishment" for years.'

Tellingly, it was in the *Sun* that Blair chose to expound his new populism. In March 1993 he wrote: 'It's a bargain – we give opportunity, we demand responsibility. There is no excuse for crime. None.'[5] The transformation of his stance and his language in just six months is shown by contrasting this with his 1992 conference speech, in which he said, 'There is no excuse for crime. But . . .'

Now he seemed to echo the words of Margaret Thatcher when the Brixton riots burst upon a horrified middle England in 1981: '*Nothing* can excuse the violence.'

Blair's attempt to 'moralise politics' took a dramatic step in the wake of the horrific murder which seemed to link crime with family breakdown – that of two-year-old James Bulger by two ten-year-olds. In a speech he gave in Wellingborough, on 19 February 1993, he described the weakening sense of community in a moral language long since lost to Labour politicians:

> The news bulletins of the last week have been like hammer blows struck against the sleeping conscience of the country, urging us to wake up and look unflinchingly at what we see . . . A solution to this disintegration doesn't simply lie in legislation. It must come from the rediscovery of a sense of direction as a country and most of all from being unafraid to start talking once again about the values and principles we believe in and what they mean for us, not just as individuals but as a community. We cannot exist in a moral vacuum. If we do not learn and then teach the value of what is right and what is wrong, then the result is simply moral chaos which engulfs us all . . .
>
> The importance of the notion of community is that it defines the relationship not only between us as individuals but between people and the society in which they live, one that is based on responsibilities as well as rights, on oblig-ations as well as entitlements. Self-respect is in part derived from respect for others.

His speech was of no direct relevance to the Bulger case, but touched a national mood of anxiety over the break-up of morals and families. It was like a Conservative politician's speech, responding to a moral panic induced by an atypical case by condemning a general moral decline. Blair's office claimed to be flooded with letters of approval and support.

The third part of his argument – the need for 'strong' fami-lies – was expressed by stealing a Conservative phrase: 'It is parents who bring up kids, not governments' (the *Sun* article again). It was the right time to reclaim it. The wave of concern about youth crime meant that both the Labour Party and the country were receptive to a new message.

Blair was emboldened to use not just Conservative phrases, but to lay claim to some of the roots of Conservative philosophy – Edmund Burke's eighteenth-century idea that a nation is built up from 'little platoons', starting with the family. In a speech in Alloa in June 1993, Blair said:

> It is largely from family discipline that social discipline and a sense of responsibility is learnt. A modern notion of society – where rights and responsibilities go together – requires responsibility to be nurtured. Out of a family grows the sense of community. The family is the starting place.[6]

Of course Blair was not consciously plundering Burke – he was merely returning to the language of John Macmurray: 'It was in the family that society originated; and it is in the family that the habit of social co-operation is learned afresh by every new generation.' It sounds like Blair in the 1990s, but it was Macmurray, writing in the 1950s.[7]

Blair's Alloa speech was also an early instance of his promotion of the two-parent family: 'All other things being equal, it is easier to do the difficult job of bringing up a child where there are two parents living happily together.' He drew attention to the 'fairly appalling' fact that ten years after marriage breakdown, half of all fathers have lost contact with their children.

Despite the 'Conservative' language, Blair was not accepting the Right's case. He was specifically taking issue with that central text of Thatcherism: 'There's no such thing as society. There are individual men and women and there are families.'[8] He saw 'strong families' as necessary to produce a 'strong society', but also the reciprocal – a strong society is needed to nurture families: 'If the old Left tended to ignore the importance of the family, the new Right ignores the conditions in which family life can most easily prosper.'[9]

This too, was a distinctive theme of the American 'communitarians'. Hillary Clinton in November 1994 made what seems on this side of the Atlantic a distinctively Blairist observation:

> In our country we have this false debate. There are those on the Right who say the family is totally responsible, society has no obligations; and there are those on the Left who say everything's the fault of society or the government and absolve neglectful parenting. They are both inadequate explanations for what's going on, and I think we ought to be more sensible.[10]

. . . or Social Conservatism?

These three elements – our duty as a society, our duty as individuals and the revaluation of the family – constitute social moralism. Blair's views are often described as socially conservative. He dislikes the label, and rejects those who use it as incorrect and 'slightly sneering':

> They're not really understanding what I'm saying here. I do not want to re-create a strong society and community as a piece of nostalgia for the past . . . I don't want a society in which women don't work or gays can't be open about their sexuality or people are inhibited about discussing sex . . . But what we do want in our country are rules and standards of conduct that people understand and can relate to. I think people are making a big mistake if they think that if you're talking the language of responsibility you're talking right-wing language.[11]

He has some justification in pointing out that the implication of the word 'conservative' is right wing and thus misleading. But his desire to strengthen the existing institution

of the family *is* conservative, even though some of the implications of the obligations that society owes to individuals can
be radical. The correct term is perhaps the American one,
'communitarian', but it has little resonance in Britain.

The conservatism of his moral language did reinforce suspicions in the Labour Party that he is simply right wing. One
anonymous critic 'close to the helm of the party' was quoted
in the *Guardian* (1 October 1994) as exclaiming: 'He's not a
Social Democrat. He's not even a Liberal Democrat. He's a
Christian Democrat.' Each of these labels contains a grain of
truth, although all are wrong. He is a social democrat in that
he rejects the Marxist socialist tradition. He is a Liberal
Democrat in the sense that he believes the Labour Party
should be capable of winning the support of third-party voters. And he is a Christian Democrat in the sense that he
believes in social solidarity and has a Christian ethical base to
his political beliefs. But continental Christian Democracy is
different from English Christian socialism, where Blair's
convictions began.

He acknowledged that some on the Left might feel uncomfortable with his moralism: 'It is easy to deny the idea of
community and some may feel unhappy with it. But, call it
community values, family values or even spiritual values, what
they have in common is something bigger than "me".'[12]

In fact, at the time, if any on the Left felt uncomfortable,
they did not say so. Part of the reason for their silence was
because Blair seemed to be merely reflecting a new moral
tone introduced into British politics by his leader, John
Smith, also a Christian socialist. Smith did not talk much
about the family or crime, but he did assert his 'profound
conviction that politics ought to be a moral activity'.[13]

Blair joined the Christian Socialist Movement in June
1992 – influenced by Smith, a long-standing member. It was
a departure for someone who, until then, had been extremely
private about his religion. It was also a good time to make
political use of long-held conviction.

Smith and Blair's beliefs were expressed in similar

language. In the R.H. Tawney Memorial Lecture in March 1993, Smith claimed to derive his political philosophy from Tawney and Archbishop William Temple, and contrasted it with the free-market doctrines of the Right:

> The fundamental flaw in the individualism of the classical writers, and their modern counterparts in today's Conservative Party, is, I believe, their assumption that human beings conduct their lives on the basis of self-interested decisions taken in radical isolation from others. This thesis grotesquely ignores the intrinsically social nature of human beings and fails to recognise the capabilities that all people have to act in response to commitments and beliefs that clearly transcend any narrow calculation of personal advantage.[14]

Smith summed up the theme which united Tawney and Temple: 'Individual freedom for them is only meaningful and achievable within society.' This was John Macmurray's central thought – which drew him to Temple's attention, just as it drew him to Blair's many years later. Because 'human beings are naturally and incurably social, freedom is best expressed in fellowship', wrote Smith. For Temple, the distinctive Christian socialist word 'fellowship' meant that people had a duty to one another: 'The combination of freedom and fellowship resulted in the obligation of service; service to family, to community and to nation.'[15]

The central idea was the same, but Blair went further than Smith in using the judgmental language of Christianity. In the Foreword to a collection of Christian socialist essays called *Reclaiming the Ground*, including Smith's Tawney lecture, Blair wrote:

> Christianity is a very tough religion. It may not always be practised as such. But it is. It places a duty, an imperative on us to reach our better self and to care about creating a better community to live in. It is not utilitarian – though

socialism can be explained in those terms. It is judgmental. There is right and wrong. There is good and bad. We all know this, of course, but it has become fashionable to be uncomfortable about such language. But when we look at our world today and how much needs to be done, we should not hesitate to make such judgments. And then follow them with determination. That would be Christian socialism.[16]

This was a rare outing for Blair the Christian Socialist. His more normal attitude was, 'I can't stand politicians who go on about religion.'[17]

Blair's social moralism, while hardly a political programme, does have practical implications. His central point is almost trivially simple: Social-ism means the principle that people can achieve more together than alone. What is important is its centrality, not its content. 'The danger for the Conservatives is not that Mr Blair has no ideas . . . it is that he has such simple ideas,' as Andrew Marr wrote in the *Independent* (26 May 1994). Blair's philosophy may not be profound, but the business of vote-getting is not profound, and his argument is robust, consistent and catches a tide.

He was engaged in the ambitious task of reclaiming the case for state intervention. He has been accused of using 'community' simply as a euphemism for 'the state'. But, while it is true that the c-word is often shallow, even when Blair uses it, his community is a moral entity, meaning a society in which people support each other. It is not synonymous with the state, but it does require state action to create it.

Blair argued against old forms of state intervention which tended to take responsibility away from individuals: 'Labour believes that action by government can help people to help themselves. The Tories believe that action by government diminishes individual responsibility.'[18] Margaret Thatcher believed in a smaller state under the rule of law, in which people would be forced to stand on their own feet and would therefore assume moral responsibility for themselves. Blair, on the other hand, started to talk about people wanting to 'stand on their own feet' as an argument for the enabling state.[19]

Interestingly, it was the new Labour MP David Blunkett who pointed out after the 1987 election that Thatcher had stolen some of the Left's best tunes. He pointed out that self-reliance does not have to exclude relying on others, though he realised that the Labour Party was riddled with misconceptions on this point:

> Although it may be misinterpreted to say so quite so starkly, democratic socialists should be appealing to the very instincts which Thatcherite Conservatism has attempted to take to its soul. Not the instincts of selfishness and greed, of materialism and self-assertion, but those instincts which are deep-rooted in the communities which made Labour great – beliefs in self-reliance and self-determination; a desire to have the dignity of looking after yourself and not having the state or local bureaucracy telling you what to do or how to do it.[20]

Blunkett is perhaps closest to Blair in his social moralism, and was appointed to the critical post of shadow Education Secretary when Blair became leader. Blair made a similar attempt to recover Labour's 'true' past:

> When you go back and read about Keir Hardie you understand that what a lot of people came to perceive as the great driving forces behind the Labour Party weren't the driving forces behind it at all. He used to talk about self-help and self-improvement the whole time.[21]

It was in 1993 that Blair started to leapfrog Thatcherism, challenging its philosophy more effectively than anyone else in the Labour Party had managed to do, and stealing Conservative words and phrases, such as 'law and order', 'the family' and 'responsibility'. In so doing, he did not appear to be capitulating to the Right but forcing it on the defensive.

Barrack Room Lawyers

The first Conservative politician to feel the heat of Blair the Social Moralist was Kenneth Clarke, who was appointed Home Secretary after the 1992 election. It was not the first time Blair had shadowed him: for a year after the 1987 election, they both held the number two position in the Trade and Industry brief. But this was a more substantial clash.

Clarke's style was breezy, accusing Blair of 'talking total and utter nonsense', although he was often sharper and better briefed than his casual manner suggested. But, even before 'tough on crime', Blair generally had the upper hand on the broad themes. He simply had to repeat 'rising crime' and 'thirteen years' before attacking the government for failing to tackle the 'causes of crime'. Clarke only levelled the playing field when they debated specific government proposals. Blair's tactics then were often to drive deep into the small print – 'pedantic nitpicking' Clarke called it, accusing him of making 'barrack room lawyer's points'.[22]

Presiding over inexorably rising crime was bad enough, but when Blair seemed to have the answers, Clarke's bluff was called. There was a trace of genial irritability when he complained in February 1993: 'Tony Blair has got the rhetoric of Bill Clinton off to perfection. But like Bill Clinton he's having considerable difficulty in finding specific measures to give effect to what he says . . . We have the measures to give effect to his slogans.' Clarke confidently and wrongly predicted that his opponent would fall into the same trap into which Labour politicians had always fallen:

> The test for this rhetoric which Tony is now applying, which is certainly closer to my own I quite accept, will come when we have actual measures . . . What the Labour Party will do when we introduce police reforms to strengthen the police as a public service. Whether they will continue to oppose changes in prison management. What

they will do when I suggest sentencing to secure accommodation for juvenile delinquents. What they will do when I propose heavier sentences for those who offend on bail. History shows they have always opposed that, and retreated into vague stuff about how this is all really a social problem, and it is all the result of economic success under Mrs Thatcher.[23]

The next day Blair outflanked him by announcing Labour's plans for locking up juvenile offenders.

There was an air of straw-clutching about Clarke the next month when it came to the renewal of the temporary powers of the Prevention of Terrorism Act. This was an annual ritual which allowed the Conservatives to present Labour as 'soft on terrorism'. Labour supported some of the powers but had a reasoned argument that other restrictions on civil liberties were not needed. Clarke could not resist the temptation to continue to play party politics. 'I am seeking to explore whether there is any substance behind the new smiling face on the opposition front bench,' he said, before accusing Blair of wanting to let terrorists 'melt into the population like snow off a ditch'.[24] It was, as Blair complained, an 'outrageous' suggestion, but his stance on crime had already taken the sting out of the charge.

The Conservatives' ritual had become transparent. Commentator Matthew Parris mocked Clarke's 'strategy for dealing with the most insidious danger Her Majesty's government has faced in decades'. Its centrepiece was the 'Prevention of Tony Blair (Exclusion of Sound Bites) Bill (1993)'. Parris's verdict was that 'Clarke was left manning a useless roadblock while, once again, the wily Blair had slipped through the net'.[25]

Only once did Clarke decisively get the better of Blair, but then he gave him 'the most comprehensive verbal thumping anyone has seen Blair receive' (Parris again in *The Times*, 14 May 1993). It was their last clash in the House of Commons before Clarke became Chancellor of the Exchequer. Clarke announced that he was abandoning the 'unit fine' system, under which standard penalties were translated automatically into cash amounts on a sliding scale according to the means of the miscreant. It was a climbdown in broad daylight, an embarrassment in which Blair could have revelled. Instead he made the mistake of demanding a statement on the bugging of the royal family alleged in that day's *Daily Mirror*. Clarke rounded on him: 'I find the honourable gentleman's choice of priorities in politics utterly absurd.' Long-dispirited Conservatives cheered Clarke delightedly on as he dismissed Blair as a 'tabloid politician'.

A chastened Blair said privately afterwards that he thought his speech that day was one of his worst performances in the House.

In May 1993, Clarke was promoted to Chancellor of the Exchequer, and Blair faced, once again, his old opponent Michael Howard. Howard is unexpectedly generous: 'I think it is fair to say that Blair did improve Labour's position on the issue of crime,' says Howard. But there is a note of impatience when he says:

> It is very hard to argue against a generalised proposition that we ought to be concerned about the causes of crime. But Tony Blair and the Labour Party tend to use that argument as a distraction from the pressing and immediate question of what you do about crime and criminals.

When they had last faced each other, at Employment, Howard and Blair had been evenly matched. Now Howard, lacking Kenneth Clarke's bounce, was fighting a losing battle. This became all too evident in a chillingly illiberal speech to the Conservative conference in October 1993 – the more chilling because Howard himself is a liberal. He announced 'twenty-seven' new measures, including the erosion of the 'right to silence', as if the number itself made them 'tough'. But the list had almost nothing to say about the causes of crime, and thus conceded Blair's ground.

When Howard came to enact some of the twenty-seven measures, in the Criminal Justice Bill, Blair yet again failed to provide the Conservatives with an easy target. Cutting against the grain of expectations on both Left and Right, he persuaded John Smith that Labour should abstain on the Bill's Third Reading rather than vote against it. This provoked howls of outrage from the libertarian Left and muted groans of despair from Conservatives. Both disappointed groups wanted Blair to oppose action against outdoor 'rave' parties and the new offence of 'aggravated trespass'. Blair cited other measures in the Bill which Labour supported – it lowered the age of consent for gay men, brought in DNA testing in rape cases, and ended the practice of judges suggesting that women witnesses in rape cases might be 'unreliable'.

As well as angering mainstream civil libertarians, the Bill became a rallying point for the hard Left, which persuaded itself that the nation's youth were rising up against these 'fascistic' measures – a term used by the leftist barrister Michael Mansfield during the Labour leadership campaign. Mansfield accused Blair of failing even to oppose the objectionable parts of the Bill:

> The police are to be given another weapon with which metaphorically to beat even more confessions out of people: the threat that silence will be interpreted by the court as a tacit admission of guilt. Again there is widespread opposition. But from Tony Blair? All mouth and no trousers.[26]

This was untrue. In fact Labour opposed most of the measures contained in the Bill when it was debated clause by clause. Blair certainly defended the right to silence under police questioning. Michael Howard argued that he wanted to deal with the problem of 'ambush defences', when a defendant suddenly comes up with a story during a trial. Blair argued that if ambush defences really were a problem, then the answer was to adopt the Royal Commission's proposal to require early disclosure of both sides' cases at a pre-trial review. This would not affect the right to silence.

Blair's decision to abstain on the Bill as a whole was tactical – Howard was desperate for Labour to oppose a Bill he could describe as 'tough on crime'. But that cannot be read as agreeing to every measure in it.

Howard must have been even more pained when he found Conservatives to the left and right of him deserting to the enemy. In April 1994, Blair's approach was endorsed by Chris Patten, the centrist former Conservative Party chairman, now Governor of Hong Kong: 'I find myself in complete agreement with somebody like Tony Blair and his stress on social cohesion and community values.'[27] No sooner had Howard recovered from this than another former chairman, Norman Tebbit, trampled him from the Right: 'I think in this area you have to approach from a direction which some might say is almost a Labour Party direction, of saying: "What are the causes of crime?"'[28]

Howard's response now is almost through gritted teeth: 'Nobody knows what the causes of crime are. We are all interested in that question. The government is doing a good deal through various projects to get at the causes of crime.' When Blair's suggestion is put to him that one of the causes of crime is the weakening of social cohesion, he says: 'We are all for social cohesion.' He says that this is 'not a socialist message, it's a Conservative message'. The trouble is that it is a small-c conservative message and it is now in the mouths of socialists.

A Turning Point for Labour?

Despite Blair's 'revolutionary' language, he did not, in fact, change perceptions of the Labour Party's stance on law and order that much. In October 1994, political analyst John

Curtice wrote: 'The proportion naming Labour as the best party for law and order has risen by 17 points over the past two years. But equally its rating on defence has improved by 19 points, on taxation by 18 points, and on inflation and prices by 16 points.'[29]

The main effect of 'tough on crime and tough on the causes of crime' seems to have been to make Blair more widely recognised among the general public, rather than to win special support for Labour's stance on law and order. (Or it could be argued that he did for law and order what Tory tax increases and the end of the Cold War did in other areas.)

However, the redefinition of socialism as to do with the moral rather than the material relationships between people is perhaps the most important philosophical change in the Labour Party since it was last in office. It was a change completed and made explicit by Blair.

When Blair joined the Labour Party in 1975, socialism was defined by the material interest of the working class. Eric Hobsbawm's essay of 1978, 'The Forward March of Labour Halted', was regarded as daringly revisionist, because it suggested that the mid-century tradition had reached a dead end. It inspired Neil Kinnock, because it spoke to his tradition of socialism. But its analysis was still framed entirely by the terms of that tradition, and it tried to explore different ways of advancing the interests of 'the working class'.

The long-forgotten 'Statement of Aims and Values' of the Labour Party, which deputy leader Roy Hattersley drafted in 1988, was a statement of individualist socialism. The statement was intended to provide the philosophical underpinning of the post-election policy review, and was a concordance to be read alongside Clause IV, because Kinnock and Hattersley judged that they would not be able to rewrite the sacred text itself. Hattersley's philosophy was a blend of John Stuart Mill with R.H. Tawney, stated most clearly in the first sentence: 'The true purpose of democratic socialism, and therefore the true aim of the Labour Party, is the creation of a genuinely free society, in which the fundamental objective of government is the protection and extension of individual liberty.'

It was entirely liberal, in its assumption that the object of politics was to maximise freedom, and it was entirely egalitarian, in its assertion that it sought the most equal possible freedom for all. This had economic implications, through Hattersley's insistence that people need resources, not merely the absence of restraint, in order to make real choices. But the implications were also confiscatory, because the doctrine contained too little emphasis either on the moral responsibility of individuals or on the dynamics of prosperity. It could be too easily caricatured as advocating that resources should simply be allocated by the state.

The nature of equality in Blair's socialism is different. It is not an equality of freedom, but an equality of respect. Again, this has economic consequences, because too great a disparity of material condition undermines mutual respect. For Blair, as for Hattersley, equal opportunity is not enough. Socialism also requires, Blair has said, 'equality of dignity, of treatment of people within society and for the notion of community to have any meaning, then there must be a certain degree of equality of outcome'.[30] But Blair's morality judges the quality of relationships, whereas for Hattersley morality lies less in judging what people do – the point of freedom being that the individual can do what he or she likes provided it does not harm others – than in judging the degree of material equality in a society.

Neil Kinnock's views, on the other hand, were always more 'communitarian'. But Kinnock's community was that of postwar working-class solidarity. His 'thousand generations' speech in 1987 was essentially backward-looking. His instinct, like Blair's, was to extend the principle of mutual support for individual advancement. But the example he gave was his own life, his origins in the Welsh mining villages. Blair's formula is more abstract and hence more universal. He recognises the general aspiration – to 'settle down', 'start a family' – rather than the history of specific communities.

A Transformation Complete

On 8 May 1994, Blair took part in Channel Four's 'deliberative polling' exercise, *Power and the People*. This was designed to give members of the public the information they needed to make informed judgments. The first programme was on law and order. Blair did not make a speech, but simply faced questions from the audience, a representative sample of the British people. They had spent a weekend cross-examining experts and discussing crime, and had become confidently opinionated on the subject. Contrary to the obvious expectations of the producers, they did not become more liberal as they became better informed. But, despite their low opinion of politicians, Blair soon had them eating out of his hand.

He talked persuasively about the need for consistency of sentencing rather than simply longer sentences. He said the problem with violent videos was often that they were 'a symptom of something that is wrong with that family', but he was in favour of legislating against 'so-called video nasties' because it would be 'sending a signal' to the broadcasters that 'we don't think this kind of thing is normal'. (He had taken a 'conservative' line on violent videos a year before, in the wake of the Bulger case: 'I do think that some films can corrode our sensitivity to what is right, diminish the boundaries between acceptable and unacceptable conduct.')[31]

He was asked about his children: 'Do you monitor what they watch on television before nine o'clock; do you ever have to turn off your television?'

'Yes. Yes, I do.'

'Doesn't that speak volumes?'

'Yes, I think it does. I'm quite surprised at things you see on relatively early. And some of the language that's sometimes used on television.'

'So that's your constant daily watching.'

'Yes. I try to exercise control the whole time. And the risk is not just what you watch at home, but what they watch with friends. And I'm sometimes very surprised at what my kids tell me other kids have watched, when they say: "Why can't we watch such and such?"'

The last question he faced was: 'What will you do to improve the discipline in schools?'

'I think the most important thing is to support the teachers when they are actually trying to exert discipline in schools. I think there has been a tendency over a period of time to regard teachers that are exerting discipline as if there was some sort of infringement of the rights of the children. Speaking again as a parent, my first instinct, if my kid has got into trouble at school, is the same instinct that my father and mother had, which is, "What have you done wrong?" And I think that's very, very important.

'The schools which are operating effectively are those where discipline is not just something which operates by itself, but there is a whole culture in the school that is geared towards improving the children. But you need that ethos reinforced not just in the school, but right throughout the community.

'And I think it's very, very important then that when the kids come out of school that they think there's something for them at the end of it, that they've got some chance of getting a job and settling down.'

Blair's appearance on that programme summed up the still-unfinished platform of social moralism, which he had developed in less than two years as shadow Home Secretary. The emphasis on discipline in schools was a new theme which was just being added. He thought he had another five or ten years to set out his credentials as a candidate Prime Minister. Four days later, John Smith was dead.

Notes

† Quoted by Tony Blair, *Sunday Times*, 14 March 1993.
1. Both examples from 'The Choices Facing the Country', speech by Gordon Brown, 17 August 1993. It is also, of

course, the J.F.Kennedy oratorical style, as in, 'Ask not what your country will do for you; ask what you can do for your country' (Inaugural Address, written by Theodore Sorenson, 20 January 1961).

2. Tony Blair, *Channel Four News*, 4 February 1993.
3. Will Marshall and Martin Schram, eds, *Mandate for Change*, pp183, 195.
4. *Independent*, 2 July 1994.
5. Tony Blair, *Sun*, 3 March 1993.
6. Tony Blair, speech on 'Crime and Society', in Alloa Town Hall, 25 June 1993.
7. John Macmurray, *Persons in Relation*, p192.
8. *Woman's Own*, 31 October 1987.
9. Tony Blair, speech on 'Crime and Society', in Alloa Town Hall, 25 June 1993.
10. Hillary Clinton, *Independent*, 11 November 1994.
11. *Independent*, 3 October 1994.
12. Tony Blair, Wellingborough speech, 19 February 1993.
13. John Smith, *Reclaiming the Ground*, p132.
14. *Ibid.*
15. *Ibid.*, pp129, 130.
16. Tony Blair, *ibid.*, p12.
17. Tony Blair, *Vanity Fair*, March 1995.
18. Tony Blair, speech on welfare in Southampton, 13 July 1994.
19. BBC TV, *Panorama*, 13 June 1994.
20. David Blunkett, *Independent*, 7 July 1987.
21. *Independent*, 2 July 1994.
22. *Hansard*, 2 November 1992, cols 30, 41.
23. BBC Radio 4, *The World This Weekend*, 21 February 1993.
24. *Hansard*, 10 March 1993, cols 958, 962.
25. *The Times*, 11 March 1993.
26. Michael Mansfield and Tony Wardle, 'Silence that should shame Tony Blair', *Guardian*, 23 June 1994.
27. *Sunday Times Magazine*, 10 April 1994.
28. BBC TV, *Panorama*, 9 May 1994.
29. John Curtice, 'What the Polls Really Say About Blair', *Parliamentary Brief*, October 1994.
30. Tony Blair, untransmitted discussion with Roy Hattersley, BBC TV, 26 May 1993.
31. *Sunday Times*, 14 March 1993.

15. THE BATTLE AGAINST THE BLOCK VOTE

One Member, One Vote, 1992–94

'The trick is to speak out on new approaches for the Labour Party without leaving people behind. It's a fine line and you worry every moment. Sometimes I feel like I'm on the end of a branch that is being busily sawed off at the trunk.'[1]

During 1993, while Tony Blair built a reputation with the voters as someone with a 'conservative' message on crime and the family, inside the Labour Party, he built his reputation as a moderniser. Both aspects had been inspired by – although they did not originate with – the Clinton campaign. The Clinton style of standing up to the American trade unions strengthened Blair's determination to change the Labour Party. Ten days after coming back from America, and a week after launching 'tough on crime', Blair came out fighting for 'one member, one vote' in the party.

'There is a conspiracy, actually. It's a conspiracy to make the Labour Party capable of winning the next General Election,' he declared on BBC TV's *On The Record*. Stung by Clare Short's attack on 'conspiratorial, secret . . . so-called modernisers of the Labour Party', he defiantly accepted the charge of being engaged in a conspiracy, and claimed 'it's a conspiracy joined by the vast majority of people in the Labour Party'.

Before he went into the BBC studio to be interviewed by Jonathan Dimbleby, Blair asked a colleague what he should say. But he had already made up his mind, because he thought that if Labour would not change its internal democracy then it would never win an election anyway. So he said, unusually bluntly: 'We have block votes determining everything. That's all got to go.'

He swept aside the idea of a compromise which had been gaining ground since the summer, and insisted on the simple principle of one member, one vote for all the important decisions in the party, with trade unions represented only through their members as full members of the party.

It was a moment of incisive clarity, one of those occasions when a politician actually says what he or she transparently believes. For many modernisers it was one of those 'I don't believe he is really going to say that' moments, as when Neil Kinnock rounded on the 'grotesque chaos' of Militant-run Liverpool in 1985. It was also a potentially dangerous thing to say, because he was, in the American phrase, 'speaking the truth to power' in the party.

It was after this programme that John Smith warned Blair that he might be endangering his chances of ever becoming leader. But the truth was that, on the contrary, it helped assure his ascendancy over Gordon Brown as the candidate of the modernisers in any future leadership contest. If Neil Kinnock had left one legacy to the party, it was to make desperation respectable. There was now a large body of opinion at grass roots and activist level that wanted to win at almost any cost. Such people had no patience with the defensiveness of trade union barons, and were beginning to despair as the tide of inertia lapped back up the party's shores as memories of defeat faded.

Smith was personally friendly with Blair – as witnessed by that openness in discussing his future leadership chances – and seems to have taken an indulgent view of what he regarded as his impossibly modernist ambitions. Blair for his part made only token attempts to hide his belief that the leader was too cautious. Smith showed no signs of opposing the compromise plan proposed by his own union, the GMB, which would give a say in party affairs to trade unionists who were merely Labour supporters, rather than members.

Blair's 'conspiracy' was an attempt to hold Smith to the unequivocal promise of one member, one vote on which he was elected leader. It was true, in one sense, that it was a conspiracy 'joined by the vast majority of people in the Labour Party'. One survey suggested that four out of five party members agreed that 'the Labour Party leader should be elected by a system of one party member, one vote'.[2] But the decision on whether to bring in the principle of one member, one vote was not going to be taken by party members. It was going to be taken by the very block votes whose power was being challenged. As John Edmonds, leader of the GMB, put it, 'It's our party too.'[3]

In his *On The Record* interview, Blair at last openly applied his anti-vested interests theme to the trade unions. Although he said he supported the principles of trade unionism, he now insisted that unions too could be vested interests, pursuing the interests of their members at the expense of, for example, those of the unemployed, or of society as a whole. 'I don't believe that the Labour Party will ever sever its relationship with the trade unions, and I don't think that it should do so,' he said. But for Blair 'relationship' means a mutual understanding, rather than institutional links, and he made it clear why those links had to go:

> What I do think is necessary, however, is that the Labour Party is able and confident when it addresses people at the next election to say, 'We are a party that is addressing the entire country and that we will form our policies and govern on the basis of the interests of the entire country.'

Of course – and it is characteristic of Blair – even the block-vote barons could not disagree with that. But it was nevertheless also a clear repudiation of the views of many trade union leaders: the idea that Labour would always side with organised labour, if its interests clashed with those of, for example, middle-income Britain. Emboldened by Clinton's success in adopting a pro-union stance while standing out against the sectional interests of the American unions, he pointed to the success of his own party in Sedgefield in recruiting trade unionists as full members:

> Now, that to me is the most healthy way of expressing the trade union link and that then leaves you in the situation not where you're anti-trade union, we should be pro-trade union, but we can be far more easily pro-trade union when that relationship is put on a proper basis.

Blair was in a uniquely strong position to make this case, because Sedgefield Labour Party by then had one of the largest memberships in the country – 1,200 members, three times greater than the average. All Labour politicians pay lip service to the need for the party to recruit more individual members, and the centre-Left had long regarded this as the key to unlocking the block vote issue.

For decades, the party's individual membership had been declining (as had the Conservatives'), from over one million in the 1950s to its low point after the 1992 election of 250,000. In 1987 Gordon Brown wrote a pamphlet for the Tribune Group of MPs, suggesting that Labour could get back to that one million figure if it cut its subscription fee and recruited trade unionists who already contributed to party funds. Blair did something about it. Sedgefield's Famous Five, who had got him into parliament, now provided him with a platform for the party leadership. Blair could argue with some authority for the renewal of the party, because they had shown in the 'Sedgefield Model' how it could be done.

The Sedgefield Experience

There is a strong urge to be sceptical about the claims made for the Sedgefield Labour Party. It is too good to be true – a mass membership party, which is part of the real sense of community which is still evident in County Durham. A party which revolves around social occasions, in which whole families are signed up, and across which extended families reach. (Most of the officers of the party seem to be called Wilson.) Sedgefield itself is a pretty village, set in rolling countryside resembling Surrey, except that it is dotted with former pit villages. The formal 'matters arising from the minutes' guff has been cut back to the barest minimum, in favour of wider political discussion and social events. And local trade unions do actually take part through their members, although they also have a few heavily-outnumbered delegates on the party's committees. There are many reasons why the Sedgefield Model cannot be copied in its entirety elsewhere, but it is nevertheless a genuine success story.

When Blair became its MP, the constituency had inherited 600 members from the other parties from which it was created by the boundary commissioners. They were a mix of traditional northern Labour and white-collar professionals. 'Under new management' it managed to draw in the younger middle-income families who are conspicuous by their absence from most Labour parties. The next year, the party was already organising barbeques instead of meetings, and John Smith came to one in May 1984. Offered a drink by the host, Peter Brookes, Smith said: 'What have you got?'

Brookes said, 'We've got brown ale and we've got claret.'

'It's a bit of a brown ale and claret constituency, this, isn't it?' said Smith.

It was during the 1987 election campaign that the groundwork for the mass party was laid. At the party conference that year, Sedgefield Labour Party seconded a motion calling for more resources for membership recruitment. For the restless Paul Trippett, here was another campaign he could throw himself into. He became Membership Secretary. Phil Wilson, who started working as Blair's assistant in the constituency after the 1987 election, became ambassador. It was not until 1989, however, that the Sedgefield party started to expand its membership. It took some time for the group to focus on membership, and perhaps for Blair to realise how important it was to have some backing for his arguments for change.

There was no secret technique. The doubling of the party's membership over three years was achieved by knocking on doors and asking people to join. In the first year, it was just the four or five members of Blair's inner circle, but then it gained a momentum of its own. It was not just about numbers. It was an attempt to give substance to 'a different kind of Labour Party'. According to Blair, it was 'more than a glorified recruitment drive. I see it as being about actually transforming the relationship of the Labour Party with the broader community.'[4] It proved that large numbers of people, including trade unionists, did want to join the party as individual members.

In 1992, the Sedgefield party won permission to run a pilot scheme, under which people were allowed to join the party on payment of what they could afford, even as little as £1. Phil Wilson says the average payment is about £5 a year. The party contracts with headquarters in London to make up the shortfall from the full membership rates from fundraising. So far, they have succeeded, and the Sedgefield party's membership is now around 2,000, compared with 470 in the average constituency.

By 1992, Blair started to use Sedgefield to make the argument covertly against the institutional link with the trade unions. 'If you have that broad membership there, then the party's organisation will start to evolve in a quite different way,' he said.[5] But in 1993 the 'battle for democracy' began in earnest, and he came out openly against the unions as institutions having a say in the Labour Party.

The History of One Member, One Vote

Barbara Castle was in favour of one member, one vote in the 1940s. Then it was a left-wing demand against the domination of the party by right-wing trade union block votes. In the early Eighties, roles were reversed. But even after the defection to the SDP of many of its advocates, Blair was by no means alone in his support for one member, one vote. A handful of constituency parties balloted their members for the deputy leadership contest between Denis Healey and Tony Benn in 1981. Wimbledon Labour Party was one, and the organiser of its ballot, David Cowling, wrote to *Labour Weekly* to report the result, which was narrowly in Benn's favour. He urged other parties to follow their example in future: 'Those comrades who fear the views of all 350,000 Labour Party members must live in absolute terror of the 40 million voters we have to face at the next general election.'[6] The Benn–Healey vote did much to discredit the idea of delegate democracy, as several union delegations ignored what was known about the views of their members to vote for Benn.

In 1984, at his first party conference after he was elected leader, Neil Kinnock tried to bring in one member, one vote ballots for choosing parliamentary candidates. The conference voted both against it, *and* against leaving things as they were. So things were left as they were. Only in the aftermath of another election defeat was Kinnock able to get a compromise through in 1987. This meant that party members voted as individuals to choose candidates, but up to two-fifths of the vote were the block votes of local trade union branches and other affiliated bodies. It was an unsatisfactory hybrid, but a bridgehead had been secured for the principle of one member, one vote.

Immediately after the 1992 General Election, there was a consensus in the Labour Party that the time had come for one member, one vote, pure and simple. The architect of this consensus was none other than John Edmonds, the leader of

John Smith's own union, the GMB. The weekend after Labour's election defeat, he appeared on television to say that there was 'one name on everybody's lips' when it came to choosing a successor to Neil Kinnock.[7] The Oxford-educated, intellectual Edmonds makes an unlikely baron, but the sight of a trade union general secretary appearing to dictate the result of a leadership election before Kinnock had even resigned looked feudal nevertheless.

Smith had never taken much interest in internal matters – he had never even been a member of the party's National Executive – but he was in no doubt that the party's internal workings needed reform. He needed no persuading to adopt the arguments of Blair and Gordon Brown for one member, one vote. Tactically, Smith also had to respond to Bryan Gould's promise that, if he were elected, it would be the last time a Labour leader was chosen by union block votes. Gould's personal view was actually lukewarm, but *he* was influenced by his political adviser Nigel Stanley. Stanley was once the organising secretary of the 'soft' Left Labour Co-ordinating Committee, in which Blair had developed his ideas in the early Eighties.

During the leadership campaign, Neil Kinnock took advantage of the resentment against the block vote barons to re-open the question of how parliamentary candidates were chosen. He used his authority as outgoing leader to per-suade the National Executive in May that local union block votes in the selection of candidates should be abolished too. He hoped his last act as leader would be to ensure that can-didates – and therefore MPs – would be chosen simply by one member, one vote in future. It seemed that the block vote in leadership elections and candidate selections was dead, and the National Executive set up a sub-committee to sort out the details. It would also have to look at a third aspect of the links between the party and trade unions – the dominance of Labour policy-making by block votes at the party's annual conference.

However, Kinnock's authority was fading fast. At the next

meeting of the National Executive, the decision on candidates was effectively reversed. The sub-committee became an all-embracing 'review group' and all three issues were referred to it to consider from scratch – leadership elections, candidate selections and conference block votes. It was the oldest bureaucratic dodge in the book, and to make matters worse for the reformers the membership of the new Union Links Review Group was dominated by the trade unions themselves. 'That will go down in history as an unforgiveable sequence,' says National Executive member Nigel Harris of the engineering union.

Kinnock was furious, and became more so when it emerged that Smith did not intend to use *his* authority as the new leader to bounce his first party conference into accepting reform. Before he had even been elected, Smith gave in to union pressure and said that the internal changes would not be finalised until the following year's party conference in 1993.[8] Smith's chief policy adviser David Ward says: 'We spoke to one or two sympathetic trade union leaders. What Neil's circle do not understand is that their position changed the moment he lost the 1992 election.' Also important in Smith's thinking was the fact that the union block votes would be cut from 90 to 70 per cent in 1993, an important shift in favour of party members.

Kinnock was convinced it would be too embarrassing for the unions to defeat the new leader, and enough of them would cave in. Ward admits that mistakes were made later, but stands by the judgment that Smith would have lost embarrassingly if he had pressed it at the 1992 conference. Instead of the dramatic showdown the modernisers wanted, Smith's first full conference speech as leader was dull, unheroic and a tremendous success. But he allowed the traditionalist forces to regroup over the next twelve months.

Trad Jazz

The traditionalists' strength lay in their emotional hold over party members. Many people would not pay attention to the substance of Blair's argument for connecting the party to individual trade unionists, because of their loyalty to 'the unions' as institutions. Equally, advocating one member, one vote was derided as wanting to turn the Labour Party into an 'SDP Mark Two'. Opposition had little to do with the merits of delegate democracy rather than direct democracy. It was an emotional argument about affinity with enemies of the party, and emotions went back to the positions held by 'traitors' who broke away to form the SDP eleven years before.

Blair's argument soon became confused with the post-election debate about electoral reform and pacts with the Liberal Democrats. Labour had lost its fourth election, and this scrap had become a regular, Pavlovian reflex. This time, the bell was rung by Liberal Democrat leader Paddy Ashdown at a speech in Chard, Somerset, on 9 May. He called for a 'new forum . . . which is owned by no particular party and encompasses many who take no formal part in politics but wish to see a viable alternative to Conservatism'. Blair's position was the same as it was after 1987. He said he was against doing deals, that Labour was prepared to have 'a dialogue of ideas', but this was not a substitute for making the changes Labour itself needed to make anyway.

Even a dialogue of ideas was too much for ultra-traditionalist Don Dixon, deputy chief whip and MP for Jarrow. At a shadow Cabinet meeting in June 1992, he gave Blair the benefit of advice given to him by his grandfather, one of the first branch secretaries of the General Workers Union in Jarrow: 'Whenever you go to a meeting, always think first and make sure what you're going to say is an improvement on silence.'[9] His attempts to patronise Blair explain one of the new leader's first – and most fiercely-resisted – actions: flooding the Labour whips' office with new recruits, including ultra-moderniser Peter Mandelson.

Dixon comes from the heart of Old Labour, from the ship-yards on the Tyne. In Jarrow today there is no shipbuilding left. The political legacy, however, survives. The boilermakers' union remained one of the most effective political machines long after they stopped making ship boilers. It sponsored a bright young Scottish lawyer MP called John Smith. And it negotiated a merger with the General and Municipal Workers Union which put its name in that of the new union – which rejoiced for a few years in the ugly acronym GMBATU, the General, Municipal, Boilermakers' and Allied Trades Union, now muffled in the redesigned initials GMB. It was Smith's remarkable achievement to be claimed as a 'boilermaker' by Old Labour and adopted as a 'moderniser' by New.

Dixon's antipathy to Blair was so obvious that Education Secretary John Patten once commented on it mischievously in the House of Commons. He said he thought Blair was 'really a Tory', and noted that, 'by the look on the face' of Dixon, 'he thinks so too'.[10]

The views of Blair and Dixon were sharply contrasted on television just after their shadow Cabinet clash in June 1992. Dixon growled: 'I don't think that you can sensibly suggest that the Labour Party should be divided from the trade union movement. Because if you do that, what you are creating is an SDP Mark Two – a party without any base or foundation.'

Blair always insisted that he did not propose that Labour should be divided from the trade unions. To that extent, he held to the view he had set out in his Australian lecture in 1982, that the SDP's founders had made a 'fatal mistake' when they 'isolated themselves from organised labour'. But his private view was that the unions had nowhere else to go. And 'one member, one vote' was recognised, correctly, as a way of weakening the role of 'the unions', as opposed to that of trade union*ists*, in the party. Blair responded to the SDP charge without knowing who made it:

I find that argument frankly fatuous. If we can't actually

trust ordinary Labour Party members with decision making within the Labour Party, how on earth are we going to go out and try and win support for the Labour Party in the broader community – the vast majority of whom aren't members of the Labour Party. So, you know, these arguments are just the arguments that people raise when they don't want change. I just think it's so clear, as we approach the twenty-first century and say, 'What does a radical, modern, progressive, left-of-centre party look like?' the answer is, it's got to look like a party in touch with its local community because its local community is part of that party.[11]

However, the forces arrayed against change argued that it was the unions which were genuinely in touch with local communities, a bulwark of common sense against the extremism and intellectualism of party members. These were weak arguments. It was the activists who had been extremist in the past, not the broader membership, and the solution was to give power to them, not to use the block vote against them.

Behind these arguments could be glimpsed the occasional unattractive sinew of raw power. 'While we continue to fund the party we'll have a say – it's as crude as that . . . No say, no pay,' said Tom Sawyer, then deputy general secretary of NUPE – and he was one of the union leaders closest to Blair.[12] He was a moderniser on policy – the architect of Kinnock's policy review – but now, as a member of the Union Links Review Group, he was being asked to abolish his own power. The urgency of the post-election impulse was being dissipated.

The Compromise

By the time the Labour Party assembled in Blackpool for John Smith's first conference as leader, the tectonic plates of

British politics had shifted. On 16 September, interest rates were raised from 10 to 12 per cent. Later that afternoon it was announced that they would go up to 15 per cent the following day. Then, just after 7pm, Chancellor Norman Lamont, with the body language of a Euro-sceptic lifer let out of prison, announced the 'suspension' of the pound's membership of the European Exchange Rate Mechanism. It was an old-fashioned devaluation crisis and a national humiliation for which the Conservative government suffered a sudden and lasting loss of support. Parliament was recalled, and John Smith was at his unforgiving best in the debate.

Some modernisers allege that Smith, having been persuaded of the case for change, now lost interest in internal reform. With the government in disarray and his public standing rising, a protracted conflict with the unions seemed to him unnecessary. But he took one important step which indicated his continuing commitment. Bryan Gould, Smith's defeated rival for the leadership, resigned from the shadow Cabinet and the National Executive. He had been a member of the Union Links Review Group, and at the end of October Smith appointed Blair in his place.

Blair and Gordon Brown had just strengthened their positions by being elected to the National Executive, along with the former leader, Neil Kinnock. (They were elected by party members under the requirement brought in the previous year for one member, one vote ballots.) The result meant there was a solid block of modernisers on both the shadow Cabinet and the National Executive – and the increasingly powerful Joint Policy Committee, the 'inner cabinet' of both overlapping bodies.

All three future leadership contenders were now members of the Union Links Review Group. As well as Margaret Beckett and John Prescott, the group included Smith's campaign manager Robin Cook, Clare Short, the MP for Birmingham Ladywood, representatives of the four largest unions in the Labour Party and Lewis Minkin, author of *The Contentious Alliance* (a history of the union-party link), the only member of the group who was not a member of the National Executive.

When Blair arrived at his first meeting, he was horrified to discover that the group was poised to reject one member, one vote. Deputy leader Margaret Beckett had surprisingly not ensured that Smith's public views were represented in the group's draft report, while John Prescott happily put himself at the head of the traditionalist faction. Until Blair joined, Nigel Harris of the engineering union had been the lone voice arguing for the simple principle of one member, one vote to be applied to all party decisions. The other three big unions were the Immovable Object – the Transport and General Workers Union, GMB and NUPE.

In the Review Group's meetings, the crude calculus of the balance of power in the party was concealed by a quasi-academic seminar on the subject of the theory of representation. This was conducted by Minkin who, in a series of discussion papers, explained and defended the existing structure of the Labour Party. He started with the origins of the party as a 'representation committee' set up by trade unions to put forward candidates for parliament. Thus the party began as a federal body, to which trade unions and other organisations – such as the Fabian Society and the Co-operative Party – affiliated. Their views were represented by means of a 'block' vote representing the number of their members (or, rather, the number of members on behalf of whom they chose to pay affiliation fees). As Minkin explained, 'block voting often occurs in organisations where representatives . . . speak for a single entity'. He cited the models of commercial companies and the World Bank. So far, so simple. But after the First World War it began to get complicated, when the Labour Party allowed people to join as individuals. Ever since, the party has been an oil-and-water mix of two different kinds of democracy. In one, organisations express a 'corporate view' through elected delegates who are accountable for their actions. In the other, individual members vote as equals. Until the reforms of 1993, the first model was dominant. But the culture that sustained it was dying, and with it the acceptance of the idea of attending meetings, having one's consciousness raised by the collective experience, and then trusting one's delegate's delegate to vote the right way at a seaside resort months later.

There was one genuine difficulty with the idea of simply switching to the more modern model of direct democracy, and that was the right of trade union members to have a say in the party they paid for. About 4 million trade unionists – about half of all trade union members in the country – pay a 'political levy' of a few pence a week, which is a more important source of funds for the Labour Party than the subscriptions of its quarter of a million individual members. The answer of the modernisers was simple – get trade unionists into the party as full members. But it was unrealistic to expect more than a small proportion of the 4 million to sign up.

The 'traditionalist' Tom Burlison, who represented the GMB union on the Review Group, came up with a compromise. The important thing, he said, was to involve levy-paying trade unionists *as individuals* in choosing parliamentary candidates. This met half of the modernisers' case, but would create two classes of membership – the full party member, and what Burlison called the 'Registered Supporter'. His idea was a little like the American system – ironically designed to take internal party decisions out of the hands of corrupt party machines. In America, candidates who want the party's nomination in a general election have to compete in a 'primary' election among registered supporters of that party. When Americans register to vote they can choose to be listed as a supporter of a party. But in America, there is only one class of Registered Supporter – there is no such thing as a party member.

Burlison proposed that the votes of Registered Supporters should be worth less than those of party members – their votes would be reduced in value so that they never accounted for more than two-fifths of the total. Burlison's plan was a genuine attempt to reconcile the irreconcilable, but some of its supporters may have backed it because they thought it would allow union bureaucracies to exercise some control over 'their' Registered Supporters.[13]

By the time Blair joined the group, a first report had already been drafted. It effectively ruled out simple one member, one vote, and endorsed the Registered Supporters scheme for choosing candidates. It was described as 'dreadful in both style and content' by John Spellar, a right-wing 'moderniser' MP and former political officer of the electricians' union. The draft report took for granted that there should be union delegates at all levels of the party, whose role was to represent the 'corporate view of the union as a whole determined through the democratic decision-making structure of the union'. Spellar described this concept as 'laughable'. He commented: 'This firstly presumes that the decision-making structure of the unions in relation to political issues is adequate. It also assumes that the public finds this degree of external control of the party acceptable.'

The report proposed no change to the block votes at party conferences, except to allow each union delegate to cast a portion of the union's vote, instead of having one official cast the whole lot. This would be called 'one delegate, one vote', but, as the party general secretary Larry Whitty explained privately to National Executive members, it was 'largely presentational'. It would avoid television pictures of a ballot paper worth hundreds of thousands of votes being posted in a box by one person. It meant, he said, that 'we will then say we don't have the block vote'. The flimsy pretence was torn away at the start of Blair's first conference in 1994. The big unions insisted that, on matters of 'union policy', their delegates would all be instructed which way to vote – as a block. (A further cosmetic change would be to express conference votes in percentages rather than in millions of notionally-represented individuals.)

For leadership elections, the report preferred to keep the existing system, simply requiring unions to ballot their members, whereas previously it had been voluntary.

Blair set about his task in the same way that he had gone about changing policy on the closed shop. Rather than try to steer a compromise and broker deals, he made his argument and worked hard to persuade individual members of the group. But he arrived in the middle of a debate, and there was an edge of intellectual arrogance to his impatience. His approach was less successful than it had been over employment law. One friend recalls:

> He was saying, 'Look, this is what you've got to do,' and they were sort of rolling their eyeballs – the idea of a rational debate about it they couldn't understand. They were taking him aside and saying, 'For goodness' sake, what's all this time being wasted at these meetings discussing it when it's all going to be fixed in advance?'

Blair was not so naive that he did not understand the politics of fixed votes. But he had to keep open the option of 'one member, one vote', so that the right outcome could be fixed later. He tried to persuade the group that, because John Smith had publicly committed himself to basing 'our internal democracy on the principle of one member, one vote, and not on the basis of block votes', they were required to give effect to that. The response of the GMB was semantic – the union's leader, John Edmonds, simply defined trade unionists who contributed to the party as 'members' too, and claimed to have given effect to the principle of one member, one vote, even though some votes would be worth more than others.

Privately, however, Blair was unsure of Smith's true position. The leader was said in some quarters to be 'persuadable' on the merits of the compromise Registered Supporters scheme. Blair remarked ruefully to friends that he was getting no support from Smith on the group, and was pessimistic about the outcome.

Blair's main contribution to the group was negative – his opposition to the Registered Supporters scheme deadlocked the discussion. As the date of the report's delivery to the

National Executive was postponed, first to January and then February, it was agreed to present a range of options – including one member, one vote – instead of a firm conclusion. 'We were on the defensive,' says Nigel Harris. 'The one thing we had to make sure was that our proposal went to the members, to the conference.'

It was against this background that Blair appeared on *On The Record*. Uncertain of the leader's true view, a more careful politician would have taken the easier route and tried to influence the compromise in the Review Group. Instead Blair dismissed it out of hand. When he was asked if he thought there was a way to allow anybody other than full party members to choose candidates, he said: 'No. I believe it should be one member, one vote . . . There should not be two classes of membership.'

Smith Digs In

When the Review Group finally reported to the National Executive in February 1993, it was evident that Blair still had the upper hand in the Battle for John Smith's Ear. It was agreed to hold a 'consultation exercise' in the party and among unions on the options in the group's report but – after months of silence – Smith spoke at last and, to the relief of the modernisers, he stood by his original position. On what was now the crux issue, the selection of candidates, he 'expressed his preference for selection by the party membership on the basis of one member, one vote; but this option need not preclude aspects of the Registered Supporters system being considered for beyond the next election'.[14] But postponing the Registered Supporters scheme was effectively to reject it. The question of how the party chose its parliamentary candidates, and therefore its MPs, was already shaping up to be the focus of a dramatic confrontation at the Brighton conference later in the year.

The party's general secretary, Larry Whitty, had come to Blair's aid by saying it was impossible to operate the Registered Supporters scheme in time to choose candidates for the next General Election. This was an unexpected intervention, as Whitty was regarded by the modernisers as unsympathetic. He was responsible for the 'conservative' composition of the Review Group, and for the muddled and daunting presentation of the various options sent out for consultation. 'It was a very complicated consultation document,' says Nigel Harris. 'It was a deliberate attempt to put any reform in a bad light.' Hence Whitty's rapid 'elevation' from his post as soon as Blair became leader.

Meanwhile, something strange was happening to John Prescott. He had come in from the cold after the Kinnock years, and was beginning to thrive under Smith's more collegiate regime. Kinnock had never forgiven him for, among other things, challenging Roy Hattersley for the deputy leadership in 1988. 'To be fair,' says Prescott, 'you were either with Kinnock or against him. Same with me. So we were against each other.'[15] But while Prescott and Gordon Brown remained on prickly terms, he and Blair began to develop a relationship of mutual respect. They did not agree, but Prescott understood Blair's arguments. And Blair realised that Prescott was both loyal to Smith and sincere in trying to resolve the apparent conflict between his commitment to the trade union movement and to participatory democracy in the party.

It was Prescott – who is now deputy leader – and Tom Sawyer – who succeeded Whitty as party general secretary – who developed a plan called 'Levy Plus'. It was a variation on an idea that had been around for years. Gordon Brown had proposed a similar idea in his Tribune Group pamphlet in 1987. It was called Levy Plus by Phil Wilson, Blair's assistant in Sedgefield, in a report written for Blair in the autumn of 1992. In return for a small payment on top of the political levy paid through the union, union members would become full members of the Labour Party. The amount eventually

agreed was £3 a year, instead of the full membership fee of
£15. It was simple, it undermined the unions' arguments,
and it was a total capitulation to the modernisers. As Wilson
put it in his report, 'The link would no longer be between
Labour and trade unions, but between Labour and trade
unionists.'

With the Registered Supporters scheme ruled out as
impractical, and the fig leaf of Levy Plus available to cover
their retreat, the unions were now divided over what to do.
The 'Gang of Six' – the six largest unions opposed to one
member, one vote – met in secret at the Trades Union
Congress with the intention of agreeing a common line. But
they could not. The Transport and General Workers Union
wanted no change, the GMB refused to accept that its
Registered Supporters scheme would not work, while the rest
wondered aloud as to whether they could sell Levy Plus to
their officials and activists.

They were thus unprepared when John Smith announced
his support for Levy Plus at the National Executive meeting
in May 1993. Smith had just embarked on a campaign of
direct appeals to trade union summer conferences. It was one
of the least successful episodes of his leadership, as he went
up and down the country stirring up hostility, and hardening
the opposition to his plan. To take one union at random, he
arrived at the dreary and cavernous Norbreck Castle hotel in
Blackpool to speak to the annual conference of MSF, the
Manufacturing, Science and Finance union. He commended
Levy Plus as not just one member, one vote but 'many more
members, many more votes'. The next day, the conference
rejected one member, one vote overwhelmingly and, just in
case there were any doubt, passed an emergency resolution to
rule out Levy Plus as well.

Over the next ten days, another four of the 'Gang of Six'
big unions voted against one member, one vote at their conferences, including Smith's own union, the GMB.

Smith Forced to Act

For all Blair's boldness at the start of the year, he had taken John Smith's warning seriously, and kept his head low while he watched the tanks roll onto Smith's lawn. Smith, meanwhile, mobilised a small committee of shadow Cabinet ministers to organise the campaign to win the vote at the party conference in Brighton, including Gordon Brown, Margaret Beckett and Robin Cook. Once again, the contrast between Brown and Blair was to work in Blair's favour.

Smith was coming round to the view that the way to win the battle that mattered – on the choosing of candidates – was to give a little ground on another aspect of the reforms, by conceding a trade union role in future leadership elections. Smith insisted that trade unionists should vote as individuals, and that their votes be counted nationally, rather than cast in blocks, union by union. On this basis, he was prepared to give trade unionists a one-third share of the vote, with one-third for party members and one-third for MPs and Euro-MPs (the old electoral college was split 40–30–30 in the unions' favour). Until this point, Smith had insisted that the vote should be divided equally between party members and parliamentarians – the option favoured by Blair and Brown.

Brown's vehement opposition to this compromise irritated Smith – one pro-Smith source accuses Brown of 'playing the Jesuit' in the group's endless discussions. Blair had publicly opposed a compromise on one aspect of the reforms, while Brown privately opposed a compromise on another. Blair persuaded the leader and won the admiration of the modernisers, while Brown merely offended the leader. But in the end Smith, with Robin Cook's support, prevailed.

Blair privately described Smith's concession as a 'disaster'. He saw it as not only a dilution of the principle of one member, one vote, but a blow to his hopes of becoming leader.[16] In fact, Blair and Brown underestimated the extent to which Smith's compromise would transform leadership elections.

Blair was aware that the compromise was better than the old system, in which trade union block votes were the property of union machines. And he could see the benefits of a 'primary'-style election among Labour supporters in the unions. In fact, Smith's apparent compromise was a dramatic change. The critical thing was that trade union members would vote as individuals. 'The GMB' would not vote as a block, but GMB members across the country would vote, along with members of other unions, in a direct ballot. In choosing the party leader, the power of the unions' activist and official structures was broken.

However, Brown and Blair feared Smith had retreated from the principle of one member, one vote – and got nothing in return. The unions were happy to accept what they saw as a concession. The question of future leadership elections was therefore settled: not one member, one vote, but one *person*, one vote. However, the unions now expected similar movement on the issue of selecting parliamentary candidates, while Smith expected *them* to move in return for his apparent concession. It was deadlock again.

As the moment of confrontation approached, Neil Kinnock came to Sedgefield in July for a party in the new Trimdon Labour Club to celebrate Blair's tenth anniversary as MP. Blair praised the former leader, contradicting Kinnock's description of himself as 'a personal and political failure'. Kinnock, on the other hand, had come to express solidarity bordering on a premature endorsement of the future leader, whom he described as a 'most considerable asset to the Labour Party'. He warned the Sedgefield faithful: 'The more you hear him attacked, the more you must cherish him, because he's in for a terrible time over the next decade, because he's so good, and if you're good in this game, that's when they want to get you down.' There was a genuine warmth between them that is rather rare in political life.

On 14 July 1993, the Union Links Review Group assembled in Westminster for its final meeting. The results of the consultation exercise had not been clear, although a

surprising number of responses from constituency parties
were opposed to one member, one vote. With the unions still
unable to agree, even at their 'pre-meeting' that morning, it
was not obvious what the meeting was going to recommend.
The problem was solved when the Labour leader himself
arrived, unannounced, in a stroke of brute politics of which
the boilermakers would have been proud. Bryan Gould once
compared him to a crustacean camouflaged on the sea-bed:
'For a long time he keeps so still that you almost forget he's
there; then, when he makes his move, he moves very quickly
indeed.'[17]

For his opponents, John Smith's arrival was a complete
surprise. Blair was in on the secret – now that the leader had
thrown in his lot wholeheartedly with the 'conspiracy'.
According to Nigel Harris, Smith said: 'There are expectations for change, proposals for change, and we haven't yet
agreed on what these proposals are going to be.' So he 'rolled
his sleeves up' and got to work. It was suggested that the
meeting should adjourn, but Smith insisted, 'No, let's do it
now.' Tom Burlison was in an exquisitely awkward position.
He represented the one union that really mattered – the
leader's own GMB. If the GMB could be persuaded to
change sides, Smith would win in Brighton. Burlison was
personally inclined to accept Levy Plus, but his boss John
Edmonds, and most of the union's regional secretaries, were
determined not to yield. Urgent consultations during a break
for lunch with union general secretaries (who usually send
their second-in-command to serve on Labour committees)
produced no movement. But six hours after he arrived, Smith
emerged to tell a waiting television crew, who had been tipped
off, that he had achieved 'consensus'.

Thus was New Labour born – in an Old Labour fix. It was
a consensus in the sense that decisions of the pre-Gorbachev
Politburo were a consensus. Smith dictated terms. Most
union representatives had no authority to accept them, so
there was no vote. Nevertheless, a document emerged, one
side of A4 – one member, one vote with Levy Plus for

choosing parliamentary candidates, individual voting in three sections for the leadership, one-third of the vote each, and cosmetic changes to the block vote at conference. Some of the six hours were spent arguing fiercely over Smith's demand that he and he alone should be permitted to speak on behalf of the group.

Five days later, the 'consensus' package was approved by 20 votes to 7 at a special meeting of the National Executive. Brushing aside the decisions of union conferences over the summer, Smith disingenuously declared: 'These are new proposals which have not yet been considered by the labour movement. I recommend them.' Although the National Executive had backed Smith, the proposals still had to be passed by the Labour Party conference in September. The votes there were still ranged against the leader. The arm-twisting was about to begin in earnest. The scene was set for a showdown in Brighton.

The Entanglement with Economic Policy

John Smith's leadership was now the issue. The one vote that mattered at the party conference was to be on rule change E, amending the party's constitution on the choosing of parliamentary candidates. As the conference approached, it became ever clearer that John Edmonds was not just taking up a bargaining position – he really was prepared to have his union vote against the leader it had so enthusiastically helped to elect. David Ward, Smith's adviser, says:

There was a misunderstanding between the two Johns on this. They were both extremely sincere in their positions. Edmonds didn't really believe that Smith believed in his position. And Smith thought that if he levelled with Edmonds, they could do a deal. But Smith had reached the point where he would have to resign if he could not win the vote. If he gave in, people could say this person was leader only so far as he was allowed to be by John Edmonds.

Edmonds says:

John said he might not be able to go on if he lost the vote. He told me he was one of the few members of the shadow Cabinet who could earn more money outside politics. I frankly didn't take that too seriously. I never believed that he really was going to resign.

This was not a position that Smith wanted to be in, although he had a steely confidence in his ability to face down Edmonds and the GMB in the end. And Smith blamed some of the modernisers for getting him into it. Some politicians relish dramatic confrontation; Smith thought it unnecessary. He was irritated with Blair, Gordon Brown, Robin Cook and Peter Mandelson. The last two he thought were responsible for newspaper stories to the effect that he was prepared to resign – it was true, but for it to be known publicly only raised the stakes still further.

According to David Ward, the beginning of September was the low point. An assessment of the likely outcome at the conference found that Smith could only be assured of 26 per cent of the vote. Smith 'expressed anxieties about what all his staff would do' if he ceased to be leader.

Smith's style was seemingly consensual, while insisting on the principle of one member, one vote. He tried to convince the unions that he had their interests at heart by moving in their direction on other issues. In his speech to the Trades Union Congress, 7 September 1993, he made a symbolic shift on economic policy. He restored the goal of 'full employment' to its prominent place in Labour's gallery of slogans:

The goal of full employment remains at the heart of Labour's vision for Britain. Labour's economic strategy will ensure that all the instruments of macro-economic management, whether it concerns interest rates, the exchange rate, or levels of borrowing, will be geared to sustained growth and rising employment.

Blair had edged towards restoring the goal of full employment before the 1992 election. And Smith committed himself to it in his manifesto for the leadership election, *New Paths to Victory*. But Smith's reference to 'all the instruments of macro-economic management' seemed to mark a change in policy. The phrase itself was rather ingeniously lifted from Gordon Brown's economic policy statement for the Labour conference, which talked of 'a better balanced use of all the instruments of economic policy' to achieve 'the right balance between a range of key economic policy goals'. These goals 'include low inflation, sustainable growth, a manageable balance of payments and the highest possible level of employment'. Smith calculatedly left out low inflation and the balance of payments to give the impression that employment was more important.

The TUC speech was an effective tactic. The GMB leader John Edmonds was due to address a meeting of Bryan Gould's economic dissidents, the Full Employment Forum, the next day. In the event, Edmonds was forced to praise Smith's speech, and the standard of rebellion was lowered again.

Blair and Brown were not happy, however. They regarded Smith's speech as conceding too much to the traditionalists – and Alastair Campbell, Blair's proto-press-secretary, accused Smith of having 'changed the chemistry inside the shadow Cabinet and widened its splits' in his column in *Today* newspaper.[18] Although no one could have thought that Smith was actually proposing, for example, more borrowing to pay for 'full employment', Brown thought the speech sent the wrong signals. He worried that, to most middle-ground voters, 'full employment' looked like a commitment to do something about somebody else's problem – hence one of his worst coinages, 'full and fulfilling employment', mercilessly mocked by John Prescott. Brown perhaps underestimated the appeal of simple 'full employment' to people feeling insecure in their jobs.

Blair, meanwhile, was annoyed that Smith had promised rights for full-time and part-time workers 'from day one' of getting a job – undermining all the cautious dodging of his time as shadow Employment Secretary. Before the 1992 election Blair had said it was 'not yet decided' whether Labour would reverse the extension from six months to two years of the period before employees are protected from unfair dismissal.[19] Edmonds says with some satisfaction of Smith's speech: 'Insiders could only interpret this as a slight kick behind the knee for Tony.' Smith's supporters had no patience with the modernisers' objections: 'We had a battle to win,' says one.

The battle for one member, one vote had become intertwined with a parallel battle in the Labour Party over economic policy. Luckily for Blair, he was out of the line of fire as shadow Home Secretary, and it was Gordon Brown who was sustaining most of the damage.

The demand for 'full employment' was the latest expression of frustration in the party at the cautiousness and orthodoxy of Brown's economic policy. He had defended the European Exchange Rate Mechanism, refused to talk about tax increases on the better-off and now seemed squeamish about tackling unemployment.

By the time of the Brighton conference, with Smith still heading for defeat by a narrow but clear margin on one member, one vote, Brown's stock in the party had touched bottom. It is an occasional feature of Brown's political caution, and one which distinguishes him from Blair, that he tries to appease his attackers. Under fire for his position on tax, he tried to get back onside with the party grassroots by sending different signals in a television interview on the eve of the conference. But he succeeded only in replacing one misunderstanding with another. 'Labour's Tax Somersault', screamed the *Daily Mail*'s front-page headline, putting its own interpretation on Brown's ambiguous words. He said, 'We will reverse the gap between rich and poor,' and 'People will have to pay their fair share of tax.'[20] The two statements were not connected, but Brown failed to make clear that 'tax and spend' was not the main way of closing the gap between rich and poor. He thought policies to get people into work were more important, but failed to spell this out.

The results of the voting among party members for the National Executive, announced the next day, marked the passing of an era, as Tony Benn failed to be re-elected after thirty-one years of continuous service. But they also marked the dawning of a new one. The damage inflicted on Brown during his past year as shadow Chancellor was all too visible. Blair increased his vote, although he only stayed in sixth place, while Brown slipped below him from third to seventh, or bottom, place. The party grass roots were not voting for future leaders – they voted from the heart for David Blunkett, Harriet Harman, Neil Kinnock, Robin Cook and John Prescott above Blair and Brown. But the reversal of positions on the 'Future Leaders' ticket was telling, even if its significance was lost in a more pressing drama.

Brighton 1993

On the Sunday night at the start of conference week, Blair, Brown, Prescott and Kinnock all spoke at a fringe meeting to rally support for one member, one vote. The hall that had been booked was too small, and was quickly packed, with many more turned away. 'I went there in order to make two points,' says Kinnock.

One was that I was outraged by the idea that the term 'moderniser' could be used as one of abuse in a democratic socialist party. It really was offensive to me. And secondly, to communicate the message that, whatever happened that week, the argument was going to go on, and the Labour Party was going to get more democratic and modernised if we had to step over people to do it.

Blair apologised for being late. He had just been on the telephone to his son, he said, who asked him, 'Who is this Omov person?' His emphasis was different from the others in that he repeated his point that one member, one vote was not just about tidying up Labour's organisation, but about political renewal. He left the audience in no doubt that he would have liked to go further. That was not the issue that night, however. The question was, How on earth could Smith get rule change E through a conference stacked against him?

Although Smith had spent the summer trying – largely unsuccessfully – to persuade the unions, it was not until the Monday that the leader's office started systematic lobbying of the hundreds of delegates from constituency parties for Wednesday afternoon's vote. Despite earlier gloomy soundings, there was a clear majority among them for one member, one vote, but Smith needed every delegate he could get. Sympathetic MPs and union officials were given groups of eight or so constituencies to work on. It was 'all hands on deck, a total swamp operation', according to one of the arm-twisters.

Extraordinary stories abound. The night before the vote, hostile delegates found themselves engaged in deeply interesting conversations over limitless pints of beer, in the hope that they would be unfit to vote the next day. One delegate who supported one member, one vote suffered from claustrophobia, and said she couldn't stay in the hall for very long. This was reported back to Sally Morgan, the party official advising the Conference Arrangements Committee, who said: 'Don't worry, we'll put a ballot box on the beach.' Blair's friend Alan Haworth, the Secretary of the Parliamentary Labour Party, argued with Phillip Whitehead, the Chairman of the Fabian Society, until 3 am to persuade him that the society should break its ancient rule of not using its vote on matters of policy. He succeeded. But the numbers still did not add up.

In the end, Smith's salvation came at the very last minute and from an unexpected source. On Wednesday lunchtime, the delegates from MSF, the Manufacturing, Science and Finance union, met to discuss how to cast their block vote. The location of their meeting was a secret, even from most of the delegation, who were told to wait after the morning's conference session to be directed. This secrecy meant that one left-wing member of the delegation was left behind, because he went to the toilet at the wrong moment and returned to find his colleagues had disappeared. They had been led a few hundred yards up the road to Brighthelm church hall, followed by a small pack of journalists (a larger pack had followed MSF leader Roger Lyons to a nearby hotel, but did not see him slip out of a back entrance into a taxi, which took him to the Brighthelm).

The MSF delegates were bound hand and foot by their union conference's decisions against one member, one vote and Levy Plus. When they had first met, at the weekend, there was a clear majority against one member, one vote. Now one of the delegates, Ann Gibson, put forward a new argument. Rule change E contained the rules for choosing parliamentary candidates by one member, one vote, and for enrolling Labour-supporting trade unionists as party members for a £3 Levy Plus payment. But it also contained new rules requiring half of all winnable seats with no sitting Labour MP to choose a woman candidate.

MSF strongly supported the policy of all-women shortlists. Gibson argued that, because the rule change contained points the union both supported and opposed, they should abstain when it came to the conference vote that afternoon. In fact she argued that if they did not abstain, they would betray all the women in the union who had voted for all-women shortlists. It was not a genuine argument, because all-women shortlists commanded wide support in the party, while one member, one vote did not. But she was trusted by some of the left-wing delegates as the guardian of the union's equal oppor-tunities policy. Gibson was the final instrument of the 'conspiracy' to make the Labour Party 'capable of winning the next General Election'.

MSF was a particularly rich example of an imperfect inter-nal democracy. Formed by a merger between the Communist-led TASS and Clive Jenkins-led ASTMS in 1988, its membership was mainly white-collar and to a large extent Conservative-voting. But its activist structures resem-bled a residential home for retired demons of the far Left. The union's conference that summer which had so definitely rejected one member, one vote was addressed by such unrep-resentatives as 'Red' Ted Knight, the disqualified leader of Lambeth council, Dave Nellist, the expelled Militant MP for Coventry, and Jim Mortimer, the gamekeeper turned poacher who had been general secretary of the Labour Party under Michael Foot.

The composition of its delegation to the Labour confer-ence was more mixed, and included two important modernisers – Hilary Armstrong, the Durham MP who was John Smith's parliamentary private secretary as well as a member of the union's national executive, and Judith Church, one of the union's officials, who held one of the two officers' votes in delegation meetings. Church is a moderniser who is close to Blair, and was elected MP for Dagenham in the mid-dle of the 1994 leadership campaign.

At Brighthelm, however, Armstrong and Church remained silent. Any intervention from known 'modernisers' might have frightened the waverers. And Gibson's argument was enough to cause four members of the delegation to change their position from the weekend. The delegation decided, by 19 votes to 17, to abstain in the vote on rule change E. A critical vote was that of the representative of the women's committee, one of the Left faction who broke ranks. If it had not been for her and the 'lost' delegate's call of nature, the vote would have gone the other way.

Within minutes, Armstrong had passed the news to John Smith. He had been inscrutably cheerful and relaxed throughout, even while he thought he was going to lose. Some of his more pessimistic advisers thought MSF's abstention would not be enough. But the happy smiles of his daughters, in the hall for the vote, gave the game away. Smith himself opened the debate, and John Prescott wound up on behalf of the National Executive. Prescott's appeal was an instant legend, a windmilling exhortation to the conference to trust John Smith:

> There's no doubt this man, our leader, put his head on the block when he said he believes, because he fervently believes, of a relationship and a strong one with the trade unions and the Labour Party. He's put his head there, now's the time to vote, give us a bit of trust and let's have this vote supported.

It is unlikely that Prescott's speech swayed all that many votes, although it certainly strengthened the resolve of some reluctant converts. But it was part of the theatre, and confirmed his high place in the leader's esteem. From that moment, Prescott became in some senses the effective deputy leader (he was promoted to shadow Employment Secretary after the conference). But it was MSF's decision that carried rule change E. With MSF's 4.5 per cent block vote abstaining, the change was carried by a margin of 3.1 per cent, against the opposition of the two largest affiliated unions, the GMB and TGWU.

When Prescott talked about the leader's 'head on the block' he was not actually referring to Smith's threat to resign, but to the fact that he had gone out of his way to back the unions' case for full employment, a minimum wage and workplace rights. Smith did threaten to resign, however, and he meant it, even though he calculated that it would probably not come to that. Prescott says he believed him:

> He called me off the platform and said to me, 'John, I think

we're going to lose this vote. I know you've always believed in this principle, will you wind up the debate?' And I said to him, naturally, 'Have you looked at all the possible compromises?' And he said, 'Yes, but there's no time for compromise now, I have to make my position clear, I've made it, and I'm going to fight for this principle.' And he then indicated that if he lost, he would resign. I was quite appalled by that, but this was the measure of this man. He had reached this stage, he had listened to the views, he'd made his mind up, now was the time to make clear his view and his party could come along with him or not.[21]

There was about Smith, as about Blair, the sense that they were stronger because they could always walk away from politics. Blair had said the same thing, privately, about the same issue, at the beginning of the year. It marks them out as different from, say, Kinnock or Brown. Smith had also told GMB union leader John Edmonds he would resign, although Edmonds had been unmoved. Edmonds's motives appear to have been a mixture of passionate conviction, pique and ambition. He honestly believed that trade unionists who paid their few pence a week to support the Labour Party should have a say in its affairs; he was piqued at being excluded from the leader's inner counsels; and he was ambitious to lead a 'super union' created by a merger with the Left-dominated TGWU. However, the GMB was also internally divided, with several regional secretaries unhappy at the thought of voting down the leader they had chosen.

If MSF had not abstained, Smith's contingency plan was not to resign immediately, but to appeal to the conference the next day and turn the issue into a vote of confidence in his leadership. Under those circumstances, the MSF and GMB delegations would almost certainly have abstained, allowing it through. Smith would have lost a damaging battle, but he would still have won the war. He knew he had to win the vote, and always thought he would – although he thought it might take two attempts to do it.

Smith's ultimate trump card was that the TGWU and the GMB did not have an alternative leader who was not also committed to one member, one vote. Or did they? John Prescott was the most obvious candidate, but he had thrown in his lot with Smith. But there was someone else whose public utterances were curiously evasive. On the Saturday before the conference, deputy leader Margaret Beckett described one member, one vote as 'not the most burning issue of the week'.[22] By Tuesday, interviewed on the BBC's live coverage of the conference, she was asked directly whether she hoped Smith would win, and said only: 'I very much hope that we will be able to reach a decision.' And she sympathised with opponents of rule change E, saying they were not really opposed to one member, one vote: 'It is really quite hard on some of our colleagues who do agree with that principle, but have differences of view about how it is expressed, that they should be somehow described as being against it.'

Especially in the light of her vaulting ambition the next year, it would seem that she was making a direct pitch for the GMB and TGWU's support, knowing that Smith had threatened to resign. It was as much an example of poor judgment as of disloyalty. Some of the modernisers never forgave her for it, although when it came to the leadership election, Gordon Brown's hostility to Prescott bulked larger, and he backed her fight to retain the deputy leadership.

Aftermath

'When on the Wednesday – after much tension and uncertainty – the vote was won, Dad was ecstatic,' wrote Sarah Smith. This was not evident in a tetchy interview her father gave to the BBC's *Six O'Clock News*, minutes after the announcement of the vote, when Anna Ford asked him if it had not been a 'stupid idea' to push the one member, one vote issue that far. He was so annoyed that he refused to give an interview to the *Nine O'Clock News* later. This only increased his growing irritation with the BBC, which suggests that, had he become Prime Minister, his relationship with the Corporation might have echoed that of Harold Wilson. But that night, all such thoughts were forgotten, according to Sarah Smith:

> That night with family and colleagues he celebrated. And for Dad celebration, like everything else he did, was not something he did by halves. Though fond of telling us we had not been put on this earth to enjoy ourselves, he could rise to occasions like that. It was a wonderful celebration. There were a lot of us, and lots of bottles of champagne. He felt the biggest test of his leadership so far was over, and there were sufficient grounds for a mighty party. At the end of a long night a deal was struck: the next really big celebration would be on the night of the General Election.[23]

That night Smith also struck a different kind of deal with himself. He wanted no more 'adventures'. He had not liked the experience of his summer tour of seaside resorts, being rebuffed by his natural supporters in one union conference after another. Nor can any politician enjoy staring over the precipice of his career's destruction, however much cold calculation told him he would still be leader of the Labour Party at the end of the week. He regarded one member, one vote as absolutely essential, and now the party seemed set on course for victory at the next election. He did not share Blair's view that the internal reforms he had just won were only a part of a wider process of renewal. He was content to play 'the long game', and confided widely that new policies would be unveiled closer to the election.

Meanwhile, the right stance for the mid-term period was to say little about Labour's plans, and let John Major get on with making a mess of things. This enabled him to reach an accommodation with the 'traditionalists', led by John Prescott, which meant that by the time of his death seven months later the party was more united than it had been for a long time.

Blair's satisfaction that a decisive breakthrough had been achieved was tempered by the feeling that Smith had built a bridge across the Rubicon and set up camp in the middle of it. For months, virtually nothing was done to take up the rhetoric of Levy Plus – 'many more members, many more votes' – and persuade Labour-supporting trade unionists to join the party. Smith's instinct to heal wounds clashed with Blair's desire to press on. Blair avoided describing the reforms passed at the 1993 conference as final – he called them *a* rather than *the* 'constitutional settlement'.

Nevertheless, rule change E *was* a decisive breakthrough. Unimportant as the issue itself seemed to the voters, the question of how MPs are selected was vitally important. It changes the culture of the party – although the leadership election changes were perhaps almost as important. But the union block votes deciding party policy at conference were left virtually untouched. Behind the presentational changes, the unions still had 70 per cent of the vote, although there was an agreement to 'review' the balance between unions and constituency parties when the individual membership of the party reached 300,000. Now that it has, the question is whether the unions' share can be cut to 50 per cent before the next election.

However, Blair has no satisfactory answer to the underlying problem that policy is decided by block votes. It is not just a matter of the unions – the constituency party delegates at conference are not necessarily representative of the wider membership, half of whom never attend meetings.[24] But it is difficult to involve the whole membership in policy making. The Swedish Social Democrats, for example, inundate individual members with enough paperwork on policy options to keep the average Cabinet minister fully occupied. The British Liberal Democrats have a provision for a 'consultative ballot' of all party members, which can be called by the party's executive committee or by its conference, on questions where the 'values and objectives of the party are in issue, or it is otherwise in the essential interests of the party'. (It has only been used once, in 1989, when the party's name was changed to its present form.)

Blair had proposed to the Union Links Review Group that it should pursue one member, one vote to its logical conclusion, and consider referendums of party members on policy. Clare Short, his most outspoken opponent on the group, was scathing:

> I've heard him argue it, but whether he will continue, I don't know, because sometimes he does change his mind. But I think it's absolutely crass and stupid. Say you've got a proposal for a housing policy – just one small area of policy – you've got housing for rent, housing for elderly people, mortgage tax relief, all these questions. So you're going to have a long and detailed document that everyone can read . . . How can you then say, 'Are you in favour, Yes or No?' and call that a rational, intelligent policy-making process? So I think that's a way of really downgrading the membership's engagement in any rational creative process and giving the power to parliamentary leaders who make proposals and then the passive membership has to say Yes. I don't like it at all.[25]

Blair's keenest supporter on the group, Nigel Harris, recalls drily: 'It didn't find much favour . . . that was a bridge too far. There was no way they would go as far as that. That was too democratic for some of them.'

However, a referendum of party members effectively took place within nine months of Blair coming to the leadership. The ballots of members of local Labour parties on the new Clause IV were optional, but three out of every four parties took part. Clearly, not all policy can be decided by referendums, but the principle has been established for important decisions.

Meanwhile, the leadership's control of policy has been

strengthened by increasing use of National Executive statements, which under party rules cannot be amended; they
have to be accepted or rejected by conference.

The final important area of internal change is the make-up
of the party's National Executive, its supreme decision-
making body in between conferences. Eighteen of the
twenty-nine places on the National Executive are controlled
by the unions, twelve directly, and six are elected by the whole
of party conference, in which the unions have a 70 per cent
share. 'If Labour is ever to escape the Tory jibe that it is a
"wholly owned subsidiary of the TUC", this has to be
changed,' says former Labour Cabinet minister Peter Shore.[26]
Blair's leadership campaign manager, Jack Straw, argues for
places on the National Executive for local councillors and
grass-roots members to dilute union control. Others argue
privately for the National Executive to be simply abolished.

The importance of 29 September 1993 cannot, however,
be underestimated in the history of the Labour Party. The
party suddenly became an open democracy. Some might say
that Smith's reforms had the truly dramatic effect of allowing
the party to elect a radical 'modernising' leader after his
death. That was not their true significance, because Blair had
already overtaken Gordon Brown, and would almost certainly
have been elected anyway, even under the old system, had
there been a vacancy. Neil Kinnock's aide Charles Clarke is
probably right to say that the overwhelming consideration
would always have been, 'Who can win the next election?'

The significance of the reforms is that Blair was elected in
a different way. The techniques required to campaign and to
win in internal Labour Party elections are now more like
those required for General Elections. The leadership campaign was thus an outward-looking rehearsal – an
American-style 'primary' – for the real thing. Blair is a mass
politician rather than a club operator. His straightforward,
clear-speaking style, combined with his openness to the
media, are qualities now needed for both kinds of contest. In
the absence of any deep ideological divisions, and in the

absence of hostility from the Conservative press, the leadership contest turned into a two-month-long advertising campaign for the party.

There are dangers in an open democracy, of course, because it gives more freedom to ambitious individuals, who then need to raise money to circulate literature, employ staff and organise events. The internal politics of the Labour Party will never be like America, because the political system is different, and British politicians cannot buy airtime (although there is nothing to stop them buying advertisements in newspapers, or trade union journals, or local papers, if they are seeking a parliamentary candidacy). At £3 a head for trade unionists to join the party, there are worries about rich people and others 'buying' parliamentary seats. Against that it should be pointed out that it might have been cheaper in the old days to 'buy' delegates to a selection conference, and that the rich have always had an advantage – such as Robert Maxwell, once Labour MP for Buckingham. However, the National Executive was alarmed by the amount of money Blair's leadership campaign raised and spent – and by Jack Straw's successful attempt to be elected by party members to the National Executive in 1994. Straw's campaign was backed by a fundraising effort aimed at raising money from individual supporters.

On A Branch, Not Waving But Sawing

The immediate impact of the successful 'conspiracy' to introduce one member, one vote was paradoxically unfavourable to Blair. Far from strengthening his position in the party, it weakened it. John Smith's rapprochement with the 'traditionalists', and John Prescott's emergence as the darling of the party mainstream, left Blair and Brown feeling increasingly isolated. Smith was irritated by the sharp difference of view which emerged between him and them, as they urged him to continue the process of change in the party. Smith's strategy was to draw a line under constitutional changes, bind the party together and begin work on policies to be unveiled later.

For three months after the Brighton conference victory, relations between Smith and Blair were cool. The modernisers were sceptical of the 'long game' strategy, fearing it was a re-run of the fallacy, 'Governments lose elections, oppositions don't win them', which they thought had lost them the 1992 election. Smith for his part was exasperated by Blair's desire to push him – as he saw it – into more trouble.

A kind of peace was made when Smith and Blair met alone for dinner in January 1994. Blair was conciliatory, and said he understood Smith's strategy, which Smith interpreted as a half-apology. But Blair still felt isolated. One friend says: 'I don't feel that Blair was right at the centre of all those day-to-day decisions that were going on, whereas he had been to a much greater extent with Kinnock.'

By April 1994, Blair was as gloomy about his and the party's future as he had ever been, telling friends that things looked bleak, and that he did not think Labour would ever be capable of winning.

That month, Tony Blair and Cherie Booth had dinner with a supporter of his in the soon-to-be famous Granita restaurant in Islington. The supporter said: 'You and Gordon are about to be wiped out. You've got to get your heads above the parapet and make the modernising case. You can't just let it all go.' Their guest felt Blair and Brown did not talk to other Labour politicians enough, especially on the shadow Cabinet and the National Executive.

On Sunday 10 April 1994, a chill ran briefly through the Labour Party when the words 'John Smith' and 'doctor' appeared in the same news agency story. It turned out that the Labour leader had twisted his ankle climbing his 108th Munro – a Scottish mountain over 3,000 feet – in Western Ross. He had not gone into hospital, but a doctor had ordered him to rest for a week. Smith's 1988 heart attack was at the back of many minds in the party, but this latest scare only seemed to confirm how fit he was.

On Monday 9 May, three days before he died, there was a macabre conversation in Smith's office. Smith told his closest adviser David Ward that his press officer Michael Elrick had laid a bet with him to encourage him to lose weight. Smith acknowledged, not for the first time, that he had to look after his heart more carefully. 'You do realise it would be pretty awful if anything should happen to you?' asked Ward.

'What would happen?' asked Smith. Before Ward could change the subject, he had answered his own question: 'It's got to be Tony, hasn't it?'

Alexander Irvine, Smith's university friend, recalls similar conversations: 'During the last six months of his life, John Smith made it clear to me on several occasions that he favoured Tony as his successor.'

Notes

1. Tony Blair, *Sunday Times Magazine*, 19 July 1992.
2. Eighty-one per cent agreed, 12 per cent disagreed, in a survey carried out in late 1989 and early 1990, Patrick Seyd and Paul Whiteley, *Labour's Grass Roots*, p240.
3. John Edmonds, speech to GMB union conference, 7 June 1993.
4. Tony Blair, interview, 8 June 1992.
5. *Ibid.*
6. *Labour Weekly*, 16 October 1981.
7. BBC TV, *On The Record*, 12 April 1992.
8. *Tribune* debate, 26 June 1992.
9. Don Dixon, interview, 8 June 1992, referring to 'one of our shadow Cabinet members'; other sources confirm the recipient of his advice was Blair.
10. *Hansard*, 23 November 1993, col 420.
11. BBC TV, *On The Record*, 21 June 1992.
12. *Independent*, 2 June 1992.

13. One other possible solution, simply to designate levy-paying trade unionists as party members, would not work because on average they only paid £1.70 a year on top of their union subscription, which would not be enough to cover the Labour Party's costs.
14. National Executive Committee minutes, February 1993.
15. *Esquire*, June 1994.
16. In the event, the trade union section did produce the lowest vote for him, at 52 per cent against 58 per cent among party members and 61 per cent among MPs. However, he still had the majority of the union vote in a three-cornered contest.
17. Andy McSmith, *John Smith*, p2.
18. *Today*, 9 September 1993.
19. *Financial Times*, Monday Profile, 27 January 1992.
20. BBC TV, *On The Record*, 26 September 1993.
21. BBC TV, *Breakfast with Frost*, 15 May 1994.
22. BBC Radio 4, *Today* programme, 25 September 1993.
23. Sarah Smith, *John Smith: Life and Soul of the Party*, p113.
24. Patrick Seyd and Paul Whiteley, *Labour's Grass Roots*, p228.
25. Clare Short, interview, 9 January 1993.
26. Peter Shore, *Leading the Left*, p182.

PART FIVE

NEW LABOUR

16. VELVET REVOLUTION

The Secret Leadership Campaign, May 1994

'But Gordon has wanted it so much. Much more than I ever have.'

The contest to succeed John Smith was over before anyone knew he was dead. His second heart attack struck at five past eight in the morning of Thursday 12 May 1994. He was pronounced dead an hour later at St Bartholomew's hospital in the City of London. The public announcement was delayed until half-past-ten to allow time for his family to be told.

He left the Labour Party more popular, more united, and more trusted by the British people, than it had been since the 1960s. Of all the tributes on his death, the most affecting are the many letters received by his wife Elizabeth from people who had never met him. A remarkable number are from people who describe themselves as 'lifelong Conservatives' or who say they 'always looked on politicians as people who promise the world but never deliver', but who admired and respected John Smith. The word 'integrity' appears again and again.[1]

Inside the Labour Party too, Smith earned the loyalty of those who expected to oppose him. He achieved a balance between modernisers and traditionalists that neither side thought possible. As a moderniser, he transformed the party's internal democracy. As a traditionalist, he restored some pride and self-confidence in the party's history. He finalised its decisive shift to a pro-European stance.

John Smith's strategy was to respect all the traditions of the party. Where Kinnock had rubbished the hard Left in order to build himself up, Smith neutralised them by making them feel they were a legitimate strand in the party.

Certainly there were doubters. There were left-wing traditionalists who would never be reconciled. And there were modernisers who were frustrated with his steadiness, which they saw as inaction. Just before he died, however, many doubters of both kinds were becoming persuaded that his strategy was working. And many more were persuaded too late, after he died, when they were taken aback by the depth of public feeling.

John Smith left an extraordinary legacy to his successor. For a party committed to solidarity, the Labour Party has had a remarkable history of disunity. Smith left a united party, fundamentally reformed. But would his strategy be continued, or would there be a reversion to the Kinnock style favoured by the modernisers?

Support for Blair, half-hidden while Smith was leader, crystallised immediately. Just at the moment when Blair and his supporters had become most gloomy about his isolation in the party, the latent strength of support for him turned out to be overwhelming.

Blair was in Aberdeen that Thursday morning, campaigning for the Euro-elections. He had just arrived at Dyce airport when Gordon Brown called him on his mobile phone. Brown called from his Westminster flat as soon as he heard the news from Elizabeth Smith at about nine o'clock. Blair spoke on lunchtime television and paid tribute to John Smith:

> He had this extraordinary combination of strength and authority and humour and humanity, and all of us who knew him closely, personally, will mourn him. I think the whole of the country will feel the loss, and our thoughts

and prayers go out to Elizabeth and the family. But it's
simply devastating.

Blair's father-in-law, Tony Booth, says: 'In that moment I
realised what this would mean for him, my son-in-law, my
daughter and my grandchildren.'[2]

Soon afterwards, outside Holborn Tube station, Cherie
Booth bumped into their friend Barry Cox, the London
Weekend Television executive who had been their next-door
neighbour in Hackney. She was on her way to Heathrow airport to meet Blair, and asked Cox if he agreed that he should
stand. Cox says: 'Cherie was worried because Tony had
always had this view that he shouldn't run against Gordon.
That had become looser in the preceding twelve months, but
he'd never actually said he would do it. It was always something that was several years away.' Cox said he thought Blair
should stand, and Cherie asked if she could call on him if
necessary to help persuade her husband. It did not turn out
to be necessary.

When Blair returned to his office in Westminster, four people were waiting with offers of support. Shadow Cabinet
minister Mo Mowlam and three of the 'Kinnocracy' had
come to offer to help elect him leader – Adam Ingram, an MP
who had been Neil Kinnock's Parliamentary Private
Secretary, Charles Clarke, who had been his Chief of Staff,
and John Eatwell, a Labour peer who had been his economic
adviser. Blair sent them all away, well aware that such discussions were inappropriate. But those close to Blair say he had
decided straight away that he would run.

That evening Blair spoke to David Blunkett, the MP for
Sheffield Brightside who was that year's Labour Party chairman. He would be responsible for organising the leadership
election. He says that when they spoke in his tiny room at the
House of Commons, he said to Blair: 'If you decide you want
to be leader of the party, you will be leader. But you've got to
make your mind up now.' To which Blair replied: 'Yes, I suppose I have.'

Blair had learned in 1992, when he hesitated over running for the deputy leadership, that decisions taken – or not taken – immediately are the ones that matter. One member of the shadow Cabinet says: 'Once you hesitate, you then learn the next time that you don't hesitate.' In 1992, while Blair hesitated, John Smith swooped and pushed Margaret Beckett, blinking, into the ring. 'So when John Smith died, Tony did not hesitate for one second.' One Labour frontbencher spoke to Blair very soon after Smith's death:

He had decided, and I was astonished how decided he was. And what he said was he had lots of other things in his life, he didn't actually need to do it for himself, but that he was going to do it. It was like the tiger had jumped out of the pussy cat's skin. And he's been like that ever since.

Another early shadow Cabinet supporter, Chris Smith, says:

He knew he was going to win and he knew right from the start he had to stand. My reading of it was that there was never any doubt in his mind that he had to be the candidate. And what Gordon decided about whether he was or wasn't going to stand was really irrelevant. Tony was going to stand. He'd made up his mind . . . I never picked up a shadow of doubt. I remember him saying to me something like, 'There are times in life when your ticket comes up with your number on it, and this is one of them.'

Blair himself kept a low profile for several days. He wanted to allow a decent period of mourning for a much-admired leader, and to preserve his relationship with Gordon Brown. And Blair certainly seemed to convince some people that he did not know whether or not to stand. Gerald Kaufman spoke to Blair the day after Smith's death, and then telephoned Roy Hattersley on Wednesday, five days later, to say, 'He's still being difficult.' Hattersley says he then telephoned Blair:

I said to him he had to do it for two reasons. One was the positive reason, that he would win, that he was the best leader. And the second was that if he didn't, nobody would ever treat him seriously politically again. And I remember what he said to me. He said, 'But Gordon has wanted it so much. Much more than I ever have.' I said to him, 'Well, there are a lot of people who wanted to lead the Labour Party who had to get used to the idea that they're not going to. And Gordon just has to join a rather long and distinguished line.'

As Hattersley himself concedes, Blair's reluctance was feigned: 'I think it was a bit put on. But it was put on for good reasons. I think it was put on for decency. He is very close to Gordon, and I think it was put on for Gordon rather than put on for the world.' Some of Gordon Brown's supporters were not taken in. One of them told Brown: 'He's going for it.'

For the first week, until John Smith's funeral, the campaign was conducted in secret, as decency almost completely suppressed open discussion in the party of the succession. Then there were three weeks of semi-secret campaigning, while the Labour Party fought the European elections. This was a period of self-imposed censorship during which the candidates still pretended not to be candidates. Only then did the official six-week campaign start. By that time, of course, it really was all over.

'It's Got to be Blair'

It is difficult to recover perceptions of politics from before such 'firebreak' events as John Smith's death. But it is worth recalling how Blair's prospects seemed in the aftermath of the 1993 conference, at the time of the shadow Cabinet elections in October. Gordon Brown was still widely, if wrongly, regarded as the 'bus' candidate (should John Smith fall under

a bus, or anything else happen to him). It was understood that
Blair would not stand against him. Brown came fourth and
Blair sixth in the shadow Cabinet poll. Robin Cook, who
came top, seemed strongly placed, although there were
doubts about the breadth of his appeal outside the party.
John Prescott, who came joint second with Frank Dobson,
was in a good position, but was not considered a serious leadership candidate – most importantly by himself. He told
Esquire in an interview that was not published until after
Smith's death: 'I'm out of that league really. I am sure a lot of
people will be glad to hear me say that.'[3]

From the moment of John Smith's death, however, the
media turned to Blair with a speed which many Labour Party
members felt was disrespectful and undemocratic.
Disrespectful because they wanted time to mourn the loss of
John Smith; undemocratic because they felt the choice of his
successor was being dictated to them. Neither feeling was
justified. Media coverage as a whole was justly respectful of
John Smith's memory. The Blair mania may have confused
comment with factual reporting but it was based on facts. It
was a fact that Blair and Brown's standing in the Labour
Party had long marked them out as possible eventual succes-
sors to John Smith. It was also a fact – although not so widely
appreciated – that Blair had overtaken Brown since the 1992
election. And it was a fact that politicians were now discussing
the leadership, making predictions and plans. The muttered
words, 'It's got to be Blair', hung over cabals all over
Westminster.

However grief-stricken they were, it was impossible for
politicians not to think and talk about the consequences of
John Smith's death. One Labour MP cynically observed that
Blair's supporters refrained from launching his campaign for
a decent period of mourning – 'about twenty minutes'. But
most Labour politicians actually conducted themselves,
through to the end of the leadership campaign, with a tact
and restraint that was rather unfamiliar in the party, and a
tribute to John Smith.

Labour Party members did not just feel that the choice was being dictated to them with unseemly haste. They felt it was a conspiracy of 'The Tory Press'. Certainly, one of the most striking articles in praise of Blair appeared in the *Daily Mail* the day after Smith's death. The Thatcherite deputy editor of the *Spectator*, Simon Heffer, wrote:

> Mr Blair is a man of rare ability. Rarer still in modern politics, he has an unblemished reputation for honesty and integrity that commands the respect even of his most committed opponents . . . Blair is a devoted and active father, practically rather than theoretically committed to family values. In the last two years, as his party's spokesman on Home Affairs, he has brought an un-selfconsciously moral tone to his pronouncements on law and order, and the nature of society.

According to Heffer, the 'conspiracy' went like this. *Mail* editor Paul Dacre asked him: 'Who's going to be leader of the Labour Party?'

Heffer said: 'If they've got any sense it'll be Blair. He'll scare the shit out of the Conservative Party.'

'Write a piece about him.'

In fact, Blair had collected two press endorsements even earlier – on the day of Smith's death. On BBC TV's *Newsnight*, Blair's chief apologist Alastair Campbell, Assistant Editor of *Today*, said: 'My own view is that it will probably be Tony Blair.' He was hardly a Conservative.

And later editions of the London *Evening Standard* carried an article headlined, 'Why I say Tony Blair should be the next leader'. It was by Sarah Baxter, former political editor of the *New Statesman and Society* – hardly a Conservative either. Some Labour MPs, determined to detect an ulterior motive of one kind or another, wrongly assumed Peter Mandelson to be in some way behind her article, on the assumption that he is responsible for anything about the Labour Party in the media.

Mandelson – Blair's other unofficial press officer – did now make a dramatic return to centre stage, however. As the architect of Labour's 1987 election campaign, and the party's original 'spin doctor', he had been one of Neil Kinnock's closest confidants. Relations between them cooled when he gave up his job as the party's director of communications to become an MP, but he remained close to Kinnock's circle. He was closest of all to Blair, and now he made a come-back, this time playing younger brother 'Bobby' to Blair's J.F. Kennedy. But for two years – his first two years as an MP – he had been out in the cold. John Smith's office was suspicious of him. When Smith once spoke disparagingly of 'the black art of public relations that's taken over politics', he probably had Mandelson in mind.[4]

Mandelson was also intensely unpopular with the conservative elements of the Parliamentary Labour Party. He was given the ritual cold shoulder reserved for people who arrive in the House already famous, and who fail to behave in the deferential way expected of new MPs (Ken Livingstone was an earlier victim).

Now, suddenly, Mandelson was important again. It was well known that he was close to both Blair and Brown. For years he championed them both, although he had favoured Blair as a future leader since at least the 1992 election, and now he became Blair's principal adviser straight away. On the death of John Smith, journalists, unable to speak to either Blair or Brown, turned their attention to Mandelson. He rekindled the resentment of many Labour MPs by being seen in the House of Commons Press Gallery several times on the day after Smith's death. At his most Mandelsonian, he apparently told journalists he knew well not to 'write Gordon off', while telling those he knew less well what he actually thought, that it had to be Blair. In order to maintain his close relationship with Brown, he needed to build him up, but he did not want to build him up too far.

On Friday, Mandelson bumped into Alexander Irvine, who was in Westminster to make arrangements for his friend's funeral. The conversation between two of Blair's closest advisers was significant, but should not be taken at face value. Irvine said the leadership was Blair's for the taking, and was surprised that Mandelson disagreed: 'I am not persuaded of that.' As he knew it would be, Mandelson's comment was reported straight back to Blair. But it only suggests that the future leader's dependence on Mandelson was so great that he was able to play hard to get.

On Saturday, Mandelson appeared on Channel Four's *A Week In Politics*. Simply going on television two days after Smith's death was guaranteed to irritate many Labour MPs but, more importantly, what he said opened a rift with Gordon Brown's camp. After a token disclaimer, claiming that neither Blair nor Brown had the 'appetite to talk about succession' at that point, he went on to talk about it for them. He listed the contenders in a very particular order: 'Tony Blair, for example, or Gordon Brown, or Robin Cook, or John Prescott . . .' And then he set out the criteria for choosing the new leader:

> Who would maximise support for the party in the country? Who will play best at the box office, who will not simply appeal to the traditional supporters and customers of the Labour Party, but who will bring in those extra, additional voters that we need in order to win convincingly at the next election?

To Brown's people this was transparent code for Blair. 'Peter shows his hand' was the message from one Brown supporter to the electronic pager of the shadow Chancellor's press officer, Charlie Whelan.

Brown's supporters also assumed that Mandelson was behind the story on the front page of the *Sunday Times* the next day, which turned a common assumption of Labour politics into an exclusive story. Where most people had assumed for some time that Blair and Brown would not fight each other for the leadership, the *Sunday Times* 'revealed' a 'secret pact' between them not to stand against each other. However, as it was clear to Brown's camp that Blair intended to stand, they thought this was an attempt by Mandelson to close off Brown's options.

So what was the nature of the 'pact' between Blair and Brown? They had been close political allies from their earliest days in parliament, and had been inseparable as they rose through the ranks in the Kinnock era. There certainly had been an 'understanding' between the two, dating from 1992, although it was ambiguous. They agreed it would be disastrous to stand against each other in a leadership election, and in 1992 they shared the view that Brown was in the stronger position.

One of Brown's supporters – although not Brown himself – claims that this agreement had not been superseded. It had simply not been discussed since – which is consistent with Cherie's desire to ensure her husband did not defer to Brown on the morning of Smith's death.

However, the agreement by its nature envisaged that the position might change. For Blair, the difficulty was how to convey to Brown that it had.

The result was an awkward impasse. Blair and Brown talked constantly but inconclusively from the moment Brown heard about John Smith's heart attack. Brown appeared to be bemused and hurt by Blair's ambition. Already devastated by the loss of Smith, he may have expected more deference from his junior partner. He was not best placed to observe the extent to which the landscape had changed over the previous two years.

Blair and Brown met face to face on the Sunday to have their first real discussion about the leadership election. It was a painful and difficult meeting. According to one of Brown's supporters, Blair was even prepared to concede that Brown could win the leadership election, but argued that he, Blair, was better placed to win the country at the next General Election.

Some of Brown's keenest supporters among MPs were still

urging him to run, but acknowledged that this would mean running against Blair.

Brown's only hope was that his support would gather momentum in the three weeks of phoney war between the funeral and the European elections. Both Blair and Brown – or their surrogates – told journalists after the funeral that they had agreed that their supporters should 'test opinion' in the party before they made any decisions. By then, however, the election had largely been pre-empted.

The First Weekend

One decisive factor in securing the leadership for Blair were the reported views of the general public. On the Sunday after Smith's death, three instant opinion polls suggested Blair was clearly ahead. Opinion polls are so influential in Labour leadership elections that they might be described as the fourth section of Labour's three-part electoral college. One part of the actual electoral college was also surveyed – a straw poll of 150 Labour-supporting trade unionists, carried out by the *Sunday Express*, which put Blair well ahead on 43 per cent, with Prescott second on 22 per cent.

Some on the old Left in the Labour Party complained that the polls were simply a mirror held up to the media's choice – a dying echo of the Bennite argument against wider democracy inside the party. Of course it is true that leader writers and political journalists generally, as individuals, were overwhelmingly pro-Blair, and that this may have reflected their peculiar biases – male, middle-class and centrist. But it also reflected many of the same judgments that the wider electorate had made or would make. Blair was also popular among women, working-class voters and Labour Party members.

By the weekend after John Smith's death, each of the leading contenders had campaign teams in the field. Nigel Griffiths, a trade spokesman, was Gordon Brown's most visible canvasser, although Nick Brown (in an awkward position as Margaret Beckett's deputy in her role as shadow Leader of the House) was his Keeper of Lists. Richard Caborn, the chairman of the Trade and Industry Select Committee, acted for John Prescott. Derek Fatchett, Robin Cook's deputy in the Trade and Industry team, acted for his boss. For Team Blair, Mo Mowlam had already appointed herself 'campaign manager', although a large number of others were already canvassing on his behalf. Peter Kilfoyle, a whip, began taking soundings among Labour MPs, with Blair's deputy on his front bench Home Affairs team, Alun Michael, acting as first-stop shop for loyalty pledges.

Kilfoyle, a new MP, had been impressed by Blair since 1990, when Blair visited Liverpool. Kilfoyle was the Labour Party's regional organiser there, and had been in the front line of the war against Militant. The local elections in 1990 were the first occasion on which Militant, who by then had mostly been expelled from the party, put up candidates against the Labour Party in Liverpool. Blair was one of the few shadow Cabinet members to go there, remembers Kilfoyle:

> He went to Netherley, where the councillor used to be one Derek Hatton, and went to this adventure playground which had been set up by the local community. Our supporters had been terribly intimidated. There were carloads of Militant there, about twenty of them in a mob, jostling people and shouting abuse, screaming. It's hard to convey to people who haven't experienced it what it was like. He handled himself not just with dignity but with courage. He didn't seem worried or intimidated.

In July 1991 Kilfoyle was elected to parliament in a by-election in Liverpool Walton against a Militant candidate who stood as 'Real Labour'.

According to Kilfoyle, Blair did not take part in campaign planning meetings until a week later, the Monday after the funeral. 'We were looking ahead to a campaign if Tony committed himself,' he says. Their first objective was to assess the level of support among the 270 Labour MPs entitled to nominate candidates. That first weekend, Kilfoyle calculated that over a third of them were already firmly pledged to Blair. Several MPs felt torn between their loyalty to Brown as the 'senior' member of the Brown–Blair partnership, and their as-yet-undeclared conviction that 'It's got to be Blair.' A minority of modernisers still preferred Brown, and thought he could win, even though they accepted it meant going 'head to head' against Blair. However, Chris Smith says that, before the funeral, 'the overwhelming consensus among the Parliamentary Labour Party was that they wanted Tony to stand rather than Gordon, and that message was getting through [to Blair] very strongly from very early on'.

There were three main knots of Blair's support among Labour MPs: Solidarity, the old right wing of the parliamentary party (which in the mid-Eighties briefly took shape in an organised faction named after the anti-Communist Polish trade union), led by Roy Hattersley and Gerald Kaufman; the 'Kinnocracy', the modernisers associated with Neil Kinnock; and the 'Class of '92', the new intake from the General Election, among whom Blair's support was significantly higher when the votes were finally counted.

The battle was being fought by indirect means. That Sunday, John Prescott was the first of the leadership non-candidates to set out his non-manifesto. He kept a longstanding engagement to appear on BBC TV's *Breakfast with Frost*, and paid a warm tribute to his former leader. He also drew attention to his role in winning one member, one vote at the previous year's conference and set out his credentials as a candidate able to unite Left and Right, in the John Smith tradition:

> I'm going to make a curious admission here. In my twenty-odd years in parliament, and my political life, coming from the Left, I've always identified very much with the Left causes, and I do now. But I've begun to learn that there's

more than Left and Right, there's about trust, there's about conviction. And that can come sometimes just as much from the Right as it does from the Left. When you have politicians that are prepared to do that, that means you might disagree with them, but you know where you stand with them, and you know they want to fight for those policies and defend them.

He associated himself again with the theme of full employment, which was to form the central plank of his platform for the deputy leadership – and indeed set off a wider debate across the political spectrum.

The one thing I do remember most of all on that fateful night before his terrible loss, was that in the shadow Cabinet I went to him and gave him a document called *Jobs and Social Justice* – he was already working out how you could achieve full employment, how you could have social justice in employment, and he gave me the great honour of actually trying to put together a document for the shadow Cabinet and the party to consider.

At the breakfast hosted by presenter David Frost after the programme, Peter Mandelson – on television again, reviewing the papers – greeted Prescott politely. Prescott was embarrassed, uncertain how to handle the olive branch offered by his enemy. In 1985 Prescott had provided Mandelson with a reference for the job of Labour Party communications director, because he knew him as a Commons researcher. But their relationship quickly became fraught, and only a few months before this meeting, Prescott had told the *Mail on Sunday*: 'I find Mandelson to be a total aberration . . . He's basically a right-wing politician who doesn't want to argue a right-wing case.'[5] Now began a rapprochement which saw Mandelson, among a group of 'modernisers', switching from Margaret Beckett, whom they had supported for the deputy leadership in 1992, to Prescott. Mandelson ended the year in the Labour whips' office, responsible for keeping in touch with the new deputy leader.

On BBC TV's *On The Record* that lunchtime, Labour backbencher Tony Wright broke the code about the succession, saying it would be 'an indulgence for the party to choose anybody but Blair'. He urged Gordon Brown to stand aside: 'This must be an agonising time for Gordon. I shouldn't perhaps say it like this because I am a great admirer of Gordon Brown, it requires an active self-sacrifice and heroism on his part, almost of a kind that we have no right to expect of him.'

Wright is a freelance thinker and High Modernist. A new MP, elected in 1992, he was a lecturer in politics and a theorist of ethical socialism, a political analyst with a good turn of phrase and the ability to subvert conventional wisdom. He once described the gloomy prediction of a fellow moderniser that Labour would lose a fifth successive election as 'much too optimistic'. He feared that Labour might win under Smith and be unprepared for government. During Blair's period of 'internal exile' in early 1994, Wright told him that he thought 'the black cars are coming whether we like it or not'.

Union Baronets For Blair

That first weekend after John Smith's death saw the start of another important part of the Blair campaign – the effort to persuade trade union leaders not to commit themselves in public to any of the possible candidates. Although the block vote had been abolished, it was still assumed that the backing of the big union machines was important and, until recently, it would have been expected that, despite their disagreements with his economic approach, the GMB and TGWU would back Gordon Brown. It was not yet clear how little influence union leaders had over their 4 million individual members who had one third of the vote in the leadership election.

The central figures in this initiative were John Monks, the new General Secretary of the Trades Union Congress, and Jack Dromey, national secretary of the Transport and General Workers Union who happens to be married to Harriet Harman. Their first objective was 'spin control' – trying to prevent an anti-Blair backlash story developing momentum in the media. That weekend they had to prevent a Prescott bandwagon picking up speed at the first conference of Unison, the new merged public sector union, in Bournemouth. Prescott was popular among the 2,000 activists and officials there.

Monday's newspapers were a tribute to their efforts. 'Unison favours Tony Blair as next Labour leader,' was the *Guardian*'s headline, a remarkable summary of a report which said: 'Among most delegates John Prescott received vocal support, but officials . . . were more cautious in private.' One of those officials would have been assistant general secretary Tom Sawyer, architect of Neil Kinnock's policy review and later Blair's choice as the party's new general secretary. When Blair saw the *Guardian*'s report he asked Dromey: 'Is that right?'

'It's half right,' replied Dromey. 'It'll soon be completely right.' He and Monks were confident that the more the decision was left to individual members, the better the result would be for Blair.

Their next objective was to prevent union executives making recommendations. Again, they were largely successful. Blair's own sponsors, the TGWU, turned out to be immune to the appeal of the 'new politics' and recommended Beckett (Dromey was a leading member of the internal opposition to the dominant old Left). But the other big general union, the GMB, eventually decided not to make a recommendation, as did Unison and MSF.

The Funeral

By the middle of the week after John Smith's death, the tensions began to show. Some of Gordon Brown's supporters imagined Peter Mandelson to be playing a double game when he told a number of Labour MPs in the Commons tea room on Monday and Tuesday that he was backing the shadow Chancellor. Brown's supporters thought he was exploiting his unpopularity in the parliamentary party to push wavering MPs towards Blair. In this atmosphere of paranoia one of Brown's most loyal lieutenants, Nigel Griffiths, launched a tactical strike on Wednesday, telling the London *Evening Standard* that there was 'dismay' among Labour MPs that Mandelson was canvassing for Blair. Griffiths – allegedly carpeted by a 'furious' Brown – then issued an immediate apology.

At the shadow Cabinet meeting that afternoon, Blair and Brown sat next to each other, chatting as if it were just another day. The meeting agreed that no contenders should declare until after the Euro-elections on 9 June.

While Blair and Brown managed to maintain decent relations in the shadow Cabinet room, Brown's supporters were busy, gently rubbishing the front runner. Journalists were being told, 'Gordon is the ideas man behind Tony', 'his speeches are so much more substantial' and 'Tony consults him before any important political decision'. But Brown's people were trying to hold back an avalanche. For example, the shadow Chancellor's deputy, Harriet Harman, had already indicated privately that she was backing Blair.

A week after John Smith's death, the entire Labour Party establishment took to the air to fly to Edinburgh for John Smith's funeral on Friday 20 May. Some of the grander ones went by private jet, former leaders Michael Foot and Neil Kinnock accepting a lift from the Labour-supporting publisher Paul Hamlyn. Brown and Blair and their respective retinues took the shuttle from Heathrow. There was an awkward encounter at the check-in, when Blair and his adviser

Anji Hunter arrived to find Team Brown (although not Brown himself, who had travelled earlier) in the queue ahead of them. It was obvious that Brown's economic adviser Ed Balls and his friends Geoff Mulgan and Barry Delaney were not going to the funeral. They were going to Edinburgh to talk to Brown about the leadership and advise him on his speech to the Wales Labour Party that weekend.

That night, Team Brown did indeed assemble at the shadow Chancellor's house in Edinburgh. They were joined by others in Brown's inner circle: his brother Andrew, a *Channel Four News* journalist, and Dr Colin Currie, an author of thrillers (under the name Colin Douglas) who helps write many of Brown's speeches. They discussed the leadership contest. Brown drily joked that when he met Blair at the funeral the next day he would ask him to be his campaign manager – an acknowledgement that his ally was in a commanding position. But their main task was to help draft Brown's speech for Sunday. This would be the shadow Chancellor's first chance to speak in public after the funeral, and would mark the opening of the 'phoney war', although obviously there could be no overt reference to the succession. He and his team worked on the speech until 3 am, and Brown started again at 6 o'clock the next morning.

The funeral service at the Smiths' parish church, Cluny, in Morningside, Edinburgh, was attended by Prime Minister John Major, former prime ministers Edward Heath and James Callaghan, and the leaders of all the other parliamentary parties, and was televised live. When the shadow Cabinet entered the church as a group, Gerald Kaufman thought that Blair looked different and said to Roy Hattersley: 'The mark is on him already.'

Alexander Irvine, the Labour peer who was head of Blair's legal chambers, delivered one tribute. He had known John Smith since they had studied law at Glasgow University in 1959:

He was then what he remained: a Highlander and so, to a

degree, a romantic; a Presbyterian, not a Puritan, reared in
the Church of Scotland; and a Labour Party family man.
He was driven by a set of moral imperatives which owed
everything to his inherited conscience.

Donald Dewar, another contemporary MA, LLB from
Glasgow University, also paid tribute, in which he captured
the national mood: 'The people have lost a friend – someone
who was on their side – and they know it.'[6]
That weekend John Smith was buried on the island of Iona
on the west coast of Scotland.

The Phoney War

After the funeral, the non-campaign became more visible.
But by now the real question was not who would win, but
who would run, and who would, or should, be Blair's deputy
leader.
It is not clear when Brown admitted defeat to himself. One
close supporter says he had all but decided not to run by the
Tuesday after John Smith's death. But he may have harboured
one of those 'small broken moments of hope' that Blair talked
about in his acceptance speech when he finally claimed victory. Brown clung to a romantic image of himself as a
politician whose empathy with the Labour movement could
yet inspire a surge of support. His speech in Swansea on the
Sunday after the funeral could be read both as a graceful
concession, or as a statement of claim.
The Wales Labour Party's annual conference was short-
ened to a single day, mostly devoted to paying respects to the
former leader. There was a simple condolence book for John
Smith at the back of the hall. Just to keep up appearances, a
few consensual motions were passed unanimously.
Originally, Blair had been listed to speak, and Brown had
not, but Brown had pushed himself onto the agenda, which

forced Blair to pull out. If they had both addressed the conference, it would have been portrayed as a head-to-head
hustings. Brown's behaviour considerably aggravated the tension in his relations with Blair.

Brown's speech was his most leaderly, and took the form
of an appeal for unity. It contained one strikingly lyrical
passage:

> To everything there is a season, and a time to every pur-
> pose. A time to mourn, and a time to renew. A time to
> reflect, and a time to move forward. A time to challenge,
> and a time to come together. A time to debate, and a time
> to unite. For us now more than ever before, this is the time
> to unite. (*Applause.*) Because we have travelled too far, too
> many miles together, for us now to lose sight of our
> destination. Together we have climbed too high for us not
> to achieve the summit. And it is near.

As Brown knew that Blair intended to run, there was a
clear implication to 'this is the time to unite'. However,
Brown's advisers did not discourage the newspapers from
reporting the speech as the opening shot of the campaign.

Partly because he was nervous, and partly because the
speech had been extensively changed at the last minute (half
a page of the text issued to journalists was in block capitals
half-an-inch high where the computer had apparently gone
haywire), Brown stumbled a few times. His speech was well
received, but the enthusiasm was contained. It 'didn't play on
TV', according to an observer with personal experience of the
same problem with Neil Kinnock's speeches: 'It was clearly
spoken to an audience and not the front room.' Journalists
noticed that Alun Michael, Blair's front-bench deputy, failed
to join the standing ovation. And Brown had nothing to say to
the press on the way out, except that he was 'glad to be in
Wales'.

The speech was seen as a pitch to the Left of the party,
which irritated some of Blair's allies. Glenys Kinnock, in the

second row, reportedly muttered 'that's more money, more money' every time Brown said something that implied public spending. The Left tilt was exploited by an anonymous Blair supporter in the shadow Cabinet, who told *The Times* that Blair had said that he would not compromise on his modernising beliefs, and 'will not be bending this way and that' to appeal to different sections of the party.

Blair's non-campaign was also raising its profile a notch. Mo Mowlam described herself to journalists as Blair's campaign manager, a role she had privately ascribed to herself on the day of John Smith's death. However, she almost immediately demoted herself, making the first mistake of Blair's campaign two days later. On a train to the Eastleigh by-election, she told Education Secretary John Patten that Blair was worried about the space for his family in 10 Downing Street. One Labour frontbencher suggested that the real question was whether Number Ten would be big enough for Mo Mowlam's mouth.

Blair gave his first speech of the non-campaign on Tuesday 24 May, to a conference on the family and crime. As he went in, he met the Welsh Secretary John Redwood, who said: 'I get the feeling they're more interested in you than in me.'

Blair began his speech by apologising for the media attention, which included four TV cameras. He said: 'I hadn't realised John Redwood was that popular.'

Blair spoke in polished seminar style, and offered a summary of his social moralism, an idea whose time had now come:

> The break-up of family and community bonds is intimately linked to the breakdown of law and order. Both family and community rely on notions of mutual respect and duty. It is in the family that we first learn to negotiate the boundaries of acceptable conduct and to recognise that we owe responsibilities to others as well as ourselves. We then build out from that family base to the community and beyond it to society as a whole. The values of a decent society are in

many ways the values of the family unit, which is why helping to re-establish good family and community life should
be a central objective of government policy, and that cannot be done without policies, especially in respect of
employment and education, that improve society as a
whole. We do not show our children respect or act respon-
sibly to them if we fail to provide them with the
opportunities they need, with a stake in the society in
which they live. Equally, we demand that respect and
responsibility from them in return.

He was beginning to connect his social moralism to
broader policies, and to identify education as a theme of his
unacknowledged campaign.

He sounded as different as possible from expectations of a
Labour politician. The contrast with Gordon Brown's speech
was deafening. Brown delivered moving oratory to a labour
movement gathering in Wales. Blair conducted a seminar
among academics in a London hotel.

At the National Executive meeting the next day, acting
leader Margaret Beckett made an unexpected announcement
which effectively threw away her chance of retaining the
deputy leadership. She said that she wanted an election for
deputy leader to take place at the same time as the leadership
election. It was normally an uncontested annual event, which
would have taken place at the October party conference, and
which need not have been affected by the succession of a
new leader. It was well known that John Prescott was itching
to challenge her, but was holding back because of the respect
she had gained during her conduct of the acting leadership.
Many National Executive members were baffled by her
announcement. Harriet Harman's face was 'a picture',
according to one of those present. Prescott and his campaign
manager Richard Caborn stayed up until 3am puzzling over
the implications of Beckett's move.

Gordon Brown, meanwhile, had worked out what Prescott
and Caborn could not. He looked 'bleak' at the meeting,

according to an observer, because he 'clearly worked out right away that she was going to run for both and lose both'. Beckett's only reason for holding both elections at the same time could be that she intended to run for the leadership, which could leave the deputy leadership vacant, so both posts would have to be contested at the same time. But that would allow Prescott to run, because he would no longer be challenging an admired incumbent. Brown realised that Prescott – who did not exactly agree with Brown about tax and economic policy – was likely to become deputy leader. For Brown, it added to his woes.

Gordon Does the Decent Thing

Gordon Brown's faint hopes that events would suddenly turn in his favour were fading. Donald Dewar, a close friend of both John Smith and Gordon Brown, played an important role in persuading Brown that he could not win. But some of Brown's supporters presented him with exaggerated estimates of his support among MPs, either because they were afraid of telling him the truth, or because they were traditionalists who wanted him to run to split the modernisers. Other Brown supporters were still telephoning union leaders to try to enlist them.

By now, however, the Brown phoney campaign's prime objective was to reinforce his position as shadow Chancellor. He had to be seen as a contender, and more of a contender than Robin Cook, who made no secret of the fact that he too wanted to be shadow Chancellor. Some of Blair's more calculating supporters were also coming round to the idea that Brown should stand, because they saw him as too cautious, and too influential with Blair. 'Perhaps it would have been better if Gordon had run,' says one. 'Not for Tony to humiliate him but to break the link. If Tony believes that he has a debt to Gordon, that's a damaging state of affairs.'

The week after his Swansea speech, the pressure on
Gordon Brown to declare his intentions was becoming
intense. It was clear to most people that he could not win, and
repeated assertions by his supporters to the contrary were
wearing thin. There would come a point where it would be
more damaging to stay in the race than to pull out. 'We're
really being drummed into this,' said one Brown supporter
who wanted to be released to declare for Blair, 'and we don't
like it.' This feeling was especially strong among Scottish
MPs who felt national loyalty to Brown, but who mostly privately backed Blair from the start.

On the evening of Thursday 26 May, Nick Brown told
Gordon Brown that he had to decide whether or not to run by
the weekend. They reviewed Nick Brown's list of Labour
MPs, marked G for Gordon Brown, T for Target, ? for don't
know and blank for supporters of other candidates. Nick
Brown claims there were fifty Gs on the list. However, he
was finding it impossible to ask Ts or ?s for their support
unless they could be assured that Gordon Brown was going to
run.

Gordon Brown asked Nick Brown to carry on canvassing
support over the weekend and suggested they review the situation on Bank Holiday Monday. But other supporters were
already preparing the ground for his pulling out. Some continued to insist to journalists that Brown's support was
growing. One talked about the importance of 'big personalities' who are not leaders – Ernest Bevin, Aneurin Bevan, Rab
Butler, Denis Healey.

That weekend the fullest possible test of opinion in the
leadership election was produced by BBC TV's *On The
Record*, with surveys of Labour Party members and MPs and
Euro-MPs. Taken together with a *Newsnight* poll of Labour-
supporting trade unionists, Blair had a convincing lead in all
three sections of the electoral college. Most significant was a
Gallup survey of party members.[7] The message for Brown
was clear:

Tony Blair	47%
John Prescott	15%
Gordon Brown	11%
Margaret Beckett	5%
Robin Cook	3%
Don't know	18%

It was also becoming obvious that shadow Trade and Industry Secretary Robin Cook would not be a candidate, with a surprisingly low 3 per cent. He was the two-time king-maker who now had thoughts of being king. He had been Neil Kinnock's campaign manager in 1983, and John Smith's in 1992. He was widely admired on the Left and centre of the party, and was respected by the Right. He was one of Labour's best parliamentary performers, and regularly came near the top of shadow Cabinet and National Executive elections. The previous week an activist in Swindon appeared to sum up the mood of the grass roots: 'My heart says Prescott, my head says Blair, so I'll probably vote for Cook.'[8]

Cook's hopes of the leadership actually faded on the weekend after John Smith's death. Chris Smith, his principal supporter in the shadow Cabinet, declared that he wanted a candidate who could appeal 'safely to all parts of the British electorate'.[9] This was a coded endorsement of Blair, the candidate who could stereotypically appeal to Southern floating voters. Chris Smith says of Cook: 'He jumped too late. He genuinely dithered about whether to stand or not for quite some time, and with hindsight I think if Robin had stood for deputy he might have done extremely well.' Cook, however, was not interested in being deputy leader.

Other potential candidates fell away. The shadow Foreign Secretary, Jack Cunningham, seems to have thought he was a serious candidate for the leadership, although he concealed his ambition with self-mocking irony. He had a solid base of support on the old Right of the parliamentary party, but had not performed well enough to avoid coming joint bottom in the shadow Cabinet elections the previous year.

Ken Livingstone, who had entertained daydreams of being the 'left-wing' candidate to succeed Neil Kinnock before he had even arrived in the House of Commons in 1987, admitted he could not muster the thirty-four nominations from MPs he needed to stand. Denzil Davies, whose career had ended six years before when he resigned as shadow Defence Secretary in a late-night telephone call to the Press Association, made a bid on a Euro-sceptical ticket. He persevered until forced out of the race, having secured only seven nominations by the deadline.

Blair's lead in the *On The Record* survey was so substantial that any last hopes Gordon Brown may have entertained of becoming leader (this time) were extinguished. Over that weekend at the end of May, Brown said in a speech to the Luton Labour Party that the party had to come before personal ambition. However, despite speaking to each other almost constantly, Blair was still uncertain of his friend's intentions. When the two of them met for dinner on Tuesday 31 May, at the minimalist Granita restaurant in Islington, Blair did not know what Brown was going to say.

The Granita dinner, or the 'Last Supper', became inscribed in political legend, mythologised as a moment of supreme self-sacrifice. In fact, its significance was as the moment when Brown chose to bow formally to the fact of Blair's impending victory. One journalist was slightly puzzled by what she thought were references to the Grim Eater, which might have been right from Brown's point of view. He did not eat much, and was seen later that night in Rodin's restaurant in Westminster enjoying a second dinner.

Brown had really decided to withdraw at another, secret dinner the night before. On Bank Holiday Monday, he dined at Joe Allen's restaurant in Covent Garden with his non-campaign manager Nick Brown and his press officer Charlie Whelan. The discussion was a run-through of what had already been recognised, after Nick Brown's weekend of trying to recruit supporters.

Gordon Brown said he knew he could win only by 'calling

on such dark and awful forces' that it would negate the attempt. It would mean having to portray Blair as SDP, non-Labour, anti-trade union. It would have been an unpleasant campaign which might have damaged the party's chances – and thus his own – of gaining office. 'There is no friendship at the top,' David Lloyd George is supposed to have said. In this case personal loyalty and self-interest coincided. Brown could not have won even by differentiating himself from his ally – he had slipped too far.

Tuesday's newspapers saw the paradoxical results of the Joe Allen's dinner: a spate of stories in the press alleging that Brown and Blair were level pegging among MPs and union leaders. This was pure nonsense and a tribute to the energy of Brown's supporters, especially his personal press officer, Charlie Whelan. The aim of this final push by Team Brown was to allow Gordon Brown to pull out from a position of strength, or at least dignity, rather than weakness.

Gordon Brown finally made the announcement by issuing a press release on Wednesday 1 June, on the grounds that news of the decision had 'leaked out'. His statement, issued at 3.30, said he would not contest the leadership and would support Blair. Neil Kinnock quickly expressed 'relief' at not being required to choose between them, on *Channel Four News*. The 'Brown pulls out' story was about as spontaneous as the Maastricht Treaty.

'He's bound to be tinged with regret,' said Donald Dewar on *Newsnight* that evening. This was a typically Dewarish understatement. Dewar hinted at the intensity of Brown's disappointment in a later interview: 'The word "driven" is often used. He's not sunny – which of us is? He works so hard it is difficult for the rest of us to live up to his high standard. If you're not on the right side of him, it can be tough.'[10]

While the relationship with Blair himself survived, Peter Mandelson was now on the wrong side of him, and had felt Brown's sharp temper a number of times since John Smith's death. Mandelson had dedicated himself to Blair's cause so abruptly that Brown resented his former ally's defection, and felt that Mandelson had been promoting Blair behind the scenes from the start. As a means of identifying a scapegoat, this charge had the advantage of being true.

The fundamentals remained, however. Regardless of the role of the cleverest spin doctor in Labour politics, Blair had made the running in the two years before John Smith's death. But Brown's position in the Labour Party is immensely strong, and his role in any future Labour government will be central. His chance may yet come – after all, James Callaghan lost to Harold Wilson in 1963 only to succeed him in 1976. Blair will owe much to Brown if Labour ever returns to government, and his party will owe him even more if he handles the nation's finances competently.

Notes

1. *John Smith: Life and Soul of the Party*, edited by Gordon Brown and James Naughtie, pp182–206.
2. Keith Dovkants, *Evening Standard*, 18 July 1994.
3. *Esquire*, June 1994.
4. *Woman's Own*, 21 June 1993.
5. *Mail on Sunday*, 20 February 1994.
6. *John Smith: Life and Soul of the Party*, pp20, 105.
7. BBC TV, *On The Record*, 29 May 1994. These findings were based on a sample of 471 members in twenty-two constituencies. In the event Blair's support was overestimated – partly because most party members did not think that Beckett would be a candidate for the leadership.
8. BBC TV, *Newsnight*, 23 May 1994.
9. BBC TV, *On The Record*, 15 May 1994.
10. BBC Radio 5, 9 June 1994.

17. MANDATE FOR CHANGE
The Public Campaign, June and July 1994

'The great task for political leaders is to show us the way. They have lost many of the old powers of direction and choice. But there remains the power of eloquence, of weaving a social vision that helps people make sense of their lives.'

Brown's self-sacrifice left the way clear for Blair, who was now regarded even more as the leader-apparent. Blair seemed curiously uncertain of the party's mood. The day after Brown withdrew, he spoke at a rally in Eastleigh to launch the final week of Labour's by-election campaign. He was reluctant to do it, and nervous, expecting the audience to be sceptical. He worked on his speech until the last minute, so that the media were only issued with 'extracts'. But he gave a strong performance to a packed and enthusiastic hall, and came away saying, according to one shadow Cabinet minister, and surely with some exaggeration, 'That's the best meeting I've ever done in my life.'

With ten days to go to the start of the official campaign, the shape of the contest became clearer. John Prescott, on BBC TV's *Question Time* the day after Brown withdrew, made it clear that he would run for the leadership. 'All elections require candidates,' he said, criticising the suggestion that

Blair should be elected unopposed. 'We had the controversy last year about extending the democratic process to more people to be involved in the election of the leader.'

The choice of candidates for deputy leader was more constrained than it looked. Some toyed with the suggestion that Harriet Harman, shadow Chief Secretary to the Treasury, should run for the deputy leadership. A 'ticket' of two middle-class modernisers might have been a bold stroke, as when Bill Clinton selected another young Southerner, Al Gore, as his running mate. However, she had not overcome the hostility of her fellow Labour MPs which had led to her ejection from the elected shadow Cabinet the previous autumn.

The real problem for Harman was the difficulty of challenging Margaret Beckett. It verged on disrespect to John Smith to question her right to continue in her post. John Prescott had said he would not run against her – although his positioning for the leadership contest was with both eyes firmly fixed on the deputy's job. Most MPs did not think that she would run for the leadership, even after she had given clear signs of her intentions. 'I assume people are going to act rationally,' said one shadow Cabinet member. 'I never thought she was going to run for leader.'

Beckett had already eyed the leadership when she thought John Smith might resign over one member, one vote at the 1993 conference. That was a misjudgment, both of the likelihood of Smith actually going and of the extent of her support. Now she misread the party again, by appearing to think it operated the US vice-presidential principle. The leader was dead; she was the leader. When she appeared on *Breakfast with Frost* on 22 May, she saw herself described as 'acting leader' on David Frost's tele-prompter, and asked for it to be changed to 'leader'. Which it was. There is, as she rightly pointed out, no such title as acting leader in Labour's constitution. But she did not ask Frost to use the phrase which *is* in the constitution, 'leader on a *pro tem* basis'.

Curiously for a politician with such a reputation for competence she seems to have misjudged how others saw her. She appeared not to have absorbed the significance of the 'Margaret Beckett Amendment'. This was another constitutional change approved unnoticed by the 1993 conference amid the drama over one member, one vote. With slightly macabre forethought, it was designed to prevent what had just happened from happening when Labour was in government. It laid down that if a Labour Prime Minister became 'permanently unavailable', the deputy leader of the party would *not* automatically stand in until a successor were elected. Instead, the Cabinet would choose a new Prime Minister from among its number, until the election of a new leader.

In the week leading up to the European elections, she firmly decided to put herself forward for the leadership, despite advice to the contrary from every high-ranking politician who chose to give it. It was nearly an act of attractive bravery, reminiscent of Margaret Thatcher's in 1975, because she appeared to stand no chance of winning. That in itself might not have mattered, but it risked losing the deputy leadership. John Prescott had already said he would not challenge her for the deputy leadership, but her bid for the leadership allowed him to argue that she had vacated that position. Perhaps she did not want it.

So it was that the first British 'primary' election had three candidates for two jobs: John Prescott, Margaret Beckett and Tony Blair. Rory Bremner called them the Lion, the Witch and the Wardrobe.

Before that contest could start, there were other elections to win. The European elections were combined with five by-elections. The day before polling, the Liberal Democrat candidate in one of them, Newham North East, Alec Kellaway, announced he was joining the Labour Party. He said the imminent election of Tony Blair as Labour leader had convinced him, a former Labour defector to the SDP, that it was time to come home (see pp63–4). His was the first in a trickle of defections, including some from the Conservatives, among candidates, local councillors and peers.

Labour held all four of its by-election seats, with hugely-increased majorities, and even pushed the Conservatives into third place in Eastleigh, a formerly safe Conservative seat outside Southampton which the Liberal Democrats took with a 22 per cent swing.

The votes in the European elections were not counted until Sunday, when most continental countries voted. When the results were announced, Labour had won sixty-two of the eighty-seven British seats in the European Parliament. The party's share of the vote, 44 per cent, was its greatest since direct European elections began in 1979, but was still short of expectations for mid-term elections – widely seen as a 'protest opportunity' – against such an unpopular government.

It's Over – and They're Off

The morning of Friday 10 June 1994 saw the official start of the Labour leadership campaign. John Prescott and Margaret Beckett held consecutive news conferences in the House of Commons. They both announced that they were seeking nominations for both leader and deputy leader. For Prescott's conference, his assistant Steve Hardwick stood on a chair at the side of the crowded room, handing out copies of the two-page statement. Photographers climbed onto two tables stacked on top of each other at the back.

'We've heard a lot about full and fulfilling employment,' Prescott growled, taking a sideswipe at Gordon Brown and setting out his theme – full employment, with no qualifying 'warm words'. 'The electorate want us to distinguish between rhetoric and reality,' he said, as if full employment was not rhetoric. The BBC's Kim Catcheside asked: 'What's your USP?' When he had affected to work out what it meant (unique selling proposition), he replied: 'Me.'

By contrast, Beckett's appeal was charmless and devoid of political content: 'For two years I have done five jobs.' Basking all-too-evidently in the glory of standing in for John

Smith – she had just attended D-Day commemorations in France – she declared:

> I've had hundreds of letters calling on me to put my name forward and much pressure not only from members of the party but from the public to stand. This has been particularly evident among women, including, earlier this week, in Portsmouth and in Normandy, whose votes Labour needs to win. I have therefore decided to offer myself for nomination to continue to lead the Labour Party.

The votes of women in Normandy, or Portsmouth for that matter, were never going to be enough to save her.

She seemed aware that she risked winning neither the leadership nor the deputy leadership. 'I fully accept that I could fall through the cracks,' she said, fatalistically, fuelling suspicions that she did not really want the deputy leadership anyway.

Despite Prescott's somewhat nostalgic appeal, Beckett managed to appear more backward-looking. In answer to a question on full employment, she said: 'We should do what we sought to do after the war – aim for full employment, in different conditions.' And, asked what her vision was, she said: 'My vision is of the party doing what it did so successfully after the war.'

The spy from Team Blair, observing from the back, did not see anything at either news conference to threaten the frontrunner's progress over the next six weeks.

Blair launched his campaign formally the next day. On a clear sunny morning, he came to Trimdon Labour Club in his Sedgefield constituency to announce his candidature. The contrast with the enclosed, metropolitan news conferences of Prescott and Beckett could not have been more marked. Like so many good ideas, it seemed the obvious thing to do once it had been done. It was Peter Mandelson's idea.

The people there were a convincing advertisement for the Sedgefield mass membership party: from pensioners to children, a mixture of traditional Geordie Labour culture with what Blair would soon start calling 'New Labour'. They burst into applause and leapt to their feet when he came in. When they sat down again, Blair said: 'Good morning, everyone.' They replied: 'Good morning.' They applauded Old Labour, when Blair pledged to remove mass unemployment and defeat the decaying and obsolete Tories, and, in turn, New Labour, when he called for a crusade against crime.

This time he *was* nervous. His delivery was shouted, and he stumbled a few times, but it did not matter. There was one thing they had come to hear, and they gave it the loudest cheer: 'This morning I am announcing my candidature for the position of Leader of the Labour Party.'

After Blair's speech, Peter Brookes, one of the 'Famous Five' who watched football on television with Blair in 1983, got to his feet and said: 'He's never let us down, and he won't let the country down.' The meeting, chaired by another of the Five, John Burton, was nominally the monthly General Committee of the Sedgefield Labour Party, but it bore only a tenuous resemblance to the rituals of Labour tradition. Instead of a motion to nominate Blair for the leadership being proposed and seconded, Burton said he assumed the nomination was unanimous, and there was enthusiastic applause rather than a vote. Blair said with a broad smile: 'I accept.' The meeting ended, and the hall was given over to a wedding reception.

Blair's Two Campaign Teams

After this sparkling start, the Blair campaign stumbled. Most outside observers would not have noticed anything amiss, but Blair failed to live up to his own high standards in his first two big tests on television. He was nervous again, and made an awkward start to his first television interview on BBC TV's *Breakfast with Frost*. David Frost started by welcoming 'the lead guitarist of the Ugly Rumours'.

'Lead singer, actually,' Blair replied, rather flatly. It was hardly worth a second thought, but it seemed to unsettle him as he threaded rather uncomfortably through the rest of Frost's unpredictable questions.

He was unable, for example, to explain why Gordon Brown had withdrawn from the election. Frost asked: 'He thought you were more of a winner than he was?'

'I don't think it's a question of thinking I was more of a winner, but we had to decide what we thought was in the best interests of the party.' The best interests of the party momentarily appeared not to include winning the next General Election.

Blair's under-performance would not have mattered if he had not been engaged at the same time in negotiations with BBC TV's *Panorama*, which was trying to organise a hustings with the three candidates the next day. All three were due to speak to the GMB union conference in Blackpool. Blair did not want to take part, as he felt unprepared, and his staff had already told the BBC that he would not do so. However, he changed his mind when GMB general secretary John Edmonds telephoned him directly. Edmonds says: 'I phoned him to make it clear that I didn't give a monkey's whether he took part in the *Panorama* debate. My first, second and only concern was that he should come to speak to the conference.' If Blair felt under pressure to take part in the debate, 'then he entirely misunderstood what I was saying'.

The *Panorama* programme could not have gone ahead without Blair, and he did not need to do it, but he agreed anyway. He was extremely nervous beforehand, reported to be white and looking ill. This was reflected in another under-par performance. He regurgitated what sounded like ready-prepared passages, and looked uncomfortable. In his anxiety to head off John Prescott's challenge on full employment, he mangled his 'line to take' with Prescottian syntax:

It's not just jobs we want, it is quality at the workplace for those in employment as well as those that are unemployed, and I don't believe you can achieve that in a modern society unless we understand that it is in the education, the skills, the talent of people, and if we're not prepared to make that commitment to education, then we will never succeed.

Blair looked isolated at one end, while Prescott, who had drawn the middle position by lot, looked as if he were amiably holding the ring in a unifying role, the confident bridge-building deputy between the two 'leadership' candidates. At one point in the debate Prescott sidled up to Blair with a stage grin, and when Blair was asked if he feared Prescott might 'get them in the gut when you're trying to get them in the head', Prescott prompted: 'They're not alternatives.' Blair agreed – 'Exactly so, they're not alternatives, we need heart and head in the Labour Party.'

Margaret Beckett easily avoided the awkward questions about her views on one member, one vote and the Maastricht Treaty. She even defused an attempt to split Prescott and Blair with a joke at her own expense, saying that Prescott had 'even called me one of the "beautiful people" and I pointed out he couldn't be more wrong'.

Prescott commented, 'We're going to love each other to death.'

He had been well briefed and rehearsed beforehand by his campaign manager Richard Caborn, MP for Sheffield Central. 'The *Panorama* programme was very good for us,' Caborn says. 'The body language was very important, and I said to John, "Remember to shake hands at the end."'

Although he was under par, Blair's par is relatively high, and much of his performance was clear and effective. He exploited his distinctive themes of crime and the family. But he was furious with himself for having agreed to take part at all. Immediately after the debate, he telephoned Peter Mandelson, campaign adviser-in-chief. There followed a pruning of Blair's media engagements, which allowed time to regroup, and the campaign was more or less technically flaw-less after that.

The extraordinary fact about Mandelson's role in the cam-paign is that, officially, he did not exist. The official campaign team had been unveiled on the day of Blair's announcement. Mo Mowlam was joined by Jack Straw as joint campaign manager. The campaign committee was made up of Peter Kilfoyle, Andrew Smith, the fraternal delegate from Gordon Brown's Treasury team, Barry Cox, the television executive and only member from outside Westminster, who was respon-sible for fundraising, and Anji Hunter, head of Blair's office. The committee met every morning, but the decisions that mattered – about media strategy and speeches – were taken elsewhere.

The central figure in the 'real' Blair campaign was Mandelson. The transparent fiction that Mandelson was 'not involved' was necessary because Mowlam and Kilfoyle were only two of many who told Blair that they would not work for him if Mandelson had anything to do with the campaign. This gave rise to bizarre incidents. In the week after Smith's death, Mowlam threatened to sue a newspaper if it reported that Mandelson was working for the Blair campaign. The paper's editor was persuaded that the story was untrue, and deleted all references to Mandelson from the article.

The hostility to Mandelson meant an elaborate deception had to be maintained. The young backroom boys, Tom Restrick, David Miliband, Tim Allan and Peter Hyman, acted as the interface between the formal campaign and Mandelson. Restrick, a former BBC TV producer, and Miliband, working at the leftish think-tank, the Institute for Public Policy Research, were friends from Oxford University, where they both took Firsts in Philosophy, Politics and Economics. Allan returned to Blair's office from a brief spell as a researcher on Channel 4's *A Week In Politics*, and Hyman transferred from Donald Dewar's office. The four regularly met Mandelson secretly at Blair's house in Islington and in Commons meeting rooms. 'Bobby' was not just a nickname for Mandelson, it was an essential codename in their office conversations.

Most of the official campaign team gradually discovered Mandelson's role, even if they pretended they did not. Kilfoyle says: 'There was always a feeling that there were other focal points outside that campaign team.' Some MPs were disillusioned by what they saw as Peter Mandelson's Restoration, but they were mistaken to think that he had ever been exiled from the court. He was the one adviser whose judgment of day-to-day media handling Blair could absolutely trust.

Most Westminster journalists knew about Mandelson's involvement too. It was extraordinary that it was barely reported until after the campaign. The silence was only broken by Blair himself on the day of his election, when he thanked 'Bobby' at his victory party. Had the secret been revealed earlier, Blair's vote would undoubtedly have been lower, because some MPs would not have voted for him if they had known how much he relied on Mandelson.

Cox, meanwhile, had raised funds to employ several staff for the Blair campaign, to rent an office and to produce a glossy leaflet for distribution among party members and trade unionists. It was called *Principle, Purpose, Power*, as if merely putting the first and third words in the title would resolve any perceived contradiction between them. The title was the work of Chris Powell, an advertising executive who worked for the Labour Party when Mandelson was director of communications. (He is also middle brother of Charles, Margaret Thatcher's Private Secretary, and Jonathan, soon to be appointed Blair's Chief of Staff.) The text was written by Alastair Campbell, then still Assistant Editor of *Today* newspaper. Their roles were not secret; they were members of the broader campaign team. As was Philip Gould, a freelance political consultant, again a Mandelson associate, who carried out small-scale opinion polling.

The final member of the broader team was Cherie. She has always been ambitious on her husband's behalf. As their

lawyer friend Charles Falconer puts it, 'She is utterly committed to Tony's ambitions.'[1] Just before John Smith's death,
she said:

> If I didn't actually believe in what Tony was doing it would
> be far more difficult to cope. But I'm very proud of him. I
> think that he's got a lot to offer and I really want him to
> succeed. The fact that Tony's fairly famous and I'm not
> doesn't bother me at all. I'm well paid and highly regarded
> in my own field.[2]

Tony Blair may have thought about his children, but says
he did not hesitate to stand for the leadership on her account.
'Cherie was in no doubt that for the Labour Party it was the
right thing to do.'[3] Once she had ensured that he would be a
candidate, however, she does not appear to have been cen-
trally involved in the leadership campaign.

John Prescott Climbs on Board

When the twelve-year-old Tony Blair stood as the
Conservative in his private school's mock election in March
1966, John Prescott, twenty-eight, was Labour candidate for
Southport in the real election. He was organising a dock
strike as a member of the National Union of Seamen, and was
denounced that summer by Prime Minister Harold Wilson as
one of 'a tightly knit group of politically motivated men who,
as the last General Election showed, utterly failed to secure
acceptance of their views by the British electorate'. He meant
they were Communists, which Prescott was not, but he could
hardly say so, as Prescott had been an official Labour candidate.[4]

Prescott left Ellesmere Port Secondary Modern school at
fifteen and trained as a chef, before working as a steward in
the merchant navy. The former Conservative minister Alan

Clark once said, 'The reason John Prescott became a socialist was probably because he met someone like me when he
was a steward on a ship,' and there is little doubt that the
experience radicalised him. But he also had 'modernising'
tendencies, which had been overlooked during a long-running
personal feud with Neil Kinnock.

Prescott was also a friend of Blair's father-in-law, Tony
Booth. Before the 1992 election, the two were a popular
double-act at union-organised rallies. Prescott would play Alf
Garnett, the racist working-class Tory bigot, while Booth
played his character from *Till Death Us Do Part*, Garnett's
militant socialist son-in-law.

Even so, Blair and Prescott make an unlikely leadership
team, and one which would have been unthinkable only eighteen months earlier. At the end of 1992, they were locked in
bitter dispute about the lessons of Labour's defeat, Clinton's
victory and the future direction of the party. But, as they
worked together on the Union Links Review Group, Blair
seems to have realised that Prescott's main motivation was a
desire to be loved and to have the confidence of the leader, a
confidence he repaid with determined loyalty. 'At the beginning of the campaign, if you'd said I would vote for John
Prescott, I would have said, "Don't be absurd",' says Roy
Hattersley. 'Prescott has grown beyond all belief and nearly
beyond recognition.'

Blair also drew the lesson of his dismay at Prescott's success in winning the heart of the party in his speech urging one
member, one vote at the 1993 conference, and his conse-
quent sitting at John Smith's right hand.

Blair was in any case hardly spoilt for choice of deputy
leader. For factional Kinnockites the charge sheet against
Margaret Beckett was longer. At the famous *Tribune* rally at
the 1981 party conference after Tony Benn had been defeated
for the deputy leadership, as Margaret Jackson she had vilified
Neil Kinnock for abstaining. Unlike Prescott, she never had a
following among the 'soft' Left. She had been rehabilitated by
the resolutely unfactional John Smith as shadow Chancellor,

and raised to the deputy leadership by him. For some 'modernisers', her disloyalty to Smith over one member, one vote at the 1993 conference was therefore all the more unforgivable.

Blair privately shared this less-than-generous assessment of Beckett, but had to be prepared to work with her as he was not in much of a position to influence the party's choice. During the leadership campaign, Beckett continued to argue for the trade unions to have a 'collective voice' – that is, block votes – in the Labour Party.[5] On that issue Blair's preference was clear. So the contest was between a traditionalist who had been loyal to John Smith over one member, one vote, and disloyal on economic policy, and one who had been the opposite. In making his choice, Blair was under fierce pressure from Gordon Brown on economic policy.

Prescott had engaged in a sustained course of conduct prejudicial to Brown's 'New Economics'. He opposed the Maastricht Treaty and a European single currency. He was also the chief opponent in the shadow Cabinet, with David Blunkett, of Brown's refusal to allow the possibility of general tax increases. Unlike Blunkett, however, he did not keep his disagreements within the confines of the shadow Cabinet and National Executive. He infuriated Brown by cutting through the shadow Chancellor's evasion on whether Labour would impose a top rate of income tax above the present one: 'There's certainly going to have to be a higher top rate than we have.'[6] Not that anyone was in any doubt, but Brown did not want it said, because the next question was, 'At what level?' – and he did not want the Conservative press to make up the answer.

Prescott continued to air his disagreement with Blair and Brown on tax during the leadership campaign. 'If everybody is going to make an effort to get our people back to work, that will involve tax payments as well as the new forms of borrowing,' he told *The Times* (29 June 1994). He repeatedly said that he would reverse the £1,000 in tax cuts that the top 1 per cent had enjoyed under the Conservatives and use the funds for training young people.[7] Brown's office sent him more than one memo during the campaign, reminding him of policy agreed by the shadow Cabinet and National Executive. Beckett, meanwhile, campaigned on the theme that the National Health Service would never have been built if the postwar Labour government had worried about where 'every last tuppence' was coming from, but was more careful not to step over the party line.

At the start of the official leadership campaign, Beckett was the favourite for the deputy leadership, nominated by Brown, most of the shadow Cabinet and Kinnock (his feud with Prescott was more recent than his denunciation by Beckett). Blair and one of his campaign managers, Jack Straw, remained neutral and did not nominate. But Blair's other campaign manager, Mo Mowlam, was so irritated by Brown's endorsement of Beckett – which could have been seen as the indirect seal of Blair's approval – that she nominated Prescott. Thus a delicate balance was maintained.

The decisive event in tilting Blair privately to Prescott, in defiance of Gordon Brown's reservations, occurred early on, on the evening that nominations for the leadership election closed. In an election which had seen almost every stage pre-empted, the formal campaign between the validly nominated candidates started at last. After the GMB union had jumped the gun with the *Panorama* debate, the rival Transport and General Workers Union now held its Leadership Election Debate at the Queen Elizabeth II conference centre opposite Westminster Abbey. It was a rather flat affair. Blair was no longer nervous, but he did not say anything new. His most striking comment in a fifteen-minute opening statement was to claim the mantle of 'the party of law and order' from the Conservatives: 'It is – and I am proud of this – our party that is backing up the police in their efforts to fight crime.'

The significant issue of the debate, however, was trade union law. Blair said, 'I don't agree that we should argue to repeal all trade union law' since 1979. Most of the audience were members of the TGWU's Left-controlled lay executive, but only two people hissed, and then it was under their breath. It was all rather different from the howling denunciations of an earlier age of Labour politics.

Beckett took a conspicuously different line. She opened her statement by announcing, 'Margaret Beckett, TGWU Region 5', to the partisan cheers of the labour movement's atavistic tendency. In answer to the same question, she said, 'We have to get rid of the framework put in place by the Tories.' It was a crude appeal to special interests, and did much to convince Blair that Prescott would be a better deputy leader – especially when she repeated it on the BBC Radio 4 *Today* programme the next morning, saying, 'There could well be a need just to sweep the board clear and start again.'

Prescott had famously said, 'It all has to go', at the time when Blair was changing Labour's stance on Tory trade union law in 1989.[8] But now he trimmed to: 'We will have to change quite considerably the trade union legislation.' And said change was needed to come into line with the European Social Chapter. It was an important nuance.

Blair made his view clear in his first conference speech as leader, four months later:

> I have heard people saying a Labour government should repeal all the Tory trade union laws. Now, there is not a single person in this country who believes that we shall actually do it. No one believes strike ballots should be abandoned. So why do we say it? We shouldn't, and I won't.

This was not the only reason for preferring Prescott, of course. His public persona had softened as John Smith drew him into his collegiate leadership, and had become less frightening to the middle classes, while he remained an effective and engaging performer.

Beckett's performance, even in front of the 'home crowd' at the TGWU hustings, lacked lustre. Nevertheless, the union executive, meeting immediately afterwards, decided to recommend her to their members. It was a forlorn effort: although the TGWU membership gave Beckett her best result, 33.5 per cent, she was still beaten by Blair on 44.0 per cent. (There is no record of how her own TGWU Region 5 voted.)

Her fellow traditionalist Prescott, meanwhile, was happily exploiting the new politics, running an energetic campaign for the deputy leadership, aiming his appeal as a mass politician at the four and a half million trade union members entitled to vote. His campaign manager Richard Caborn explains the strategy:

> We decided that we had a very simple message. Full employment was our only issue. We didn't pay any attention to the other candidates. It became shaky after ten days. People said you've only got one theme. But we stuck to it, and it came through. We took the view that you've got four and a half million people, you've got to stick to a simple message . . . I don't think we turned down any TV or radio interview. And all on less than £10,000.

(Blair spent £79,000, which came from donations from individuals, including sums of up to £5,000 from rich individuals such as the former SDP benefactor David Sainsbury.)

However, Blair's move towards Prescott as his favoured deputy was discreet until the last two weeks of the campaign – in other words, until it became reasonably clear that Prescott was going to win. Gordon Brown continued to try to persuade Blair not to back him, and the issue provoked another row with Peter Mandelson. The Sunday papers on 10 July ran stories which suggested that Beckett would lose. When Brown saw the early editions the night before, he rounded on Mandelson, accusing him of briefing journalists in Prescott's favour.

Brown's case had just been strengthened by a renewed outbreak of Prescott's Euro-scepticism. He was interviewed by a panel of experts as potential Prime Minister on BBC TV's *Newsnight* on 5 July. When asked, 'You don't want a single currency?' Prescott said, 'I'm not a fan of the single currency, no.' This prosaic admission was the flat opposite of party policy – repeated by Blair in an interview in *The Times* and in a speech on European policy the next day – which was in favour of a single currency in principle. Indeed, Blair went further in *The Times*, insisting that Labour must be the pro-European party and must not trim to prevailing scepticism. Although the newspapers mostly ignored Prescott's candid disagreement, Brown feared that such differing views in the leadership team might be damaging in the long run.

However, it was too late to hold back the tide, now running strongly in Prescott's favour. Once again, the Sedgefield posse acted as Blair's deniable line of communication. At the Darlington hustings on 11 July, dominated by a huge contingent from neighbouring Sedgefield, Blair's local party chairman, John Burton, spoke to Prescott: 'I know Tony Blair can't speak to you, but I wanted to let you know you had support in the Sedgefield constituency.'

Some senior Conservative strategists privately cheered Prescott on. As deputy leader, he seems determined to be as loyal as possible, but his election contained significant risks for Blair. Above all, his sceptical hostility to European integration has pushed the fault-line in the Labour Party to the top. Initially, however, the publicists' version of the Blair–Prescott relationship passed into conventional mythology – the complementary opposites, middle-class public schoolboy and working-class product of a secondary modern, mod and trad, working in harmony. Just because they are such an unlikely team who have evidently grown to respect each other, however, does not mean that the tensions will not weaken the Labour Party at the next General Election or in government.

Mandate for Change

Blair's formal campaign was remarkable for two things: the utter blandness of his platform, and the favourable media coverage it received. In fact the leadership campaign as a whole escaped much analysis of the issues. The main differences pointed up during the campaign were those selected by the candidates themselves, such as John Prescott's advocacy of targets for reducing unemployment. The potentially damaging differences between them on Europe, tax and party reform remained little examined.

The media's failure to analyse Blair's platform is surprising in the light of the refrain, 'Where's the beef?' There was some anxiety in the Blair campaign over how to respond. One of Blair's early decisions was that he should not go beyond existing party policy. However, it was occasionally argued that Blair needed one or two new symbolic policies that would define the positive modernising programme. Education policy was an obvious candidate, as 'education and training' was central to the modernisers' economic analysis. It was, like law and order, a chance to exploit Conservative weakness on a middle-class concern. And it was one of the few areas where the Liberal Democrats had made any impression.

Blair had already marked out education as 'vital' to his personal crusade to build strong families and strong communities in his first speech after John Smith's death. He said, 'We should not be afraid of using the education system actively to promote good parenting', and described nursery education as 'the best investment a country can make'.[9]

The 'beef' question became acute in the drafting of Blair's campaign statement. Blair and his team at first assumed that the task of setting out his personal manifesto would be an exhilarating one. At last, he would be able to set out where he wanted to take the party. But, in fact, without John Smith's conservatism to overcome, the modernisers' programme had lost its focus.

The drafting of the document also exposed the youth of

some of Blair's team. Some were unversed in the recent history of the Labour Party, let alone the last Labour government. Roy Hattersley recalls that Tony Blair wanted a copy of his 1987 book, *Choose Freedom*, an elegant essay on libertarian socialism:

> When he was writing his statement, one of the children who was working for him came over to one of the children who works for me and said: 'Tony's looking for a book called *Choose Freedom*, have you heard of it?' And the child who was working for me said: 'No I haven't, Roy Hattersley never has any of those obscure things.' I think it was about two days later he said to me: 'Tony's looking for a book called *Choose Freedom*, have you ever heard of it?' So I was able to say: 'Yes, and what's more I've got a few remaindered copies in the cupboard.' So I sent him a copy.

The first draft of Blair's manifesto was written by Andrew Smith, an MP in Gordon Brown's Treasury team, and David Miliband, later to join Blair's office as policy chief. Then it suffered a sort of 'You've got to have something about the United Nations' syndrome, as everyone from the shadow Cabinet downwards commented on drafts. Martin Kettle, a friendly journalist on the *Guardian*, rewrote it. The final document, *Change and National Renewal*, ran to 5,000 words, but all it did was dress up existing Labour policy in what John Prescott derided as 'warm words'. Caution had prevailed: with the campaign running smoothly, it was argued, why frighten the horses?

The document's thinness was evident as Blair's campaign team invented two themes to define what the document was about, just before it was launched on 23 June at Church House, Westminster. In the airy room overlooking Dean's Yard and Westminster school, Blair set them out: 'The twin engines of national renewal for the next Labour government must be the modernisation of industry . . . and lifelong education and learning available to all.' The first, 'the modernisation of industry', was a curiously Wilsonian phrase at a tangent to the economic section of the document. The second, the most substantial plank of Blair's platform, had been garbled by the 'warm words committee'. The tautologous 'education and learning' had been coined to avoid the usual pairing of education with 'training', which Labour Party research had shown to be a 'cold' word.

'Education is at the heart of our project for national renewal,' the document declared boldly. But this declaration had been 'liberated', as Blair put it in another context, 'from particular policy prescriptions'. Nursery education 'for every three and four year old whose parents want it' was 'an objective' without a deadline. This was party policy. The document was in favour of good schools and against bad schools (while recognising the 'challenges' of their 'surrounding social environment'). It wanted to 'overcome the debilitating divide between academic and vocational courses', which Harold Wilson promised to do in 1963, and it wanted to 'make a reality of lifelong learning', enhancing the skills of people in work. But how?

The novelty of Blair himself, however, was enough to distract journalists from a document which had little to say, but said a little about everything. His performance at the news conference was sharp, with just a hint of a White House briefing. He stood at a podium at the front and fielded all questions himself, while his campaign managers, Jack Straw and Mo Mowlam sat to one side to 'dress the set'. The journalists had come to enjoy the show, and found the gravitational force around the Man of Destiny too beguiling to resist.

Blair's most passionate answer was to an Austrian radio journalist who asked if it was not disastrous to do away with the cloth cap image. No, said Blair. 'The hope of a better life for your children than you yourself had – that used to be the Labour dream, and will be the Labour dream again.' This is instantly recognisable as – the American Dream.

It was subtly different from a dream he had dreamt in the *Daily Mirror* the week before: 'It's about taking the lives of

ordinary people and developing their extraordinary potential. It is about people having sufficient hope to have
ambitions for themselves and for their families.'[10] Blair
described this as the 'British Dream', and it does indeed echo
Aneurin Bevan's complaint against the 'poverty of aspiration'
of the British working class.

The weekend after launching *Change and National Renewal*,
Blair did begin to move – cautiously – beyond party policy. In
a television interview on 26 June, he became animated just
once, when he declared:

> Under the next Labour government, if I'm leading it, edu-
> cation is *there*, right at the heart, and the whole business of
> government would be to make sure that we raise the skills
> and talent of people because that raises their ambitions, it
> raises their horizons, and it allows them to make the most
> of their own lives.[11]

He contradicted the party line by accepting the principle of
government policy on testing and school league tables: 'It is
absolutely vital that parents get as much information as possible.' This was the only issue during the leadership campaign
on which Blair stood against party policy.

It is revealing that this one example of independence
involved accepting the Conservative government's changes,
rather than giving substance to the priorities of 'New Labour'
with a novel proposal.

A positive signal could have been sent by promising nursery education for all by the end of a five-year parliament, a
possible pledge which by coincidence was discussed by the
party's Joint Policy Committee on the day after Blair's interview. But the committee decided not to put a timetable on its
'objective', because that would have been a firm promise to
spend public money. Blair stuck to Gordon Brown's line that
it was too early for that.

Rhetorically, however, Blair remained a big spender. One
of his finest sound-bites, delivered at the TGWU debate on

16 June, was his commitment to 'the best obtainable system of nursery education and care – so no one has to choose between the work they need and the family they love'. Using a phrase from Clause IV – 'the best obtainable system' – was a nice touch.[12] In a speech devoted to the subject of education on 4 July, he repeated an implausible finding from the United States that every dollar invested in pre-school education produces a return of seven dollars. What is the point of citing a spurious 'fact' like that if you are *not* prepared to find the money for nursery schools for all who want them?

Thus Blair won the leadership on a platform of 'change' with only the vaguest outline of what the change might involve, apart from changing some of Labour's policies to accommodate Conservative changes. It turned out that the shift of style, language and priorities which he represented was dramatic enough to avoid awkward questions. Blair was hailed as so different from political life as we know it that detailed position papers seemed unnecessary.

As he acknowledged in his first conference speech, many Labour Party members voted for him because they thought he could win, not because they believed in what he was doing. In the *On The Record* survey at the end of May, 86 per cent of party members described Blair as 'a winner', but by a 46–42 per cent margin they thought he was a social democrat rather than a socialist. Unlike Foot and Kinnock, but like Gaitskell and Wilson, Blair's relationship with his members is based on respect rather than affection. His unwillingness to be explicit with the party, however, could rebound later.

At the time, Blair responded to the charge of vacuity directly. He said it would be a mistake to write the Labour Party manifesto two or three years before a General Election – 'We've done that before.' But he also said:

> We shouldn't get bounced by the Tories or a bit of twittering in various parts of the media, who say, 'If you don't produce all your detailed policies then we can't take you seriously.' Rubbish. Out there, what the public actually

want is a clear vision of what Britain would look like and a
clear set of ideas, and those are the things that I want to set
out now. The detailed policy work will come, but it should
come within that intellectual and political framework.[13]

In this he was happy to admit to learning a lesson from
Margaret Thatcher, whose 'clarity' and 'conviction' he
admired a number of times during the campaign. It is certainly true that one of the more significant qualities of a
national leader is the ability to tell a country 'stories' about
itself which make sense of what a leader and a party are trying to achieve. Andrew Marr wrote before the official
campaign began: 'The great task for political leaders is to
show us the way. They have lost many of the old powers of
direction and choice. But there remains the power of eloquence, of weaving a social vision that helps people make
sense of their lives.'[14]

Indeed, much Conservative dissatisfaction with John Major
seemed bound up in his non-visionary style. But Major was
determined to compete on his own ground. In his 1994 conference speech he declared: 'Alongside the vision thing, I
must tell you that I remain rather attached to the "action"
thing. To the "practical" thing.'

Blair's homilies of families and community, of opportunity, of new versus old, even of the British Dream, however
derivative, are thin compared to Thatcher's. But simplicity is
essential. One of the concepts which Blair had discussed with
Bill Clinton's pollster, Stanley Greenberg, was that of 'low
information rationality'. This is the idea that voters behave
rationally, but on the basis of little information. Greenberg
explained:

People don't have a lot of time for politics, so they develop
a story out of a small set of facts. We spent a lot of time
thinking about what were the small set of facts that would
enable people to tell the story that was consistent with our
message and consistent with our candidate. So it was

important to tell the story that Bill Clinton came from Hope, Arkansas, small town, working class family, worked hard, did well. What it said was that he believed in work and that work was the route to success.

The accusation that Blair is shallow misses the point. His intelligence is sharp, pragmatic and simplifying. What is more important is the danger of a gap between rhetoric and reality, with all the potential for disappointment which Clinton, for example, has fulfilled so richly. Blair's campaign for the leadership was important for confirming the fact that he is a politician who is at least *capable* of winning a General Election although Blair's belief that it was a 'dry run' for the rigours of a General Election campaign is touchingly naive. It told us less about his quality as a potential Prime Minister. To judge that, we need to assess his brief record as Leader of the Opposition.

Election of Leader and Deputy Leader of the Labour Party, 21 July 1994

	Total	MPs and Euro-MPs	Party members	Labour-supporting trade unionists*
Leader				
Tony Blair	57.0%	60.5%	58.2%	52.3%
John Prescott	24.1%	19.6%	24.4%	28.4%
Margaret Beckett	18.9%	19.9%	17.4%	19.3%
Deputy Leader				
John Prescott	56.5%	53.7%	59.4%	56.6%
Margaret Beckett	43.5%	46.3%	40.6%	43.4%
Votes cast	952,109	327	172,356	779,426
Turnout		98.8%	69.1%	19.5%

*And Labour-supporting members of affiliated socialist societies.

Notes

1. *Daily Mail*, 16 January 1995.
2. *New Woman*, May 1994.
3. Tony Blair, *The Times*, 1 October 1994.
4. Ben Pimlott, *Harold Wilson*, p407.
5. For example, in the BBC TV *Panorama* debate, 13 June 1994.
6. *Observer*, 27 February 1994.
7. John Prescott, BBC TV, *Newsnight*, 5 July 1994; Darlington hustings, 11 July 1994.
8. John Prescott, *Labour and Trade Union Review*, December 1989.
9. Tony Blair, speech to Family Breakdown and Criminal Activity Conference, 24 May 1994.
10. *Daily Mirror*, 14 June 1994.
11. BBC TV, *On The Record*, 26 June 1994.
12. The rest of the sound-bite was not original, either. Blair used it in his first party conference speech in 1990. It is a line which he and Gordon Brown shared freely – its most recent outing had been in Brown's Swansea speech, on 22 May: 'There should be no need for any woman to choose between the work they need and the care of the children they love.'
13. BBC TV, *On The Record*, 26 June 1994.
14. Andrew Marr, *Independent*, 25 May 1994.

18. Minds and Hearts
Leader, July 1994 to April 1995

'This young man has not faintest idea of how socialists think, and does not begin to understand the mentality of the party which he has been elected to lead.'

Tony Blair's first act as Leader of the Opposition was to launch a rhetorical offensive. On the day after his election, he said that the trade unions would have no more influence over the next Labour government than employers: 'They will have the same access as the other side of industry . . . We are not running the next Labour government for anyone other than the people of this country.'[1]

That Sunday, Brian Walden pursued the logic of social moralism in a television interview. Blair finally agreed with Walden's statement that 'single parents who have chosen to have children without forming a stable relationship . . . are wrong'. Pressed three times, he conceded: 'Yes, I disagree with what they have done.' It was hardly surprising, in the light of what he had said before – Blair was reluctant only because he wanted to avoid offending people who had become lone parents through family breakdown. But Walden seized on Blair's words as the final break with one of the dominant ideas of social liberalism, that individuals should decide their own family arrangements without interference from politicians. Or, as the novelist Will Self put it, 'I don't want some pol like you telling me that I represent social disintegration because I'm separated from my wife and children. Mind your own bloody business.'[2]

The next day he commandeered his shadow Education Secretary's news conference. Where Ann Taylor was opposed to league tables of school exam results, he said he was in favour of publishing information. In case journalists did not spot the difference, they had been briefed beforehand by Blair's staff that his words would contradict those of Taylor's education policy document, which said: 'Test results and league tables are not acceptable management tools in the assessment of school performance.' On the lunchtime television news Blair was asked what the main points of the document were, and his first comment was that unfit teachers should be sacked – another 'tough' message, designed to distract attention from the document itself.

In themselves, these were three small steps in the long march to a different kind of socialism. As shadow Employment Secretary, he had insisted on 'fairness not favours' for the trade unions. As shadow Home Secretary, he had talked about strong families. And during the Labour leadership election campaign, he had advocated parent power in education. But now he was leader, his statements carried greater authority and impact.

The Conservative press welcomed his election with more enthusiasm than it can ever have expressed for a Labour leader. The editorial in the *Daily Mail* on 26 July said: 'This paper is not in the habit of congratulating leaders of the Labour Party, but then few politicians recently have spoken with the courage and conviction of Mr Tony Blair.' On the same day, the *Daily Telegraph* devoted precious column inches to an interview in which Blair appealed to its readers,

in their own interests, to consider the alternative – not how we are parodied, but how we are . . . Many of those who voted Conservative are now asking serious questions about their quality of life and living standards and prospects for their children under the Conservatives.

After a week of exhausting interviews, Blair went on holiday with his family to the south of France.

For the first five months of his leadership, the adulation continued unabated. The Blair Bubble was a phenomenon of British politics without parallel since the launch of the Social Democratic Party. At the end of 1981, the Liberal-SDP Alliance briefly touched 50 per cent in the opinion polls. By the end of 1994, the Labour Party under Blair reached an improbable 61 per cent.[3] The ghost of the SDP was abroad.

As the SDP had done, Blair engaged the moderate leftish sympathies of most individual journalists while satisfying their desire for a 'big story'. And, within a fortnight of his election, three of the SDP's Gang of Four who led the exodus from Labour endorsed Blair 'from the other side', in the SDP's successor party, the Liberal Democrats. Roy Jenkins said he accepted 'even with enthusiasm' that a non-Conservative government 'necessarily involves Mr Blair as prime minister', and urged Blair to enter into 'friendly relations with the Liberal Democrats, within whose ranks are many whose thought-out instincts are very close to his own'.[4] Shirley Williams said Labour and the Liberal Democrats 'have a great deal in common and ought to work together towards a common programme',[5] while Bill Rodgers said he hoped Blair would win the next election.[6] The fourth member of the Gang, David Owen, who had endorsed John Major but not the Conservative party in 1992, kept his own counsel.

Blair maintained the raised tempo when he came back from holiday. On 31 August, within an hour of the Irish Republican Army announcing a three-month ceasefire in Northern Ireland, the Labour leader took to the BBC's new twenty-four-hour news network, Radio 5 Live, to welcome the 'opportunity' that this presented. Labour's Northern Ireland spokesman, Kevin MacNamara, got as far as the BBC studio in Hull to give his reaction, to be told that the leader would be speaking for the party on the issue. MacNamara, soon to be replaced, had long been distrusted by the Unionists, who suspected him of seeking to impose a united Ireland against their will. The next day, Blair confirmed his desire to accommodate Unionism by moving away from Labour's logically-challenged position of 'unity by consent', developed as an uneasy compromise in 1980. He emphasised the 'consent' rather than the 'unity', and made it clear that the Labour Party did not see itself as a 'persuader' for a united Ireland. 'The important thing is not that the government takes up the role of pushing people in one direction or another, but that they allow the wishes of those in Northern Ireland to be paramount.'[7]

If the newspapers and old-time Social Democrats were delighted by Blair's energetic start in his new job, the leaders of the Liberal Democrats and the Conservatives seemed unable to respond effectively to the threat. Paddy Ashdown took a collection of Blair's speeches on *his* holiday in France in the summer of 1994, but appeared irritated whenever he was asked questions about the author of his holiday reading.[8] John Major took a personal dislike to Blair, complaining privately that he found him 'cold', humourless and hard to get on with, contrasting him unfavourably in these respects with John Smith and Neil Kinnock. But he found it difficult to focus his tactics against Blair, uncertain how to deal with such a bold raid on what he thought was his own political territory. 'If you have to choose between a real Conservative party and a quasi-Conservative party, where the Labour Party says one thing but the party's heart and soul is elsewhere, then I believe people will go for the real thing,' he said.[9] This was called the 'Coke' strategy in Conservative Central Office – selling the Tories as the 'real thing' – but it was vulnerable to consumers deciding for themselves that they preferred the taste of Pepsi.

The Conservatives' problem was that, though Blair was more like Neil Kinnock than John Smith, their line of attack against Kinnock did not damage Blair. They had accused Kinnock of changing policy out of lust for power, and described the party's modernised programme as a 'mask', concealing its true socialist face. It was a charge which had some support in the Labour Party – Peter Shore, one of Kinnock's rivals when he took over the leadership in 1983, was withering:

> At the unripe age of forty-one, he had had few testing experiences or challenges to help develop his own political convictions . . . He was politically unformed and immature. He had a complete kit of then-fashionable left-wing viewpoints but, as events were to show, no settled convictions on any of them.[10]

The Conservative 'lust for power' charge did not work with Blair, because the message is the man. Blair's rhetorical offensive, on trade unions, social moralism and schools, was a middle-class message delivered by a former self-employed barrister, a family man and an assertive parent of school-age children. Kinnock had used similar language, but did not embody the message (partly because he rarely referred to his family). Blair is at ease with his message, where Kinnock gave the impression of reading, somewhat uncomfortably, from a script.

Only Michael Heseltine, the President of the Board of Trade, was able to land a punch on the new leader. In a variation of the 'Coke' strategy, he attacked Blair's judgment. 'Why should you believe a man who has got all the major judgments wrong in the first half of his life, when he tells you he is going to get them all right in the second half of his life?' he thundered on the *Today* programme. He cited Blair's past support for the Campaign for Nuclear Disarmament, and his positions on trade union reform, privatisation and low taxes. It was a superb performance, which reduced interviewer James Naughtie to squawks of indignation.[11]

Heseltine was obeying the first law of American politics, 'Define your opponent before he gets the chance to define himself.' Many people had still not formed a settled view of

Blair, and Heseltine tried to disrupt Blair's control over his image. The attack drew blood immediately, with a Labour official quoted in *The Times* the next day, 16 September, denying that Blair had ever been a member of CND. Three days later this was amended to an admission that he was 'briefly' a member of Parliamentary Labour CND, after Conservative Central Office produced a copy of its advertisement bearing Blair's name in the CND magazine *Sanity* in May 1986. But Labour officials – incorrectly – repeated their denial that he had ever been a member of 'mainstream CND'.[12] Blair claimed he was a member of CND when he wanted to be an MP, and Parliamentary Labour CND was organised by, and its members were members of, 'mainstream CND'. The only difference was that the parliamentary body had a corporate opt-out from CND's policy of withdrawal from 'nuclear alliances', because Labour supported the North Atlantic Treaty Organisation.

Since then, it has been argued on Blair's behalf that he was 'never *really* a unilateralist'. This cannot be squared with the evidence from 1982, when he argued for unilateral nuclear disarmament in the Beaconsfield by-election campaign (see pp82–3). Nor is his present position clear. During the leadership election campaign he touched on the question of defence policy only tangentially. In his policy speech on Europe, he warned of the disintegration of the former Soviet Union, with

> a still powerful, and indeed nuclear, military machine, and a people both fiercely nationalistic and utterly humiliated by their slide from superpower status to hospital case. We know well what can arise from such a combination and we should prepare for it, actively, today.

However, all the preparation he proposed was that Western Europe should be 'strong and confident' and 'opening up' to the East.[13]

Another effective line of attack used by Michael Heseltine

was the 'head and body' approach, stressing the gap between the leader and his party. The party membership was clearly to the left of and more traditionalist than the leader at its head, while party policy-making and the National Executive were still dominated by trade unions. Blair was only too aware of his vulnerability to the 'head versus body' problem – it was one of the reasons why he launched his battle to rewrite Clause IV of Labour's constitution.

Clause IV

Blair's holiday in the south of France consisted largely of discussions with a steady procession of visitors about the strategy for his next big test, his first Labour Party conference as leader. The decision to try to revise Clause IV was taken there, with Peter Mandelson and Gordon Brown the central confidants. Neil Kinnock and John Smith had both wanted to rewrite the clause, which committed the party to the 'common ownership of the means of production, distribution and exchange', but both had calculated that the time was not ripe.

At the start of the leadership campaign, Blair was unsure whether to tackle Clause IV. In order to keep his options open, he tried to close down the debate by appearing to rule out change. He said no one wanted the debate about Clause IV 'to be the priority of the Labour Party at the moment'. Nor did he think the vast majority of British people 'sit out there and debate the intricacies of the Labour Party constitution'.[14]

However, it would have been his and Peter Mandelson's style to plan a *coup de théâtre* for Blackpool. Mandelson had long wanted to get rid of Clause IV. Soon after he became Labour's communications director in 1985, new membership cards were printed without the hallowed wording on the back. Such a change was hardly likely to go unnoticed, and it did not. Mandelson claimed it was a 'printing error', the cards were pulped and new cards ordered.

Rewriting Clause IV was also an easier fight to choose and to win than some of the other changes Blair could have pressed for. Even with the huge authority conferred on him by mid-term elevation, he could not hope to attack directly the 70 per cent domination of party policy by union block votes, or the built-in majority of union seats on the party's National Executive. And it is arguable that, instead of starting a fight over internal affairs, he should have pressed for the important policy changes he wanted – for example on education. That he did not reinforces the suspicion that he did not have a clear idea of the positive policies he wanted, as opposed to the existing policies he did not want, and used the Clause IV debate partly to buy time.

Traditionalists accused Blair of resuming what they saw as the exhausted Kinnockite 'project' of trying to persuade the public that the Labour Party had really changed by winning an internal battle. One of Blair and Mandelson's arguments for rewriting Clause IV was that the party's private polling showed 'there is still too great a fear of the unknown as far as the Labour Party is concerned', because voters did not believe that the party had changed sufficiently.[15] John Smith's view, on the contrary, had been that if the only thing people heard about the party was that it was repudiating its past, it would betray a lack of self-confidence – people would distrust the party's motives and be ready to believe the worst about what it really intended.

When he died, Smith had been preparing a less confrontational initiative on Clause IV. He felt that the party would only accept a supplementary statement side-by-side with the original, but hoped to use such a statement to deflect criticism of the clause.

He made it clear he did not agree with the clause, but described the debate about getting rid of it as 'academic'.[16] Privately, he felt he could not take on Clause IV as well as the block vote, and was extremely angry with Jack Straw, shadow Environment Secretary, for calling for Clause IV to be scrapped in a pamphlet in the middle of the battle for one

member, one vote in 1993. His chief policy adviser, David
Ward, says Smith intended to publish a personal statement of
values at the 1994 Labour conference, and had consulted Blair
about it. 'It would have been a rewrite and purely secular version of his Tawney lecture in March 1993,' says Ward. This
was Smith's exposition of his Christian socialist beliefs, identical to Blair's, centred on the conviction that 'the individual is
best fulfilled in the context of a strong community bound
together by fellowship'.[17] One of Smith's last acts before he
died was to set a date in June 1994 for a meeting with his
advisers to draft the statement. The plan was to ask the party
to discuss it and then to adopt it – possibly amended – at the
following year's conference in 1995. Smith's intention, says
Ward, was then to deflect any questions about Clause IV by
saying it had been 'superseded' by the new document.

Smith's approach to Clause IV was symptomatic of his
wider strategy, to put the Left to sleep and allow people to
forget about them, whereas Blair's was deliberately to open
Pandora's box to let out more dragons to slay.

Clause IV has been described by one historian as 'the red
lamp which attracted socialist political myth'.[18] The words
(reproduced in the Appendix) were drafted in the month of
the Russian Revolution in 1917 by Sidney Webb and Arthur
Henderson, and adopted in February 1918, before the end of
the First World War. It was very much the product of its
time, and was already out of date six years later, when the
first, minority, Labour government took office. It had no
intention of nationalising all the 'means of production'.

The words of Clause IV, Part Four – 'the common ownership' part – first appeared on membership cards only in 1959,
the very year when Hugh Gaitskell asked the party to delete
it.[19] Only then did it become central to an invented history of
the party, a fake tradition which was used to bolster the
argument that the party has always been essentially 'socialist',
while its leaders have always been temporising pragmatists.

By the 1950s, few in the party read Clause IV literally. Its
defenders tended to advocate neither the abolition of private

capital and markets, nor their replacement by a planned, collectively-owned economy, which is what Clause IV said. (It also promised to secure for workers the *full* fruits of their industry, a stark statement of simple Marxian economics, about which few had thought and with which fewer would have agreed.) For them it only meant *more* public ownership, and stood for the distant hope of an economic system that was morally different from 'capitalism'. It was 'symbolic of values rather than policy', as Blair himself put it in an interview with the *Daily Telegraph*, after he had decided to try to get rid of it, but before he had admitted as much.[20]

In 1959, Gaitskell mishandled the attempt to change Clause IV because his rational mind paid attention to the words rather than the symbolism. He allowed the party to believe that his response to a third election defeat was to abandon the party's principles, and he was forced to settle for a National Executive statement adopted at the following year's conference to 'reaffirm, amplify and clarify' Clause IV. The statement declared that the Labour Party's 'central ideal is the brotherhood of man. Its purpose is to make this ideal a reality everywhere.' It retained the phrase 'common ownership', calling for 'an expansion of common ownership substantial enough to give the community power over the commanding heights of the economy'. These were Aneurin Bevan's words, inserted as an amendment just after his death in 1960 by his widow, Jennie Lee. But the scope of common ownership was at least limited: 'Further extension of common ownership should be decided . . . with due regard for the views of the workers and consumers concerned.'[21] The statement was a reasonable reflection of the actual beliefs of the party at the time, which were only a little to the left of Gaitskell's, but his real defeat was that Clause IV was left untouched.

In 1994, John Smith planned to repeat the exercise, but hoped it would codify his expressed belief that ownership was 'largely irrelevant'. The sleeping dogs of the Left and the unions would have been left to lie, but Clause IV itself would also have remained. Smith's 'quiet life' approach was defended by Roy Hattersley: 'I have learned, during the forty years since Clement Attlee was Prime Minister, that the party does best when it is at peace with itself.'[22]

Blair had decided to go to war instead. In France, he discussed his plan for Clause IV with Alastair Campbell, the Assistant Editor of *Today*. He offered, and Campbell accepted, the job of his press secretary. Campbell's first task was to sell the ditching of Clause IV.

Essential to this exercise, however, was the support of John Prescott. It was an early test of Prescott's loyalty to the new leader. Prescott knew he was being used to give traditionalist cover to the modernisers' 'project', but there was nothing he could do. Nor did he disagree in principle with rewriting Clause IV, although he made it known that he had doubts about whether it was the right time to do it. He consented to the idea, on condition that he could assure trade union leaders that there would be no more party reforms before the General Election. This understanding was ambiguous, however, because the party had already agreed to review the 70 per cent union vote at Labour conferences when party membership reached 300,000. Blair's latest 'open conspiracy' to make Labour 'capable of winning the next General Election' was under way.

There was a whiff of Gaitskellism in the air in Blackpool, as the Labour conference opened on 2 October 1994, revealing the slogan 'New Labour, New Britain' on a green backdrop. Gaitskell's ally Douglas Jay had suggested changing the Labour Party's name in 1959 (one of his suggestions was 'Radical Labour'). Now Blair had made his change.

The more important parallel between 1959 and 1994 was not revealed until the end of Blair's first conference speech as leader. At the 1959 Labour conference, when Tony Blair was six, Gaitskell said it was better explicitly to accept the mixed economy, 'instead of going out of our way to court misrepresentation'. Thirty-five years later, Blair used almost the same words to demand a new Clause IV, to set out Labour's aims in terms 'the Tories cannot misrepresent'.

The manner of Blair's request, however, was indirect. Immediately after declaring, 'Let us say what we mean and mean what we say,' he failed to mention 'Clause IV', when he said he and John Prescott would propose a new statement of the party's objects to 'take its place in our constitution for the next century'. It was not until after his standing ovation that many delegates realised that he meant rewriting Clause IV – although a vigilant Arthur Scargill was already denouncing Blair's betrayal to journalists under a balcony during the applause.

The announcement came as a surprise to all but a few trusted advisers and union leaders. Unusually for a modern party conference speech, the press were not given copies in advance. Television journalists, who use the text to decide camera moves, were issued with a copy with the last three pages missing. Much of the press coverage afterwards was devoted to the subject of who knew what was in those last three pages and when, and how it had been kept a secret for so long. However, it is the politics of the move that are of lasting importance. In his speech, Blair had acknowledged the party's reservations about him. 'Some of you, I hear, support me simply because you think I can win,' he said. There was laughter, as embarrassed delegates recognised themselves. 'Actually, that's not a bad reason for supporting me. But it is not enough. I want more. We are not going to win despite our beliefs. We will only win because of them.' The delegates applauded, but Blair was raising the awkward question of what those beliefs actually were, and whether there was agreement on them.

Even though a new draft was not promised until December (it was actually published in March 1995), it was assumed that Blair would win the debate on rewriting Clause IV, but only because the trade union block votes would reluctantly back him. The party's doubts seemed to be confirmed two days after Blair's speech, when the conference carried a motion affirming Clause IV by 50.9 to 49.1 per cent.

After this early setback, the campaign for a new Clause IV

was slow to start. It was not until 14 December that the National Executive agreed a timetable for a special Labour Party conference to vote on the change in spring 1995. This was designed to pre-empt trade union conferences over the summer, which might see unrepresentative activists trying to ensure block votes were cast against change – as they did over one member, one vote. At the same time, a survey of local Labour parties by *Tribune* found that 59 of the 61 who had voted on Clause IV had voted to keep it. The parties included Gordon Brown's, Dunfermline East, and Harriet Harman's, Peckham. These were decisions by activist-led General Committees, and Blair already had plans to encourage ballots of all party members, but the omens did not look good.

The battle had begun. Superficially it was merely a battle over words drafted seventy-seven years before. In reality, it was a battle to change the party's soul. And the suspicions of the traditionalists, now including much of the Smithite mainstream, were stoked by a decision which touched the party's soul more than any other.

The London Oratory

It was during the leadership election campaign that the *Daily Express* first reported that Tony and Cherie were 'poised' to send their elder son Euan to the London Oratory, a traditionalist Roman Catholic state boys' school which had taken advantage of Conservative law to opt out of local council control.[23]

A few days later Blair said on television:

Parents are going to choose whatever is the best choice of school for their kids. We have disagreed with the government opting out schools, but you can't say to parents they then can't choose them – that would be manifestly absurd –

any more than you could say with a National Health Service trust that you shouldn't use it.[24]

Just before John Smith's death, Cherie expressed her worries about the effects of public interest in her family:

I'm quite a private person and want to protect our children. When Tony takes them to school the other kids are always saying, 'We saw you on the telly last night.' I don't want my children growing up thinking that they're special, just because of what their daddy does.[25]

This seemed a forlorn hope as Euan, then aged ten, found himself at the centre of a national controversy. The seeds of doubt sown during the leadership campaign were reaped after the Blairs' decision was confirmed in December. This co-incided with the end of Blair's long honeymoon, and crystallised anxieties in the party both about the timing of the Clause IV debate and about Blair himself.

Many party members thought it hypocritical of Blair to attack the government for favouring certain schools over others, and yet to benefit from that advantage for his own family. The school's head, John McIntosh, a former adviser to Education Secretary John Patten, unhelpfully said, 'He can't sacrifice his son to his own political values,' implying that there was a conflict between the two.[26] Blair even more unhelpfully said: 'Any parent wants the best for their children. I am not going to make a choice for my child on the basis of what is the politically correct thing to do.'[27]

The Blairs had run up against the conflict between freedom and equality that socialists have sought to sidestep through the ages. If people can choose between schools, differences will be exaggerated. And where there are only so many 'good' schools, choice for some is opportunity denied for others.

Blair repeatedly stressed that the London Oratory is a state comprehensive, as indeed it is supposed to be, in that it is required to admit children regardless of ability or background – apart from religion. But children have to be interviewed before they are given a place, according to the school's prospectus, to 'assess whether the aims of the parents and the boy are in harmony with those of the school'. This allows the school effectively to select its pupils by academic ability. The Roman Catholic church's own education service complained that this did not conform with Department for Education guidelines, which say: 'Church schools should take care to ensure that interviews are used *only* to judge religious suitability and that their purpose is made clear in their written admission policies.'[28] As with any popular, over-subscribed school, admission policy in practice is opaque, to say the least.

Another reason why the decision caused trouble in the party was that it ran counter to Blair's vision of 'strong communities'. The Oratory, in Fulham, is eight miles from his home in Islington, where there are other Roman Catholic secondary schools. Schools are an essential component of any realisation of the concept of community in the practical world. Unsurprisingly, Blair explains what the word means to him in terms which reduce it to vapid generality: 'The notion of community for me is less a geographical concept than a belief in the social nature of human beings.'[29]

The problem of choice and equity in education is probably ultimately insoluble for the Left, even if a Labour government removes the financial incentives to opting out. Blair and his new shadow Education Secretary, David Blunkett, sought instead to focus attention on immediate measures to raise standards and direct resources to failing schools. After a bumpy start, Blunkett began to deliver what Blair wanted: a policy aimed at raising standards that would offend the National Union of Teachers. (Blunkett's 'fresh start' plan to close failing schools and re-open them under a new head, new governing body and new name was a Blairist strike which ensured he was harangued by Socialist Workers Party teachers at the NUT's conference in March 1995.)

Meanwhile, on New Year's Day 1995, in a sharp reminder of how unready Labour was for office, the party performed a U-turn on the issue of VAT on private school fees. This was nothing to do with the Oratory (although it was a widespread misconception that it was a private school), but that controversy had made the issue of educational privilege highly sensitive in the party.

David Blunkett thought he was repeating the party line in interviews with the *Sunday Times* and *Mail on Sunday* when he said the party was considering charging VAT on school fees. But Blair and Gordon Brown reacted immediately to front-page headlines warning of this 'threat' to private schooling. By lunchtime, Blunkett was on the radio to rule out what that morning had been an option. He said: 'The shadow Chancellor and the leader think it is helpful to rule out that possibility in order to avoid confusion.'[30] In his irritation, he made sure that Brown was associated with the change, and preserved some of his own left-wing credentials.

Blair and Brown were clearly anxious not to send signals that Labour wanted to penalise aspiration, and Brown's team had certainly identified technical problems in imposing VAT on school fees and not on other charges for education or training. But it was a presentational inelegance which, combined with unease over the Oratory and Clause IV, gave the impression that Blair's grip was already weakening.

Against this background, the battle to replace Clause IV – especially with no alternative form of words yet proposed – seemed to many in the Labour Party to be an attempt to abandon their basic values. Blair appeared to confirm their fears when he refused to say Labour would renationalise British Rail if it were privatised.

On 10 January 1995, a majority of Labour's Euro-MPs sponsored an advertisement in the *Guardian* defending Clause IV, saying it could be 'perhaps added to, but not replaced'. It was a strategically-timed repeat of an advertisement in *Tribune* in November, which had gone virtually unnoticed. Blair, in Brussels for a conference, rounded on them, accusing them of 'infantile incompetence' and 'gross discourtesy'. The intemperate language spoke of weakness rather than strength, but the air of crisis spurred Blair's supporters to begin fighting for a new Clause IV. Later that month the National Executive agreed to urge local Labour parties to ballot their members on Clause IV; Robin Cook, an important centre-Left figure, came out for rewriting the constitution; and Blair began a tour to meet party members all over the country to argue for change.

It was only then that the debate over Clause IV really began. With the defenders of common ownership forced to spell out their arguments, the process immediately turned in Blair's favour. Face to face, the party was surprised by its new leader, and the leader seemed, not for the first time, surprised by himself. Blair turned the corner, and was on a rising trend up to the special conference in April.

The End of the Beginning

At the Scottish Labour Party conference in Inverness on 10 March 1995, Blair cleared the way for a new Clause IV. The party in Scotland is more traditional than the English party, but it also has a history of loyalty to Labour leaders. With the confidence gained from speaking to party rallies around the country, Blair overcame the ties of tradition. The autocue had broken down, so he was forced to improvise, appealing directly to his audience and moving away from his text:

> If we have the courage to change, the country will . . . There will be people voting at the next election who will barely have been born at the time of the last Labour government. When that day comes, the next election is going to be every bit about us as about the Conservatives. Make no mistake about that . . . The question people will ask is,

'Do we trust Labour?' I believe it is essential, for that trust to be won, that we are clear about the values we hold dear. We need the people with us . . . The only thing that stands between us and government is trust. Trust will be gained, not by clinging to icons for fear of thinking anew, but by seizing the spirit without which all thought is barren.

Like the debate in 1959, but unlike the later debate of the whole party in London, the hall in Inverness heard repeated biblical references. 'Nothing stands still,' said the delegate from the Western Isles, 'not even the authorised version of the Bible.' The conference voted for a Revised Standard Version of Labour's sacred text.

But it was only now that the final form of the new Clause IV began to take shape. For weeks a collection of uninspiring drafts had been circulating among shadow Cabinet members and union leaders, one of whom described what he saw as like a 'raggedy composite'. While in Inverness, Blair wrote a draft (reproduced in the Appendix) of the new Clause IV Part One, the paragraph that was to replace the words on the back of party membership cards. It began with the faintly biblical declaration which is the distinctive heart of the new clause, 'By the strength of our common endeavour . . .'

The new Clause IV was completed that weekend, with the cameras invited to Blair's Islington house to record John Prescott's presence at the scene of the crime (as the traditionalists saw it), and the words (also reproduced in the Appendix) were unveiled at the National Executive meeting on 13 March.

In one sense, the rewriting of Clause IV was a rather inconclusive symbol. The economics of the old clause were so archaic that little credit can be claimed for doing in 1995 what should have been done in 1959, which is after all when the German Social Democratic Party wrote all traces of Marxism out of its programme at Bad Godesberg.

However, despite the apparent universality of the

sentiments of the new Clause IV, it would be a mistake to underestimate the ideological significance of the rewriting. It marks the rejection of all the dominant traditions of socialist philosophy, to leave only the most attenuated system of public ethics as Labour's core belief. In *She* magazine, Blair provided a 24-word summary of the new 340-word Clause IV: 'Social-ism . . . is not about class, or trades unions, or capitalism versus socialism. It is about a belief in working together to get things done.'[31] It is not just Marxists who define socialism in terms of class, trade unions and opposition to capitalism – but the lowest-common-denominator definition which Blair offers is not, however thin, an ideological vacuum. It is ethical socialism, which does not require a belief in rival systems of economic organisation called Capitalism and Socialism to sustain it, and which reflects the current ideological debate on the Left about the different kinds of capitalism which are possible.[32]

Of course, Blair and Prescott insisted repeatedly that the new clause simply expressed the values that lay behind the old one in the modern context, but it is not just the mechanism – common ownership of the whole economy – that is different. The values expressed are different and, indeed, incompatible. Sidney Webb, the main author of the original clause, is perhaps the best authority on what it means. But he offered two interpretations. 'The Labour Party stands essentially for revolt against the inequality of circumstance that degrades and brutalises and disgraces our civilisation,' he wrote in 1917. That may be consistent with the new Clause IV. But he went on:

> It abhors and repudiates the unscientific and immoral doctrine that the competitive struggle for the means of life is, in human society, either inevitable or requisite for the survival of the fittest; it declares, indeed, in full accord with science, that competition produces degradation and death, whilst it is conscious and deliberate co-operation which is productive of life and progress.[33]

The new clause, however, espouses both competition *and* co-operation.

Two Labour Party Special Conferences, in Wembley, 24 January 1981, and in Westminster, 29 April 1995, bracket Labour's wilderness years – also the history of the party as Blair knows it. The Wembley Special Conference, to decide the form of electoral college which would take the choice of Labour leader out of the hands of MPs, was the high point of Tony Benn's ascendancy, and triggered the SDP breakaway. The Clause IV Special Conference at Methodist Central Hall saw New Labour break away from its past, and its leader exceed expectations. It marked the end of the beginning of Blair's leadership.

Methodist Central Hall was also where the original Clause IV was adopted during the First World War. In the very chamber where it was agreed without debate to abolish private capital in 1918, Blair's polite endorsement of 'the enterprise of the market and the rigour of competition' was approved by a 65 per cent vote in 1995. It was an unexpected result. First, the public service union, Unison, normally loyal to the Labour leadership, decided to cast its 11 per cent block vote against the new clause without balloting its members. But then the results from local party ballots started to come in, running at an average of 85 per cent in favour of change. The left-wing MP Diane Abbott claimed party members were so keen to win the next election that they would have voted 'for the healing power of cabbage' if the leader had asked them to. It was an insulting and unconvincing explanation of the size of the majority.

After the result was announced, Blair spoke briefly, without notes:

> I wasn't born into this party. I chose it. I've never joined another political party. I believe in it. I'm proud to be the leader of it and it's the party I'll always live in and I'll die in. (*Applause.*) If sometimes I seem a little over-hasty and over-urgent, it's for one reason only: I can't stand these

people, these Tories, being in government over our country.

The short speech was similar in style and content to his private speech to the victory party on the day of his election as leader. In it, too, Blair had tried to convince his supporters that he was not a Tory. It was an indirect response to the question posed by Clare Short, the Bevanite shadow minister for women and National Executive member, which was, 'Is there a bottom line to Blair's politics?'

The vote was a decisive rejection of the judgment of Labour Euro-MP Ken Coates: 'This young man has not the faintest idea of how socialists think, and does not begin to understand the mentality of the party which he has been elected to lead.'[34] In an interview after the vote, Blair conceded that Coates *had been* right:

I know the Labour Party very well now. It may be a strange thing to say but before I became leader I did not. The Labour Party is much nicer than it looks. Labour often looks as if it is about to engage in class war, but in fact it is full of basically rather decent and honest people.[35]

In fact the party had changed substantially, even since he became leader. Membership had risen from 250,000 to 330,000. One activist complained: 'There are people becoming members who would actively dislike the idea of socialism.'[36] But, by defining it, Blair had redefined British socialism.

Blair had turned the Clause IV debate into a personal triumph. He recalled Conservative predictions that he would have to be rescued from a suspicious party by the trade union block vote. David Hill, the party's chief spokesman, produced a list of quotations from Conservatives saying how significant it was that Labour still had the old Clause IV, and a new list saying how insignificant the change was. Just before his victory over Clause IV, Blair trounced John Major at Prime

Minister's Questions. It was the day after Major brought the rebel Conservative MPs back into the party, without any concessions on their part. The contrast with Blair's facing down his (admittedly weaker) Clause IV rebels was sharp, and Major unwisely tried to point out that both parties were divided over Europe. But there *was* a difference, said Blair: 'I lead my party. He follows his.' Enjoying the smack of firm government, Labour MPs roared their delighted approval.

In victory, Blair created expectations of further change. He played on this in his unscripted speech after the Clause IV vote to make a politically risqué joke: 'I want to say something about the party's name.' He paused, as delegates looked at each other in surprise. 'It's staying as it is.' This was a bit too close to the bone for John Prescott, who did not look pleased. It is inconceivable that any previous Labour leader could have said the same.

In any case, the name had effectively been amended already, to 'New Labour'. The real area for change defined itself. One potential drawback of holding a Special Conference had been that it would draw attention to the continuing dominant role of trade union block votes in Labour's affairs. Instead, the balloting of party members, and of members of unions such as the Communication Workers Union, who voted overwhelmingly for change, humiliated the leaders of the Transport and General Workers Union and Unison, the two main opponents of change. The block vote was bound to be challenged, especially as the party's membership had passed the 300,000 level which triggered a review of the trade unions' 70 per cent share of Labour conference votes. Blair himself did not need to draw the obvious conclusion, because journalists drew it for him by asking when the share might be reduced to 50 per cent.

Blair was noncommittal, but Prescott was furious with him and his advisers, feeling that he had reneged on their Clause IV deal, in which his support was conditional on there being no more party reforms before the General Election. In television interviews, Prescott said, 'I personally don't see that change taking place this side of an election,' and warned 'those in victory' of the need to hold the party together.[37] The fault-line at the top of the party threatened to widen.

Since becoming leader, Blair has acted on Harold Wilson's famous dictum: 'The Labour Party is like a vehicle. If you drive at great speed, all the people in it are either exhilarated or so sick that you have no problems. But when you stop, they all get out and argue about which way to go.' There is of course a danger in the love of movement for its own sake, encouraging the sense that Blair has a direction, but not a destination. And, if the destination is only the centre ground of British politics, the risk, by definition, is of overshooting.

Blair's leadership election manifesto, which did not even suggest that any of Labour's policies should be changed, turned out to be a misleading prospectus. In his first nine months as leader, Labour changed its policy or general stance on, among other things, the single European currency, low taxes, low inflation, the minimum wage, exam league tables, opted-out schools, Northern Ireland, regional assemblies and the House of Lords. In every case, the change moved Labour closer to the Conservatives.

The pace set by Blair's leadership has left opponents in and out of his party unable to fix him. The significance of his various nicknames – Bambi, Tony Blur, Tory Blair – is that none has stuck. And, regardless of the strategic rightness of the positions Blair has adopted, he has not made any obvious blunders.

There remain large questions over the detailed policies of a Blair government, but there is no doubt that in his first nine months as Labour leader Blair demonstrated the qualities of judgment needed in a prime minister. The departure from the 'long game' strategy of John Smith already appears to have been vindicated, not just by the vote on Clause IV, but by the revitalisation of the Labour Party generated by the campaign for change. Whether the new Clause IV and the repositioning of the party more emphatically in the centre ground yield the ultimate electoral dividend in bringing Labour to power, they have already boosted the party's performance in opinion polls, local elections and by-elections. Blair has shown himself to be wholly worthy of the title Leader of the Opposition; indeed, it is difficult to imagine a more potent electoral challenger to a Conservative government. But winning a second election is a very different proposition from winning once, requiring coherence, competence, and economic success in government. Like all prime ministers, Blair would be transformed by power, but from his record as party leader, it is possible to discern the outline of what a Blair administration would be like.

Notes

1. BBC Radio 4, *Today*, 22 July 1994.
2. Will Self, *Independent Magazine*, 3 June 1995.
3. Gallup polls, December 1981 and December 1994. The two figures are not comparable, however, because opinion polls are not what they used to be: as with by-elections, they have increasingly been used as a way of voicing a protest.
4. *The Times*, 23 July 1994.
5. BBC Radio 4, *Today*, 1 August 1994.
6. *The Times*, 3 August 1994.
7. BBC Radio 4, *Today*, 1 September 1994.
8. *Observer*, 25 September 1994.
9. BBC TV, *Panorama*, 3 April 1995 (7 April in Scotland).
10. Peter Shore, *Leading the Left*, p155.
11. BBC Radio 4, *Today*, 15 September 1994.
12. *The Times*, 19 September 1994.
13. Tony Blair, speech to the Foreign Press Association in London, 6 July 1994.
14. BBC TV, *Breakfast with Frost*, 12 June 1994.
15. Tony Blair, in a note of a discussion between Blair and Peter Mandelson, kept by Mandelson, and quoted by Jon Sopel, *Tony Blair: The Moderniser*, p273.
16. BBC Radio 4, *Today*, 24 February 1994.
17. John Smith, *Reclaiming the Ground*, edited by Christopher Bryant, p138.

18. Roger Eatwell, *The Labour Government, 1945–51*, p20.
19. Steven Fielding, 'Mr Benn and the Myth of Clause IV', *Parliamentary Brief*, April 1995.
20. Tony Blair, *Daily Telegraph*, 26 July 1994.
21. The statement is reprinted as an appendix in Philip M. Williams, *Hugh Gaitskell*, p572.
22. Roy Hattersley, *Observer*, 15 January 1995.
23. *Daily Express*, 21 June 1994.
24. BBC TV, *On The Record*, 26 June 1994.
25. *New Woman*, May 1994.
26. BBC Radio 4, *PM*, 1 December 1994.
27. Tony Blair, BBC TV *Good Morning*, 1 December 1994.
28. Department for Education Circular 6/93 (8 July 1993), p9; *Independent*, 10 December 1994. The Oratory's admissions criteria were not new: they had been tolerated by the Labour-controlled Inner London Education Authority. Nor are they likely to change: the Roman Catholic church has not pursued its complaint.
29. *New Statesman*, 28 April 1995.
30. BBC Radio 4, *The World This Weekend*, 1 January 1995. The removal of charitable status remained an option.
31. *She*, March 1995.
32. See, for example, William Keegan, *The Spectre of Capitalism*.
33. Sidney Webb, *Observer*, reproduced in Ken Coates, editor, *Clause IV: Common Ownership and the Labour Party*, p10.
34. *Daily Telegraph*, 13 January 1995.
35. *Guardian*, 1 May 1995.
36. BBC TV, *On The Record*, 18 December 1994.
37. BBC TV, *On The Record*, 23 April 1995; *Westminster On-Line*, 2 May 1995.

19. SHADOW PRIME MINISTER
The Future

'If Blair turns out to be as good as he looks, we have a problem.'

John Maples, Conservative Deputy Chairman[1]

It has twice taken the death in office of its leader to put the Labour Party ahead of history. Hugh Gaitskell's death in 1963 allowed Harold Wilson to catch the tide. The parallels between Wilson and Blair were commented on – not least by Blair himself – when Wilson died in May 1995.

They had in common a love affair with television. Writing about Wilson, Blair said: 'Communicating with the people, and speaking up for them in public, is a vital part of the politician's role.'[2] The forty-seven-year-old Wilson was presented as Labour's answer to John F. Kennedy, capturing the excitement of modernity. 'In the sense that he appeared to embody the desire of the country to move on and address a new age with its technological and economic and social challenges, then there are parallels,' the New Wilson claimed, immodestly.[3]

There is a less flattering similarity, too, in the sometimes meaningless rhetoric of Wilson then and Blair now. Wilson said in April 1964 that Labour's policies

are the application to the world of the Sixties and the Seventies of the basic truths that have inspired this

Movement from its earliest days, truths and ideals that
express abiding values, but which in their detailed expression are dynamic, urgent, up-to-date, relevant, worthy of a
great people.[4]

But there were important differences between Blair and
Wilson in their route to power. Despite the 'white heat' of his
futurist language, Wilson was in most senses the traditionalist
and his predecessor the moderniser. After he became Prime
Minister, Wilson explained why he opposed Gaitskell's attempt
to rewrite Clause IV: 'We were being asked to take Genesis out
of the Bible. You don't have to be a fundamentalist to say that
Genesis is part of the Bible.'[5]

Blair is privately more critical of Wilson's governments
than he was in his public tributes, and believes he has learnt
important lessons from Wilson's failures – particularly the
1967 devaluation, the failure to reform trade union law and
the neglect of Labour's ideology and organisation. In his
interview in *Vanity Fair* (March 1995), Christopher Hitchens
asked: 'What is your *real* opinion of Harold Wilson?'

'Ah, well, I'm afraid I'll have to go off the record to answer
that,' Blair replied.

The successes of Wilson's government, such as progressive
social legislation and the creation of the Open University,
were relatively modest – his main political achievement was
the negative one of keeping the Conservatives out of office for
eleven years. Could Blair achieve more than that?

As a politician, Blair has shown an inexhaustible capacity
to learn, adapt and discover his strengths. From the moment
in 1982 when he spoke at the Newcastle meeting of the soft-
Left pressure group, the LCC, and swayed it in favour of
loyalty to Michael Foot, he seems to have learnt things about
himself. And he learns from his mistakes – he never made
another like his 1987 slip, when he talked of Margaret
Thatcher's 'unbalanced mind'. His ditching of the closed
shop in 1989 has been exaggerated as an act of political heroism – its real significance lay in the fact that Blair surprised

SHADOW PRIME MINISTER 433

himself with the soundness of his judgment and the decisive-
ness of his action. He learnt from his hesitation over standing
for the deputy leadership in 1992. He then expanded his
horizons as a communicator, as a force in the Labour leadership team and as an ideologist of social moralism. And, as
Leader of the Opposition, he has exceeded expectations in a
more intensely testing position. The tests would be different
in government, but Blair faces them in an unusually strong
position.

With the voters, the Blair Phenomenon – a combination of
youth and 'normalness' – will wear off. *Private Eye*, in a dry
aside at the end of 1992, described him as 'the only member
of the Labour Party a normal person could ever vote for.'[6]
Part of Blair's appeal was that he did not sound like a politician, an impression he seeks to reinforce – not surprisingly at
a time when politicians are held in such low esteem:

> I *feel* a perfectly normal person. I look at politicians who are
> older than me and I wonder when was the last time they
> had their own thoughts to themselves in their own way
> without feeling they had to programme their thoughts to
> get across a message. I think you can totally lose your
> humanity . . . My friends aren't that impressed, you know.
> I'm very lucky in having good, close friends. This may
> sound like an odd thing to say, but I don't actually feel
> much like a politician.[7]

However, Blair *is* a politician, whose mind is always on the
message he wants to get across, and he will increasingly be
seen as one. Hence his cultivation of a persona in which
Margaret Thatcher's 'resolute approach' is the model, rather
than Harold Wilson's political adroitness.

'She was a thoroughly determined person and that is an
admirable quality,' he says. 'It is important in politics to have
a clear sense of direction, to know what you want. I believe I
know what Britain needs.'[8] The evidence suggests that, as a
whole, the voters are rather more sceptical of Blair's claim to

'know what Britain needs' than most political commentators, and remain suspicious of 'New' Labour, but he has had a better start with the British public than any other party leader in recent times.

In parliament, Blair would probably face a weak and divided opposition – although not perhaps for very long. It is conceivable that the Conservative party may split, but equally it may be that, after a short and vicious ideological civil war, the party would be an energetic and effective opposition.

In the Labour Party, Blair's election under a system of one member, one vote and the endorsement of his ideology in members' ballots on Clause IV gives him a powerful mandate. In office, this would put him in a stronger position than Wilson and Callaghan, who had to govern against the party. The views of the members on policy are more traditionalist than Blair's, but their expectations are modest and there is no alternative parliamentary leader of the status of Aneurin Bevan or Tony Benn.

In a Labour Cabinet, Blair's lack of potential leadership challengers would be unprecedented. One reason for his success was that the party was so weak. When he began his rise in the party, its powerful politicians were fading: Denis Healey, Tony Benn, Peter Shore. Only Gordon Brown and Robin Cook in his Cabinet would be of comparable intellectual and political weight. And it is safe to predict that Brown and Cook – and John Prescott – would not be conspiring to replace him. His relationships with these three would be the central axes of his administration, although David Blunkett at Education and Jack Straw at the Home Office would also be important. Blair's main difficulty is that the personal antagonisms between his lieutenants are sharp, although no more so than the fratricidal loathings that characterised past Labour governments. The particular problem is that Brown, Cook and Prescott all want to run economic policy.

A Blair administration would be the first Labour government containing no one with experience of serving in

Cabinet. Even in 1924, Arthur Henderson had served in the wartime coalition government. Before he became leader, Blair's attendance at shadow Cabinet was dilatory, and he always sat at the corner seat near the door so that he could arrive late and leave early. But as leader he is judged an effective chairman by his colleagues. Unlike Margaret Thatcher and Neil Kinnock, he has the advantage that they all voted for him, apart from John Prescott, Margaret Beckett and Michael Meacher (who voted for Prescott).

In addition to the real Cabinet, a prime minister's kitchen cabinet needs talent too. Gordon Brown, Alexander Irvine and, in time, Peter Mandelson are likely to be members of both, while Cherie, in what is increasingly the quasi-constitutional role of prime minister's spouse, Alastair Campbell, his press secretary, and Anji Hunter, his 'personal political secretary', would wield influence from outside the Cabinet room.

These are the key relationships which would shape a Blair government, and influence its policy and style.

Gordon Brown and the Economy

Aside from Blair himself, Gordon Brown is the dominant force in the Labour leadership, and would be in government, not just in strictly economic matters, but across policy-making. Despite the tensions of the leadership struggle, the after-effects of which were lasting, the Blair–Brown axis would still be the engine-room of a Labour government.

It would be Brown's primary task to avoid repeating Harold Wilson's first failure, being blown off course by macroeconomic errors. Wilson's mistake was to refuse to devalue when the balance of payments problem first emerged. In opposition, Brown has successfully pursued a political strategy of moving onto the centre ground. But in government, that strategy could be Brown's undoing.

Brown and Blair have raised the control of inflation to the first priority of Labour economic policy – thus rewriting John Smith's 1993 speech which placed full employment 'at the heart' of Labour's economic strategy. And they now try to compete with the Conservatives as the low-tax party. During the Lawson boom years the government was able both to raise public spending and cut taxes. Blair offers a sustainable version of the same thing: 'A healthy, prosperous economy with stable growth will lead to an economy where you can spend money on the services you want and you can reduce the burden of taxation.'[9] This was the culmination of the plan devised by Brown after the 1992 election.

Brown's strategy was designed to allow the Labour Party to use the language of the 'dynamic market economy' in the cause of left-of-centre values. High pay for privatised utility directors and scandals concerning the private interests of Conservative MPs have helped him move the dividing line between Right and Left. Blair has even written:

I believe in a society where you get where you are on your own merit, not one based on privilege or who you know. When we reward hard work we will get more of it. And if someone goes on to become wealthy, best of luck to them. We need entrepreneurs – men and women prepared to use their brains and talent to take an idea and develop it. They deserve the success that comes with it. I came into politics to fight against injustice and poverty, not wealth.[10]

The Brown–Blair partnership continues to operate: Brown the strategist, Blair the communicator. Brown is not a flashy politician, easily outclassed by Blair on television. But his time may yet come. Reflecting on his own sudden elevation, Blair commented: 'You have to come to terms with the fact that you will probably do something else before you retire . . . It is unlikely – I sincerely hope not – that I will be leader of the Labour Party for twenty-five years.'[11] Eleven Downing Street does not appear a promising base for Brown's long-term ambitions, however, as Roy Jenkins and Denis Healey might testify.

If Chancellor Brown's room for manoeuvre on taxes, spending and borrowing would be limited, he could face an even greater constraint on exchange rate policy – it was, after all, in the 1967 devaluation that Wilson's promise of an economic revolution foundered. It was Brown who took the strictest anti-devaluation line, differing from John Smith and Neil Kinnock, when the Conservative government ran into the sterling crisis in 1992, and Blair thought he was right to do so. The exchange rate issue has returned, as the European Union prepares for the single currency. But Brown's control of exchange rate policy is challenged by his rival for 11 Downing Street, Robin Cook.

Robin Cook and Europe

As shadow Foreign Secretary, Cook is jointly responsible for Labour's policy on European monetary union, which has direct implications for the management of the economy. Under cover of Blair's ruthlessly effective exploitation in the Commons of the government's open divisions on Europe, Cook engineered a shift in Labour's strategic stance which is of great significance for the future: the Euro-sceptic turn.

The first time Blair came face to face with John Major at Prime Minister's Questions was on 18 October 1994. (He had rehearsed in the empty Commons Chamber with Peter Mandelson beforehand.) He used his first question to con-gratulate the Prime Minister on the ceasefire in Northern Ireland, but then asked if he agreed with his Chancellor, Kenneth Clarke, who had ruled out a referendum on further moves to European integration. It was an effective tactic, as Major avoided the question, but it implied that Blair favoured one.

In ensuing weeks, Blair and Major both edged carefully

towards the possibility of a referendum, Blair trying to embarrass the Prime Minister and Major trying to avoid being boxed in. In the event of 'a major and fundamental constitutional change, there is clearly a case for ensuring that the decision can be very clearly taken by the British people', said Blair.[12] Major said 'a referendum could be necessary, it could be desirable, and I am prepared to keep that option open'.[13]

Both were contradicting their previous positions. Blair had rejected the idea of a referendum on the Maastricht Treaty: 'The right place for the debate to take place is in parliament, where people can express different views.'[14] MPs alone should decide, he said: 'Our mandate is derived from our ability as members of parliament to represent our constituents.'[15]

A referendum is demanded by some Euro-sceptics because they believe public opinion is on their side. But some pro-Europeans in the Labour Party also support a referendum, which fits with the Left's arguments for greater democracy in the European Union. John Smith could have forced the government to hold a referendum on Maastricht: he chose not to mainly because he thought the people would vote 'No'.[16] As in France, it might have turned into a vote on the government's popularity. But he did privately intend, in government, to hold a referendum on the single European currency.[17]

Meanwhile, Cook was working on the substance of Labour policy. Blair himself had shifted subtly during the leadership election campaign: he started off saying simply that he was in favour of the single European currency in principle. Towards the end he said only that there were 'potential benefits', and became 'techno-sceptical' about the conditions for joining: 'It is not enough that the indicators interlock with the requirements of the Maastricht Treaty at one point of the economic cycle.'[18]

In appointing Robin Cook shadow Foreign Secretary in November, he co-opted a converted anti-European. Cook opposed Britain's entry into the EEC and, as a new MP, campaigned for a 'No' vote in the 1975 referendum. But he had helped Neil Kinnock change Labour's policy as his campaign manager for the leadership election in 1983, and then as his European spokesman.

In December, Cook hardened Labour's conditions for joining the single currency, requiring a politically accountable bank and convergence on employment and growth as well as on inflation and public borrowing. As these were not in the Maastricht Treaty, they nullified support for the single currency 'in principle'. And Cook made it clear that Labour would not give up Britain's right to opt out of the single currency, a concession negotiated by John Major and condemned at the time by Neil Kinnock and John Smith.[19]

In January, Cook was asked if a Labour government would rejoin the European Exchange Rate Mechanism. 'No, we've said quite clearly that the ERM poses very clear problems for Britain,' he said.[20] This cast further doubt on Labour's position, because Britain must rejoin the ERM by the end of 1996 in order to be eligible to join the single currency, which comes into force in 1999 – in countries which meet the conditions – under the terms of the Maastricht Treaty.[21] Cook's new line brought together most of the divided Parliamentary Labour Party, allowing Blair to present a united front throughout the time when the Conservative Euro-rebel MPs were outside the party.

As Cook edged away from the single currency, Gordon Brown took a half-step towards it. In May 1995 he and Blair set out a policy of semi-independence for the Bank of England, allowing it to set interest rates in order to meet an inflation target which would still be set by the government.[22] This was intended to establish Labour's anti-inflationary credibility with the City, but an independent central bank – which would form part of a European Central Bank – is also a condition of joining the single currency. It was not clear whether a Labour government would want at least to be eligible to join the single currency. The party's position was inconsistent. It was in favour of the single currency in principle, but against the practical arrangements agreed by all the members of the European Union.

It was significant that Gavyn Davies, one of the Treasury's 'six wise men' who is close to Blair and Gordon Brown, had become sceptical about handing the power of monetary policy to a European Central Bank:

> No country has yet entirely ceded these powers to an untried foreign quango, which is what the Maastricht Treaty invites us to do. My heart has always been with the pro-Europeans. But on this issue my head has more than a few nagging doubts, and these have become much greater since the ERM debacle. I did not expect that to happen, and cannot entirely shrug off the fact that it did.[23]

The note of uncertainty encapsulated Blair's problem. But most of the 'modernisers' who argued for the ERM had neither apologised nor explained after the 'debacle'. Indeed, Derek Scott, Blair's chief economic adviser, and Peter Mandelson were publicly associated in June 1995 with calls for Britain to join the single currency when it starts in 1999, even if Labour's additional conditions could not be negotiated.[24] However, Labour's position escaped scrutiny.

Blair scored a parliamentary triumph in an opposition debate on the government's European policy on 1 March 1995, mocking John Major's refusal to decide the government's position. He asked five questions which he said the Prime Minister could not answer, the last of which was to ask if John Major agreed with his own earlier statement that it was 'unrealistic' to believe that 'economic and monetary union as set out in the Maastricht Treaty will be a step in the direction of a federal Europe'.[25] Blair taunted the Conservatives:

> Can the Prime Minister agree with that? I can; can he? . . . I find it odd that he cannot agree with his Chancellor, I find it strange that he cannot agree with his Secretary of State for Employment [Michael Portillo] and I find it unbelievable that he cannot agree with himself.[26]

But the 'clarity' of Blair's answers to the questions he put was illusory. The Labour Party had not answered the fundamental questions about handing monetary policy to an 'untried foreign quango'.

When it is examined, Blair's policy was as unsatisfactory as Major's, a rhetorical look-both-ways and an insincere invitation to debate, as set out in an overture to Labour's own Euro-sceptics in April 1995: 'I am strongly pro-European although I think that Europe must be greatly reformed. But there's a perfectly justifiable intellectual argument against it. I don't merely not disapprove of having that debate, I positively welcome it.'[27] The triple negative was a grammatical metaphor for Blair's lack of true clarity on one of the most significant issues which faces the nation in the second half of the 1990s.

If the single European currency starts as planned in 1999, would Blair stand out against it, or confront a sceptical public with the dangers of being left out? This is an important question, because Blair has not, so far, argued for a policy that is unpopular with the voters. But the question that must also be asked of him and Cook is, 'What is their vision of the kind of Europe they would like to see in 2000 or 2010?' It is worth noting that the new Clause IV does not even name the European Union, committing Labour only to 'co-operating in European institutions'.

John Prescott and Full Employment

The third member of the economic policy troika in a Labour Cabinet would be John Prescott. If Cook is a semi-sceptic on Europe, then Prescott is the real thing, although he was able to work with John Smith when Bryan Gould, for example, was not. He would like to have charge of some kind of over-arching economic department for driving through the objective of full employment. This would not happen, and Prescott's role in a

Blair government remains undefined. In March 1995, Blair gave him a regional and employment policy brief, but Prescott has neutralised himself by also running for deputy leader on a party organisation ticket, and his credibility now depends on the half-million members target he has set himself.

He also plays a role in learning the lessons of Harold Wilson's second failure – his surrender to trade union special interests. 'Had he been allowed to implement *In Place of Strife*, the recent history of our country would have been hugely different. But he wasn't, and there are many of his colleagues and his enemies alike who must share the blame for that,' Blair wrote.[28] The nature of the relationship between the unions, especially the public sector unions, and a Blair government is nonetheless hard to predict. The refusal to put a figure on the minimum wage until in government demonstrated that policy is not dictated by the unions, but the climate may change if a Labour government is the employer. As a politician trusted by union leaders, and who has ruled himself out as a leadership contender, Prescott is more Blair's human shield against union discontent than the standard-bearer of revolt.

Alexander Irvine and the Constitution

Blair calls Alexander Irvine nearly every day, usually early in the morning – Irvine gets in to work at 6.30 – and respects his former pupil-master's advice. 'What is so impressive about Derry Irvine is that he can peel away the layers of a problem. He has a combination of fierce intellect and a fairly brutal approach to hard work – if you hadn't done the work, there was no point coming into the room,' Blair said of his mentor in 1991.[29]

Irvine is Labour's legal affairs spokesman in the House of Lords, and would become Lord Chancellor in a Labour government. He worked with Blair on trade union law when

Blair was shadow Employment Secretary, and on reform of the House of Lords when Blair was shadow Home Secretary. Blair's desire for Irvine to serve in his Cabinet appeared to produce a reversal of policy which his legal affairs spokesman in the Commons, Paul Boateng, found awkward to explain. Until Blair became leader, Labour intended to do away with the Lord Chancellorship, a post at the head of the judiciary held by a politician. Boateng said in June 1994: 'Labour will take executive functions away from the Lord Chancellor and give them to a Ministry of Justice headed by an MP.'[30]

By March 1995 his tune had changed:

We are not really going to get hung up on the issue of the Lord Chancellor, whether or not he should be in the Cabinet, or anything like that . . . We have a very consider-able constitutional agenda anyway. There's always a danger of constitutional overload.[31]

The status of the Lord Chancellor is an anachronism which is hard for 'New' Labour to justify. But it is true that a Labour government would face a heavy load of difficult constitutional issues, and Blair and Irvine have pared back the party's plans in order to minimise the risk of parliamentary log-jam.

Although Scottish and Welsh assemblies would go ahead in the first year of a Labour government, joint boards of local councillors would be as far as devolution would go in English regions for the foreseeable future. On the House of Lords, Blair has adopted a two-stage plan: 'A short Bill introduced in the House of Commons, for which Labour would have a manifesto commitment,' would abolish the rights of heredi-tary peers, 'as a minimum first step' towards the replacement of the House of Lords by an elected second chamber.[32] Shadow Home Secretary Jack Straw made it clear that the second step would 'probably not' happen during the first term of a Labour government.[33]

The legislative and logical complexity of Scottish and Welsh devolution alone is daunting enough, even disregarding the law of unintended consequences. Add the incorporation of the European Convention on Human Rights into British law, and Blair and Irvine would be responsible for one of the largest programmes of constitutional change in the country's history.

Courtiers

Blair does not yet have a 'kitchen cabinet' in the sense of Harold Wilson's informal coterie around Marcia Williams at 10 Downing Street. But he has a number of confidants outside the shadow Cabinet whom he consults individually, the most important being Peter Mandelson, Alastair Campbell, Anji Hunter and Cherie.

Mandelson, a few months younger than Blair, was at Oxford University at the same time as him. Asked if he knew him then, Mandelson is said to have replied: 'No, I was interested in politics.'[34] It was the later discovery of his genius for media management which brought him and Blair together. He is immensely influential with Blair now, regarded by many as his alter ego, and in government it is likely that he would be more influential with the prime minister than anyone else except Gordon Brown. But Mandelson does not have his own power base; his power derives from his closeness to the leader. This leads to constant conflict, varying from petty sniping to total (but mostly private) war, with many of the shadow Cabinet and the wider Parliamentary Labour Party. Brown, in charge of the day-to-day implementation of political strategy, has not forgiven him for his role in the leadership election – although in government, Brown would have an economy to run, giving Mandelson more scope.

His relations with Alastair Campbell, as the prime minister's press secretary, would also be rich with the possibility of friction. After Blair's 1994 conference speech, Campbell, still a *Today* columnist although already acting as Blair's spokesman, paid barbed tribute to Mandelson's role in orchestrating the unprecedented press acclaim:

> Many newspapers rightly spotted the hand of Peter Mandelson, legendary MP for Hartlepool and the spin doctor's spin doctor, of whom John Smith once memorably said that he was so devious he would one day disappear up his own something or other.
>
> Few people are as capable of arousing strong passions as Peter, who is both admired and loathed.
>
> Having been a close friend of his since the days before he started wearing cufflinks, I have none of the traditional hang-ups about Peter, and fully intend on becoming Blair's press secretary to exploit his expertise, which in some areas is second to none.
>
> Speech-writing, however, is not one of them, but such is his ubiquitous appeal that *The Times* yesterday suggested he had helped write Blair's speech.
>
> I know from the days when Peter was a *People* columnist that writing was never his strong point, and that he had to look to his friends to help him out. Know what I mean?[35]

Campbell is an aggressive propagandist, and had been an informal press adviser to Blair as long ago as 1989 when, as political editor of the *Mirror*, he was 'in and out of Blair's office all day' discussing how to handle the closed shop, according to one source. He is popular with other journalists, and would be a robust Downing Street press secretary, reminiscent of Bernard Ingham under Margaret Thatcher.

In Blair's private office Anji Hunter is the central figure. If access is power, she would be in a powerful position in government. Inevitably, she invites comparison with Marcia Williams, Baroness Falkender. She has known Blair since they were at school, and has worked as his assistant in the Commons since 1988 – but, as with Marcia, 'never with the sense that her job was permanent'.[36] She left in 1991 – despite Blair's desperate pleas – to spend more time with her young children, but politics had taken hold. During the 1992 election campaign, she worked for Neil Kinnock, and then, returning to Blair's office, she was seconded to Margaret Beckett's deputy leadership campaign.

She is a 'fixer, charmer and tactician', according to one of the pre-1994 Blair entourage. Ben Pimlott's description of the relationship between Wilson and Williams applies equally to Blair and Hunter: 'The precise nature of her duties was unspecified . . . Her important role was to be the person who thought about Wilson's needs and cared about his well-being more than anybody else outside his family.'[37] Hunter's job is to provide reassurance, to tell Blair how wonderful he is. 'She deals with the emotional side very well, mothers him, calms him down,' says one observer.

Like Williams, Hunter keeps the leader in touch with Labour MPs and officials at party headquarters. She gossips with them and tells Blair to whom he should speak. She also sees it as part of her job to keep Blair in touch with a part of the real world – the Southern middle classes. She lives in Sussex with a non-political husband and two young children. She is not as influential with Blair as Williams was with Wilson, because there is always Peter Mandelson. But she is ever-present, while Mandelson is usually on the telephone.

Blair hardly had a private office before John Smith's death. By the time he became leader, he had accumulated a staff of about a dozen, and Hunter was nominally in charge. But if her role has a title, it is Williams's, Personal Political Secretary, more than 'head of private office': that post was filled when in January 1995 Jonathan Powell arrived from America to take over as Chief of Staff. Blair met Powell in January 1993 in Washington, where Powell was at the British Embassy. This was just as Powell's brother Charles met Margaret Thatcher, whom he served for six years as Private Secretary. Charles (the only one of three brothers to pronounce his name Pole) was First Secretary at the British Embassy in Bonn when Thatcher met him on a visit soon after her election as Leader of the Opposition. The middle brother, Chris Powell, is now in charge of Labour's advertising, as director of the agency BMP. The persistence of Powells recalls the influential private court of Margaret Thatcher: Bernard Ingham, Charles Powell, Alan Walters and Denis Thatcher. Derek Scott plays the Walters role as Blair's part-time economic adviser. He is director of European economics at City dealers BZW, and was special adviser to Chancellor Denis Healey, 1976–79, and stood as the SDP candidate in Swindon in 1983.

The final figure is Cherie. She is a political wife, more like her predecessors Elizabeth Smith and Glenys Kinnock than Mary Wilson or Norma Major. Until 1985, she was a politician in her own right. She is a successful barrister, becoming a QC in April 1995, and earns about £200,000 a year. Blair dismisses press speculation that she still wants to exercise political power through him: 'It's not worth being irritated about, but it is curious that, because she is a successful career woman, some people find it impossible to believe that she doesn't want to do my job as well as her own. But in fact she doesn't.'[38]

Her main influence on her husband has been to reinforce his ambition as he rose through the ranks. Her political views appear to be indistinguishable from his, and it may be that her most significant contribution in 10 Downing Street would be to act as a role model for career women. Her stated ambition is to become a judge: 'If one day I was asked to be a judge, I would love to be one.'[39]

Her legal career gained momentum when in 1991 she transferred to the chambers of Michael Beloff, a large set which did a lot of work in the expanding areas of judicial review and European Community law, after Alexander Irvine telephoned Beloff to suggest it. 'She was obviously getting restless,' says Beloff. 'I was rung up by Derry Irvine, who said, "I think she deserves to be in a set that's reputed to be better and looks stronger than the set she's presently in."'

Beloff says he was 'bowled over' by her, and she was eventually taken on.

One of the things I find absolutely amazing, and I think her
colleagues do here, is that sometimes you get these rather
hostile profiles – I think some said, 'She's very chippy, she's
charmless' – it's simply incredible. It's like saying Marilyn
Monroe is ugly or Linford Christie can't run. She's one of
the most obviously charming people that I've ever met.

She is, however, forceful and determined. Beloff admits
that there have been 'collisions' over Cherie's 'progressive
views' about the administration of chambers. But it was her
use of the old-fashioned system of personal pupillages which
got her into trouble after Blair became leader. She took on
Buster Cox, son of Barry, family friend and chief fundraiser
for the Blair campaign, for an unpaid traineeship. It was
understood that Buster was not competing for a permanent
place at her chambers, but he was clearly benefiting from the
six months' experience.

A potential problem for Blair in the future is that she is
engaged in activities which intrude on public life. A newspaper story about her demanding that a poll tax defaulter
stay in jail serves as a warning that she would act in prominent cases which could be used by the Labour Left or the
Conservatives against her husband.[40]

Paddy Ashdown and Pluralist Politics

There is one further relationship which would influence a
Blair government, and that is between Blair and Paddy
Ashdown, the Liberal Democrat leader.

In opposition in the House of Commons, Blair has shown
himself to be formidable in adversarial debate. But in government he would face the challenge of a different kind of
politics – that of coalition-building. Whether Labour has an
overall majority or not, the Liberal Democrats would matter.

Labour backbencher Dennis Skinner made the problem

explicit in June 1994: 'When we get in, I and other members of the Socialist Campaign Group will have the balance of power . . . We shall need a few socialists when the Labour government's in to make sure that we try to keep them on the straight and narrow.'[41] Based on his experience of the early Eighties, Blair fears that a section of the party would immediately go into internal opposition. Of course, the Labour Left is not the ideological force it once was. But the Parliamentary Labour Party does contain about forty MPs whom the whips would find hard to control. As with the Conservative Euro-sceptic rebels, it is difficult for other parties to construct alliances with them, but embarrassing defeats would be possible, especially on constitutional reform. Devolution and the reform of the House of Lords have seen unlikely alliances between the Labour Left and Conservatives in the past.

Ultra-modernisers urge co-operation with the Liberal Democrats: 'Given the choice of relying on the votes of unreconstructed traditionalists in the Campaign Group or progressives in the Liberal Democrats to sustain a Blair agenda, I know what I would prefer,' says Neal Lawson, a former adviser to Gordon Brown.[42] This is partly a practical argument, partly an argument for the principle of 'new' pluralist politics.

At Blair's other elbow is Jack Straw, shadow Home Secretary, who has built a following in the Labour Party by bashing the Liberal Democrats. But Blair leans to the ultras, and told Straw off for attacking the Liberal Democrats after the shadow Cabinet were asked not to at a 'strategy meeting' in September 1994. At the time of Labour's 1994 conference, Blair set out the most friendly stance towards the third party ever adopted by a Labour leader:

> It is foolish for us to pretend that the left of centre is solely occupied by the Labour Party, and it is only Labour that ever has good ideas. It would be absurd of me to say that my views and Charles Kennedy's are a million miles apart.

They're not. But this has to happen through a process of developing ideas, not in pacts or deals or working out who sits in what position. I try not to be tribal in my thinking. Indeed, there are Liberal Democrats and Labour people co-operating at a local level. The most important thing is that the left of centre develops a political philosophy with meaning for the modern world and the Liberal Democrats clearly have a place in that.[43]

Blair's favourite label, 'left of centre', had always contained a suggestion of 'left *and* centre', which he made explicit in February 1995, when he said Labour 'is increasingly the party of the centre and the left of centre'.[44]

Blair's personal relations with Liberal Democrat leader Paddy Ashdown, however, have not been warm. In 1992, Ashdown told friends he had never had a real conversation with Blair, and a meeting was arranged. 'They didn't get on as well as might have been hoped,' according to a Liberal Democrat MP.[45]

Ashdown, like Blair, is under pressure against co-operation from parts of his own party. On the eve of Blair's election as Labour leader, Liberal Democrat MP Robert Maclennan, a Labour defector to the SDP, travelled to Sedgefield to give a hostile television interview on the doorstep of the Trimdon Labour Club: 'The trouble with the Labour Party is that it's so slow to change, so resistant to democracy, that it would be quite inappropriate to do any sort of business with it.'[46] He was elected President of the Liberal Democrats in September 1994.

At Ashdown's other elbow are Labour defectors who believe their former party has reformed but feel, like Macbeth, that they are 'in blood Stepp'd in so far that, should I wade no more, Returning were as tedious as go o'er.' They are led by the Gang of Three Liberal Democrat peers, one of whom, Bill Rodgers, urges Blair to include Liberal Democrats in his government even if Labour wins an overall majority in the Commons, so that a coalition could govern on behalf of a clear 'majority of our nation'.[47]

Ashdown, like Blair, has moved step by step towards co-operation. In May 1995, he dropped the policy of maintaining 'equidistance' between the Conservatives and Labour, saying it was inconceivable that his party would sustain the Conservatives in office in a hung parliament.

A central issue between Labour and the Liberal Democrats is the question of changing the voting system. When he was still shadow Chancellor, John Smith spoke to Ashdown in a taxi on the way to a television studio, in May 1991, saying he was ready to concede electoral reform for the Commons in return for Liberal Democrat support in a hung parliament.[48] During the Labour leadership campaign in 1992 Smith said he did not like the one-party domination in Southern England and Central Scotland produced by the present voting system, but he wanted to keep single-member constituencies.[49] The next year he decided he did not dislike one-party domination enough to want to change the system for the House of Commons, but promised a referendum under a Labour government, so that the people could decide.

In the 1994 leadership election campaign, Blair was defensive when asked about electoral reform, saying simply, 'My policy is exactly the same as John Smith's.'[50] He did not try to claim the democratic high ground, and his muted hostility to proportional representation remained:

If people pose the question, 'Is the present electoral system unfair?' in my view the answer to that is yes. What is more difficult is answering the question 'Is there a less unfair electoral system?' . . . My concern is that under proportional representation you can get disproportionate power wielded by a small party.[51]

A referendum on electoral reform is another part of the overgrown thicket of constitutional reform Blair would like to prune. The issue would split a Labour Cabinet (Robin Cook is a strong advocate of electoral reform), and Blair would be in a lose–lose situation: either the people would vote for reform, which would look like defeat for him, or they would reject it, which would make the exercise seem a sop to the Liberal Democrats. And there is the possibility of another referendum on the single European currency. In practice, Paddy Ashdown would not be in a strong position to demand it, as it lacks the weight of public opinion behind it. In the 1992 election campaign, Ashdown said the promise of a referendum was the 'key that unlocks the door' to co-operation. This time the door already seems to be open.

Character

In the end, the character of a Blair government would be determined by its leader, whose true character can only be provisionally sketched here. While he is certainly eager to give the impression of 'strong leadership', behind the rather self-conscious facade he has in fact already turned out to be a strong leader, showing genuine determination and a sound strategic sense. But he has yet to face the test of failure – so far all that can be said is that in adversity blandness is his main defence. Personally, he is detached, self-disciplined and moral, charming without being charismatic, engaging without being warm. He inspires loyalty. He consults widely, but partly as a tactic, and only defers consistently to advice from three people: Gordon Brown, Peter Mandelson and Alexander Irvine. He makes quick and firm decisions when he has to, but will avoid them until a deadline looms.

Some who have worked with him say he responds badly to pressure, describing him as 'petulant' and behaving like a 'spoilt child' when criticised, with a tendency to exaggerate – 'it's all terrible' – when he suffers a minor setback.

His personal integrity has never been seriously questioned. Attempts by Conservative backbenchers to challenge his entries in the Register of Members' Interests have been generally unconvincing. True, he did not say which trade union financially supported his office, only that it was not affiliated to the Labour Party. And his first explanation for not registering his Concorde trip to the United States in 1986, paid for by business interests, was misleading. He claimed he had been asked to go by the government, whereas he had been one of an all-party lobby (which still meant the trip did not have to be declared). The group lobbied against the State of California's double taxation of British companies, a cause supported by the government. But he is undoubtedly honest, both as a citizen and a legislator.

In his political style, he wants to be seen to follow Margaret Thatcher's more than any other prime ministerial example. Jonathan Powell, his Chief of Staff, says:

> Thatcher is his model. And she once said that her single greatest success was the change she had brought about in the Labour Party. That's also Tony Blair's job – in reverse, of course. If he can pull that off, then he can become 'the new paradigm', the thing people hoped Bill Clinton was going to be.[52]

As Thatcher did, he uses a strong and consistent rhetoric to give a greater sense of purpose to a political 'project' less well-defined than it seems. Significantly, one aspect of her approach he recalls favourably was that the Conservatives 'travelled very light' in opposition before 1979.[53]

Thatcher's 'project' was, and certainly became, more substantial than Blair's to date. One of his most overworked perorations is his claim to want to win power, or turn the Tories out, not just for a parliamentary term, but for a generation. This was a much used line, partly because he is rather bad at finishing speeches, and stuck with a good device when he found it. But it begs the question, what does he want three or four parliamentary terms *for*?

In his ruthless appeal to a conservative electorate, Blair's ambition seems to many of his party so modest, so right-wing or so illiberal, that the central uncertainty about him is whether he would do anything to be elected, and re-elected, or whether he has a principled core.

In fact, he does have a vision of 'good society' which appears to be rooted in a genuine, almost spiritual belief, although he has also given the impression that he developed his political philosophy by trial and error according to what evoked the best response. And he has drawn a bottom line under his political principles in the new Clause IV – there are two parts of it with which moderate Conservatives would not be entirely at home.

The first is the superiority of common endeavour over individualism, which sustains the ideal of community. There are problems with this ideal which Blair is slow to acknowledge – for example, the difficulty of creating real communities in a modern economy, as identified by his philosophical mentor, John Macmurray:

> The mobility of labour means a continuous breaking of the nexus of direct relations between persons and between a person and his natural environment . . . The end result can only be the destruction of the family and the production of the 'mass-man'.[54]

The problem posed by communitarianism for the Left is that a sense of community requires a sense of tradition. For many socialists, radicalism – that is, the rejection of tradition – is central to their beliefs.

More immediate problems arise from trying to translate social moralism into practical policies. American communitarians have introduced measures which would disrupt Blair's consensual language here. 'Workfare' – requiring people to work or train in return for welfare benefits – is implied by much of what Blair says, but is controversial and difficult to operate in practice. However, the principle of 'duty' is barely conceived of as a policy programme – instead, Blair the superb communicator offers a shift in public language and values, which could still make a significant difference to national life.

The second distinctive concept in the new Clause IV is the just society, 'which judges its strength by the condition of the weak as much as the strong'. Blair clearly intends to reverse the trend towards greater inequality in British society since 1979, although his means would be unfamiliar to the Left. Rather than expanding tax-funded welfare, Blair would try to subsidise people into work.

Of course, principle is pointless without determination. Blair *is* determined, but he has not yet, as leader, taken a principled stand against public opinion – although, as he says, the distinction between principle and electoralism is partly a false choice. The leaders who give electoralism a bad name, like Harold Wilson and Bill Clinton, are those who come to power by telling the voters what they want to hear but who then fail to deliver in government.

The main weakness of Labour governments in Tony Blair's lifetime has been the clash between what the *party* wants of the government and what the *public* wants. One of his reasons for changing Clause IV was to persuade the party to accept in advance the modesty of his ambition. That acceptance is not complete, and there is no doubt that Blair as prime minister would offend many of his own party. Equally, however, there is every likelihood that, as his ethical socialist programme becomes better defined, he will build support for it among the public.

In the increasingly constrained arena of national government action, Blair is likely to be a highly effective prime minister. In his relations with Europe – particularly over the single currency – and with the subsidiary parts of the United Kingdom, there are no easy answers. But if he can surprise the country as he has surprised his party on these difficult issues, and deliver modest progress towards a more 'just' and 'moral' society, he could become one of the most successful prime ministers.

Notes

1. Memo leaked to the *Financial Times*, 21 November 1994.
2. Tony Blair, *Independent*, 25 May 1995.
3. Tony Blair, BBC Radio 4 *The World At One*, 24 May 1995.
4. Harold Wilson, speech, 5 April 1964, in *The New Britain: Labour's Plan Outlined by Harold Wilson*, p126.
5. *Listener*, 29 October 1964, quoted by Ben Pimlott, *Harold Wilson*, p227.
6. HP Sauce, *Private Eye*, 1 January 1993.
7. *The Times Magazine*, 1 October 1994.
8. *Sunday Times*, 2 April 1995.
9. BBC TV, *On The Record*, 26 June 1994.
10. Tony Blair, *News of the World*, 28 August 1994.
11. *The Times Magazine*, 1 October 1994.
12. *Sunday Telegraph*, 11 December 1994.
13. *Hansard*, 1 March 1995, col 1069.
14. BBC TV, Labour Party conference programme, 27 September 1992.
15. *Hansard*, 1 February 1993, col 32.
16. James Naughtie in Gordon Brown and James Naughtie, eds, *John Smith: Life and Soul of the Party*, p51.
17. Interview with David Ward, chief policy adviser to John Smith.
18. BBC TV, *Newsnight*, 12 July 1994. An example of an early endorsement of the principle of the single currency, BBC Radio 4 *The World This Weekend*, 29 May 1994.
19. BBC TV, *On The Record*, 11 December 1994.
20. Channel Four, *A Week In Politics*, 28 January 1995.
21. These conditions and the timetable may be reviewed at the Inter-Governmental Conference in 1996.
22. Gordon Brown, speech on 'The Macroeconomic Framework', 17 May 1995; Tony Blair, Mais lecture, 22 May 1995.
23. *Independent*, 13 February 1995.
24. Derek Scott and Peter Mandelson were members of a Federal Trust 'round table' which produced a report, 'Towards a Single Currency', on 6 June 1995.
25. Chancellor Kenneth Clarke had, in a speech to the European Movement on 9 February 1995, said the single currency did not 'herald the end of the nation state'.
26. *Hansard*, 1 March 1995, col 1057.
27. *New Statesman*, 28 April 1995.

28. Tony Blair, *Independent*, 25 May 1995.
29. *Harpers & Queen*, January 1991.
30. Quoted in the *Independent*, 22 March 1995.
31. *Independent*, 22 March 1995.
32. Tony Blair, speech in Cardiff, 15 July 1994.
33. BBC TV, *Breakfast with Frost*, 5 February 1995.
34. Peter Mandelson was a member of the Young Communist League before he went to Oxford.
35. Alastair Campbell, *Today*, 6 October 1994.
36. Ben Pimlott, *Harold Wilson*, p341.
37. *Ibid.*, p344.
38. *The Times Magazine*, 25 April 1995.
39. *Channel Four News*, 22 January 1995.
40. *Independent on Sunday*, 22 January 1995.
41. BBC Radio 1, *Nicky Campbell Show*, 16 June 1994.
42. Neal Lawson, *Renewal*, April 1995.
43. *Observer*, 2 October 1994.
44. Tony Blair, speech, 15 February 1995.
45. *Guardian*, 8 August 1994.
46. BBC TV, *Look North*, 20 July 1994.
47. BBC Radio 4, *The World At One*, 26 May 1995.
48. Andy McSmith, *John Smith*, p326.
49. *Tribune* debate, 26 June 1992.
50. Tony Blair, at the launch of his leadership manifesto, 23 June 1994.
51. Tony Blair, unbroadcast BBC *Talking Politics* interview reported in the *Guardian*, 19 September 1994.
52. *Vanity Fair*, March 1995.
53. *Evening Standard*, 21 February 1995.
54. John Macmurray, *Persons in Relation*, p187.

Appendix
Clause IV

The Old

Clause IV, 'Party Objects', of the Labour Party constitution

1. To organise and maintain in parliament and in the country a political Labour Party.
2. To co-operate with the General Council of the Trades Union Congress, or other kindred organisations, in joint political or other action in harmony with the party constitution and standing orders.
3. To give effect as far as may be practicable to the principles from time to time approved by the party conference.
4. To secure for the workers by hand or by brain the full fruits of their industry and the most equitable distribution thereof that may be possible upon the basis of the common ownership of the means of production, distribution and exchange, and the best obtainable system of popular administration and control of each industry or service.
5. Generally to promote the political, social and economic emancipation of the people, and more particularly of those who depend directly upon their own exertions by hand or by brain for the means of life.

6. To co-operate with the labour and socialist organisations in the Commonwealth overseas with a view to promoting the purposes of the party, and to take common action for the promotion of a higher standard of social and economic life for the working population of the respective countries.

7. To co-operate with the labour and socialist organisations in other countries and to support the United Nations Organisation and its various agencies and other international organisations for the promotion of peace, the adjustment and settlement of disputes by conciliation or judicial arbitration, the establishment and defence of human rights, and the improvement of the social and economic standards and conditions of work of the people of the world.

Published in 1917 and adopted by conference at Methodist Central Hall, Westminster, in 1918. The words 'distribution and exchange' were added to Part Four in 1928, and Part Seven was added, at the suggestion of Tony Benn, in 1960. Parts One and Three have been retained and moved to Clause I.

The Nascent

Early draft of Part One of the new Clause IV, written by Tony Blair on an aeroplane from Glasgow to London, 10 March 1995, returning from the Scottish Labour Party conference in Inverness, and copied from drafts written in Inverness.

The New

'Aims and Values'

1.   The Labour Party is a democratic socialist party. It believes that by the strength of our common endeavour we achieve more than we achieve alone, so as to create for each of us the means to realise our true potential and for all of us a community in which power, wealth and opportunity are in the hands of the many not the few, where the rights we enjoy reflect the duties we owe, and where we live together, freely, in a spirit of solidarity, tolerance and respect.

2.   To these ends we work for:

A dynamic economy, serving the public interest, in which the enterprise of the market and the rigour of competition are joined with the forces of partnership and co-operation to produce the wealth the nation needs and the opportunity for all to work and prosper, with a thriving private sector and high quality public services, where those undertakings essential to the common good are either owned by the public or accountable to them;

A just society, which judges its strength by the condition of the weak as much as the strong, provides security against fear, and justice at work; which nurtures families, promotes equality of opportunity and delivers people from the tyranny of poverty, prejudice and the abuse of power;

An open democracy, in which the government is held to account by the people; decisions are taken as far as practicable by the communities they affect; and where fundamental human rights are guaranteed;

A healthy environment, which we protect, enhance and hold in trust for future generations.

3.   Labour is committed to the defence and security of the British people, and to co-operating in European institutions, the United Nations, the Commonwealth and other international bodies to secure peace, freedom, democracy,

economic security and environmental protection for all.

4.   Labour will work in pursuit of these aims with trade unions, co-operative societies and other affiliated organisations, and also with voluntary organisations, consumer groups and other representative bodies.

5.   On the basis of these principles, Labour seeks the trust of the people to govern.

Approved by the National Executive on 13 March 1995, with three small changes. The word 'will' before the first 'achieve' in Part One was deleted. In the second paragraph of Part Two, 'family life' was replaced by 'families' on the suggestion of David Blunkett. Part Four was changed to delete 'with its affiliated organisations such as' before the trade unions and co-operative societies, and insert 'and other affiliated organisations' after them. Adopted by a Special Conference, again at Methodist Central Hall, on 29 April 1995.

BIBLIOGRAPHY

The place of publication is London unless specified.

Clement Attlee, *As It Happened*, Heinemann, 1954.

Tony Booth, *Stroll On: An Autobiography*, Sidgwick & Jackson, 1989.

Gordon Brown and James Naughtie, editors, *John Smith: Life and Soul of the Party*, Edinburgh: Mainstream, 1994.

Christopher Bryant, editor, *Reclaiming the Ground*, Hodder & Stoughton, 1993.

Trevor Burridge, *Clement Attlee*, Jonathan Cape, 1985.

David Butler and Dennis Kavanagh, *The British General Election of 1983*, Macmillan, 1984.

Alan Clark, *Diaries*, Weidenfeld & Nicolson, 1993.

Ken Coates, editor, *Clause IV: Common Ownership and the Labour Party*, Nottingham: Spokesman, 1995.

Michael Crick, *Militant*, Faber & Faber, 1984.

Norman Dennis and A.H. Halsey, *English Ethical Socialism: Thomas More to R.H. Tawney*, Oxford: Clarendon Press, 1988.

Roger Eatwell, *The Labour Government, 1945–51*, Batsford Academic, 1979.

Roderick Floud and Donald McCloskey, editors, *The Economic History of Britain since 1700, Vol 3: 1939–92*, Cambridge: University Press, 1994.

Michael Foot, *Another Heart and Other Pulses*, Collins, 1984.

Eric Hammond, *Maverick: The Life of a Union Rebel*, Weidenfeld & Nicolson, 1992.

David Hare, *Asking Around*, Faber & Faber, 1993.

Robert Harris, *The Making of Neil Kinnock*, Faber & Faber, 1984.

Bob Hawke, *The Hawke Memoirs*, Heinemann, 1994.

Anthony Heath, Roger Jowell and John Curtice, *How Britain Votes*, Oxford: Pergamon Press, 1985.

Anthony Heath and others, *Understanding Political Change*, Oxford: Pergamon Press, 1991.

Dave Hill, *Out for the Count: Politicians and the People*, Macmillan, 1992.

Colin Hughes and Patrick Wintour, *Labour Rebuilt: The New Model Party*, Fourth Estate, 1990.

Mervyn Jones, *Michael Foot*, Victor Gollancz, 1994.

David Kogan and Maurice Kogan, *The Battle for the Labour Party*, Fontana, 1982.

David Kusnet, *Speaking American: How the Democrats Can Win the Nineties*, New York: Thunder's Mouth Press, 1992.

Jack Lawson, *Peter Lee*, The Epworth Press, 1949.

Nigel Lawson, *The View from No 11*, Corgi, 1993 (paperback edition, first published by Bantam Press, 1992).

Ken Livingstone, *If Voting Changed Anything, They'd Abolish It*, Collins, 1987.

John Macmurray, *The Self as Agent*, New Jersey and London: Humanities Press International, 1957, new edition 1991.

——*Persons in Relation*, New Jersey and London: Humanities Press International, 1961, new edition 1991.

Andy McSmith, *John Smith: A Life 1938–1994*, Mandarin, 1994 (revised edition of *Playing the Long Game*, Verso, 1993).

Will Marshall and Martin Schram, editors, *Mandate for Change*, New York: Berkley Books, 1993.

Mary Matalin and James Carville, *All's Fair: Love, War and Running for President*, Hutchinson, 1994.

Austin Mitchell, *Beyond the Blue Horizon*, Bellew, 1989.

Michael Oakeshott, *Rationalism in Politics*, Methuen, 1962.

Matthew Parris, *Look Behind You!*, Robson Books, 1993.

Ben Pimlott, *Harold Wilson*, HarperCollins, 1992.

Michael J. Sandel, *Liberalism and Limits of Justice*, Cambridge: University Press, 1982.

David Selbourne, *The Principle of Duty*, Sinclair-Stevenson, 1994.

Patrick Seyd and Paul Whiteley, *Labour's Grass Roots: The Politics of Party Membership*, Oxford: Clarendon Press, 1992.

Peter Shore, *Leading the Left*, Weidenfeld & Nicolson, 1993.

Jon Sopel, *Tony Blair: The Moderniser*, Michael Joseph, 1995.

R.H. Tawney, *Equality*, 1931, fourth revised edition, 1952, George Allen & Unwin, 1964.

Norman Tebbit, *Upwardly Mobile*, Futura, 1989 (paperback edition, first published by Weidenfeld & Nicolson, 1988).

Margaret Thatcher, *The Downing Street Years*, HarperCollins, 1993.

Alexis de Tocqueville, *Democracy in America*, first edition 1835 edited by Phillips Bradley, New York: Vintage, 1945.

Philip M. Williams, *Hugh Gaitskell: A Political Biography*, Jonathan Cape, 1979.

Harold Wilson, *The New Britain: Labour's Plan Outlined by Harold Wilson*, Selected Speeches 1964, Harmondsworth: Penguin Books, 1964.

PICTURE CREDITS

INDEX

Numbers in **bold** denote chapter/major section devoted to subject.